# Victoria Crosses on the Western Front
## Battles of the Hindenburg Line – Havrincourt and Épehy

### September 1918

Paul Oldfield

Pen & Sword
**MILITARY**

First published in Great Britain in 2022 by
Pen & Sword Military
an imprint of
Pen & Sword Books Ltd
47 Church Street
Barnsley
South Yorkshire
S70 2AS

Copyright © Paul Oldfield 2022

ISBN 978 1 52678 807 8

The right of Paul Oldfield to be identified as the Author of this Work has been asserted by him in accordance with the Copyright, Designs and Patents Act 1988.

A CIP catalogue record for this book is available from the British Library

All rights reserved. No part of this book may be reproduced or transmitted in any form or by any means, electronic or mechanical including photocopying, recording or by any information storage and retrieval system, without permission from the Publisher in writing.

Typeset by Mac Style
Printed and bound in the UK by CPI Group (UK) Ltd,
Croydon, CR0 4YY.

Pen & Sword Books Ltd incorporates the imprints of Pen & Sword Archaeology, Atlas, Aviation, Battleground, Discovery, Family History, History, Maritime, Military, Naval, Politics, Railways, Select, Social History, Transport, True Crime, and Claymore Press, Frontline Books, Leo Cooper, Praetorian Press, Remember When, Seaforth Publishing and Wharncliffe.

For a complete list of Pen & Sword titles please contact

**PEN & SWORD BOOKS LIMITED**
47 Church Street, Barnsley, South Yorkshire, S70 2AS, England
E-mail: enquiries@pen-and-sword.co.uk
Website: www.pen-and-sword.co.uk

Or

**PEN AND SWORD BOOKS**
1950 Lawrence Rd, Havertown, PA 19083, USA
E-mail: Uspen-and-sword@casematepublishers.com
Website: www.penandswordbooks.com

# Victoria Crosses on the Western Front
## Battles of the Hindenburg Line – Havrincourt and Épehy

September 1918

# Contents

*Master Maps* vi
*Abbreviations* ix
*Introduction* xii

## Battle of Havrincourt (Master Map 2)   1

425. Sgt Harry Laurent, 2 New Zealand Rifle Brigade, NZEF, 12 September 1918, Gouzeaucourt France
426. Sgt Laurence Calvert, 5 King's Own Yorkshire Light Infantry, 12 September 1918, Havrincourt, France

## Battle of Épehy (Master Maps 2 & 3)   13

428. Cpl David Hunter, 5 Highland Light Infantry, 16 September 1918, Moeuvres, France
429. Sgt Maurice Buckley aka Gerald Sexton, 13 Battalion, AIF, 18 September 1918, Le Verguier, France
430. Pte James Woods, 48 Battalion, AIF, 18 September 1918, Le Verguier, France
431. LSgt William Waring, 25 Royal Welsh Fusiliers, 18 September 1918, Ronssoy, France
432. LCpl Allan Lewis, 6 Northamptonshire, 18 September 1918, Ronssoy, France
433. 2Lt William White, 38 Machine Gun Corps, 18 September 1918, Gouzeaucourt, France
434. 2Lt Frank Young, 1 Hertfordshire, 18 September 1918, Havrincourt, France

## Local Operations (Master Maps 1 & 3)   47

435. Lt John Barrett, 5 Leicestershire, 24 September 1918, Pontruet, France
436. Lt Donald Dean, 8 Queen's Own (Royal West Kent), 24 September 1918, Cité St Emilie, France

**Biographies**   55
**Sources**   245
**Useful Information**   251

*Index*   255

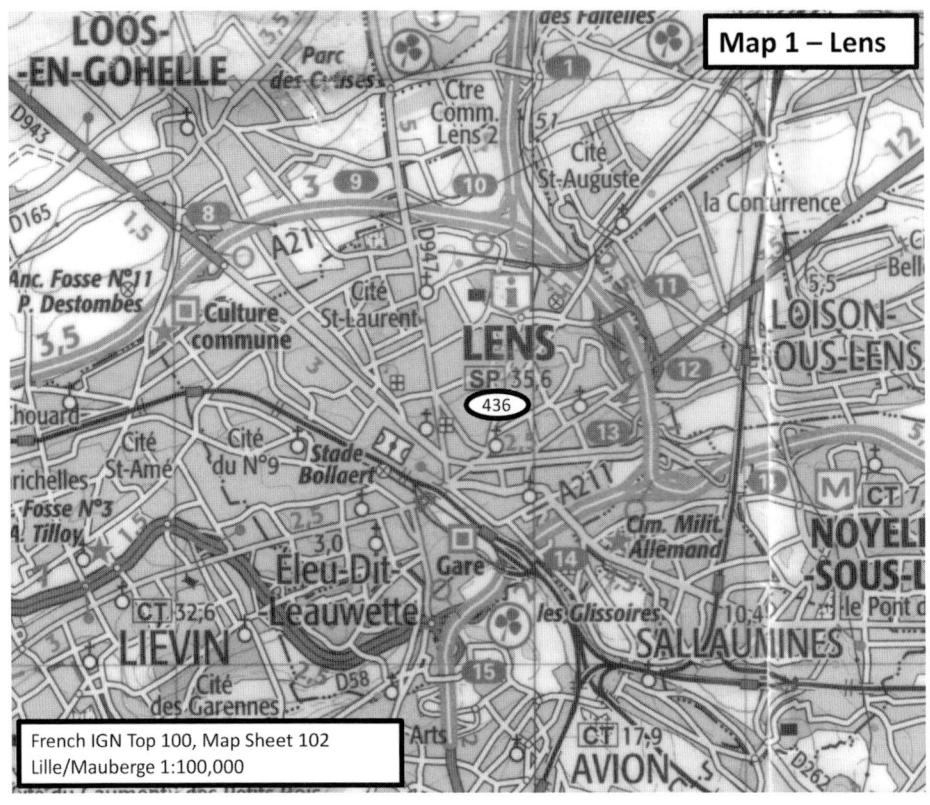

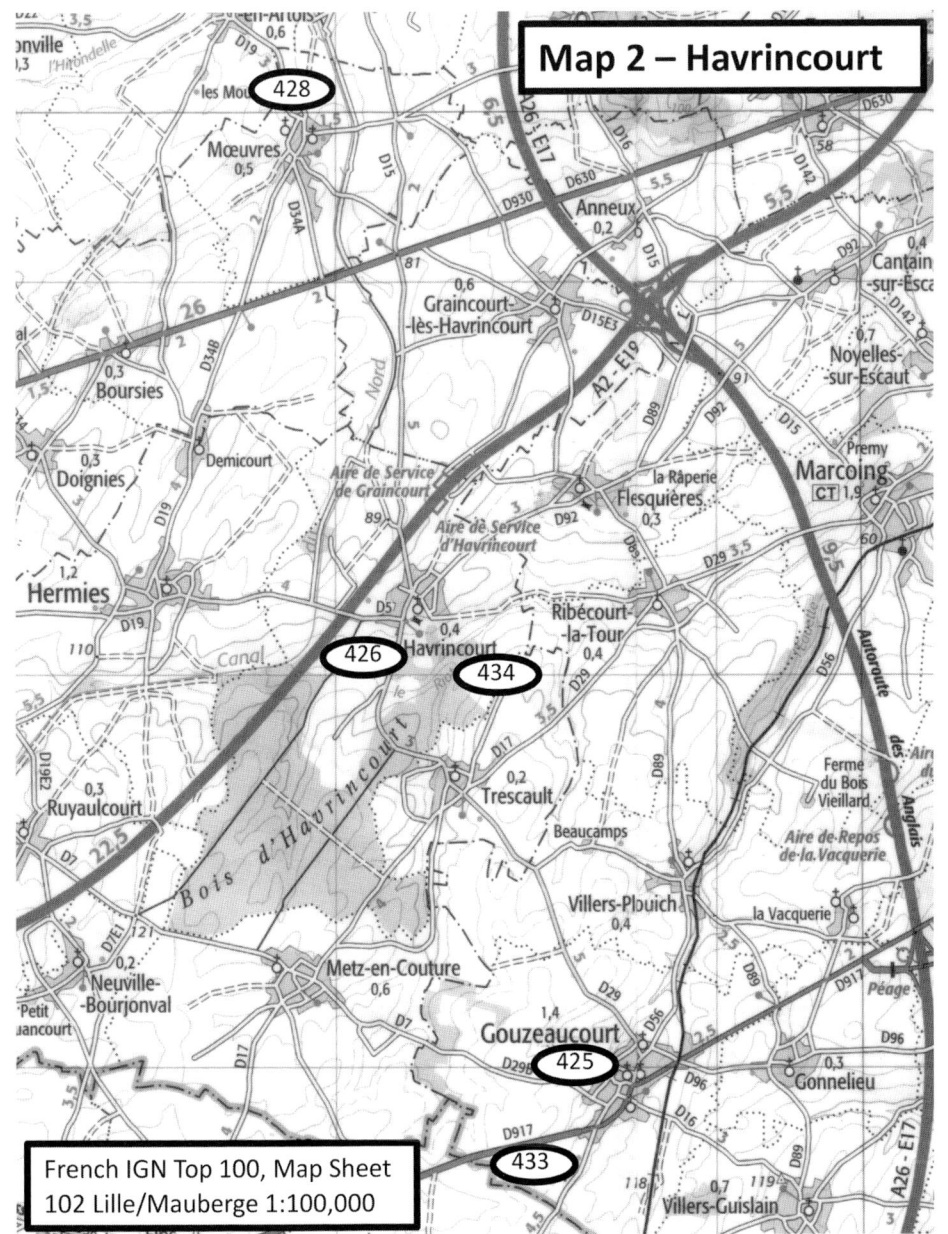

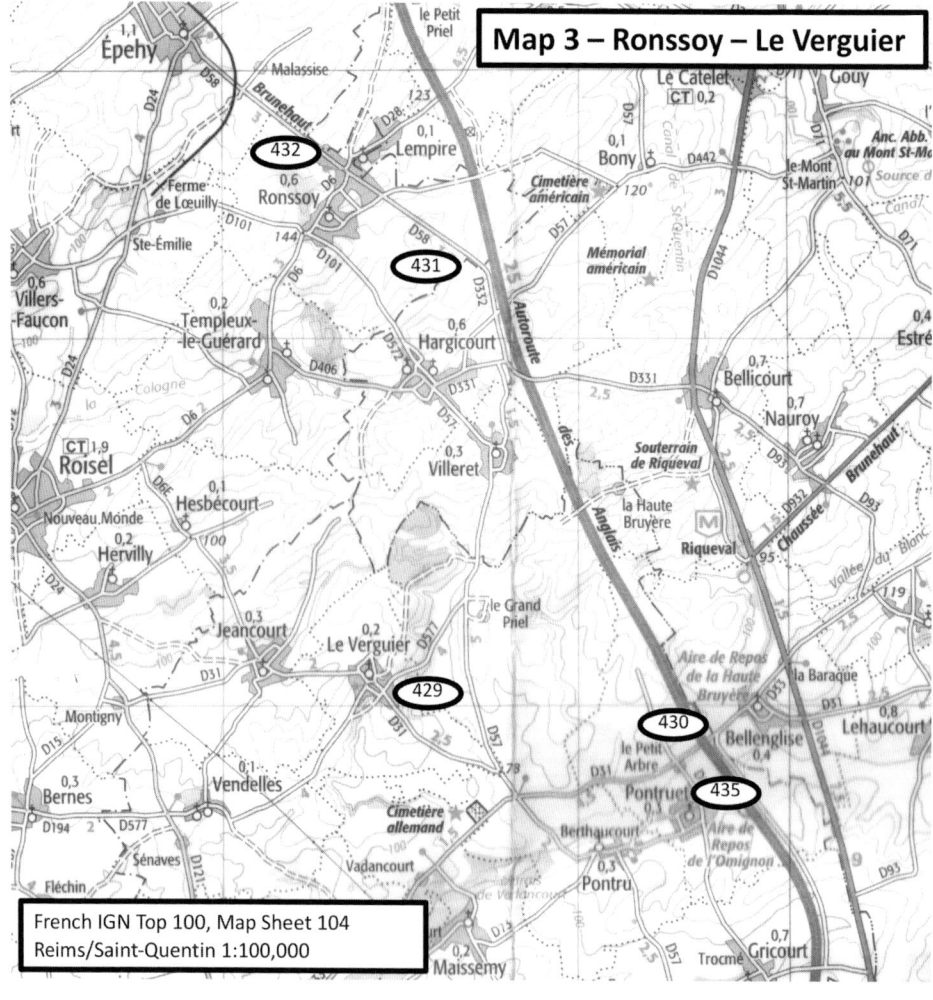

Map 3 – Ronssoy – Le Verguier

French IGN Top 100, Map Sheet 104
Reims/Saint-Quentin 1:100,000

# Abbreviations

| | |
|---|---|
| AASC | Australian Army Service Corps |
| AWM | Australian War Memorial |
| ADMS | Assistant Director Medical Services |
| AE | Australian Engineers |
| AFA | Australian Field Artillery |
| AFC | Australian Flying Corps |
| AIF | Australian Imperial Force |
| Aka | also known as |
| AMF(L) | ACE (Allied Command Europe) Mobile Force (Land) |
| AMPC | Auxiliary Military Pioneer Corps |
| AT | Auxiliary Transport |
| Att'd | Attached |
| BEF | British Expeditionary Force |
| BM | Brigade Major |
| BS | Bachelor of Surgery |
| Capt | Captain |
| CBE | Commander of the Order of the British Empire |
| Ch | Chateau |
| C-in-C | Commander-in-Chief |
| CO | Commanding Officer |
| Col | Colonel |
| Cpl | Corporal |
| CSM | Company Sergeant Major |
| Cty | Cemetery |
| CWGC | Commonwealth War Graves Commission |
| DBE | Dame Commander of the Order of the British Empire |
| DCM | Distinguished Conduct Medal |
| DSC | Distinguished Service Cross |
| DSM | Distinguished Service Medal |
| DSO | Distinguished Service Order |
| FC | Football Club |
| FRCS | Fellow of the Royal College of Surgeons |
| FRSM | Fellow of the Royal Society of Medicine |
| GBE | Knight/ Dame Grand Cross of the British Empire |

| | |
|---|---|
| GCSE | General Certificate of Secondary Education |
| GEC | General Electric Company |
| GHQ | General Headquarters |
| GOC | General Officer Commanding |
| GSO1, 2 or 3 | General Staff Officer Grade 1 (Lt Col), 2 (Maj) or 3 (Capt) |
| GWR | Great Western Railway |
| HMHS | Her/His Majesty's Hospital Ship |
| HMS | Her/His Majesty's Ship |
| HMT | Her/His Majesty's Transport/Troopship/Hired Military Transport |
| HT | Hired Transport |
| KBE | Knight Commander of the Most Excellent Order of the British |
| KCB | Knight Commander of the Order of the Bath |
| Kia | Killed in action |
| Kms | Kilometres |
| LCpl | Lance Corporal |
| LG | London Gazette |
| LLP | Limited Liability Partnership |
| LRCP | Licentiate, Royal College of Physicians |
| Lt | Lieutenant |
| Lt Col | Lieutenant Colonel |
| Lt Gen | Lieutenant General |
| Maj | Major |
| Maj Gen | Major General |
| MB | Bachelor of Medicine |
| MBE | Member of the Order of the British Empire |
| MC | Military Cross |
| MD | Medical Doctor |
| MGC | Machine Gun Corps |
| MID | Mentioned in Despatches |
| Mk | Mark |
| MM | Military Medal |
| MO | Medical Officer |
| MRCS | Member of the Royal College of Surgeons |
| MSM | Meritorious Service Medal |
| MS | Motor Ship |
| MT | Motor Transport |
| NCO | Non-Commissioned Officer |
| NSW | New South Wales |
| NZEF | New Zealand Expeditionary Force |
| OBE | Officer of the Order of the British Empire |
| Obj | Objective |
| OC | Officer Commanding |

| | |
|---|---|
| OTC | Officers' Training Corps |
| P&O | Peninsular and Oriental Steam Navigation Company |
| Pte | Private |
| PWRR | Princess of Wales's Royal Regiment |
| QF | Quick Firing |
| QM | Quartermaster |
| RA | Royal Artillery |
| RAAF | Royal Australian Air Force |
| RAFVR | Royal Air Force Volunteer Reserve |
| RAMC | Royal Army Medical Corps |
| RAN | Royal Australian Navy |
| RAOC | Royal Army Ordnance Corps |
| RASC | Royal Army Service Corps |
| RDC | Royal Defence Corps |
| Res | Reserve |
| RNAS | Royal Naval Air Service |
| RNZAF | Royal New Zealand Air Force |
| RNZE | Royal New Zealand Engineers |
| RSM | Regimental Sergeant Major |
| SA | South Australia |
| Sgt | Sergeant |
| SNCO | Senior non-commissioned officers |
| Sp | Support |
| SS | Steam Ship |
| Sw | Switch |
| TA | Territorial Army |
| TD | Territorial Decoration |
| TF | Territorial Force |
| Tr | Trench |
| TSS | Twin Screw Steamship |
| VAD | Voluntary Aid Detachment |
| VC | Victoria Cross |
| VD | Venereal Disease |
| VSEL | Vickers Shipbuilding and Engineering Ltd |
| WA | Western Australia |
| WO1 or 2 | Warrant Officer Class 1 or 2 |

# Introduction

The twelfth book in this series covers the beginning of the Battles of the Hindenburg Line, specifically the battles of Havrincourt and Épehy in September 1918. The book tells the story of eleven Victoria Crosses, three of which were awarded to Dominion troops.

As with previous books in the series, it is written for the battlefield visitor as well as the armchair reader. Each account provides background information to explain the broad strategic and tactical situation, before focusing on the VC action in detail. Each is supported by a map to allow a visitor to stand on, or close to, the spot and at least one photograph of the site. Detailed biographies help to understand the man behind the Cross.

As far as possible chapters and sections within them follow the titles of battles, actions and affairs as decided by the post-war Battle Nomenclature Committee. VCs are numbered chronologically 428, 429, 430 etc and, as far as possible, they are described in the same order. However, when a number of actions were fought simultaneously, the VCs are covered out of sequence on a geographical basis in accordance with the official battle nomenclature. As a result it may appear that 427 is missing. However, it appeared in the previous volume.

Refer to the master maps to find the general area for each VC. If visiting the battlefields it is advisable to purchase maps from the respective French and Belgian 'Institut Géographique National'. The French IGN Top 100 and Belgian IGN Provinciekaart at 1:100,000 scale are ideal for motoring, but 1:50,000, 1:25,000 or 1:20,000 scale maps are necessary for more detailed work, e.g. French IGN Serie Bleue and Belgian IGN Topografische Kaart. They are obtainable from the respective IGN or through reputable map suppliers on-line.

Ranks are as used on the day. Grave references have been shortened, e.g. 'Plot II, Row A, Grave 10' will appear as 'II A 10'. There are some abbreviations, many in common usage, but if unsure refer to the list provided.

I endeavour to include memorials to each VC in their biographies. However, every VC is commemorated in the VC Diary and on memorial panels at the Union Jack Club, Sandell Street, Waterloo, London. To include this in every biography would be unnecessarily repetitive.

In any work of this scale, it is almost inevitable that some errors will be included unintentionally. Every effort is made to cross-check facts. If mistakes occur, I apologise for them and urge readers to let me know so that future revisions can be made.

Thanks are due to too many people and organisations to mention here. They are acknowledged in 'Sources' and any omissions are my fault and not intentional. However, I must mention the contribution made by fellow members of the 'Victoria Cross Database Users Group', Doug and Richard Arman, and those no longer with us, without whom I simply could not complete these books. The cooperation of Steve Lee and the Memorials to Valour website team, who carry out amazing work, is also invaluable.

Paul Oldfield<br>
Wiltshire<br>
November 2021

# Battle of Havrincourt

## 12th September 1918

> 425 Sgt Harry Laurent, 2nd New Zealand Rifle Brigade NZEF (3rd New Zealand (Rifles) Brigade, New Zealand Division), Gouzeaucourt, France
> 426 Sgt Laurence Calvert, 5th Battalion, The King's Own Yorkshire Light Infantry (187th Brigade, 62nd Division), Havrincourt, France

The BEF spent the period 4th-11th September 1918 following up the retreating Germans as they fell back on the Hindenburg Line. On the 4th, Fourth Army crossed the Canal du Nord but, due to the tiredness of the troops, the pursuit was not vigorous. Third Army also crossed the Canal on its right and centre and on the left closed up to the Hindenburg Position. Advanced guards were ordered to remain in contact with the enemy but to refrain from large scale encounters. First Army was in contact with the Germans on the Canal du Nord and the Sensée, but the positions there could only be taken by a large operation. No major movement took place in this area until 26th September, except for the extreme left, which cooperated with Fifth Army and made a series of small advances.

For the rest of this period only Third and Fourth Armies made any progress. The other Armies had reached as far as they could without launching major offensive operations. Marshal Ferdinand Foch issued a directive for all allied armies to attack simultaneously on 10th September, which was later delayed to the 12th. The offensive was to be further extended on the 26th by additional French and American attacks on the Meuse-Argonne Front. In the meantime, Fourth Army made good progress following the German withdrawal, which pivoted on Havrincourt, north of which the Germans remained west of the Canal du Nord. Third Army swung its right and centre forward to keep pace with Fourth Army. A number of small but sharp actions were fought and further passages over the Canal du Nord were secured.

On 8th September German resistance stiffened. During the next few days forward movement slowed as the outposts of the main defences were reached and also because of the atrocious weather. The Germans intended to stand on the line from which they launched the March offensive. Only a deliberate and well-prepared attack would succeed in shifting them. By 11th September, Fourth Army had come to a halt almost everywhere as it prepared for a major operation on the

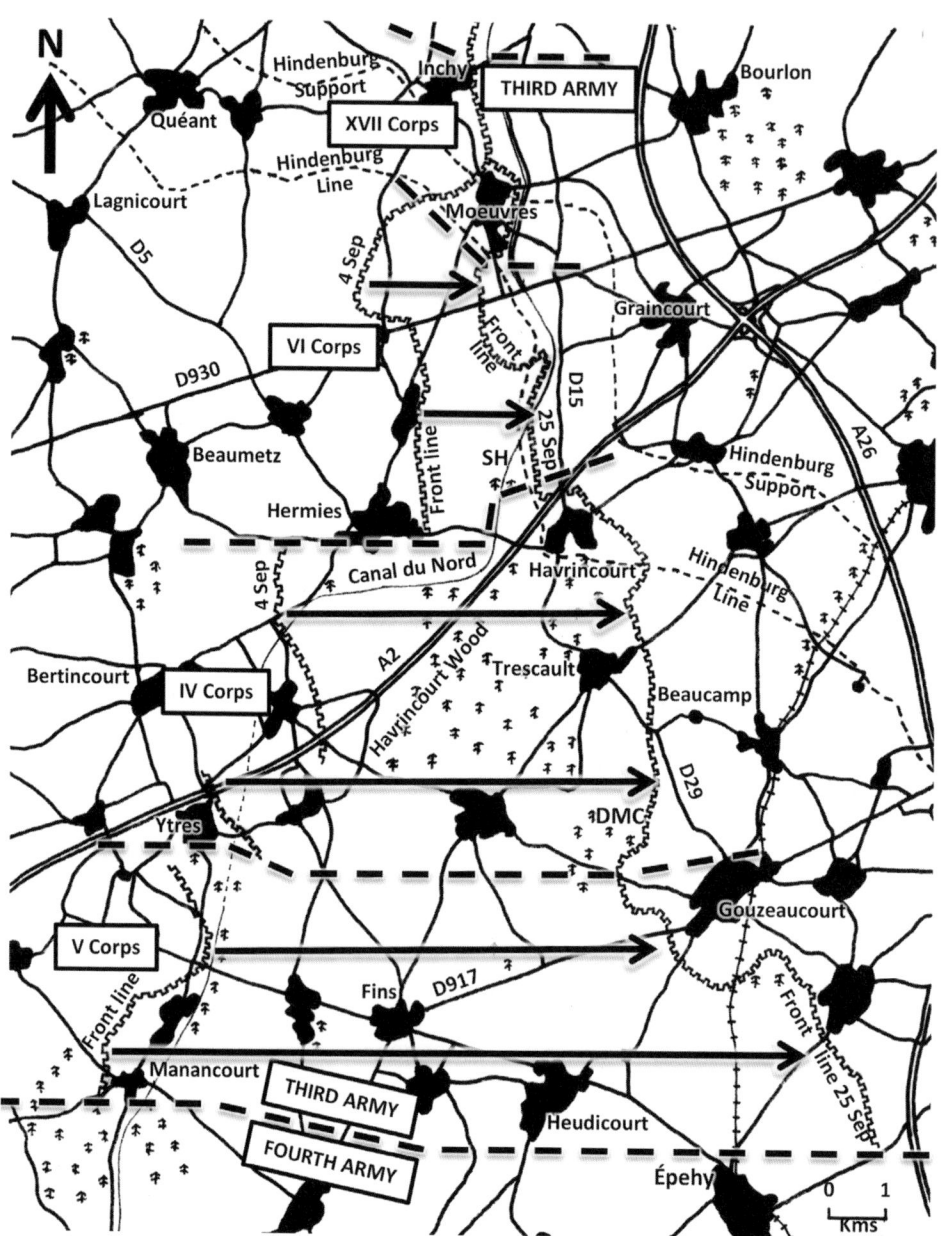

DMC = Dead Man's Corner, SH = Spoil Heap.
Third Army's progress from 4th to 25th September.

18th. Third Army used the 11th to make final improvements to its positions for an attack next day.

Foch asked Haig to attack the whole enemy position before they had the opportunity to properly prepare it. However, the British faced an enormous task. In

Fourth Army's area the Germans had six separate defence lines, including three old British lines and the Advanced, Main and Reserve Hindenburg Systems. Despite the scale of the task, the longer the British delayed the stronger the defences would become. In addition, although their spirit was not yet broken, the Germans were

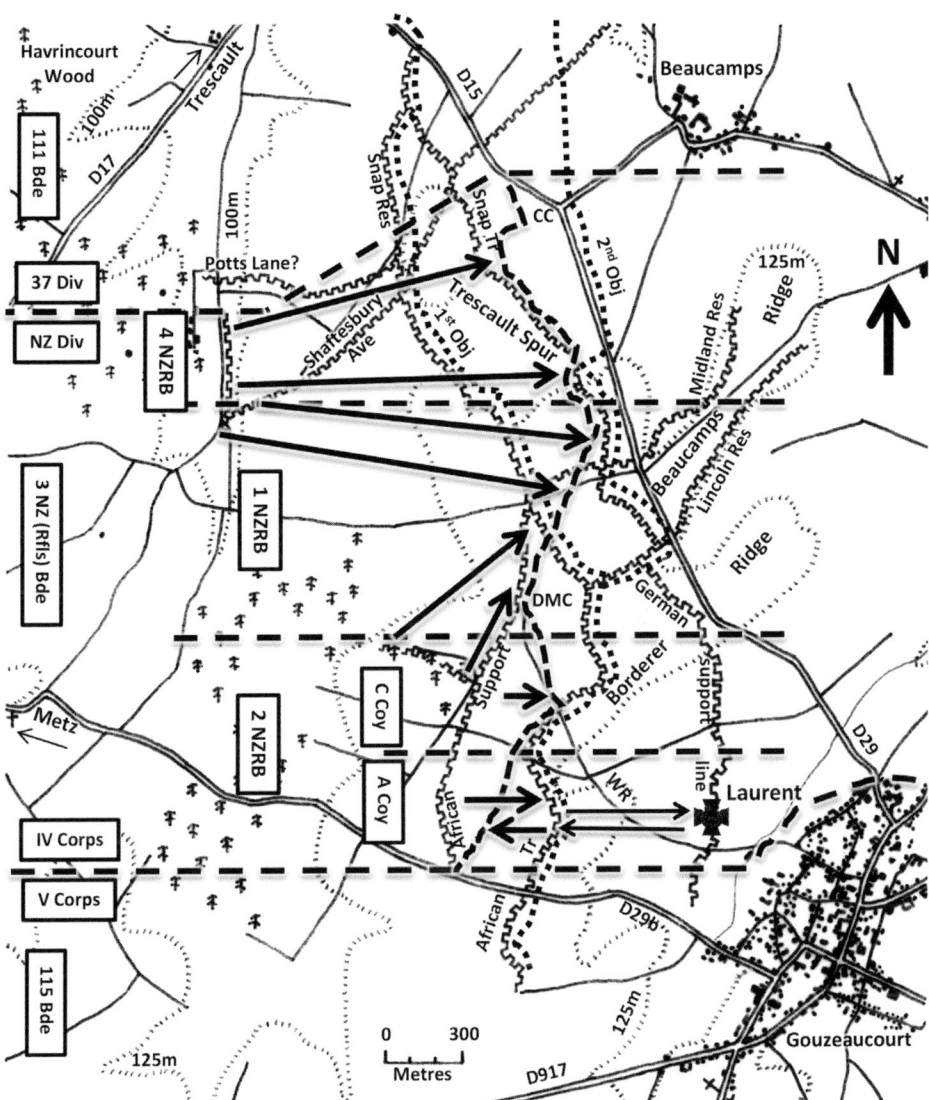

CC = Charing Cross, DMC = Dead Man's Corner, WR = Wood Road,
In Gouzeaucourt drive north along the D917 (Avenue du Général de Gaulle) until it swings to the right. Go straight on along the D29 (Rue de Villers Plouich). After fifty metres turn left onto Rue Blanche and follow this for 800m into open country beyond the north-western edge of the town, passing a large white barn on the left. Look back towards Gouzeaucourt. The trench captured by Laurent ran across the fields in front of you.

demoralised and the downward spiral had to be maintained. Rawlinson, commanding Fourth Army, advocated storming the first lines as quickly as possible, in order to gain observation over the main enemy Hindenburg positions. Byng, commanding Third Army, came to a similar conclusion, to attack as soon as possible to continue eroding the enemy's morale. The time for offensive action in Flanders was also approaching and Haig agreed for Second Army to operate under the command of the King of the Belgians.

Operations to reduce the outlying defences of the Hindenburg Position commenced on 12th September with Third Army fighting the Battle of Havrincourt and Fourth Army joined in on the 18th (Battle of Épehy). On the evening of 11th September, in a preliminary operation for the main attack next day, 2nd Division (VI Corps) secured the Spoil Heap on the west bank of the Canal du Nord. On 12th September the objective was the Trescault and Havrincourt spurs, running parallel to the front line and separated by the Grand Ravin.

In the centre of Third Army two of IV Corps' divisions made the attack against Trescault spur. On the right was the New Zealand Division and on the left was 37th Division. To the north, on Third Army's left flank, VI Corps attacked Havrincourt with 62nd Division alongside 37th Division.

The New Zealand Division led with its 3rd New Zealand (Rifles) Brigade. The right flank was protected by 115th Brigade (38th Division, V Corps). V Corps also prolonged the barrage to the south for two hours after zero on African Trench, Gouzeaucourt and the approaches from it to the ridge. The objective was 2,750m of the crest northwards from the main Gouzeaucourt road. On the right, 2nd New Zealand Rifle Brigade was to take African Trench. In the centre, 1st New Zealand Rifle Brigade was to pass through 3rd New Zealand Rifle Brigade, clear Dead Man's Corner and capture a sector of Snap Reserve as its first objective, and Snap Trench as the second. On the left, 4th New Zealand Rifle Brigade's objectives were similar, except that the second objective was on the crest road from Gouzeaucourt to Trescault, 275m beyond Snap Trench. 3rd New Zealand Rifle Brigade was in reserve, with two companies on immediate call to 1st and 2nd New Zealand Rifle Brigade.

Six field artillery brigades were to provide the creeping barrage, moving forward ninety metres every three minutes, with a pause of fifteen minutes at each objective. The 4.5" howitzers had targets ahead of the field guns. Three batteries of 6" Howitzers were for counter-battery fire and other targets in Couillet Valley beyond the ridge. Four 6" Newton mortars were to bombard Dead Man's Corner, another crossroads 450m to the north and two strongpoints in front of 1st New Zealand Rifle Brigade. Six light trench mortars would supplement the creeping barrage. Two machine gun companies (Otago and Wellington) and a section of a third (Auckland) were to fire a barrage on the Brigade's first objective. The three remaining sections of the Auckland Company were to accompany the attacking troops, one with each battalion. The assault battalions were in position an hour before dawn. Although the weather had turned cold and wet, the morning of 12th September was fair and cool. When the barrage opened at 5.25 a.m., the leading elements pushed forward close to the line of bursting shells.

2nd New Zealand Rifle Brigade had consolidated its position in African Support following the attack on 9th September. Light mortars were deployed on the right flank and to deal with Dead Man's Corner on the left. On the evening of the 10th the Germans made a final effort to recover African Support. They attacked in captured British helmets, regained Dead Man's Corner and then bombed from it and from African Trench towards the Support line, but were repulsed by Lewis guns and were chased back to Dead Man's Corner and their trenches. By the end of 11th September, the Battalion had joined up with V Corps on the right.

In the attack on 12th September 2nd New Zealand Rifle Brigade was led by A Company (Lieutenant Donald Kennedy MC – DSO for this action) on the right, and C Company (Captain Wallace Charles Ivan Sumner), on the left. D Company (Second Lieutenant ROC Marks) and B Company (Lieutenant HB Pattrick) were in support, with two platoons of each company detached to the forward companies as immediate reserves.

The barrage came down on the opening line for six minutes, then lifted onto African Trench for another fifteen minutes. Under its cover the attacking companies pushed through the wire and closed up behind the bursting line of shells. When the barrage lifted, the Battalion stormed forward. Although some stiff opposition was encountered, it was overcome quickly and African Trench, the Battalion's only objective, was taken.

However, A Company on the right discovered that the company of 115th Brigade that was to cover the flank had not come up in line. C Company on the left also had its flank open as 1st New Zealand Rifle Brigade had drifted northwards. The enemy put pressure on both flanks, which had to be bent back but they were held by sections of the support company fighting their way forward. Sergeant Frank Ellery (later DCM as a temporary company sergeant major) led a platoon of A Company in the attack, then found himself cut off with a few men on the right flank. Aided by Corporal William Smith O'Brien, who commanded one of the Lewis gun teams, he held out against repeated attacks until the Battalion was relieved after nightfall.

Before the attack each Battalion had detailed sections for exploiting success. These sections formed reconnaissance patrols which, immediately after the capture of the objective, were to work forward and maintain touch with the enemy. One patrol in 2nd New Zealand Rifle Brigade's A Company, consisting of twelve men with a Lewis gun, was commanded by **Sergeant Harry Laurent**. It moved forward from African Trench, which was hardly recognisable, having killed a number of the enemy there. Although the Germans were numerous elsewhere, this patrol happened to be in an area that was not garrisoned and the wire had been destroyed. Laurent led his patrol forward cautiously but steadily, taking advantage of the little cover available. The ground was swept by machine gun bullets and shells and a

Looking eastwards towards Gouzeaucourt. The section of the enemy support line captured by Laurent's section ran from the camera position towards the end of the tree line on the left of picture. The sunken road is on the right.

number of casualties were suffered, but there was no sign of the enemy. The patrol advanced down the slope and, as it approached a sunken road near Gouzeaucourt, identified a trench across its line of advance about 700m east of African Trench. Laurent realised that he had gone too far but before withdrawing decided to attack the enemy's support line, despite it being held strongly. He deployed his men, reduced by this time to just seven, and charged the trench. The aggression and ferocity of the attack surprised the Germans and very quickly about twenty had been killed. Rifleman Maurice Healey/Healy, alone on the flank, killed ten enemy with bayonet and bomb, including an officer who was frantically working the telephone. The telephone wire was cut and more of the enemy who continued to resist were killed. Corporal Edward William Wood (MM for this action) moved along the parapet firing his Lewis gun from the hip. An attempt by a German machine gun crew to come into action was thwarted and the enemy, demoralised by the sudden and fierce onslaught, threw up their hands. About thirty had been killed and wounded. The patrol was under heavy fire from all around. Some of the

Reverse of the previous view from the north-western edge of Gouzeaucourt looking west, with the sunken lane in the foreground running over the hill left of centre. The trench captured by Laurent's section ran across the field in the centre beyond the distinctive field boundary on the right.

enemy showed signs of making trouble and a number were shot, which had the effect of quietening down the remainder. The prisoners, an officer, 111 men and two messenger dogs, were bundled back to the Battalion's line, bringing the patrol's casualties, two dead and two wounded, with them. One member of the patrol was killed during the withdrawal. The prisoners were the survivors of a whole support company, whose position was extremely strong, with many concrete emplacements mounting machine guns and field guns firing over open sights. Laurent said later, *I never had a rifle. I had a revolver, and I don't think I ever took it out of the holster*.

Two particularly strong counterattacks were made by the Germans. The first at 6 a.m. was against the left of the Battalion, where C Company came under pressure from strong German bombing parties in African Trench and from a communication sap. Although they suffered heavy casualties, sheer weight of numbers enabled the Germans to work around the rear. C Company had to give up African Trench, as did the right of 1st New Zealand Rifle Brigade, and it fell back to the sunken Wood Road. Repeated attempts to regain the lost trench failed.

Despite the pressure on the flanks, the Battalion made efforts to regain parts of the objective that had been lost. One thrust by a support platoon under Sergeant AI Batty, captured twenty-six prisoners and seven machine guns. At 2 p.m. the Jägers attacked in greater strength from sunken roads on the right flank and managed to outflank the Battalion from the south. When bombs ran out, A Company was

gradually driven up African Trench to 200m south of Wood Road, which was held by C Company on the left. African Trench in this area had to be given up and a new line was established about halfway between African Support and African Trench. After being twice pushed back north of the Metz Road, A Company bombed south and regained it.

Fortunately Wood Road from Dead Man's Corner on the left, another sunken road on the right and a communications trench in the centre afforded covered approaches from the support positions. Fresh supplies of bombs were brought forward and all further German efforts from the flanks and in front were resisted. The flanks were strengthened by sections brought up from the supports and the leading companies were well established. On the right, A Company continued to resist stubbornly.

In the centre of the Brigade, 1st New Zealand Rifle Brigade had a hard struggle to gain the first objective in the face of heavy machine gun fire, but Snap Reserve was reached and cleared. When the barrage moved on, the attackers were swept by numerous German machine guns in Snap Trench and from Beaucamp Ridge. Continuing the advance over the open was impossible. Use was made of various saps and parties bombed forward against determined opposition. Three posts were established in the southern end of Snap Trench, the only part of the second objective to be captured. The left company established blocks to hold the enemy. Heavy showers from 9 a.m. made movement in the muddy trenches increasingly difficult. During the afternoon the Battalion launched a series of attacks along the saps and some progress was made, but the gains did not improve the hold on the forward trench. The Germans maintained pressure with repeated counterattacks. At 10.30 p.m. they launched a final counterattack along Lincoln and Midland Reserve saps from Borderer and Beaucamp Ridges. The forward posts were pushed back to the road running north from Dead Man's Corner, leaving the southern portion of Snap Trench in this area in enemy hands. Touch was maintained with the right of 4th New Zealand Rifle Brigade by a communications sap in the northern part of Snap Trench.

On the left, despite encountering serious opposition, 4th New Zealand Rifle Brigade, pushed along Shaftesbury Avenue and Potts Lane to secure the first objective in Snap Reserve on time. However, the Battalion faced a broader area to cross to the second objective, with Snap Trench lying midway between the two. Despite persistent efforts little progress was made. A party on the left succeeded in reaching the objective at Charing Cross but, being isolated, had to fall back again. Elsewhere posts were established in the saps. At 7 p.m. the Battalion launched a fresh attack supported by an artillery barrage, with 1st New Zealand Rifle Brigade co-operating. Although not a complete success, by 7.30 p.m. the whole of Snap Trench was captured within the Battalion's boundaries. On the left a post was established one hundred metres west of Charing Cross, close to the second objective and in contact with troops on the flank. In the final German counterattack at 10.30 p.m., the right platoon was all but annihilated and a support platoon had to re-establish the position.

Despite not gaining all its objectives, 3rd New Zealand (Rifles) Brigade had secured the greater part of the line on the crest of Trescault Spur, gained a footing in African Trench, cleared Dead Man's Corner for good and held the northern part of Snap Trench to the left boundary in contact with 37th Division. The enemy had suffered at least 300 killed and the New Zealanders had taken 492 (502 in some accounts) prisoners. The Brigade had 620 casualties between 1st and 12th September (128 killed, 477 wounded and fifteen missing). 2nd New Zealand Rifle Brigade's share was 149 (thirty killed, 114 wounded and five missing). During the night the Brigade was relieved by 1st New Zealand Brigade in pouring rain. 2nd New Zealand Rifle Brigade was relieved by 1st Auckland. The Brigade went into divisional support near Ytres and on 14th September the New Zealand Division became Corps reserve.

37th Division was led by 111th Brigade, which initially made good progress until reaching Trescault and a strongpoint to the east of it. The objective on the right and centre was eventually secured, but the left had to be bent back to remain in touch with 62nd Division to the north.

62nd Division had taken Havrincourt on 20th November 1917 during the Battle of Cambrai. The orders issued for this attack were therefore to 'recapture' it. On the left flank was 2nd Division (VI Corps), which was to support 62nd Division by rolling up London Trench and London Support in the Hindenburg Line. The initial advance by 62nd Division was to be north-easterly before swinging east to the final objective beyond the front Hindenburg Position. Havrincourt was then to be cleared from the west. Initially it was planned to use tanks but on 9th September it was learned that none were available.

On the right, the leading battalions of 186th Brigade (2/4th Duke of Wellington's and 2/4th Hampshire) overcame considerable opposition to capture the Hindenburg front system by 7.30 a.m. Another battalion then began the capture of the village. The chateau fell quickly, but resistance stiffened elsewhere and it was 11.30 a.m. before the eastern edge of the village was reached. The Divisional Pioneers, 1/9th Durham Light Infantry, attached to the Brigade for the operation, advanced 800m beyond the front Hindenburg Position, but was later forced back due to casualties.

187th Brigade on the left completed its move into Velu Wood by 2.00 a.m. on 11th September. That day officers reconnoitred routes to the assembly positions and as many as possible went forward to overlook the ground. That night the move forward went ahead without problems and the control posts and taped routes worked well. The Brigade was in position by 1.30 a.m.

187th Brigade attacked with 5th King's Own Yorkshire Light Infantry and a company of 2/4th King's Own Yorkshire Light Infantry on the right and 2/4th York and Lancaster on the left. 2/4th King's Own Yorkshire Light Infantry (less one company) in support, was to take over from 2/4th York and Lancaster after the first objective to secure the final objective. A Company, 62nd Battalion

# 10 Victoria Crosses on the Western Front – Battles of the Hindenburg Line

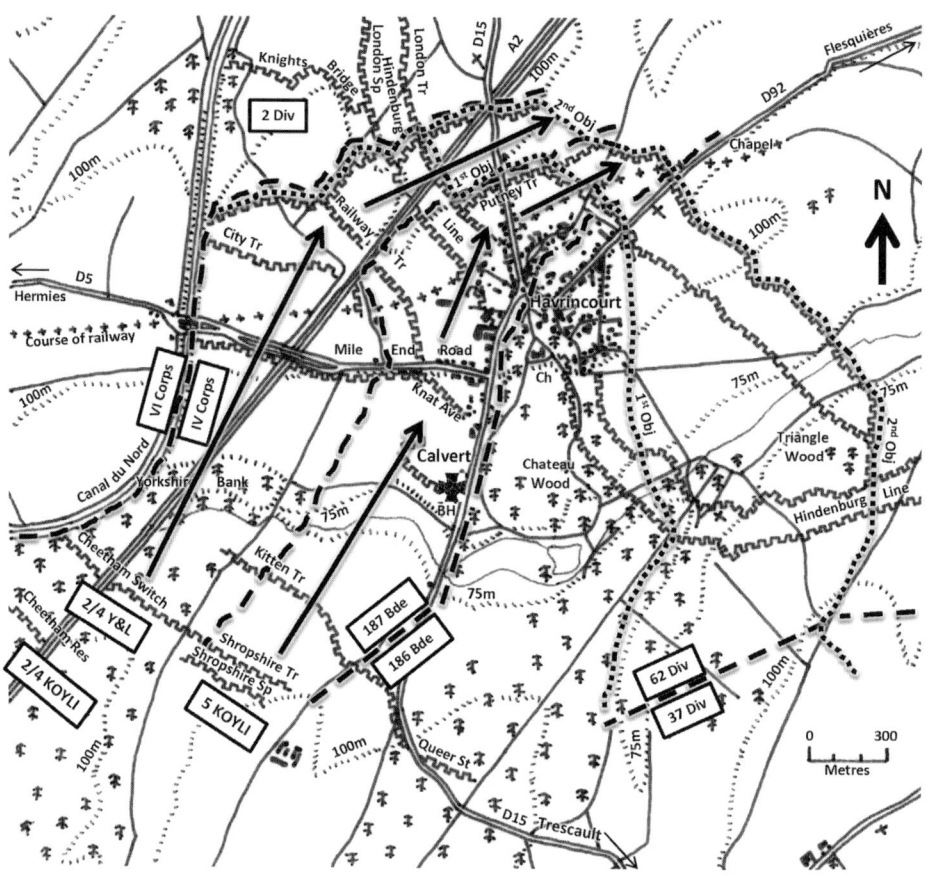

BH = Boggart's Hole, Ch = château.
Leave Havrincourt southwards on the D15 towards Trescault. Pass the right turn to Hermies (D5) and continue downhill for almost 600m, where there is a track on the right. Pull in here and look back up the hill towards Havrincourt. The hollow immediately in front of you is Boggart's Hole. Alternatively continue downhill for another 350m to where there is a layby on the left side of the road. Opposite the layby is a rough track leading to a large farm. A more elevated view can be obtained by walking southwest along this track for a few hundred metres.

MGC was attached and one of its sections was to assist the attack with direct fire from Yorkshire Bank. The attack was supported by a creeping barrage, which would pause for forty-five minutes on the first objective. The heavy artillery was to fire on selected points to the east of the creeping barrage. Two other companies of 62nd Battalion MGC and a company each of the Guards Division and 2nd Division Machine Gun Battalions were to fire a barrage in advance of the creeping barrage. After firing the barrage, one of the 62nd Division MGC companies was to move to Havrincourt Chateau Wood to support the advance to the second objective and to guard the valley south of Flesquières. One section of 187th Trench Mortar Battery was allocated to each battalion, with the remaining section kept in reserve. Two platoons of 2/4th Duke of Wellington's (186th Brigade) were to follow behind 187th Brigade's right to form a defensive flank along the edge of Havrincourt Chateau Wood.

At 4 a.m. the outposts of 63rd Brigade (37th Division), holding the forward line of Queer Street and Kitten Trench, withdrew. Just before zero the Germans fired a counter-preparation bombardment. 2/4th King's Own Yorkshire Light Infantry in particular suffered casualties from the shelling in Cheetham Reserve. At 5.25 a.m. the British artillery opened fire and the infantry launched their attack, keeping close to the creeping barrage. The vacated assembly trenches were occupied by 185th Brigade.

5th King's Own Yorkshire Light Infantry assembled in Shropshire Trench and Support. It advanced initially with C Company on the right and B Company on the left. C Company was to clear the triangle at the southwest corner of the village formed by Knat Avenue and Mile End Road. D Company was to pass through C Company to seize the quadrangle in the village formed by Railway Trench, Mile End Road and a line running northwest through the village square to where London Trench crossed the railway. On the left, B Company was to press on regardless to take Putney Avenue on the first objective, so that if C Company on the right experienced difficulties the flanking movement would assist it considerably. Putney Avenue was then to be occupied by the attached company of 2/4th King's Own Yorkshire Light Infantry, and B Company was to press on to the final objective. A Company moving behind B Company was to secure the ground north of the railway, regardless of any opposition that B Company might meet.

Almost immediately the advance was raked by heavy machine gun fire from Boggart's Hole, a depression west of the Trescault – Havrincourt road and 400m south of Havrincourt. The advance was held up as the attackers were caught in frontal and enfilade fire. **Sergeant Laurence Calvert** in C Company charged two machine guns on his own, bayoneted three of the crew and shot four more. The rest of the garrison were so shocked at the speed of Calvert's action that four officers and eighty soldiers gave themselves up immediately. A number of machine guns and six trench mortars were also taken. The way was clear for the advance to resume. B Company had a few problems on the left and all its officers were lost, but OC A Company led his Company through. The Battalion seized all its objectives by 7.30 a.m., suffering fewer than one hundred casualties.

The CO of 2/4th York and Lancaster reported at 9.00 a.m. that the Battalion was in contact with 2nd Division in London Trench. The left company had cleared London Trench and Support as far north as Knights Bridge, while the right company was in contact with 5th King's Own Yorkshire Light Infantry. 2/4th King's Own Yorkshire Light Infantry passed through for the final objective, which was reported to have been captured at 10.50 a.m. However, there was no touch with 186th Brigade on the right until midday.

From the farm track looking northwards along 5th King's Own Yorkshire Light Infantry's line of advance, with the D15 road, 187th Brigade's right boundary, on the right. Beyond the road are the grounds of Havrincourt château, with the village at the top of the picture in the centre. Boggart's Hole is the hollow to the left of the road with a scrubby hedge line running away from it to the left.

5th King's Own Yorkshire Light Infantry was resupplied by a supply tank and was tasked with clearing pockets of the enemy in the northeast corner of the village. The Brigade spent the rest of the morning and early afternoon mopping up and consolidating. 2/4th York & Lancaster was gradually withdrawn to London Support, Railway Trench and City Trench.

At 5.20 p.m. orders came from Division for 187th Brigade to take over the whole of Havrincourt, thereby relieving 186th Brigade. This meant that 5th King's Own Yorkshire Light Infantry had to extend to the right. At 6.50 p.m., while this relief was being organised, the Germans opened a furious bombardment, supported by low flying aircraft and heavy machine gun fire, against the junction of 186th and 187th Brigades. At 7.03 p.m. a very determined counterattack was launched by two fresh battalions of 20th Infanterie Division from Triangle Wood and the Chapel. Although there were some penetrations of 187th Brigade's line, the front was maintained throughout. The attack was broken up by concentrated small arms fire from 5th King's Own Yorkshire Light Infantry and 2/4th Hampshire (186th Brigade). At 7.30 p.m. the artillery joined in, in response to SOS signals.

Although the attack was driven off, the line was somewhat disorganised afterwards, making the readjustment of the front extremely difficult. The precise positions of the battalion being relieved were indefinite and so the relief was carried out by a series of fighting patrols. A company of 5th King's Own Yorkshire Light Infantry, assisted by some men of 2/4th York & Lancaster, worked south-easterly from Putney Trench, while another company advanced easterly along the Brigade boundary to meet a company working from the north, its place being taken by a company of 2/4th York & Lancaster from City Trench. Two companies of 1/5th Devonshire were sent up to occupy City Support in close support to 187th Brigade.

The conditions could not have been worse. Runners took three hours to cover 900m from company to Battalion HQ. The ground was extremely badly broken, with much discarded wire and collapsed buildings to negotiate, whilst also under heavy enemy shell and machine gun fire. Added to which, the relief was conducted in pitch darkness and heavy rain. However, it was completed at 9.30 p.m., but not without heavy casualties amongst 5th King's Own Yorkshire Light Infantry. There remained some doubt about contact being maintained in the northeast corner of the village.

Strong counterattacks continued for the next few days and the Germans pushed the British back 200m through the village before the situation was restored. Despite this, favourable positions for the grand attack on the Hindenburg Line had been secured.

## Battle of Épehy

> 428 Cpl David Hunter, 5th Battalion the Highland Light Infantry (157th Brigade, 52nd Division), Moeuvres, France

## 16th September 1918

Following the Battle of Havrincourt on 12th September, the British prepared for a major operation on the 18th (Battle of Épehy), involving First, Third and Fourth Armies. Some small scale operations were fought at key points along the line as the British manoeuvred into position for the main attack, including one at Moeuvres on Third Army's left flank. Moeuvres, on the Hindenburg Line, covered the southern end of the dry section of the Canal du Nord and the approaches to the key communication centre of Cambrai. While the Germans held the village, it prevented the British from rolling up the Hindenburg Line from the northwest: its possession was vital for both sides.

On the nights of 15th-16th and 16th-17th September, 52nd Division relieved 57th Division. 155th Brigade took over the line on the right at Moeuvres. The village had already changed hands several times and was badly battered. The defences consisted of a dozen posts (glorified shell holes) on the eastern side of the village facing the Canal du Nord. Next day, 155th Brigade extended left to take over an isolated post from 57th Division. It was in a shallow hollow, known as E14 Central from its map reference, and was 135m north of the village. Meanwhile 157th Brigade moved into the line vacated by 172nd Brigade (57th Division) on the left.

5th Highland Light Infantry, on the right of 157th Brigade, took over the Hindenburg Support Line between Inchy and Moeuvres from 1st Royal Munster Fusiliers at midnight on 16th September. B Company on the left and C Company

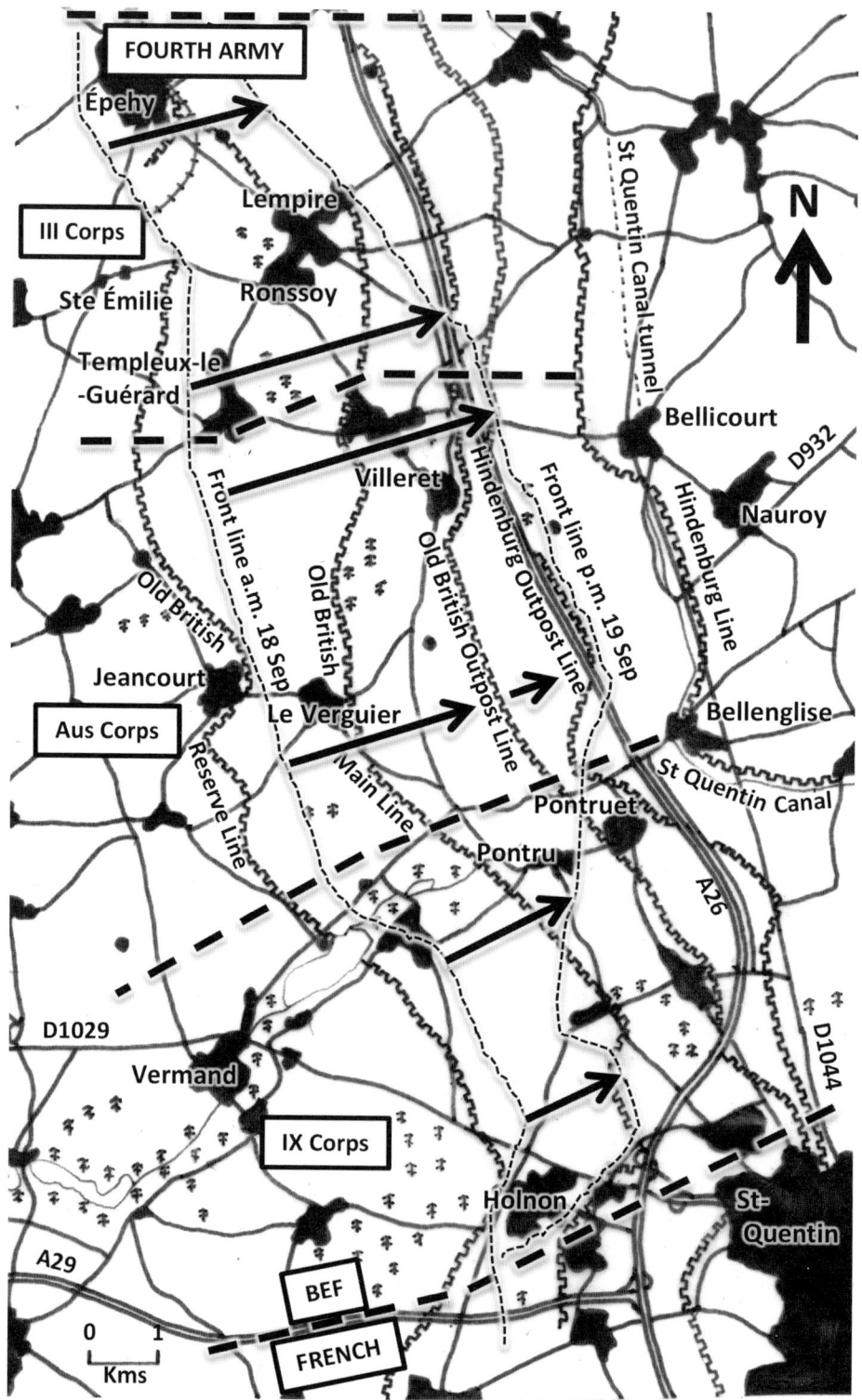

Fourth Army's progress during the Battle of Épehy.

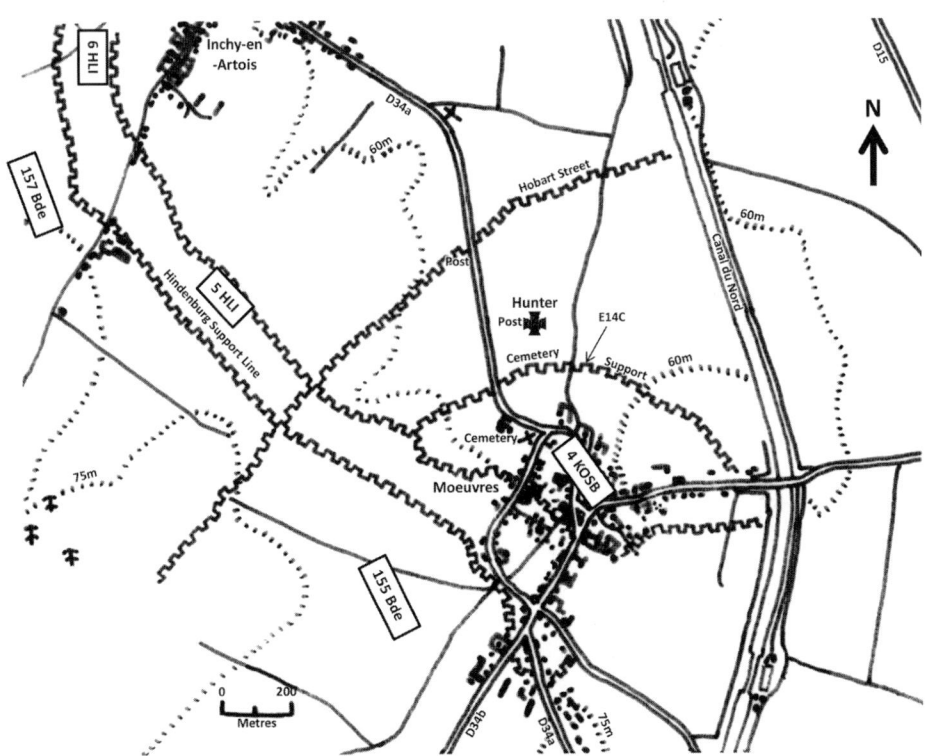

Drive into Moeuvres from the south and continue northwards, passing the church on the right. Just before leaving the village on the D34a towards Inchy, park at Moeuvres Communal Cemetery Extension on the left. Look across the road to Hunter's Post, which was 300m due north of this position. Continue driving towards Inchy. On the left side of the road is a brick pillar. Hunter's Post was 140m east of it in the field on the right side of the road, just about in line with a mast on the distant hillside.

on the right were in the front line, with A and D Companies in support. 4th King's Own Scottish Borderers (155th Brigade) was on the right and 6th Highland Light Infantry was on the left in Inchy, with 7th Highland Light Infantry in support, reinforced by two companies of 156th Brigade. A number of posts were occupied forward of the main line by 5th Highland Light Infantry, but the Battalion had only one third of its established strength and was hard pressed to cover its front. Very few men were available for the forward posts. C Company, only thirty-five strong, had to hold two posts in addition to a stretch of the line. One of these posts was about 500m forward of the main line, close to an enemy post in Hobart Street, just beyond the Inchy – Moeuvres road. The second post, 200m to the right of the first, was on the far side of the road and completely devoid of cover. It was occupied by **Corporal David Hunter** and six men with a Lewis gun. The post was essentially a large shell hole measuring about three metres by one and a quarter metres and was one and a half metres deep.

Looking south-eastwards with Moeuvres in the right background and the D34a road on the right. The brick pillar can be seen on the right side of the road, with three prominent poplar trees beyond it. Hunter's Post was 140m into the field on the left in front of the hedge. The Canal du Nord is marked by the line of trees running across the middle of the picture from the left towards Moeuvres.

At 10.30 a.m. on 17th September a German barrage fell on 155th Brigade's front on the right. The SOS signal was fired, a counter barrage came down and no major attack developed. A party of thirty Germans tried to rush E14 Central, but was driven back by small arms and artillery fire. By 11.30 a.m. the situation was once again calm.

It was planned to relieve C Company with D Company that night, as the former did not have sufficient men for its task. Before this took place, a heavy barrage of gas and high explosives fell on the village at 6.25 p.m. and extended northwards as far as Inchy. Thirty minutes later a strong attack was launched from the northeast, east and southeast simultaneously. 4th King's Own Scottish Borderers (155th Brigade) pushed the Germans back from the high ground south of Moeuvres but, in the low ground on the left, it was driven back to the Hindenburg Line on the western edge of the village, losing Cemetery Support Trench. The attack also pushed back 5th Highland Light Infantry's right flank, held by C Company. It was assumed that the two isolated forward posts had been overrun.

Hunter saw no reason to withdraw his post and decided to hold on and await a counterattack. The Germans tried several times to destroy the post. Bombers crawled close on a number of occasions but were either killed or driven back by small arms fire. One enemy machine gun persistently sprayed the post and Hunter was determined to get rid of it. At night, covered by his riflemen, he crawled towards the machine gun post. About twenty metres from it he threw in a grenade and charged with fixed bayonet to find the crew of six dead. Other enemy posts alerted by the explosion blazed away into the darkness and it took Hunter almost three hours to get back to his post, loaded down with the machine gun and ammunition. During

one of the days a British aircraft circled low over the post and Hunter hoped that this meant they had been found. However, nothing occurred afterwards.

The Battalion's flank, reinforced by two platoons of D Company, was drawn back to face southwest along Hobart Street. The extreme right was in the Hindenburg Support Line in contact with 155th Brigade. The other two platoons of D Company were to relieve C Company when the situation allowed. During the evening, companies of 4th and 5th Royal Scots Fusiliers reinforced 4th King's Own Scottish Borderers and linked up with the right of 5th Highland Light Infantry. Heavy fighting continued but the Germans were contained at the western edge of the village by 10.30 p.m.

A C Company stretcher-bearer, Private Chester, returned down the communications trench from the northern post and reported that it was holding out. A patrol was despatched with instructions to also find out what was happening at the other post. Corporal I Ross and three men had been lent to C Company by D Company to form a connecting link between the main line and the northern post. Ross had been wounded in the barrage but refused to fall back and had continued to hold the post. He was sent back to Battalion HQ and was awarded the MM for this action. Sergeant Glover and a corporal from this post then set off over the open towards Hunter's post. After thirty metres they were met with a shower of grenades and were driven back. Corporal M'Ewing (sic) and Private J Adams tried later but were caught in the light of Very flares just before reaching the Inchy – Moeuvres road. Coming under heavy fire they also had to give up. A third attempt also failed and, in view of the number of Germans in the area, it was assumed that Hunter's post had been overwhelmed. The whole of D Company became available later and relieved C Company, which was by then only seventeen strong.

Artillery duels continued and during the 18th the Germans pushed reinforcements into the village. The 5th Highland Light Infantry post on Hobart Street was driven back for a short period but managed to recover its position. The Germans attacked again at 5.30 p.m. but, despite gaining a footing, they were repulsed. 4th King's Own Scottish Borderers was replaced by 4th and 5th Royal Scots Fusiliers and that night D Company, 5th Highland Light Infantry was relieved by A Company. Artillery action and enemy attacks continued throughout the 19th. Early that morning several bombing attacks on 5th Highland Light Infantry's right were pushed back. In the afternoon an attack on a 5th Royal Scots Fusiliers post south of the village was also resisted.

At dawn on the 19th a wounded man from Hunter's post, 203406 Private D McFarlane, came in through B Company's right post. He had been sent by Hunter with 55784 Private Terence Mulhill, who was killed by a grenade on the way (Moeuvres Communal Cemetery Extension – V A 29), to make contact with the Company. McFarlane had been wandering around for five hours before he found the main line. With the light spreading nothing could be done immediately. Meanwhile, just before daylight, Hunter sent Private Jones back but he returned having been unable to find a way through the German positions. The men in Hunter's post faced another day without food or water.

At 7 p.m. the British launched a major attack. In 155th Brigade, 5th Royal Scots Fusiliers on the right headed northeast through Moeuvres and then along the Hindenburg Line, while 4th Royal Scots Fusiliers in the centre attacked eastwards through the village. Two companies of 7th Highland Light Infantry (157th Brigade) on the left, attached for the operation, attacked eastwards. They were to re-establish posts around the cemetery, recapture the two posts that it was assumed had been lost two days before and maintain contact between 5th Highland Light Infantry and 4th Royal Scots Fusiliers. Elements of 4th Royal Scots Fusiliers reached the east of the village by 8.45 p.m., but could get no further. Confused fighting took place in Moeuvres throughout the night and it was not cleared until 10.30 a.m.

The companies of 7th Highland Light Infantry formed up in Hobart Street and the Hindenburg Support Line on the left of 155th Brigade just in time for zero hour. They captured a post on the northern edge of Moeuvres. At 8 p.m., A Company, 5th Highland Light Infantry advanced from Hobart Street. Half the Company went forward along the trench, but could not get over the Inchy road. The other half attacked from half way along the trench, but the company commander, Captain William Francis Maxwell Donald, was killed (Moeuvres Communal Cemetery Extension – I C 1), one of many casualties, and the party lost direction. D Company was sent to reinforce, but the situation was unclear. About 8 p.m. it became clear that 7th Highland Light Infantry had succeeded on the right. Shortly afterwards two men, including 200062 Private John L Phillips, came in from Hunter's post and announced it was still holding out. A platoon was sent immediately and Phillips volunteered to guide it, despite being utterly exhausted.

A corporal of 1/7th Highland Light Infantry was challenged as he approached the post and that was the first contact Hunter had had with friendly troops for three days. The corporal then guided the exhausted men back. A few minutes later

Hunter and his two remaining men returned to their Company HQ in Hobart Street. However, the Germans held onto the area around the post, which was retaken by 5th Canadian Brigade next day.

With just six men behind enemy lines, Hunter had resisted all attempts to seize his post. They had no shelter against the lashing rain and only a day's ration and a water bottle each, but they held on in the open for almost seventy-two hours, during which they were shelled by the Germans and British twice each. Hunter was congratulated by the CO and was told to write home immediately as he had been posted missing. In addition to Hunter's VC, every man with him who survived received the DCM – Privates John Fleming (940668), W Gray (41617), William J Jones (55770), D McFarlane (203406) and John L Phillips (200062). Only two were not wounded during the ordeal.

That night, 157th Brigade was relieved by 5th Canadian Brigade, having suffered 118 casualties during this tour of duty in the forward area. 5th Highland Light Infantry was relieved by 25th Canadian Battalion by 11 p.m., having endured what it described as one of the most trying periods of the whole war. Hunter was asked if he would prefer to ride in an ambulance. He refused and insisted on taking his place in the ranks with the men of his company.

## 18th September 1918

> 429 Sgt Maurice Buckley aka Gerald Sexton, 13th Battalion AIF (4th Australian Brigade, 4th Australian Division), Le Verguier, France
> 430 Pte James Woods, 48th Battalion AIF (12th Australian Brigade, 4th Australian Division), Le Verguier, France
> 431 LSgt William Waring, 25th Battalion Royal Welsh Fusiliers (231st Brigade, 74th Division), Ronssoy, France
> 432 LCpl Allan Lewis, 6th Battalion The Northamptonshire Regiment (54th Brigade, 18th Division), Ronssoy, France
> 433 2Lt William White, 38th Battalion Machine Gun Corps (38th Division), Gouzeaucourt, France
> 434 2Lt Frank Young, 1st Battalion The Hertfordshire Regiment (112th Brigade, 37th Division), Havrincourt, France

The British launched another major attack on 18th September (Battle of Épehy), involving Fourth and Third Armies, supported by the French First Army to the south. The aim was to make inroads into the Hindenburg Line defences and close up to the line St Quentin – Cambrai, within attacking distance of the main Hindenburg Line. Six lines of defence were available to the Germans, including the overgrown former British reserve, main and outpost lines. The total attack frontage was twenty-seven kilometres.

Fourth Army had already overtaken the old British reserve line. Its objectives on 18th September were to seize the main and outpost lines and, if possible, exploit as far as the Advanced Hindenburg Line (also known as the Outpost Line). On 11th September, 32nd Division, which was attached to the Australian Corps, was relieved by IX Corps, which took over Fourth Army's right flank. Next day, General Rawlinson, Commander Fourth Army, met his corps commanders to plan the forthcoming attack. Three objectives were set. The first was the old British main line (Green/Brown Line) and the second was the old British outpost line (Red Line). The third objective was the Hindenburg Outpost Line (Blue Line), to be seized by exploitation. It was recognised that this would be a tall order in most places. On the same day it was announced that shipping had been found to take the 1914 men home on overdue leave. This resulted in 358 men from already severely under strength units in 1st and 4th Australian Divisions, the two assault formations, being removed just days before the attack.

The period 12th-17th September was used to improve start positions for the main attack, during which the far right moved forward 3,700m. Eight assault divisions faced twelve German divisions sited in reverse slope positions. In order to retain a degree of surprise there was no preliminary bombardment. The creeping barrage, containing ten percent smoke shell, would pause on the first objective to allow some of the field artillery to move forward. In total there were 1,488 guns and howitzers available. Tanks were to be used sparingly, with the majority in reserve for the main task of breaching the Hindenburg Line later. Only twenty machines were allocated for where resistance was expected to be strongest – four to IX Corps and eight each to the Australian and III Corps. The night before the attack, the RAF made a number of bombing raids on villages opposite Fourth and Third Armies.

Zero hour was 5.20 a.m. It rained heavily in the early hours, turning the ground very muddy, and thick mist hung in the valleys, making direction keeping difficult. IX Corps, on the right, was hampered by preliminary operations failing to secure the desired start line and poor French assistance. The few tanks available either ditched or were knocked out. Some progress was made, but the objectives were not taken. Another attack by 2nd Brigade (1st Division) at midnight on the left flank managed to reach Fourmi Trench and make contact with the Australians to the north. However, it later fell back 300m to a sunken road.

The Australian Corps, in the centre, spent the days before the offensive nibbling away at the enemy in order to establish a clear start line. There were significant differences in the Australian Corps' plan compared to the other Fourth Army corps. For example, the Australians only wanted to pause on the first objective for an hour but, because of IX Corps to the south, 4th Australian Division had to plan on two hours' delay. At the second objective the Australians planned to begin exploitation to the third after just fifteen minutes. However, the left of IX Corps would not be ready to do so for two hours. There was considerable concern when Lieutenant Colonel TR Marsden DSO, CO 5th Australian Machine Gun Battalion, was captured. He had wandered beyond the outposts while reconnoitring for the forthcoming attack and was carrying a map with the objective marked on it.

Fifteen brigades of field artillery were available. The barrage would fall 175m ahead of the infantry start line and remain there for three minutes before moving forward. The infantry were directed to keep as close as possible to it. Air dropped smoke bombs were to be used in certain areas, in addition to smoke fired in the barrage. In addition to the eight tanks allocated to the Corps, ten dummy tanks of hessian on wooden frames were to be used to give the impression of a larger armoured threat to the Germans. Each assault division was allocated another division's machine gun battalion to double the concentration of the machine gun barrage. When the barrage opened at 5.20 a.m. it included 200 machine guns in the Australian Corps alone.

The Australian Corps attacked with 4th Australian Division on the right and 1st Australian Division on the left. Having decided, for sound tactical reasons, not to reduce brigades to three battalions, in line with British formations, Australian battalions were by this time very weak. In 1st Australian Division they averaged just under 360 all ranks and in 4th Australian Division about 425. Having also lost men on home leave, most battalions reorganised into three rifle companies, each of three platoons. The four brigades leading the assault totalled just 5,822 men.

4th Australian Division attacked with 12th Australian Brigade on the right and 4th Australian Brigade on the left. 12th Australian Brigade advanced on a one-battalion front with 48th Battalion to the first objective, 45th Battalion to the second and 46th Battalion to the limit of exploitation. White bursting rifle grenades were to be fired on each objective to signal success. On the Green Line they were to be fired southwards, on the Red Line northwards and on the Blue Line vertically. Attached for the operation was 12th Australian Machine Gun Company, with its A Section to 48th Battalion, C and D Sections to 45th Battalion and B Section to 46th Battalion. Also attached were two sections 13th Field Company AE, B Company of 4th Australian Pioneer Battalion, 10th Field Brigade AFA, half a troop of 13th Australian Light Horse and a Mk V Tank of B Company, 2nd Tank Battalion, which was not to go beyond the Green Line. Two mortars of the Brigade Light Trench Mortar Battery were attached to each assault battalion. The two mortars attached to 48th Battalion were to join 46th Battalion as it passed through, in preparation for the attack on the Blue Line later.

At 5.23 a.m., 48th Battalion advanced with three companies leading – C Company on the right, D Company in the centre and B Company on the left, with A Company in support. When the real tank moved forward, a number of dummy tanks followed about 400m behind until they reached the start line and were then parked and concealed. The Battalion crossed a valley to the old British main line on a low spur opposite. The left company captured its sector easily, having advanced 1,100m. The centre was fired on at Dean Copse but quickly overcame the opposition there. The right company came under heavy fire between Dean and Cooker Trenches and the

The advance of 4th Australian Division on 18th September.
AF = Ascension Farm (site of), AW = Ascension Wood, BBC = Big Bill Copse, BG = Buisson-Gaulaine Farm (site of), CP = Coronet Post, CQ = Cooker Quarry, GC = German War Cemetery, Maissemy, LBC = Little Bill Copse, MS = Mill Spinney, PC = Parker Copse, T = Tumulus, TC = Thierru Copse (Bois Chenaveaux), VCR = Victoria Cross Roads.

commander was seriously wounded. The tank attached to the Brigade went through the Australian barrage to the Green Line and then turned south across the front to the boundary with IX Corps. On the way it destroyed several enemy positions and, having completed this mission, returned to its rallying point. Then C Company jumped into the German trenches and bombed along them. The Germans pulled back to their battalion HQ in Parker Copse behind the spur and a sunken road, where they reorganised. They had numerous casualties from artillery fire in this area. The old British main line was taken everywhere. C Company alone took 350 prisoners. Overall resistance had been negligible. The Battalion war diary records the objective being taken at 6.30 a.m. The success signal was seen at 6.45 a.m. but it was not until 7.35 a.m. that 48th Battalion formally reported to Brigade HQ that the whole of the Green Line had been captured.

During the seventy minutes pause on the first objective, the protective barrage was much lighter. The mist and smoke thinned and German snipers and machine gunners in the next objective fired on the troops digging in. On the right, 1st Division (IX Corps) had advanced slower, although the right company of 48th Battalion was joined by elements of 2nd Royal Sussex in the old British main line (Mareval Trench).

The platoon commanded by Lieutenant W Parry MC worked around the shoulder of the spur into the valley in which the German battalion was being rallied in Parker Copse and the sunken road. Two other platoons also moved over the spur. The Lewis gunners took up positions and forced the Germans into cover. Corporal TA Price DCM got behind the German HQ and bombed a dugout. Sixty prisoners were taken, including the battalion commander. Other enemy were surrounded and a total of 187 were taken prisoner. Casualties had been light with a total of sixty-one, of which only four were killed. About 500 prisoners were taken as well as a field gun, a minenwerfer and numerous machine guns.

45th Battalion, following 400m behind 48th Battalion, which failed to keep up with the leading assault troops, was hit by the German artillery. There were many casualties including the CO, adjutant, signals officer, intelligence officer and a company commander. Cover was sought in a sunken road and shell craters. Not all the artillery was in position at 8.20 a.m. when the second phase was to begin. The second objective was about 1,350m ahead on a higher spur. A tumulus on the right flank was expected to cause trouble but was taken by British troops, according to one source. However, 12th Australian Brigade's war diary maintains that enemy fire from 2nd Brigade's area caused a number of casualties, particularly from Cooker Quarry, a trench northeast of it and the tumulus north of Pontru.

Although the British were behind on the right, 45th Battalion pushed on, taking the hilltop and several hundred prisoners. This was partly due to the enemy being demoralised and disorganised and the lack of enemy artillery fire. A battery of 5.9" Howitzers was seen trying to limber up to get away, while being protected by some machine guns. It was shot up by the Lewis gunners and the survivors were captured, along with the howitzers. Another battery was abandoned to the north. Some of the Germans displaced by 48th Battalion on the left were also captured. The advance swept on and posts on the hilltop were seized while the garrisons sheltered in their dugouts. The Red Line was reached by 9.35 a.m. Beyond was a wide valley with another spur on which was the Hindenburg Outpost Line. Visibility was much improved and the cathedral in St Quentin could be seen. A German battery in Pontruet was shelled out of the village. Ahead German batteries and transport were moving back to safety.

Meanwhile on the left, 4th Australian Brigade's assault troops had formed up on a taped line about 135m behind the forward posts, which were withdrawn half an hour before zero. The Brigade advanced with three battalions leading. 13th and 15th Battalions were to pass around le Verguier, south and north respectively, to the first and second objectives. 16th Battalion in the centre was to clear the village and then hold the Brown Line as Brigade reserve. 14th Battalion was to pass through after the second objective and exploit to the Blue Line. Three tanks were allocated to the Brigade but they were not to go beyond the Green Line. Two tanks were with

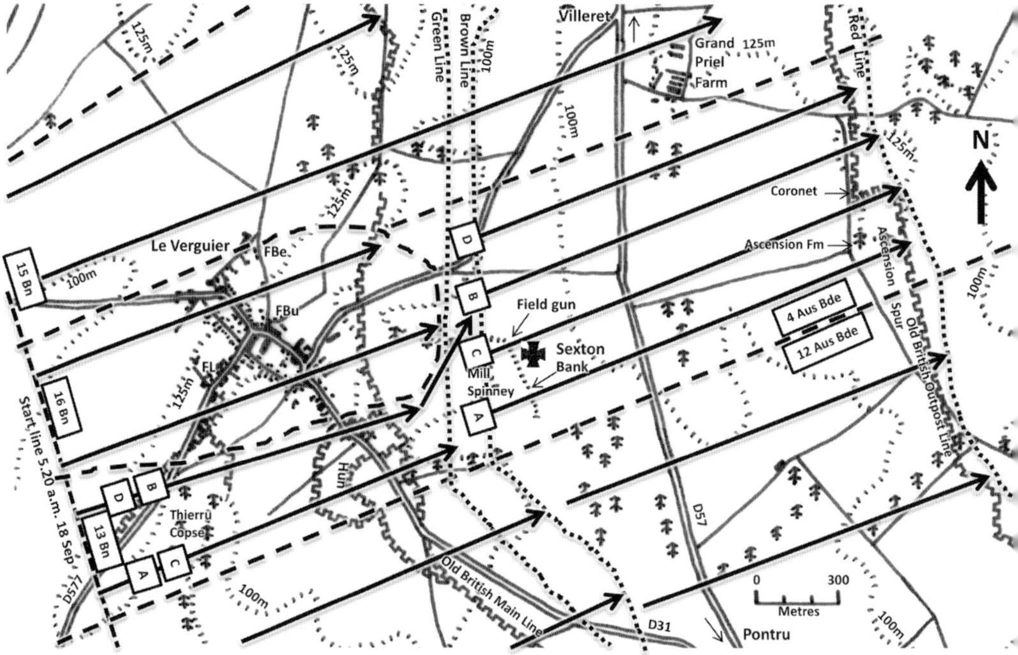

## 24  Victoria Crosses on the Western Front – Battles of the Hindenburg Line

FBe + Fort Bell, FBu = Fort Bull (Dyce), FL = Fort Lees,
Leave Le Verguier south-westwards towards Vendelles on the D577. After a few hundred metres park on the left, where there is a recycling centre and a new cemetery. Behind the cemetery is Thierru Copse, now named Bois Chenaveaux on modern maps. This is the area in which the first actions that led to the award of the VC to Sexton took place. To view the later actions, drive north on the D57 from Pontru towards Villeret. Pass the left turn onto the D31 to le Verguier, continue uphill for 1,100m and park on the left side of the road, where there is hard standing next to a gas installation. Look to the west. In the low ground is the tree covered bank at Mill Spinney that was captured by Sexton. For a better view walk back down the hill for sixty metres and turn right along a faint track that skirts a copse on the left. After 175m there is a clear view of the bank and the three-sided Mill Spinney.

Thierru Copse (Bois Chenaveaux) in the centre, with the D577 Vendelles road on the right. Sexton cleared the first machine gun post and trench on the far side of the road before entering and clearing Thierru Copse.

16th Battalion to assist in the capture of the village and were then to accompany 15th Battalion. The third tank was with 13th Battalion. Each of the three leading battalions was allocated two sections (four guns) of the Brigade Machine Gun Company and two mortars from the Brigade Light Trench Mortar Battery.

The barrage fell on time and stood for three minutes to allow the infantry to close up. It then crept forward and was so effective that there was little opposition, although frequent belts of wire were encountered, often running diagonally across the line of advance. The tanks were unable to reach the start line on time and were of little assistance in the attack.

13th Battalion's strength on paper was 541 men but only 415 went into action, with companies just over eighty strong. When the advance commenced the Battalion was on a frontage of 500m but, after passing around the south of le Verguier, it expanded to 900m. There were complaints that the smoke was overdone and caused difficulties in maintaining direction. However, it did allow the assault troops to close with enemy positions largely unseen until the last moment.

A few men were hit by their own guns at the start, but the Battalion kept moving ahead and cleared some outposts in order to reach the old British main line, Hun Trench. **Sergeant Gerald Sexton (Maurice Buckley)**, leading a Lewis gun section in D Company, immediately ran into an enemy machine gun post. Calling on his section to follow, he rushed the post and killed the crew, which allowed the rest of the company to resume the advance. They had not gone much further when they came under fire from some bombers and riflemen about sixty metres ahead. Sexton rushed the trench, firing from the hip and either killed or captured everyone in the post. He then entered Thierru Copse (now Bois Chenaveaux) and killed or captured everyone there as well.

The advance continued over the ridge and B Company swung to the left around the eastern side of le Verguier to make contact with 15th Battalion. As the barrage moved ahead the smoke began to thin and soon visibility was up to 400m. Lieutenant RL Price pointed out to Sexton a bank at Mill Spinney from which a party of Germans firing a field gun, a large trench mortar and two light mortars,

The copse near the gas installation on the D31 (out of sight far right) is on the extreme left of picture. Le Verguier is on top of the hill in the centre. 13th Battalion advanced down the hill towards the camera position and to the right. The bank at Mill Spinney runs across the centre of the picture.

were causing casualties. Sexton pressed ahead once more, firing short bursts from the Lewis gun and calling on his section to follow him. He jumped a trench and tore his clothing as he passed through barbed wire belts. Rushing down the bank, he shot the gun's crew and then, under fire from two machine guns, rushed over a flat area to shoot another group of twelve and then back to the bank near the field gun. There he fired into some dugouts and thirty Germans surrendered, including a battalion commander. It was the HQ of a battalion of 58th Infanterie Regiment (119th Division). As a result of Sexton's bold action, B Company on the left was able to resume its advance to meet up with 15th Battalion east of le Verguier. Corporal Alfred David Edwards, who joined Sexton in capturing the field gun, was awarded the DCM.

On the right was C Company supported by A Company. 48th Battalion had been held up to the south and a gap opened between the two units. A Company came up on the right of C Company and worked south a little to make contact with 48th Battalion. C Company under Captain HW Turner captured an aid post and seven machine guns without opposition. However, a party marching along the Pontru road about 175m ahead was mistaken for Australian and managed to get away. C Company reached the objective on the Brown Line at 6.30 a.m. B and A Companies were a little later. 13th Battalion dug in while contact was made with 15th Battalion on the left at almost the exact spot envisaged.

16th Battalion approached le Verguier under fire in small groups. The defences were strong and the wire was largely uncut. However, many machine gun posts were found abandoned. At three large strongpoints the attackers were engaged by machine guns and grenades but these were quickly surrounded. The occupants retreated into deep dugouts and were bombed until they surrendered. At Fort Bell

seventy were captured, including a regimental commander. At Fort Lees another twenty-eight prisoners were taken with six machine guns. The main position, Fort Bull behind the village centre (this appears as Fort Dyce on trench maps), also fell, along with thirty-seven prisoners. Overall, for twenty casualties, 16th Battalion took 450 prisoners, sixty machine guns, four or five field guns and two anti-aircraft guns.

15th Battalion on the left met only slight opposition, which was overcome quickly, to reach the Brown Line. 4th Australian Brigade, which had started closest to the objective, then had two hours to wait before commencing the advance to the second objective. 13th and 15th Battalions were to continue leading. In the meantime, several hundred Germans slipped away with their machine guns and reorganised. However, the delay allowed some field batteries to move forward and the renewed creeping barrage cowed the defenders successfully.

13th Battalion's plan was for A and D Companies to pass through C and B Companies to the second objective. However, the Battalion was so weak that it had to advance with all four companies in line, with A Company on the right, C Company centre right, B Company centre left and D Company on the left. They climbed Ascension Spur and a number of farms were taken. Sexton's company (D) was held up by three machine guns, two on the right and one on the left. A platoon had gone to ground and was engaging the gun on the left but it was not silenced. Standing upright Sexton engaged the post on the left and silenced it. He then switched attention to the two machine guns on the right, which were pouring fire into the area around him, and also silenced them. He then moved forward, followed by the platoon, and entered a trench, where he killed a number of Germans and advanced along a sap to take five prisoners.

Coronet Post on the summit held twelve machine guns but the crews had taken shelter in dugouts due to the barrage. 13th Battalion rushed in as the barrage lifted and found them there. Eighty prisoners were taken in a trench near Ascension Farm. Sexton cleared three more machine gun posts and on the second objective he was made responsible for the post on the left of D Company. He silenced a machine gun that was firing across the company's front from about sixty metres away, enabling the rest of the men to dig in. Sexton then went forward again along a sunken road and captured fifteen more prisoners.

13th Battalion suffered 109 casualties (eleven killed and ninety-eight wounded) between 17th and 21st September. One of those killed was 1109 Sergeant Albert Dawson, an original member of the Battalion, born in Scotland, who was due to go on home leave on 21st September (Villers-Bretonneux Memorial). In the same period the Battalion captured 560 prisoners, two field guns, eight light and medium mortars and over thirty intact machine guns. The battle on 18th September was 13th Battalion's last major action in the war. In addition to Sexton's VC, a number of other awards were made to the Battalion for this action:

DSO – Lieutenant Henry Seymour Baker.

DCM Bar – Sergeant James Lihou DCM MM.

DCM – Sergeant Arthur John Acton, Corporal Alfred David Edwards and Privates Thomas Andrew Denny & F Shepherd.

MM Bar – Private Edward Carlton Wicks MM.

MM – Sergeants Leonard Climpson & Frederick James Darke, Corporals John Banks, Joseph Henry Duncan, Henry Martyn, William McRay McDonald & Keith Miller and Privates Aubrey James Robert Cornell & Keith Leslie Chambers.

MSM – RQMS Jack Mitchell and Sergeant R Hill.

15th Battalion also kept up with the barrage and resistance was weak. Several hundred prisoners were taken. By 9.35 a.m. both battalions had seized the second objective and dug in on the eastern slope of Ascension Spur under machine gun and sniper fire from the Hindenburg Outpost Line.

The main enemy trench in the third objective was between 1,100m and 1,800m from the old British outpost line, higher up and well protected by dense wire entanglements. It was not possible to attack it with patrols alone and therefore whole battalions were committed to the third stage – 46th Battalion in 12th Australian Brigade and 14th Battalion in 4th Australian Brigade. They set off at 9.49 a.m.

On the right, 46th Battalion advanced with C Company on the right and D Company on the left, supported respectively by A and B Companies. The left cooperated with 14th Battalion and the whole line was supported by the machine guns attached to 45th Battalion on the Red Line. Spare Lewis guns followed on mules. The right company echeloned back in order to cover the open southern flank, where 1st Division (IX Corps) was pausing for two hours before launching its exploitation phase. There was no creeping barrage but the heavy guns engaged the Blue Line until 10.03 a.m. and then lifted onto targets beyond. The advance came under heavy fire but platoons dribbled across Ascension Valley with few losses. The bank of the road running north-south through Victoria Cross Roads was reached and the Battalion had established a line there by 2 p.m. This road was also held by 14th Battalion to the north and it was swept by intense fire from the Hindenburg Outpost Line. A Lewis gun managed to set up in a position from where it could engage the German machine guns as they popped up. At 5 p.m. the British heavy artillery opened fire on the German lines and a field battery shelled the enemy wire. The shells burst so close that the Australian troops withdrew from the bank down into the road. It was arranged that another attack would be launched at 11 p.m.

14th Battalion advanced into the wide Ascension valley and immediately came under machine gun fire from the Hindenburg Outpost Line on the opposite crest. The two leading companies advanced by short rushes using shell holes for cover on the bare slope. It was expected that Australian machine gunners would fire overhead to suppress the enemy fire but this did not appear to materialise. There were many casualties but Ascension Wood was reached and the defenders fled. By then 150 men were advancing on a frontage of 1,375m, too weak for the task in hand, and the support companies came up in line. German machine gunners in Big and Little Bill Copses were hit by the Lewis gunners and forced to retreat. The right of the Battalion worked up the hillside to a low road bank but, whenever they showed themselves above it, were hit by a storm of machine gun fire. All attempts to get forward here were halted. However, bombing parties got into the German trenches south of Buisson-Gaulaine Farm and pushed on several hundred metres to the southeast. A German party got between two of the bombing parties via a communication trench and a sharp fight followed, in which the Germans lost six men killed. Despite this setback, enemy opposition increased.

About 11 a.m. it was learned that 3rd Australian Brigade to the north was getting into the German line. A 14th Battalion company was withdrawn to work around into 3rd Australian Brigade's area and bomb southwards along the German line and eastwards to the support line. The attack southwards began at 12.45 p.m. but, despite initial success, was held up in a straight section of trench covered by a machine gun. The attack was halted.

Another attempt was arranged for 11 p.m. after a bombardment in cooperation with 46th Battalion. With the 1st Division (IX Corps) still some way behind, two companies (A & B) of 48th Battalion (12th Australian Brigade) were to attack on the right of 46th Battalion to cover the open flank. However, it was learned later that 2nd Brigade (1st Division, IX Corps) was to attack at midnight to link up with the Australian right flank. Accordingly one of the two assault companies of 48th Battalion was instructed to form a defensive flank. The other was put under command of 46th Battalion but was to be kept out of the fight for as long as possible in support.

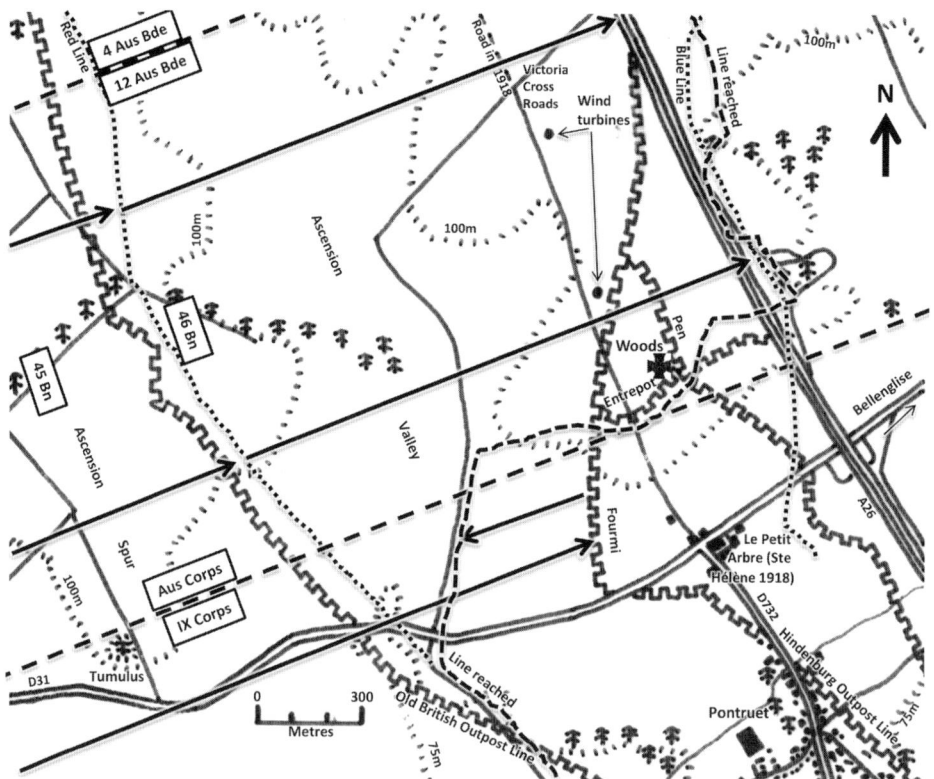

Approach Pontruet from the west along the D31. At a crossroads, where the right turn leads to Pontruet on the D732, turn left along a rough track that climbs uphill towards a series of wind turbines. Go as far as the first one (No.8) and use the hard standing below it to turn round and head back the way you came. Stop just over the brow of the hill. Woods' VC action was in the field half left from this position.

At 10.55 p.m. a short but heavy rainstorm burst overhead and the barrage opened on the German wire. After three minutes it lifted onto the German front line for two minutes, while the assault troops made their way through the wire. It was extremely dark and negotiating gaps in the wire proved difficult. 46th Battalion was led by A Company on the right and B Company on the left. The defenders opposite them, who far outnumbered the attackers, were sheltering in dugouts from the artillery and rain, and left their machine guns unmanned. They were bewildered by the attack, which had been expected at dawn. Many surrendered and others fled southwards. The assault moved on to the second enemy trench, where there was some severe fighting before it was secured. The positions were mopped up and a barricade was constructed in Pen Trench, where the Germans were still active. Although the Blue Line was reported captured at 1 a.m., pockets of enemy held out within the captured lines until next day. About 450 prisoners were taken. By 3 a.m. preparations had been made to meet a German counterattack at dawn.

One company of 14th Battalion was to attack south along the Hindenburg first trench. Another company was to charge over the open from the same trench to the second and then turned south to bomb parallel with the first. Another company would follow and bomb northwards along the second trench. One company was caught between the two trenches by heavy machine fire and went to ground but a Lewis gun silenced the machine guns and allowed the trench to be rushed. Both trenches were then cleared for about 800m with just a few losses. Those bombing to the north made contact with 3rd Australian Brigade but no contact was made with 46th Battalion to the south until just before dawn, when it was discovered that the two battalions were separated by 550m. 4th Australian Brigade captured a total of 1,137 prisoners, fifteen field guns, 150 machine guns, fifteen medium mortars and two anti-tank guns.

By dawn on 19th September almost all the exploitation objective in the Australian Corps area had been captured. On the right flank of 12th Australian Brigade, a patrol of three men of 48th Battalion was sent to investigate the junction of Pen and Etrepot Trenches at the southern end of the ridge. It had been reported that 1st Division was there, which seemed unlikely as it had only reached Fourmi Trench 250m to the west the night before and had been forced to fall back 300m. In the patrol **Private James Woods** rushed the German post at the trench junction, captured one German and wounded another. The rest of the garrison fled, leaving behind six machine guns (four heavy and two light). One of Woods' companions was wounded and about thirty Germans counterattacked along the trenches and over the open. Woods lay on the parapet under heavy fire and threw bombs passed up by his comrades. He thus managed to hold off the attack on his own. More men of 48th Battalion arrived along Pen Trench and this flank was secured. However, the area was contested bitterly and the Battalion suffered more casualties in this part of the battle than in securing the first objective. 12th Australian Brigade suffered 239 casualties up to 19th September (twenty-six killed, 211 wounded and two sick). In the period ending on 21st September, the Brigade took 1,411 prisoners, seventeen artillery pieces, three minenwerfers and ninety-three machine guns.

1st Australian Division attacked with 3rd and 1st Australian Brigades, each on a two-battalion frontage. The assault battalions set off into the dawn mist, which was thickened by the smoke shells, and direction was maintained by compass bearing. Scouts in pairs moved about 135m ahead of the assault companies, which were in section lines. Many enemy outposts were taken from the rear.

3rd Australian Brigade had fierce fighting in Grand Priel Wood and lost the barrage. However, with the support of a tank, progress was made and the first objective was gained. The support battalions passed through at 8.30 a.m. Heavy fire was met from machine guns and the barrage was lost again. Other tanks helped in capturing Villeret and the old British outpost line, which was seized after some hard fighting. Those enemy who were not killed, either surrendered or fled. East of Cologne Farm and Villeret the old British and German outpost lines ran close

Looking south from near the first wind turbine, which is behind the camera. The line of trees disappearing over the horizon, just left of centre towards the cluster of wind turbines, mark the A26 Autoroute. The lane on the right leads downhill to Pontruet, which is mainly hidden by trees in the low ground. 46th Battalion advanced from right to left across the lane to just beyond the line of the A26 on the far left. The junction of Pen and Etrepot Trenches was in the middle of the field left of the lane.

together for 1,800m and in places were interlaced. Patrols were sent ahead while the second objective was being consolidated. Aggressive action by these patrols led to more of the disorganised enemy surrendering, while others fell back even further. Posts were established in the Hindenburg Outpost system, overlooking the Canal, the tunnel entrance and Bellicourt and Nauroy. By 10.30 a.m. the right of 1st Australian Division was consolidating the third objective.

By 10 a.m. next day, 1st Australian Brigade on the left had cleared almost all of the Cologne Farm ridge but not all of the third objective, although observation over the St Quentin Canal was gained. Contact was made with III Corps to the north, which had only managed to reach the second objective at Malakoff Farm. In total the Australian Corps captured 4,243 prisoners, seventy-six guns, over 300 machine guns and thirty mortars. It suffered 1,260 casualties.

Prior to the attack, III Corps, on the left of Fourth Army, had taken some prisoners, who confirmed that the attack was expected and that the German positions would be stoutly defended. The strong defences around Ronssoy, Lempire and Épehy, which covered the tunnelled section of the St Quentin Canal, assumed great importance, as a breakthrough there would obviate the need for an assault over the canal elsewhere. III Corps used all four divisions in the initial attack. Each division committed a single brigade to lead the advance, except for 74th Division, which employed 230th and 231st Brigades, right and left respectively, each reinforced by an extra battalion from a reserve brigade.

After dark on 16th September 231st Brigade was relieved by 18th Division and then took over the line held by 230th Brigade. This allowed the latter to sideslip southwards. That night 15th Suffolk (230th Brigade) slipped into the Australian Corps area to the south, in order that the attack could head in an east-north-easterly

direction. At zero hour the Battalion swept into Templeux-le-Guérard and the Quarries, taking the garrison by surprise. The rest of the Brigade also reached all its objectives and beyond. However, the advanced troops were forced back from Triangle Trench in the evening, due to being under British artillery fire. They fell back to Rifle Pit Trench and a counterattack forced the Division back even further.

231st Brigade was led on the right by 16th Devonshire (attached from 229th Brigade) and 24th Welsh on the left. Two sections of C Company, 74th Machine Gun Battalion were attached to the attacking battalions throughout, as were two

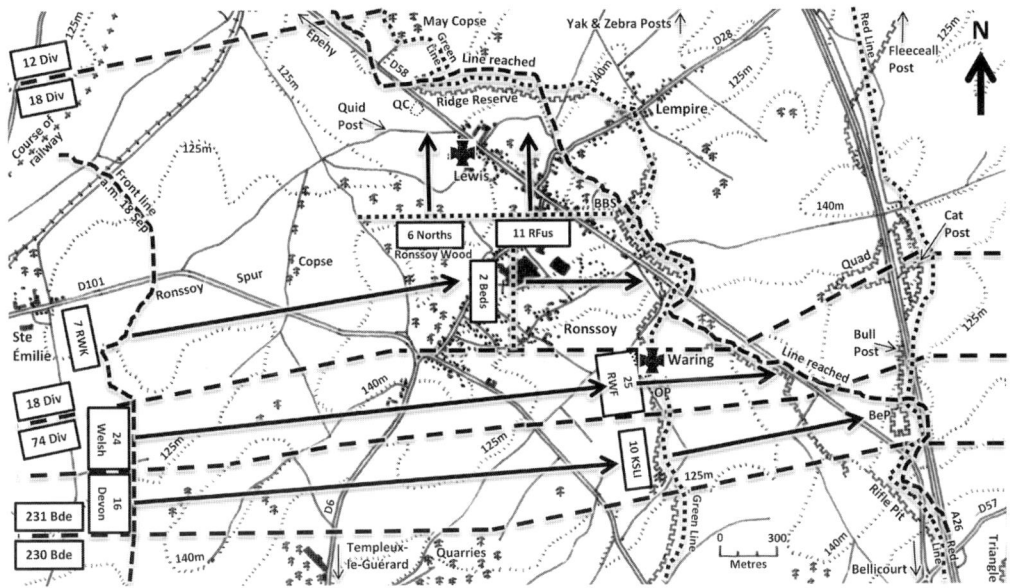

The right of III Corps on 18th September.
BBS = Basse Boulogne South, BeP = Benjamin Post, Copse = the small copse attacked by 7th Royal West Kent and 2nd Bedfordshire, OP = Site of Orchard Post, Quad = Quadrilateral, QC = Site of Quid Copse.

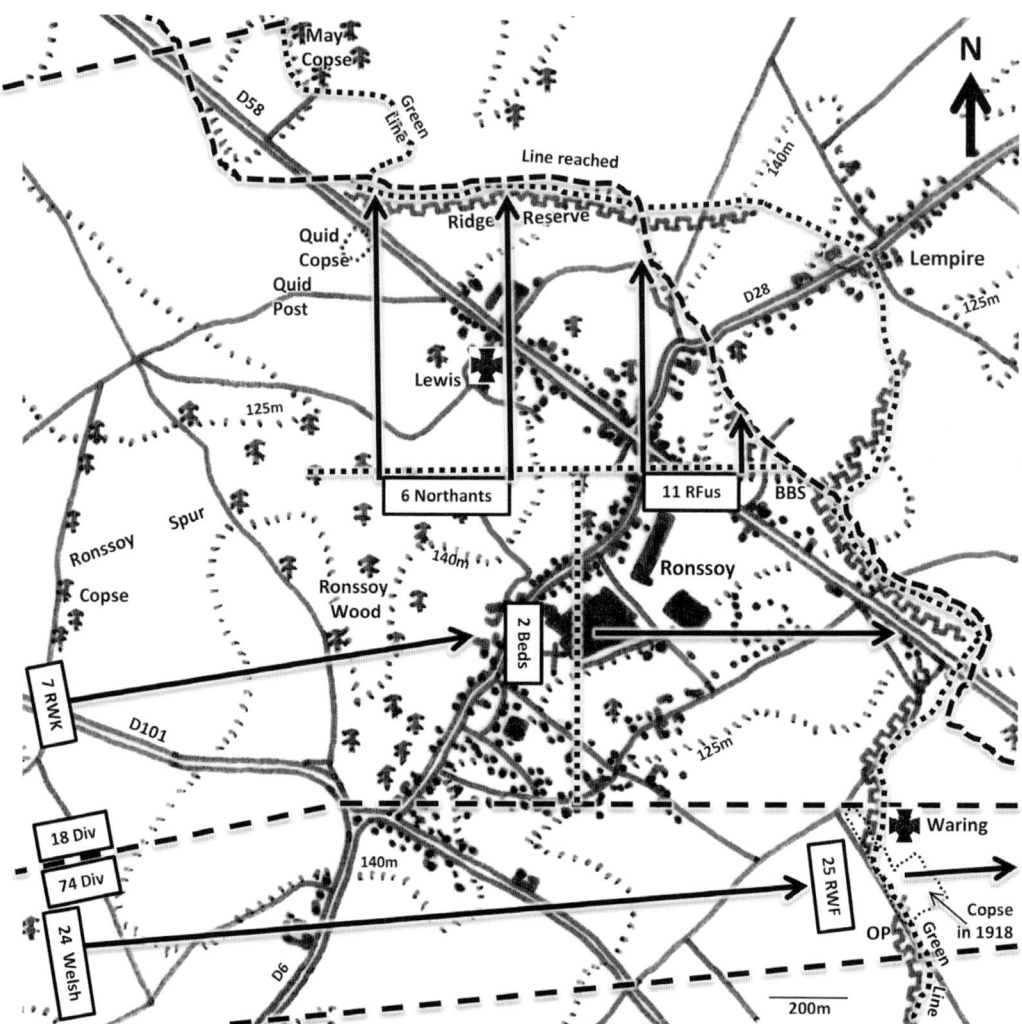

The complicated operation conducted on the boundary between 18th and 74th Divisions on 18th September that resulted in the award of the VC to William Waring and Allan Lewis.

To view the site of the Waring VC action, approach Ronssoy along the D58 from the southeast. Just before the village sign (Le Ronssoy) turn left onto a track and follow this for just over 100m to where there is space to park and turn round. Continue walking along the track to the southwest for 200m. Look to the left over the fields to where Waring rushed the strongpoint. Alternatively, particularly in wet weather, pass the village sign on the D58 and after 220m turn left at a crossroads onto Rue Franklin Roosevelt. Drive along this road for a few hundred metres and park on the roadside on the right. Look left to the southeast and the position of Waring's VC action.

To view the site of the Lewis VC action, approach Ronssoy along the D58 from the southeast and drive through the village (Rue Winston Churchill) until the end of village sign appears on the right side of the road. There is a small layby just before it. Park and cross the road, where there is a track junction. Look back to the southeast towards the village. Lewis's VC action was amongst the houses and this is the closest vantage point without entering private property.

mortars from the Brigade Light Trench Mortar Battery. At the first objective (Green Line), the troops were to consolidate about 275m ahead of it, in order to avoid the anticipated enemy artillery reaction. Meanwhile, the creeping barrage would pause for ninety-eight minutes from 6.52 a.m. At 8.30 a.m., when it commenced moving forward again, 10th King's Shropshire Light Infantry and 25th Royal Welsh Fusiliers, right and left respectively, would continue the advance to the second objective (Red Line). Consolidation there was to be just behind the objective trench, on the reverse slope, with posts dug in along the line of the trench to give warning of any counterattacks. The barrage would rest for fifteen minutes and then die away. Patrols were then to press ahead to the line of exploitation (Blue Line), whilst field batteries moved forward to support the new line. As platoons reached the first and second objectives, they were to fire Very lights of the same colour as the line reached, i.e. green or red. Three men from 182nd Tunnelling Company were attached to each battalion to search for booby traps.

The moon set at 2.37 a.m. on 18th September. Thereafter parties moved forward to cut gaps in the wire, while patrols covered them to the front. The assault troops were on the start line tapes by 4.30 a.m. 24th Welsh was instructed to detail one company to clear buildings to the west of Ronssoy and the southern street of the village. The company was not to leave the area until all cellars and dugouts had been cleared.

There was heavy rain overnight and, as dawn approached, thick fog developed. The advance commenced on time and initially there was not a great deal of opposition. The leading battalions reached the first objective (Green Line) at Orchard Post by 7.35 a.m. and took many prisoners. When the barrage began moving forward again at 8.30 a.m., 10th King's Shropshire Light Infantry and 25th Royal Welsh Fusiliers continued the advance to the Red Line. 25th Royal Welsh Fusiliers advanced with A Company on the right and B Company on the left, supported by C and D Companies respectively. Heavy resistance was encountered from numerous machine guns on the objective and the barrage was lost. **Lance Sergeant William Waring** led an attack against machine guns holding up neighbouring troops. Single-handed he rushed a strongpoint, despite devastating fire from front and flank, bayoneted four of the garrison and took twenty prisoners, together with their machine guns. Then, still under heavy artillery and machine gun fire, he reorganised his men and led them forward another 375m until he was mortally wounded. The advance ground to a halt 450m from the Red Line.

A renewed bombardment was arranged to fall along the Red Line. At 3.50 p.m. 10th King's Shropshire Light Infantry managed to get forward on the right and seize Benjamin Post from the west and south simultaneously. However, 25th Royal Welsh Fusiliers was unable to keep up. This was because 18th Division, on the left, was behind due to the resistance of the Quadrilateral. A defensive flank was formed along the Bellicourt road from Benjamin Post to near Basse Boulogne South, where touch was gained with 18th Division. Counterattacks on Benjamin Post that

From the track southeast of Ronssoy, which is on the extreme right of picture. Waring's VC action was in the field to the left of the track in line with the prominent copse on the far hillside.

evening and at midday on the 19th were driven back by 10th King's Shropshire Light Infantry, with heavy losses being incurred by the attackers. At 2 p.m. there was an unsuccessful attempt to capture Bull and Cat Posts but they were held in strength by the Germans and proved too strong to overcome.

25th Royal Welsh Fusiliers took over one hundred prisoners and twenty machine guns, while suffering sixty-five casualties (thirteen killed, forty-seven wounded and five missing). In total 231st Brigade recorded 279 casualties, of which eighty-two were missing. At the time that this was recorded in the Brigade HQ war diary, it was assumed that most of the missing had got lost in the fog and were with other units.

In the centre of III Corps, 18th and 12th Divisions had the formidable task of seizing the high ground of the Ronssoy – Épehy position. It was decided that the triangular basin between Ste Émilie, Ronssoy and Épehy would be avoided in the attack. Although this caused difficulties, it concentrated the attack by both Divisions onto narrower fronts and avoided the defences overlooking the basin itself. When

From Rue Franklin Roosevelt looking southeast. The D58 road is on the far left. Waring's VC action was in the low ground in the centre of the picture just beyond the telegraph pole.

the initial attacks had succeeded, both Divisions were to wheel inwards to roll up the main defences on the ridge joining Ronssoy and Épehy. The Royal Engineers made some dummy tanks that appeared to be entering the basin. However, on the day of the attack visibility was so poor that they failed to draw any fire.

18th Division was led by 54th Brigade in an unusual operation. The leading battalion, 7th Royal West Kent (attached from 53rd Brigade), was to advance along the south of the Ronssoy Spur to a north-south line through the eastern end of the cemetery in the village. From there 2nd Bedfordshire (a few days later it was commanded by Lieutenant Colonel Arthur Percival, who as a lieutenant general surrendered Singapore to the Japanese in 1942) would pass through to the road junction east of Ronssoy and south of Basse Boulogne. With the left flank protected by a standing barrage, 11th Royal Fusiliers and 6th Northamptonshire were to follow, form left and seize the first objective (Green Line) from the south. Later 11th Royal Fusiliers was to continue northwards to seize Yak and Zebra Posts. With the Green Line secured, 55th Brigade was to pass through and continue eastwards to the second objective (Red Line). 53rd Brigade was in reserve. Eight tanks were available to the Division. The northern part of 18th Division's front was not to be attacked but would be subjected to a heavy bombardment.

On the night of 16th-17th September, 8th Royal Berkshire (53rd Brigade) took over the front line positions from where the attack was to the launched. It carried out a programme of active patrolling and, early on the 17th, four prisoners were taken from 2nd Guards Regiment. They provided valuable information about the enemy that would be faced in the attack.

Forming up went smoothly, in spite of the atrocious weather, except for the rear company of 6th Northamptonshire, which arrived ten minutes late and suffered casualties from shellfire. When the attack got underway, the enemy barrage was strong at first but became progressively weaker. As a result, there were few casualties. The tanks found the ground conditions difficult and only six made it to the start positions.

7th Royal West Kent lost the barrage in the mist and drifted to the right. As a result the leading companies of 2nd Bedfordshire following in support found themselves involved in the early fighting. Both battalions became embroiled in

capturing a copse west of Ronssoy Wood. 2nd Bedfordshire pressed on, assisted by three tanks, and had continuous fighting all the way to its objective. The intended line was reached on time by 7 a.m., except on the left. It took 24th Royal Welsh Fusiliers (231st Brigade) on the right some time to clear the cellars. Considerable numbers of prisoners were taken. However, it was some hours before the whole of the village had been cleared, even with the enthusiastic assistance of two tanks of A Company, 2nd Tank Battalion.

11th Royal Fusiliers, on the right, and 6th Northamptonshire, on the left, formed up in the wake of 7th Royal West Kent and 2nd Bedfordshire. They moved off on time at 7.16 a.m., supported by a new enfilade barrage. Both battalions had already encountered pockets of the enemy and 6th Northamptonshire had suffered casualties in clearing Ronssoy Wood before reaching its start line. Once the attack commenced, they came under very heavy artillery and machine gun and became somewhat mixed up. By this time the fog was beginning to lift and they also came under long-range fire from Épehy, where 12th Division was held up.

11th Royal Fusiliers was hit by almost point blank artillery and machine gun fire from the right flank, but gained its objective and threw back two counterattacks. 6th Northamptonshire was led by B and C Companies, with A Company in support and D Company in reserve. The Battalion was in position just eight minutes before the appointed start time.

On the right of 6th Northamptonshire, **Lance Corporal Allan Lewis** managed to keep his section together when the fire became so intense that forward movement became impossible. The barrage went on and the Battalion was held up. Working through the ruins with his section, Lewis observed two machine guns enfilading the whole Battalion's front. On his own initiative he went forward and bombed both gun teams. The survivors tried to escape but he opened fire and wounded six with his rifle. Four others surrendered immediately.

6th Northamptonshire attacked from right to left into the northwest corner of le Verguier on 18th September. The main road through the village is on the left, with Ronssoy Wood in the right background. Lewis's VC action was behind the houses left of centre.

The Battalion was then able to continue. The northwest of the village was secured and some guns were seized. By 10 a.m., Quid Copse and Quid Post on the left had been captured. Touch was gained with 11th Royal Fusiliers in Ridge Reserve. Two field guns, fourteen machine guns and about 160 prisoners were taken. On the right two tanks assisted 11th Royal Fusiliers in securing Basse Boulogne. Patrols from Quid Post linked up with 12th Division at Knoll Post, but further forward movement was held up by heavy fire from Zebra Post and Fleeceall Post.

At 8.30 a.m., 55th Brigade continued the advance eastwards towards the Blue Line, but the task was almost impossible as the timetable did not allow sufficient time to clear the village. Renewed attacks in the afternoon ran into German reinforcements and the advanced parties were in danger of being cut off. At 7 p.m. they were withdrawn to the first objective. After dark, 6th Northamptonshire attempted several times to take May Copse on the Division's left flank, but it was not until 5 a.m. next morning that it was secured. On 21st September, Lewis' company was caught in a German barrage. Displaying excellent powers of command he rushed the men through the shellfire until they came under heavy machine gun fire and were forced into the cover of some shell holes. About this time he was killed by a shell.

To the north, 12th Division took Épehy with relative ease, but could get no further. 58th Division's experience was similar. In summary the flanks of Fourth Army had limited success and did not achieve all their objectives, whereas the Australian Corps in the centre had been successful almost everywhere.

Only the right of Third Army (V Corps) took part in the operations on 18th September. The centre had already closed up in front of the Hindenburg Line and the left was beyond it. There were three objectives on the right to bring V Corps into line with Fourth Army, but only two on the left. Three divisions made the attack, from the right these were 21st, 17th and 38th Divisions. 33rd Division (Second Army) and a brigade of 38th Division were in reserve.

21st Division's right reached the second objective with few casualties but was hit by enfilade fire and was held up 900m from the third objective, due to the failure of

the left flank of Fourth Army to keep up. The centre reached the third objective but was forced back, while the left reached and held the third objective.

17th Division attacked successive objectives with one brigade, each deploying all three battalions in line. The first objective fell to 52nd Brigade by 5.50 a.m. and the second, except on the left, fell to 50th Brigade by 7.55 a.m. but the left flank had to be strengthened. At 7.47 a.m., 51st Brigade passed through towards the third objective, leaving a company to assist clearing the left of the second objective. The third objective fell following hard fighting in places. Guns from the Machine Gun Battalion moved up in support and broke up a counterattack. A counterattack on the right was also stopped at 9.45 a.m. Counterattacks at 2 p.m. forced the attackers back, but the lost ground was regained. 17th Division attacked again at 9 p.m. in conjunction with 114th Brigade (38th Division). The aim was to sweep northwards

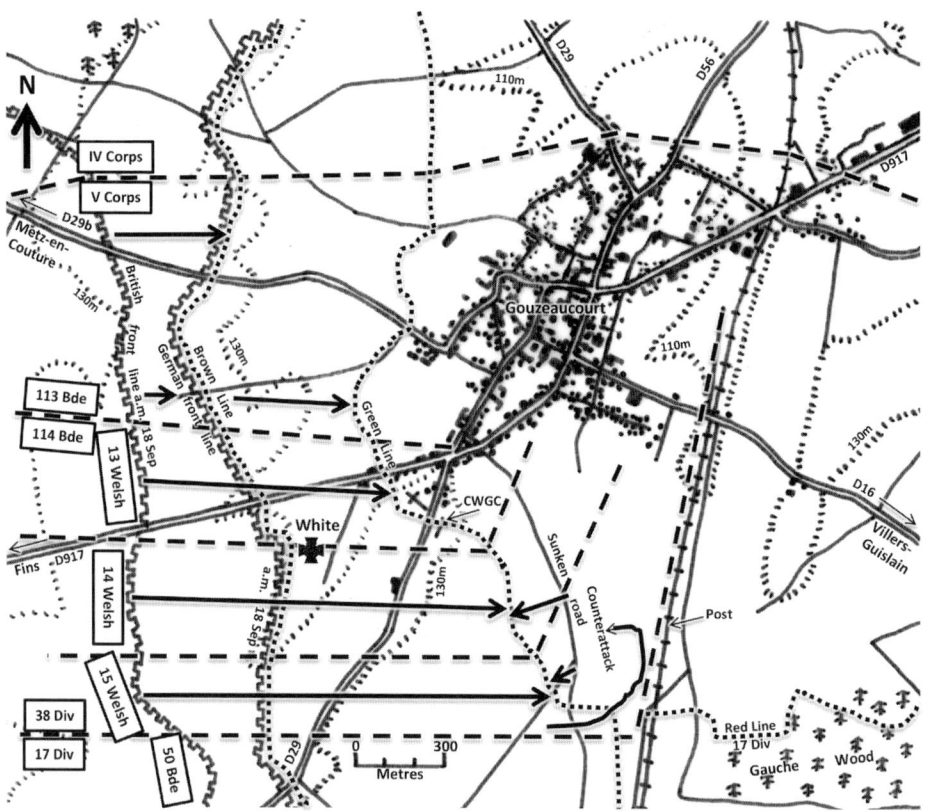

Leave Gouzeaucourt on the D917 westwards towards Fins. Drive almost to the top of the hill, where there is some hard standing on the left side of the road, and park there. This is about the midpoint between the British and German lines on the morning of 18th September. Look back towards Gouzeaucourt. The German front line crossed the road 275m in front and the British line 110m behind. This location is just north of the boundary between 13th and 14th Welsh. White's VC action took place somewhere between here and Gouzeaucourt.

from the Green Line to seize Gouzeaucourt, with the two brigades either side of the railway, but the infantry could not be organised in time. Strong patrols were sent out instead and, although they failed to penetrate into the village, a patrol on the right of 114th Brigade linked up with 50th Brigade and established a post.

38th Division had taken over the line in the Gouzeaucourt area on 11th September and had been subjected to repeated enemy action since. On 18th September it had only two objectives and advanced with 114th Brigade on the right and 113th Brigade on the left. The Divisional Machine Gun Battalion assigned D Company to 114th Brigade and B Company to 113th Brigade, while A and C Companies were to fire barrages under B Company's overall direction. 115th Brigade was in reserve under cover of Fins Ridge, to be prepared to counter any enemy counterattack across the whole of the V Corps front.

114th Brigade attacked with three battalions in line. From the right these were 15th, 14th and 13th Welsh. A section of D Company, 38th Battalion MGC and a platoon of A Company, 19th Welsh (Pioneers) were attached to each battalion. The remaining section of machine guns was to fire a barrage on the Green Line at zero hour and then advance behind the infantry to set up in the first objective (Brown Line). The night before the attack, 13th Welch completed cutting gaps in the front line wire, while the other battalions moved forward. The Germans fired gas shells most of the night and the approach march of 14th Welch was particularly affected. However, gas did not have much effect on the troops once they were in their assembly positions. Rain fell intermittently all night, making the going heavy. By 4.30 a.m. all units were in position and at 5.20 a.m. the attack commenced. All three battalions advanced with three companies forward, each led by a single platoon. The field artillery fired the usual creeping barrage, whilst the light trench mortars engaged the enemy front line and the wire beyond it.

In the darkness the infantry found direction keeping was difficult to maintain. On the right, 15th Welch swamped two machine gun posts west of the barrage line with rifle grenades. A number of enemy dead and wounded were found there as the advance swept over them. Little resistance was encountered by 114th Brigade initially. The enemy front line (Brown Line) was found to be held by fifteen or sixteen machine gun posts, spaced about thirty-five metres apart. By 6.50 a.m. reports were reaching Brigade HQ that the Brown Line had been taken. However, a gap had opened as the Brigade swept forward quicker than 113th Brigade on the left.

Stronger resistance was encountered beyond the Brown Line, including machine guns firing in enfilade from Gouzeaucourt southwest along the valleys. Reports that the Green Line had been captured about 6.40 a.m. began to arrive at 7.50 a.m. The Germans resisted strongly and many were killed there. Despite the Green Line falling, movement forward of the Brown Line was still under enemy observation, resulting in the area being under heavy and accurate machine gun fire.

On the right, 15th Welch repulsed a counterattack from a sunken road in front of the Green Line. In conjunction with 50th Brigade on the right, the Battalion moved

From the hard standing on the D917 Fins road looking to the east. The D917 is on the left with Gouzeaucourt in the left background. The buildings on the skyline just right of centre are on the D29 Heudicourt road.

around to the south and got behind the sunken road. The enemy were surrounded and many were killed. About one hundred prisoners were taken in addition to two anti-tank guns and three anti-tank rifles.

114th Brigade was subjected to intermittent shell and machine gun fire for the rest of the day. A warning order was issued at 2.25 p.m. for 13th and 14th Welsh to attack again with 50th Brigade at 9 p.m. against the southwest of Gouzeaucourt. 10th South Wales Borderers (115th Brigade), from reserve, was attached to relieve the troops of 114th Brigade in the Brown Line so that they could rejoin their battalions for the attack. However, due to the difficulty in moving between the Brown and Green Lines, and the disorganisation of the assault troops in the Green Line, it was not possible to reorganise and prepare for the attack. Orders did not reach some forward companies until after zero hour and the attack did not take place. Patrols sent forward instead achieved little. However, 15th Welsh managed to establish a post with 50th Brigade on the railway.

At some point in the attack, **Second Lieutenant William White** in D Company, 38th Battalion MGC, supporting 114th Brigade, observed the infantry being held up by a machine gun. He rushed it single-handed and shot the crew of three. A little later he attacked another machine gun post with two other men, who were shot down before closing with it. White went on and dealt with this position, inflicting heavy losses on the garrison. On the objective he assisted with consolidation and brought his own and captured machine guns into the position. These he used with great skill later to break up a counterattack.

The war diaries of 38th Machine Gun Battalion, HQ 38th Division, HQ 114th Brigade and its battalions do not specify where White was during this action. It is known that Second Lieutenant Harry Nellis commanded the machine gun section attached to 15th Welsh and was awarded the MC for this action. When the left flank was threatened he pushed his guns to the front and beat off several

attacks. Then, singlehanded, he attempted to capture fifty prisoners in a sunken road. Having secured twenty-five of them, the rest scattered and opened fire on him. Although wounded he returned fire with a machine gun and inflicted many casualties. It is therefore clear that White was commanding the section with either 13th or 14th Welsh but which one is not known. The war diary of 13th Welsh states that it took its objectives with relative ease and suffered few casualties, perhaps indicating that White was attached to 14th Welsh. However, the Brigade casualty return for 18th-20th September shows that 13th Welsh actually suffered more casualties than the other two battalions (13th – 153, 14th – 128 and 15th – 141).

113th Brigade's left was covered by two companies of IV Corps. Almost every officer was hit by flanking fire in the left battalion and a CSM took command. The right battalion (14th Royal Welsh Fusiliers) managed to take the first objective, but was isolated on both flanks. Its right reached the Green Line, where it hung on and beat off several counterattacks. Another section of the objective was gained by bombing parties in the afternoon. However, further attempts to get forward on the left of 113th Brigade failed. After dark a flank was formed on the right from the front line to 114th Brigade in the first objective.

38th Battalion MGC fired a total of 258,000 rounds in the barrage alone that day and suffered fifty casualties, eighteen of whom were gassed. Relief came early on the morning of the 20th. The frontage of 114th Brigade was taken over by elements of 52nd and 115th Brigades and the relief was completed by 5 a.m. The Brigade had suffered 429 casualties.

Apart from the two companies in IV Corps covering V Corps' left flank, the British did not launch any large attacks further north than Gouzeaucourt. However, 112th Brigade (37th Division) fought a local action northeast of Trescault. The Brigade had all three battalions in the line, with 13th Royal Fusiliers on the right, 1st Essex in the centre and 1/1st Hertfordshire on the left. The left of 13th Royal Fusiliers and the right of 1st Essex pulled back from the front line prior to 5.20 a.m., when a heavy artillery and trench mortar bombardment fell on the German front line. Ten

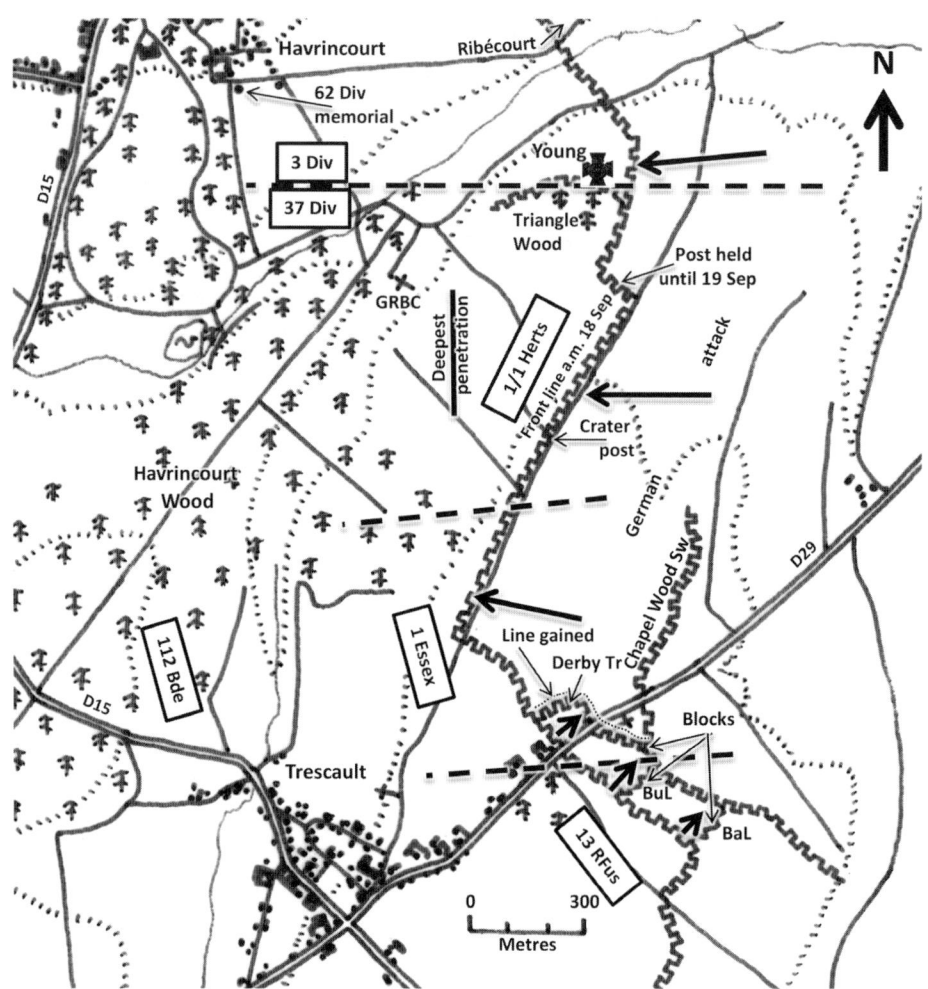

BaL = Bass Lane, BuL = Burton Lane, GRBC = Grand Ravine British Cemetery.

Approach Havrincourt from the northeast along the D29E2 and drive through the village until reaching the crossroads in the centre, where the main road (D15E2) swings to the right. Turn left here into Grand Place, passing the war memorial and the church on the right, and continue to the end, where the road swings left (Rue de Ribécourt). Pass the 62nd Division memorial on the right and 130m beyond turn right, signed for Grand Ravine British Cemetery. Take care along this section of track as it can be difficult in wet weather. Pass through Havrincourt Wood and park when the track emerges from it. The track to the cemetery is on the right. Walk along the track to the left north-eastwards. Triangle Wood, where Young's VC action took place, is on the hillside on the right. However, a better view of the Wood can be obtained from the single lane road (Rue de Ribécourt) running east from the 62nd Division memorial. Instead of turning right for Grand Ravine British Cemetery carry straight on. It is possible to turn a car around in places along this road but, particularly in wet conditions, it is best to park at the 62nd Division memorial and walk 700-800m to gain a clear view of Triangle Wood across Grand Ravine. Alternatively, after viewing Triangle Wood, continue straight on along Rue de Ribécourt which, as the name suggests, will eventually bring you to Ribécourt village. However, note that the road is narrow and farm vehicles may be encountered coming in the opposite direction.

minutes later the barrage lifted to the east and the two battalions attacked. A footing was gained in Derby Trench by 1st Essex and a bombing block was established in Chapel Wood Switch. Strong German bombing parties were encountered at the junction of Derby Trench and Burton Lane, Meanwhile 13th Royal Fusiliers attempted to force a way along Burton and Bass Lanes. All efforts failed and a series of bombing blocks was established. Both battalions attacked again at 7.30 a.m. but without improving the positions held.

Later in the day the Germans attempted to recover Havrincourt and Moeuvres. At 3.15 p.m. a heavy barrage, including masses of gas shell, fell on the battery positions around Havrincourt Wood that were supporting 112th Brigade and 8th and 9th Brigades in 3rd Division to the north. At 4.15 p.m. this bombardment shortened and a barrage opened on the front line trenches. In addition, German aircraft dropped bombs and machine-gunned the trenches. The barrage built in intensity over the next hour, when it lifted onto Trescault and the valley to the north of the village. At 5.15 p.m. the Germans attacked the line held by 1st Essex and 1/1st Hertfordshire. Five minutes later the British SOS barrage came down.

On the left, north of Havrincourt in 3rd Division's area, the Germans penetrated the support trench of the front Hindenburg System. There was also fierce hand to hand fighting southeast of Havrincourt in 112th Brigade's area, where some front line posts held by 1/1st Hertfordshire and 1st Essex were overwhelmed. However, one post in a crater east of Havrincourt Wood, held by a party of 1/1st Hertfordshire under Corporal Smith, held out throughout this action and was able to inflict severe casualties on the enemy. Two German parties managed to penetrate up to 400m behind the front line, to Kut Lane and Femy Trench, before being destroyed there by small arms fire.

On the left in No. 4 Company, 1/1st Hertfordshire, **Lieutenant Frank Young** continued to visit his posts during the bombardment to encourage his men. When

The north-eastern corner of Havrincourt Wood is on the extreme left, with Triangle Wood on the skyline in the centre. Grand Ravine British Cemetery is behind the camera.

Looking over Grand Ravine to Triangle Wood from Rue de Ribécourt. Young's VC action was on the northern (left) end of the Wood.

the attack started, he rescued two of his soldiers captured by the Germans, who had penetrated the front line in this area. He then led a counterattack north of Triangle Wood, during which he bombed and silenced a machine gun. Several prisoners were taken. He was surrounded but knocked two of his would be captors down with his fists. He fought his way back to the main barricade and drove off a party of the enemy assembling for another attack. He fought on for four hours and was last seen in hand-to-hand combat with a number of the attackers, before being killed. His actions allowed the Battalion to maintain its positions.

None of the German gains were held, except for one post in 1/1st Hertfordshire's front line, which was recovered at 3.15 p.m. next day. Otherwise, by 11 p.m. the line had been restored. Thirty-six prisoners from three German infantry regiments (3rd, 64th and 396th) were taken. Next day 112th Brigade was relieved by 63rd Brigade, having suffered 192 casualties (sixteen killed, 146 wounded and thirty missing). One of the missing, Lance Corporal Robinson of 1st Essex, escaped from the Germans near Cambrai on 26th September, passed through the British barrage next day and entered the lines held by 5th Division that night.

Although the BEF did not attain all its objectives on 18th September, over 9,000 prisoners were taken and substantial gains were made towards the main Hindenburg Position.

# Local Operations

## 24th September 1918

> 435 Lt John Barrett, 5th Battalion, The Leicestershire Regiment (138th Brigade, 46th Division), Pontruet, France
>
> 436 Lt Donald Dean, 8th Battalion, The Queen's Own (Royal West Kent Regiment) (72nd Brigade, 24th Division), Cité St Emilie, France

During the attack on 18th September (Battle of Épehy), the flanks of Fourth Army had not made as much headway as the centre. Operations continued to close up to the Hindenburg Line over the next few days. On the right, IX Corps fought a subsidiary action on 24th September to gain observation over the Hindenburg Line, in preparation for the forthcoming offensive. The attack commenced at 5 a.m. and was made in conjunction with the French First Army on the right, which succeeded in taking some of their objectives. IX Corps attacked with three divisions, from the right these were the 6th, 1st and 46th. 6th Division took Gricourt and pressed on overnight to complete the capture of its objectives next day. 1st Division seized its objectives after heavy fighting, in which tanks gave valuable assistance. Heavy fire from Pontruet, on the left flank in 46th Division's area, was partly neutralised by bringing up machine guns and trench mortars.

Pontruet, lying in a shallow valley overlooked by high ground to the north, east and south, was the objective of 138th Brigade in 46th Division. The aim was to protect the left flank of 1st Division to the south. Ahead of the attack, 5th Lincolnshire was to occupy Ste Hélène (Le Petit Arbre on modern maps), in conjunction with 6th Sherwood Foresters (139th Brigade) to the south, and mop up some trenches on the left flank. Ste Hélène was to be bombarded for two hours on 23rd September, following which the houses were to be occupied, as it was believed that the Germans only occupied them at night. Should the Germans be found to be holding them, they were to be taken by force.

5th Leicestershire was to make the main attack. Two mortars from 138th Light Trench Mortar Battery were attached, each with a carrying party of ten men from 4th Leicestershire. A section of 468th Field Company RE was also attached to the Battalion, as were eight runners from the Brigade HQ signallers to maintain communications with the Advanced Brigade HQ. The plan was to outflank the village by advancing from the north to the east of the village and then turning west to take it from the rear. All four companies were to advance over the Bellenglise–Vadancourt road in line, with A Company on the right, then B, C and D Companies, the latter on the left. When they were in line with the southern edge of Pontruet the two companies on the right (A and B) were to turn ninety degrees right and sweep through the village to the western edge. D Company on the left was to swing ninety

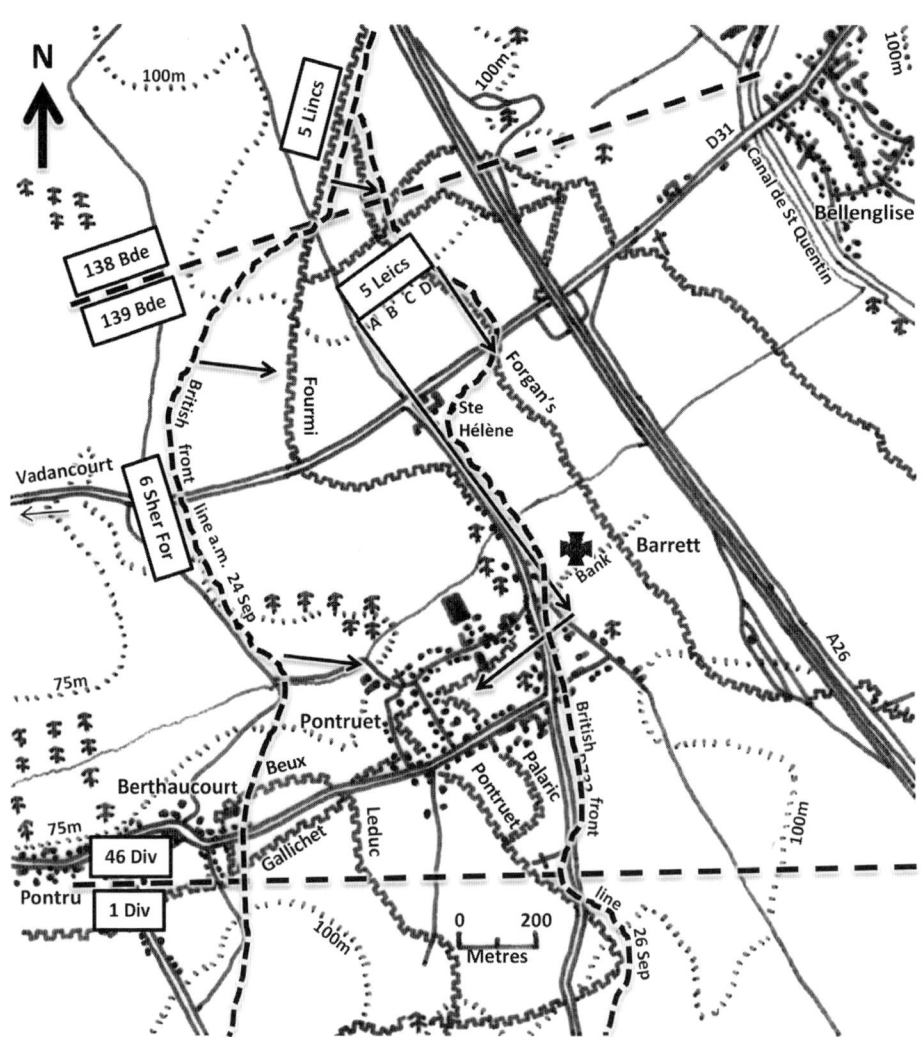

Approach Pontruet from the west along the D31. Go straight on at the crossroads, where the right turn leads to Pontruet on the D732. After 430m, just before the road passes under the autoroute, park on the right where there is an access road onto the autoroute. Look south across the ground over which 5th Leicestershire advanced.

degrees left to seize Forgan's Trench, assisted by a platoon of C Company. The remainder of C Company was to assist whichever flank needed it.

On the right flank, 6th Sherwood Foresters (139th Brigade) was to set off seventeen minutes after the main attack to seize a section of Fourmi Trench and mop up Beux and Leduc Trenches and Gallichet Alley southwest of Pontruet. In addition to the creeping barrage, the artillery concentrated on pinning the defenders inside the village until the position could be outflanked.

From the bank on the north side of the D31 Bellenglise–Vadancourt road looking southeast, with Pontruet in the right background. 5th Leicestershire advanced from the right over the road towards the high ground in the left distance. Forgan's Trench ran approximately along the boundary in the field on the south side of the road. The stream is marked by the line of trees running across the middle of the left side of the picture. The bank ran across the slope beyond the stream but has all but disappeared due to ploughing.

Just after midnight, 5th Leicestershire was relieved by 6th South Staffordshire (137th Brigade) and formed up on a taped line facing south. A few hours previously 5th Lincolnshire had been raided on the road at Forgan's Trench. It was possible that Germans were still in the area and so D Company formed up in the trench rather than in the open. The mist thickened just before the attack and a smoke barrage, fired against the western edge of Pontruet, much against the Battalion's wishes, added to it.

The advance began on time but became confused in the smoke and darkness. A Company, guided by the road on its right flank, swept over Ste Hélène and reached the turning point at 5.14 a.m., despite heavy flanking fire from Forgan's Trench on the left and 4 Platoon losing direction for a time. Visibility was a few metres at best. There was heavy fighting in the village, mainly at bayonet point, but the northern part was overcome after just over an hour and 120 prisoners and four machine guns were taken. About fifty more Germans were driven into 6th Sherwood Foresters. The heaviest fighting was in the southwest of the village, where the Germans were well dug in, in two trenches around a blockhouse that resisted all attempts to take it.

B Company became confused in the smoke and mist, but two platoons made their way into the village and mopped up behind A Company. However, they too failed to clear the blockhouse area. The other two B Company platoons and C Company suffered from heavy fire from Forgan's Trench.

C Company overcame the Germans in the east of Pontruet and occupied a trench facing east. Further south another party crossed a small road bridge and also took up a position facing east. The rest of C Company, led by **Lieutenant John Barrett**, with Sergeant Spencer, reached the far side of the valley, where they were joined by

The reverse of the previous view. 5th Leicestershire advanced from the high ground to the right of the wind turbines, beyond the building in the foreground, towards the right of the picture. The trees lining the stream run across the middle of the picture. The remains of the bank, marked by a slightly darker smudge in the field in line with the bottom of the end wall of the building in the foreground, are in the centre closer to the camera.

some men of B Company. Barrett was surprised to find a newly dug trench up a bank full of Germans but he did not hesitate in rushing it. Having gained the trench, he turned east to push towards Forgan's Trench. He was hit but reached Forgan's with his party and captured three machine gun posts, two of them personally. The party remained under heavy fire and was bombed from several directions simultaneously. Barrett was wounded again but he held up one bombing party with his pistol, while Sergeant Spencer dealt with another. Shortly afterwards Barrett's pistol arm was hit by a bomb burst. He realised that the position could not be held and, despite his utter exhaustion, climbed out of the trench to assess the situation. He then called his NCOs together and gave them instructions on how to get away. Barrett refused all help and crawled through the wire, where he was wounded again. He was carried back to the RAP, where the MO believed that he would die.

On the left, D Company found that Forgan's Trench was not held by just a few posts, as was previously believed. It was strongly manned and was well wired in front and laterally. Reaching the Bellenglise–Vadancourt road, the Company walked into a hail of fire from three machine guns in a post near the road. Attempts to rush it failed with heavy casualties. However, a little later another attack managed to overcome two of the guns, but the third held out and continued to cause heavy casualties at almost point blank range.

By 7.45 a.m., when the wind cleared the smoke and mist, the village had been taken except for the southwest corner, where the blockhouse held out. A and B Companies were established in the northwest corner and C Company held about half of the eastern edge. Although earlier the smoke had caused confusion, it had also provided protection. The Battalion was now totally exposed in a precarious situation and resupplying ammunition was almost impossible. The attention of a tank, that was supporting 1st Division to the south, was sought but it was knocked out before it could render any assistance. Heavy small arms fire from the south forced the defenders of Pontruet back to the north-western portion of the village, where contact was made with 6th Sherwood Foresters, which had also been held up. The defenders of Forgan's Trench built a block and held from the northernmost point of Pontruet to Ste Hélène on the Bellenglise–Vadancourt road.

The Germans reoccupied Forgan's Trench and infiltrated around the south of Pontruet to trenches on the west side. Forgan's Trench was shelled for an hour to prevent an enemy counterattack from it. At 7.30 p.m., a company of 6th Sherwood Forester and survivors of 5th Leicestershire tried to get into Pontruet from the Ste Hélène side without success. By 2.30 a.m. on the 25th the village had been abandoned and posts were held to the north and west of it. In this action 5th Leicestershire suffered 164 casualties (fourteen killed, twenty-four missing and 126 wounded).

On 26th September, when the Germans pulled back into the Hindenburg Line, 1st Division got into the eastern edge of Pontruet with very little fighting. As a result IX Corps had closed up everywhere to the main German defences in preparation for the next offensive.

III Corps, on the left flank of Fourth Army, also continued to move forward after 18th September, taking most of its objectives but not everywhere. Third Army was relatively quiet, except for the actions around Moeuvres for which Corporal David Hunter of 5th Highland Light Infantry was awarded the VC. Fourth and Third Armies had achieved good start lines for the attack on the Hindenburg Line and the bombardment started at 10.30 p.m. on 26th September.

A small action was also fought in First Army's area, unconnected with Fourth Army's operations to close up to the Hindenburg Line. Throughout September the Germans had made a number of small withdrawals in the Lens area and the British had followed up with aggressive patrolling. 8th Royal West Kent had been involved in these operations early in the month and returned to the line on 19th September to take over from 9th East Surrey. Days and nights of active patrolling followed until it was decided to retake a post at the junction of Claud and Canary Trenches. This position had changed hands on a number of occasions previously.

On the night of 23rd-24th September a party of C Company seized the post and set about consolidation. At 6.40 a.m. on the 24th a party of forty Germans bombed into the northeast of the post from Canary Trench and from the junction of Claud with Twisted Alley (not identified). Six men were captured by the Germans. A counterattack was launched following a barrage with rifle grenades from Canary Trench. Two subalterns (Claude Trenchard-Davis and Norman Edward Beynes) led parties along either side of the trench. The Germans fled up Canary, allowing two British prisoners (one was Lance Corporal Binks) to turn the tables on their captors and brought them in as prisoners. By 7.30 a.m. the situation had been restored completely.

52    Victoria Crosses on the Western Front – Battles of the Hindenburg Line

Due to the extent of the built-up area, only a few trenches are shown as white and black lines. In 1918 much of this area was open ground. In the centre of Lens, drive north-eastwards on Rue de Londres from the junction with Rue Emile Zola. After 390m turn left onto Rue Jean Moulin. Drive north for 260m and turn left onto Rue Jean Baptiste Charcot. Walk back to the junction and look northwest to where Claud Trench met Canary Trench at Dean's Post.

At 9 p.m. that evening two sections of 16 Platoon, D Company, commanded by **Lieutenant Donald Dean**, relieved C Company in the contested post. Dean's men were mainly young soldiers with almost no combat experience. A great deal of work was required to consolidate the post but there was no time to remedy the situation as, within ten minutes of taking over, the enemy attacked again. Covered by heavy machine gun fire they attacked from the northeast but Dean's men drove them back with their small arms. Dean moved about constantly, encouraging his men, always exposed to the fire all round him.

As soon as the attack had been driven off, Dean set his men to work deepening the trench and establishing blocks in Canary and Claud. The work was carried out under constant machine gun fire and the trench in places was only two feet deep.

The junction of Rue Moulin (right) with Rue Jean Baptiste Charcot (left). Dean's Post was behind and to the right of the large silver birch in the centre of the picture.

Just after midnight there was another attack, in which two men were wounded and the Germans were on the brink of getting into the post. Dean led a counterattack and the post was saved again. Digging continued.

By dawn the platoon was exhausted, but there was to be no rest as the Germans attacked again at 6 a.m. The enemy artillery blocked contact with the rear and the post was hit with mortars. Attacks down Canary and over the open were met by rifle grenades and small arms fire. The enemy faltered and Dean charged after them in the open in an attempt to grab a prisoner, but he was forced back by sheer weight of fire. For hours afterwards the Germans were seen moving around their trenches removing casualties. For the rest of the day and night Dean and his men worked on under fire. By the morning of the 26th, Dean had strengthened the post significantly. His other two sections came up to relieve the first two, although Dean remained in command.

At 10.15 a.m. the post, and communications leading to it, were shelled by 5.9″ Howitzers and grenatenwerfen, setting off two Bangalore torpedoes that had been brought up for a raid that afternoon. The explosion severely shook Dean but he positioned his men and beat off the attack that followed. He then went to call his CO on a field telephone that Dean had arranged to be brought into the position the previous night. While he was away the Germans attacked again, after scoring a number of direct hits on the post. Having suffered a number of casualties, the sergeant decided to pull back fifty metres temporarily and the enemy occupied the post. Dean saw what was happening and broke off the conversation with the CO saying, *The Germans are here. Goodbye*. He immediately collected his two sections and charged across the open, giving the enemy no time to reorganise. The platoon to the right in Cinnabar Trench, under Second Lieutenant Horace Cambrook, also attacked to cut off the enemy's retreat and heavy fire was brought to bear on them by 1st North Staffordshire on the left. The attack from two sides was too much and the Germans fled. Dean himself shot four of the enemy. Cambrook was severely wounded in the chest and died on 17th October (Houchin British Cemetery – III A 8).

At 3 p.m. a party of two officers and four sections of 8th Royal West Kent, supported by four sappers with Bangalore torpedoes, attacked the junction of Claud and Cinnabar Trenches covered by machine guns and trench mortars. A machine gun post was captured and a number of significant maps and documents were recovered from a dead officer. The rest of the garrison fled into dugouts and refused to come out. The dugouts were therefore destroyed by explosive charges. That night Dean and 16 Platoon were relieved, having resisted five of the six attacks made by the Germans in forty-eight hours. Dean's performance in handling young and inexperienced soldiers in a very tight situation was remarkable. 21103 Sergeant Thomas Henry Skipper received the DCM and three men received the MM for their parts in the defence of Dean's Post. Skipper died of wounds on 20th October 1918 and is buried in Tunbridge Wells Cemetery, Kent (C 13 554).

# Biographies

## LIEUTENANT JOHN CRIDLAN BARRETT
### 1/5th Battalion, The Leicestershire Regiment

John Barrett was born on 10th August 1897 at 30 Regent Street, Royal Leamington Spa (usually shortened to Leamington Spa), Warwickshire. He was known as Jack within the family. His father, Josephus Teague Barrett (1850–20th March 1929), born at Lifton, Devon, was living with his uncle and aunt, William and Mary Barrett, at 26 Garden Street, Stoke Damerel, Devon in 1861. By 1871 he was living with his uncle and aunt, Thomas and Lavinia Barrett, at 36 Waterloo Street, Devonport, by when he was an apprentice chemist. He was a pharmaceutical chemist, living at 30 Regent Street, Leamington Spa, Warwickshire in 1881. Josephus married Fanny Ada née

Cridlan (21st October 1860–16th March 1953), born at Paddington, London, in 1894 at Upton-upon-Severn, Worcestershire. They were still living at 30 Regent Street, Leamington Spa in 1901 and had moved to 68 Queen's Gardens, Bayswater, London by 1911. Josephus continued in business as a chemist until retiring in 1926 and then they moved to Razmak, Park Road, Watford, Hertfordshire. Josephus died at Mardale, Stratford Road, Watford. Fanny was living with her nephew, John Lionel Cridlan and wife Florence at Felden Park, Hemel Hempstead, Hertfordshire in 1939. She died at 35 Park Road, Watford. John had three siblings, one of whom died in infancy:

- Cyril Cridlan Barrett (31st August 1898–24th August 1933) enlisted in 2/28th London Regiment (Artists' Rifles) on 6th February 1917 (765077). He was

John was born on Regent Street, Leamington Spa, seen here at about the turn of the 19th century.

admitted to the Royal Military Academy, Woolwich on 12th June 1917 and was commissioned in the Royal Garrison Artillery on 6th June 1918. Cyril served in France from 31st July. He also served in the Afghanistan and North West Frontier campaign in 1919 and in Waziristan. He was promoted lieutenant on 6th December 1919 and captain on 6th June 1931. He was appointed Adjutant and Quartermaster, School of Artillery, Kakul, India on 19th December 1931. He married Dorothy Mary Nares (8th January 1906–4th December 1988) on 24th July 1930 at Holy Trinity Church, Brompton, London. They lived at Razmak, Park Road, Watford. Cyril died at the Hospital de Monaco, Monaco. Dorothy married Gustav Adolf Karl Von Dippe (20th September 1910–18th September 1976), born in Berlin, Germany, in 1936 at Westminster, London. They were living at 17 Ladbroke Walk, London in 1959 and at 8 Pentlow Drive, Cavendish, Suffolk at the time of his death there. Dorothy died at Chilton Croft Nursing Home, Newton Road, Sudbury, Suffolk.

John's father, Josephus, was born at Lifton, Devon, close to the border with Cornwall. The village was founded by the Saxons and was first recorded as *Liwtune* in the will of King Alfred in the late 9th century. Queen Elizabeth I sold it to local landowner, William Harris of Hayne, in the parish of Stowford. There has been a church in Lifton since Norman times but the existing St Mary's Church dates from the 15th century. The local economy was based upon agriculture and mining and the dairy company, Ambrosia, has been there since 1917. The railway station on the South Devon and Tavistock Railway opened on 1st June 1865 and the line remained open until February 1966.

- Winifred Alice Cridlan Barrett (18th September 1900–18th October 1994) was a physical training instructor in 1939, living with her cousin, John Lionel Cridlan and his wife Florence, at Felden Park, Hemel Hempstead. She never married and died at Tenterden House Nursing Home, Lye Lane, Bricket Wood, Hertfordshire.

John's paternal grandfather, John Barrett (c.1825–53), born at Lifton, Devon, married Eliza née Teague (c.1825–54), born at Stowford, Devon, in 1849 at Tavistock, Devon. He was a manganese miner in 1851, when they were living at Tinney, Lifton. Both of their deaths were registered at Tavistock. In addition to Josephus they had a daughter:

- Amelia Teague Barrett (4th March 1851–1903), born at Lifton, married Alfred Bertram Toms (24th March 1852–18th November 1921), born at Grouville, Jersey, Channel Islands, on 9th August 1875 at Plymouth, Devon. He was indentured as an apprentice for four years in the Merchant Navy at Brocklebank Dock,

The Royal Military Academy, Woolwich trained officers for the Royal Artillery and Royal Engineers and later for the Royal Corps of Signals and other technical corps. It was known as 'The Shop' because its first building was a converted workshop of Woolwich Arsenal at the Warren. After a false start earlier in the century, the Academy opened by authority of a Royal Warrant in 1741, to produce 'good officers of Artillery and perfect Engineers'. The gentlemen cadets were initially aged from ten to thirty and were lodged in Woolwich but this proved unsatisfactory, as the cadets gained a reputation for riotousness. In 1751 the Cadets' Barracks (demolished in the 1980s) was built and stricter military discipline was imposed. The Academy outgrew the available accommodation and a new complex of buildings at the southern edge of Woolwich Common was built between 1796 and 1805 and opened the following year. One hundred and twenty-eight senior cadets moved to the new Academy, sixty remained at the Warren (renamed Royal Arsenal) and another sixty were sent to a new college for junior cadets at Great Marlow. In 1810, military cadets of the East India Company moved to a new college at Addiscombe. After the Crimean War the minimum age for cadets was raised to fifteen and more specialist training was added. The Academy was enlarged in the 1860s. In 1873 the central block had to be entirely rebuilt following a devastating fire. The Royal Military Academy closed in 1939, on the outbreak of the Second World War, as did the Royal Military College, Sandhurst, which trained officers for the infantry and cavalry. The last Commandant at Woolwich was Major General Philip Neame, who was awarded the VC in 1915 and whose story appears in the first book in this series, *Victoria Crosses on the Western Front, Mons to Hill 60, August 1914–April 1915*. In 1947 the two institutions joined into a single Royal Military Academy at Sandhurst to train officers for all arms and services of the British Army. The old Academy site became part of Woolwich Garrison and housed various units in the following years. The central block was taken over by the Royal Artillery Institution and housed its museum, archives and offices. The chapel became the Garrison Church when the Garrison Church of St George was destroyed during the Second World War. The strength of Woolwich Garrison gradually reduced in the second half of the 20th century and by 2002 the site was no longer required. The buildings have since been converted into houses and apartments.

John's paternal grandmother, Eliza, was born at Stowford, Devon, just west of Dartmoor.

Liverpool, Lancashire on 12th May 1868. He served aboard the *Alexandra* and *Cedar*, deserting from the latter at Liverpool on 22nd September 1869. In 1891 he was a licensed victualler and they were living at Navy Hotel, 34 Southside Street, Plymouth. He was living at 5 Durham Avenue, Plymouth when his son Alfred enlisted in 1897. Amelia died in Plymouth. Alfred married Elizabeth Arden née Fisher (c.1849–3rd August

1925), born in Liverpool, in 1904 at Plymouth. They were living at 17 Lidderdale Road, Wavertree, Liverpool in 1911 and both of them subsequently died there. Elizabeth had married Charles Arden (1846–29th November 1897), a grocer born at Burrington, Herefordshire, in 1870 at West Derby, Lancashire. They were living at 361 Mill Street, Toxteth Park in 1871 before moving to 212 Windsor Street, Toxteth Park by 1881. They were still living there at the time of his death, when his business was at Devonshire Road, Liverpool. Amelia and Alfred had five children:
- Henry Josephus Bertram Toms (1876–81).
- Alfred Bertram Toms (1878–1944) was a clerk when he enlisted in the Welsh Regiment (5336) in London on 15th September 1897. He was described as 5′ 5¾″ tall, weighing 147 lbs, with fair complexion, blue eyes, black hair and his religious denomination was Church of England. He joined the 1st Battalion on 2nd October and gained 2nd class army education on 2nd June 1898. Alfred passed for corporal on 13th April 1899 and was promoted on 27th July. He served in South Africa 4th November 1899–8th August 1904 (Queen's South Africa Medal with clasps *Relief of Kimberley*, *Paardeberg*, *Driefontein*, *Johannesburg* & *Diamond Hill* and King's South Africa Medal with clasps *South Africa 1901* & *South Africa 1902*). He was reduced to the ranks and forfeited good conduct pay by Regimental Court Martial on 21st March 1900 for conduct to the prejudice of good order and military discipline. Good conduct pay was restored on 21st March 1901 but was forfeited again on 12th November, restored on 12th November 1902, forfeited on 9th April 1903 and restored on 9th April 1904. Alfred transferred to the Army Reserve on 14th September 1904 and was struck off strength while absent on 1st January 1905. He was discharged at the end of his engagement after twelve years (seven years full time service and five years on the Reserve). He re-enlisted at Falmouth on 13th May 1915 in 1/2nd Cornwall (Fortress) Royal Engineers TF (946 & 512554) and was embodied the same day. He served in 2/2nd Works Company, later redesignated 575th (Cornwall) Works Company, and was appointed temporary lance corporal on 25th May and temporary corporal on 5th June (later substantive from this date). He was appointed unpaid acting sergeant on 21st March 1918. He joined No.5 Dem (sic) Train Depot RE on 1st July and reverted to corporal on 19th July. He was discharged from the Labour Corps Camp, Codford, Wiltshire no longer fit for war service on 20th September 1918. Alfred married Jubilee Agnes E Claydon (31st January 1887–1971) at Falmouth in 1915. They had two children – Victor A Toms 1921 and Daniel K Toms 1923.
- Amelia Mary Toms (1880–1911) married William Henry Cooper in Plymouth in 1904.
- Henry Josephus B Toms (1883–87).
- Victor Emilio Toms (19th September 1886–28th January 1956) emigrated to Australia, where he married Rose Emily Neumann (1880–1965) in

Victoria in 1911. They had a son, Alfred Victor Neumann Toms, born at Clifton Hill in 1912. Victor was an electrician when he enlisted in the AIF in Melbourne, Victoria on 23rd February 1916 (32352). His wife was living at Dunearn, Clarke Street, Northcote, Victoria and later at 50 Roseneath Street, Clifton Hill. He was described as 5′ 6½″ tall, weighing 155 lbs, with dark complexion, blue eyes, brown hair, a tattoo on his right forearm and his religion was Protestant. He joined the Field Artillery Reinforcements on 16th October as a driver and was assigned to 14th Field Artillery Brigade, 10th Reinforcements on 5th January 1917. He embarked at Melbourne aboard RMS *Osterley* on 14th February and disembarked at Plymouth on 11th April, joining the Reserve Brigade Australian Artillery, Larkhill, Wiltshire the same day. He was treated at Fargo Military Hospital, Larkhill for influenza 24th-30th May and re-mustered as a gunner on 8th June. He went to France via Southampton on 8th August, arriving next day to join the Australian General Base Depot, Rouelles. He joined 3rd Australian Division Ammunition Column on 13th August and transferred to 30th Battery, 8th Field Artillery Brigade on 15th August. On 23rd September he was wounded in the face and was treated at 6th Australian Field Ambulance, No.10 Casualty Clearing Station and 30th General Hospital, Calais the same day. He was transferred to the Base Depot, Calais on 14th October and the Australian General Base Depot, Le Havre next day. He joined 3rd Australian Division Artillery on 21st October and rejoined his unit on 24th October. He was admitted with an old septic wound on his face to 8th and 5th Australian Field Ambulances on 23rd November and rejoined his unit on 3rd December. He was gassed (phosgene) on 11th May 1918 and was admitted to 11th Australian Field Ambulance, transferred to No.61 Casualty Clearing Station next day and was transferred by 37 Ambulance Train to 9th General Hospital, Rouen on 13th May. He was evacuated to Britain on 16th May aboard HMHS *Guildford Castle* and admitted to Exeter War Hospital next day. He was transferred to 1st Australian Auxiliary Hospital, Harefield on 25th June. He was granted leave 27th June–11th July, then reported to No.4 Command Depot, Hurdcott, Wiltshire. On 5th November he transferred to the Overseas Training Brigade and to the Reserve Brigade Australian Artillery, Heytesbury on 22nd November. He was absent without leave from midnight on 5th December until 8 a.m. on 6th December, for which he forfeited one day's pay and was confined to barracks for a day. He transferred to the Overseas Training Brigade on 28th December and embarked on HT *Ceramic* on 25th January 1919, arriving in Australia on 23rd March. Victor was discharged from 3rd Military District on 22nd April 1919. He was issued War Service Badge No.108475 on 10th April 1919 but it was lost later. In May 1941 he applied for a replacement, which was provided on repayment.

His maternal grandfather, John Cridlan (1827–6th April 1919), born at St Pancras, London, married Hannah née Boxall (1829–11th June 1897), born at St Marylebone, London, in 1852 at St George, Hanover Square, London. He was a butcher and farmer, employing twelve men and four boys, in 1881, when they were living at Abbey Cottage, Abbey Road, Great Malvern, Worcestershire. By 1891 they had moved to 14 Bishop Road, Paddington, London. They were living at the Regent Hotel, Leamington, Warwickshire (owned by the Cridlan family 1904–98) at the time of his death there. She was living at Fairlawn, Great Malvern, Worcestershire at the time of her death there. In addition to Fanny they had three other children:

The Grade II* listed Regent Hotel (on the right) opened on 19th August 1819 as the Williams Hotel but, just three weeks later, was renamed The Regent by permission of the Prince Regent (later George IV). In 1830 Princess Victoria (later Queen Victoria) stayed at the hotel with her father, Prince Edward, Duke of Kent. Eight years later from the balcony of the hotel it was announced that Victoria had granted the prefix Royal to be added to the name of the town. At the time the hotel was one of the largest in Europe with over one hundred rooms. It catered for wealthy tourists who were in town to take the waters, as well as being an important meeting place for local gentry and landowners. Other prominent visitors included the Hollywood actor Douglas Fairbanks, and the author Charles Dickens. On 8th April 1882, Warwickshire Country Cricket Club was formed at the hotel. In the 1940s to 1960s the England football team used to meet there before travelling to fixtures abroad. The Hotel was owned by the Cridlan family from 1904 until it closed in 1998. It reopened after being completely refurbished in 2005.

* John Joseph Cridlan (1853–22nd December 1938), born at Kensington, London, was a butcher. He married Ann Harrison (died 1st September 1905) in 1879 at Upton-upon-Severn, Worcestershire. They were living at 38 Gloucester Gardens, Paddington, London at the time of Ann's death there. John married Abeth Julia Cox née Cave (1871–25th January 1957), born at Edmonton, Middlesex, in 1911 at Bingham, Nottinghamshire. She had married Arthur Cox in 1895 at Edmonton. John and Abeth lived at Maisemore Park, Maisemore, Gloucestershire, where he subsequently died, leaving effects valued at £169,355/10/9 (£11.6M in 2020). Abeth was living at Oak Tree House, Redington Gardens, Hampstead at the time of her death there. John had six children from his two marriages:
    ○ John Lionel Cridlan (15th January 1880–1951) married Florence Mudd (1875–1962) in Birmingham in 1905.
    ○ Daisy Louise Cridlan (1882–25th June 1955) never married.
    ○ Nellie Violet Cridlan (1884–11th June 1933).
    ○ Lilian Ethel Cridlan (1885–22nd June 1965) married Harry S Ferguson (c.1878–1959) at Paddington in 1915.

- Evelyn May Cridlan (1890–1961) never married.
- Frank John Cridlan (11th November 1913–8th November 1993), born at Gloucester, was a barrister-at-law. He was granted an Emergency Commission in the RAFVR, Administrative & Special Duties Branch as a pilot officer (77747) on 27th February 1940. He was confirmed in the appointment and promoted to flying officer (war substantive) on 27th February 1941. He was promoted flight lieutenant on 1st June 1942 and relinquished his commission, retaining the rank of flight lieutenant, on 11th November 1958. Frank married Patricia Alice Helena Bane (1920–7th June 2004), born at Croydon, Surrey, in 1944 at Gloucester Rural. They were living at Oak Tree House, Redington Gardens, Hampstead, London in 1960 and subsequently divorced. They had two children – Anthea Elizabeth Cridlan 1948 and Jeryl Margarat Cridlan 1952. Frank married Mary Elizabeth Rawlings (22nd October 1936–7th June 2004), born at Bath, Somerset, in 1981 at Camden, London. Mary was elected Mayor of Bath in 1976 and was a Liveryman of the Worshipful Company of Butchers. They owned the Regent Hotel, The Parade, Leamington Spa, Warwickshire and in 1984 named the lounge bar, The Victoria Cross Lounge, to commemorate Leamington VCs, John Barrett and Henry Tandey. Frank died at Allens House, 39 Mill Street, Warwick, leaving effects valued at £1,192,706 (£2.5M in 2020). Mary closed the hotel in May 1998 but it reopened as a Travelodge in March 2005.
- Louise Emma Cridlan (8th August 1858–5th January 1931), born at 8 Chichester Street, Bayswater, London, married Frederick George Underwood (1852–15th February 1892), born at Taunton, Somerset, on 28th October 1879 at the Priory Church, Great Malvern, Worcestershire. He was a coal merchant in 1881, when they were living at Manor House, Henwick Road, Worcester. By 1911 they had moved to Malvernbury, Rainbow Hill, Claines, Worcestershire, where they both subsequently died. They had eight children:
  - Louisa Fanny Underwood (19th June 1880–1880).
  - Frederick William Underwood (17th May 1881–1881).
  - Frederick John Underwood (26th June 1882–1954) married Marguerite A Adams (1882–1914) in Worcester in 1913. She died giving birth to a daughter, Margaret L Underwood, who survived, in 1914.
  - Harold Trevor Underwood (15th March 1884–1884).
  - Evelyn Louise Underwood (16th March 1885–1965) never married.
  - Gladys Violet Underwood (20th December 1886–1970) never married.
  - Elsie Amy Underwood (26th March 1888–1972).
  - William Frank Cridlan Underwood (2nd September 1890–1962) served with the British Red Cross and St John's Ambulance in the Balkans from 18th May 1916 and was awarded the British War Medal and Victory Medal.
- Alice Florence Cridlan (22nd December 1865–4th April 1947), born at Kensington, London, married Henry Foster (5th May 1839–1921), a merchant

born at Sutton-on-Trent, Nottinghamshire, on 28th June 1904 at Lillington Parish Church, Warwickshire. They were living at The Lawn, Leamington Spa, Warwickshire in 1911. Alice was living with her sisters-in-law, Katie E Florence, wife of Sydney Foster, and Ethel Mary Mitchell, at Guyscliffe, Durham Road, Bishop Auckland, Co Durham in 1939. She was living at Fort Royal House, Worcester at the time of her death. Henry had married Mary Jane Veitch (1843–28th April 1901) in 1864 at Bishop Auckland, where she was born. They were living at Hillcrest, Bishop Auckland in 1871 and at The Lawn, Leamington Spa at the time of her death there. Henry and Mary had six children – Frederick Veitch Foster 1865, Arthur Lee Foster 1867, William Lee Foster 1868, Thomas Denison Foster 1872, Sydney Foster 1875 and Ethel Mary Foster 1879.

John was educated at Arnold Lodge School, Kenilworth Road, Cubbington, Leamington Spa, Warwickshire and at Merchant Taylors' Boys' School, Crosby, Liverpool, Lancashire 1907–16. He was a cadet sergeant in the Merchant Taylors' Junior Division of the Officer Training Corps. In 1916 he was awarded a medical scholarship to study at St Thomas's Hospital, London.

John was commissioned in the Leicestershire Regiment (TF) on 27th January 1916 and joined 3/5th Battalion for training at Bulwell, Chesterfield and Catterick, Yorkshire. He was posted to 1/5th Battalion in France on 2nd July and served as the Battalion Signals Officer February 1917–May 1918. He was wounded at Gommecourt in February 1917 and was involved in the fighting at Lens that summer. He was promoted lieutenant on 27th July 1917 and was gassed at Gorre in May 1918.

Arnold Lodge School was founded in September 1864 by Alfred Kirk, a former assistant master at Leamington College. It was named after Dr Thomas Arnold, Headmaster of Rugby School 1828-42. In 1972, the Douglas and Eileen Hall Building was opened by Secretary of State for Education and Science and future Prime Minister, the Right Honorable Margaret Thatcher. In 1977 the school became coeducational. Although originally it was the only prep school in Warwickshire, Arnold Lodge extended the admission age to GCSE in 2008 and a sixth form was added in 2013 (David Stowell).

**Awarded the VC for his actions at Pontruet, France on 24th September 1918, LG 14th December 1918.** John returned to England in October 1918. The VC was presented by the King in the ballroom at Buckingham Palace on 13th February 1919. He was granted the Freedom of the Borough of Leamington on 11th August together with Private Henry Tandey VC, and was presented with a gold wristwatch. He was presented with a cheque for £330 and a silver cigarette box by General Sir Ian Hamilton at

The Merchant Taylors' Boys' School was founded in 1620 and until 1910 was run by the Merchant Taylors' Company. The first Headmaster, the Reverend John Kidde, was also Minister of Crosby and a farmer. He is understood to have been removed from the post in 1651 due to mismanagement, although it may have been caused by Roman Catholic sympathisers because of his Puritan ways. In 1878, the school moved to its present site and the original site formed part of the Merchant Taylors' Girls' School. Until the 1970s, Merchant Taylors' was also a boarding school but now educates over 700 day pupils. It remains independent and fee paying. Amongst the School's famous alumni are:

- John Richard Heaton Greenwood OBE (born 11th September 1941) former England rugby union player and coach.
- Simon Jack (born 10th May 1971) the BBC business journalist and news correspondent.
- Benedict James Kay MBE (born 14th December 1975), former England rugby union player. He played throughout every match in the 2003 World Cup, except for that against Uruguay, including the final in which England beat Australia in the last minute.
- Robert Alexander Kennedy Runcie, Baron Runcie MC PC (2nd October 1921–11th July 2000), Archbishop of Canterbury 1980-91.

27 Devonshire Terrace, Lancaster Gate, London in April 1920.

John began studying medicine at St Thomas's Hospital in 1920. He qualified MRCS (Eng), LRCP (Lond) and MD in 1924 and graduated MB and BS (with Honours in Pathology) in 1925. He was awarded the Bristowe Medal for Pathology by St Thomas's Hospital in 1925 and was appointed FRCS February 1928 and FRSM by 1937.

John held numerous medical appointments during his career:

- St Thomas's Hospital – house surgeon 1924 and later a casualty officer, clinical assistant and Senior Resident Surgical Casualty Officer.
- General Practitioner in Watford, Hertfordshire c.1928–29.
- Leicester Royal Infirmary – Senior House Surgeon 1929–30, Honorary Assistant Surgeon 1930–37, Honorary Surgeon 1937–47, Senior Honorary Surgeon 1947–62 and Emeritus Surgeon 1962–77.

Henry Tandey VC DCM MM (1891-1977). His story will be related in the next book in this series – *Battles of the Hindenburg Line – Canal du Nord, September – October 1918.*

St Thomas' Hospital, named after Saint Thomas Becket, was originally run by a mixed order of Augustinian canons and canonesses in Southwark and has provided free healthcare since the 12th century. In the 15th century, Richard Whittington endowed a lying-in ward for unmarried mothers. One of the first printed English Bibles was produced there in 1537. When the monastery was dissolved in 1539, the hospital closed until 1551, when it was reopened by the City of London, which obtained the site and a charter from Edward VI. The hospital has remained open ever since. The hospital and church were largely rebuilt at the end of the 17th century. In 1721 Sir Thomas Guy, a governor of St Thomas', founded Guy's Hospital to treat 'incurables' discharged from St Thomas'. The Nightingale Training School and Home for Nurses opened at St Thomas' Hospital in 1860 and is now the Florence Nightingale Faculty of Nursing and Midwifery, part of King's College London.

The hospital left Southwark in 1862, when the site was compulsorily purchased for the construction of Charing Cross railway viaduct. It was housed at Royal Surrey Gardens, Newington until new buildings on the present site in Lambeth on the Thames opposite the Houses of Parliament, were completed in 1871. The foundation stone was laid by Queen Victoria in 1868. There were 600 beds in six separate ward buildings set at right angles to the river and linked by low corridors. It was one of the first hospitals to adopt the 'pavilion principle', popularised by Florence Nightingale, to improve ventilation and to separate patients with infectious diseases. Some parts of the old St Thomas' Hospital survive on the north side of St Thomas Street, Southwark. The hospital was taken over by the War Office in 1914 and became 5th London General Hospital. Three ward blocks were destroyed during the Second World War and there was some limited reconstruction in the 1950s. However, complete rebuilding was agreed in the 1960s and a new thirteen-storey block was completed in 1975. The three remaining Victorian ward pavilion blocks were refurbished in the 1980s and are now Grade II listed. In 1949, Harold Ridley performed the world's first implantation of an intraocular lens and was subsequently knighted 'for pioneering services to cataract surgery'. When Guy's and St Thomas' Hospitals merged into a single trust, accident and emergency services were consolidated at St Thomas' Hospital in 1993.

St Thomas' Hospital Medical School was established in 1550 but in 1825 Guy's Hospital established its own separate medical school. They remerged in 1982. Other medical training facilities joined and in 1997 there was a merger with King's College School of Medicine and Dentistry to form The Guy's, Kings & Thomas' Schools of Medicine, Dentistry and Biomedical Sciences. It became King's College London School of Medicine and Dentistry at Guy's, King's and St Thomas' Hospitals in 2005.

> In 1948 he instituted the Modern Records Department and set up a Genito-Urinary Outpatients Department.
> - Hinckley and District Hospital – surgeon 1939–46.
> - Leicester City General Hospital – Consulting Surgeon 1942–48.
> - Leicester Isolation Hospital & Sanatorium – Consulting Surgeon 1959–62.

He also contributed specialist papers to the British Journal of Surgery on gangrenous cystitis, malignant tumours and giant prostatic calculi. He held a number of other appointments:

- Military Member, Leicestershire Territorial Army & Air Force Association from 1939.
- Vice-Chairman, Leicester No.2 Hospital Management Committee – 1948–53.
- Deputy Lieutenant, Leicestershire 20th December 1950 (LG 2nd January 1951).
- Military Member, Leicestershire & Rutland Territorial & Auxiliary Forces Association 1953–62.
- Member of the Accident Services Review of Great Britain & Ireland 1958–60.
- Member of the Council of the Royal College of Surgeons 3rd July 1958–6th July 1966.
- President of the Provincial Surgical Club of Great Britain 1961–63.
- Leicestershire Branch, British Red Cross Society – Director 1962–67, Regional Representative 1964, Deputy President 1967–71 and Honorary Vice President 1971–77.

John married Ernestine Helen Wright (10th November 1905–11th February 2000), born at Leicester, on 3rd September 1935 at St John the Divine, Leicester. They were living at 1 Elmfield Avenue, off London Road, Leicester in 1939 and later at 7 University Road, Leicester before moving to Selby Lodge, 11 Southernhay Road, Leicester. Ernestine died at Selby Lodge. There were no children.

Ernestine's father, Ernest Wright (12th February 1874–25th August 1952), born at Leicester, married Sarah Edith Wright (27th August 1879–18th January 1964), born at Whitley Bay, Northumberland, in Leicester in 1903. He was a clerk in 1891, living with his parents at 29 Humberstone Road, Leicester and at 10 Salisbury Road, Leicester in 1901. In 1911 he was a coal merchant's manager, when they were living at 48 Clarendon Park Road, Leicester. By 1939 he was a company director, living with his wife at the home of his daughter and son-in-law, John Cridlan Barrett VC, at 1 Elmfield Avenue, Leicester. They were living at 218 London Road, Leicester at the time of his death. Sarah was living at 1 Elmfield Avenue, Leicester at the time of her death at 312 London Road, Leicester.

John continued serving in the 5th Battalion after the Great War. He was promoted captain on 1st July 1925 and major on 1st April 1930. In 1931 he was appointed Second-in-Command of 5th Battalion and was promoted brevet lieutenant colonel on 1st January 1935. **Awarded the Efficiency Decoration (Territorial), LG 19th June 1936.** On 16th February 1937 he was promoted lieutenant colonel and was appointed CO of 5th Battalion until 1939. John was mobilised on 24th August 1939. On 26th January 1940 he relinquished the rank of lieutenant colonel and transferred from the Leicestershire Regiment (TA) to the Royal Army Medical Corps (TA) General List (21885) as a major with seniority from 20th August 1934. He was promoted to temporary lieutenant colonel on 26th February 1940 and commanded the Surgical Division, No.30 General Hospital in Reykjavik, Iceland until being transferred to the RAMC (TA) Unemployed List in 1941. He last appears in the Army List in March 1943 and was later transferred to the TA

The Efficiency Decoration was instituted in 1930 for part-time officers of the Territorial Army of the United Kingdom and of the Auxiliary Military Forces of the British Dominions, Colonies and Protectorates and India after twenty years efficient service as a thoroughly capable officer. It superseded a number of awards including the Volunteer Officers' Decoration and the Territorial Decoration. In 1949 the qualifying service was reduced to twelve years of commissioned service. A clasp was awarded for each further period of six years of qualifying service. In the Commonwealth it has been superseded by national decorations in Canada, South Africa and Australia. In the United Kingdom it was superseded by the Volunteer Reserves Service Medal in 1999. New Zealand continues to award the Efficiency Decoration.

Reserve of Officers as a major and was granted the rank of honorary lieutenant colonel. **Awarded three clasps to the Efficiency Decoration (Territorial), LG 13th April 1951.** John ceased to belong to the TA Reserve of Officers on 10th August 1952, having attained the age limit of liability to recall. However, his connections with the TA did not end then as he was appointed Honorary Colonel, 5th Battalion, Royal Leicestershire Regiment (TA) 1st September 1953–1st September 1958 and retained the honorary rank of colonel.

John was keen on sport, particularly golf and swimming, and was also a philatelist. He attended a number of VC reunions – VC Garden Party at Buckingham Palace on 26th June 1920, VC Dinner at the Royal Gallery of the House of Lords, London on 9th November 1929, the VC Centenary Celebrations at Hyde Park, London on 26th June 1956 and the third VC & GC Association Reunion at the Café Royal, London on 18th July 1962.

John died at his home at Selby Lodge, 11 Southerhay Road, Leicester

St Mary Magdalen, Knighton dates back to 1097 but there was a chapel of St Margaret's Church, Leicester there before the Norman Conquest. The earliest part of the current building, the tower, is 13th century. The Parish was served by a curate and did not have its own vicar until it was made a separate parish in 1878. The church was restored in at least two phases c.1860 and in 1894 but by the early 20th century the church was too small for the increased population of the parish. However, due to the outbreak of war, it was not until 1960 that the foundation stone for the extension was laid. In 1978 four of the five bells were removed and replaced with six bells from the disused Church of St Michael, Stamford and two new bells.

on 7th March 1977, the last surviving VC of his Regiment. His funeral was held at the Church of St Mary Magdalen, Knighton, Leicester on 15th March, followed by cremation at Gilroes Crematorium, Groby Road, Leicester. His ashes were scattered in Rose Bed 14 there. He is commemorated in a number of other places:

The memorial to the Leicestershire Regiment VCs in Leicester Cathedral.

- Leicester Cathedral, St Martin's, Leicester:
  - Memorial plaque in St George's Chapel.
  - Named on the memorial to the four Leicestershire Regiment VCs.
- A painting of the VC action by Terence Cuneo was commissioned by the Royal Leicestershire Regiment in 1958.
- A Department for Communities and Local Government commemorative paving stone was dedicated at Leamington Spa War Memorial, Euston Place, The Parade, Leamington Spa, Warwickshire on 23rd September 2018.
- Named on the Freemen of the Borough Board, Town Hall, Royal Leamington Spa, Warwickshire.
- Replica VC and photograph in the entrance to Arnold Lodge School, Leamington Spa, presented by the Royal Leicestershire Regiment on 21st November 2014.
- A Leicestershire County Council green plaque was dedicated on the site of the former Glen Parva Barracks, Wigston, the home of The Leicestershire Regiment and later the Royal Leicestershire Regiment 1881–1960, on 12th March 2020.

In addition to the VC he was awarded the British War Medal 1914–20, Victory Medal 1914–19, Defence Medal, War Medal

The Defence Medal was instituted in May 1945 for non-operational military and certain types of civilian war service (Home Guard, Civil Defence, Royal Observer Corps, Fire Service and other approved civilian services) from 3rd September 1939 to 8th May 1945 and for the Pacific Theatre until 2nd September 1945. In the United Kingdom military personnel in headquarters, training units and airfields were eligible for the award. Qualifying service varied. In the United Kingdom the requirement was three years or three months in a Mine and Bomb Disposal Unit. In a non-operational area, not subjected to air attack and not closely threatened, the requirement was one year's service overseas outside the individual's country of residence. In a non-operational area subjected to air attack or closely threatened, the requirement was six months.

Newarke Houses Museum, which is in the middle of the De Montfort University campus, includes the Royal Leicestershire Regiment Museum and exhibits of post-medieval and contemporary Leicester. There are two buildings – Wyggeston's Chantry House, built c.1511, and Thomas Skeffington's House, built in the 17th century. Both were used during the Siege of Leicester in 1645, during the English Civil War. They were sold in 1908. Chantry House remained a private residence, while Skeffington House became a boys' school. Both properties were converted for museum use in 1953 as part of the celebrations of the Queen's coronation.

The War Medal 1939–1945 was instituted on 16th August 1945 to be awarded to those who served full-time in the armed forces or Merchant Navy for at least twenty-eight days between 3rd September 1939 and 2nd September 1945.

1939–45, George V Silver Jubilee Medal 1935, George VI Coronation Medal 1937, Elizabeth II Coronation Medal 1953 and Efficiency Decoration (Territorial) with three clasps. He stipulated in his will that the VC should go to the Royal Leicestershire Regiment on the death of his wife. The VC is held by the Royal Leicestershire Regiment Museum, Newarke Houses Museum, The Newarke, Leicester.

### 6594 SERGEANT MAURICE VINCENT BUCKLEY
### 13th Australian Infantry Battalion AIF

Maurice Buckley was born on 13th April 1891 at Upper Hawthorn, Melbourne, Victoria, Australia. His father, Timothy Buckley (1854–23rd October 1943), a brickmaker born in Ireland, emigrated to Victoria, Australia from Co Cork and settled at Taku, 35 McArthur Street, Malvern, Victoria. He married Hanora/Honora Mary Agnes née Sexton (1859–1945), born at North Melbourne, Victoria, in 1887. She was known as Agnes. Maurice had seven siblings:

- Daniel John Buckley (26th May 1887–1st November 1980), a railway employee, married Marguerita Kathleen Bourke (4th July 1897–15th February 1989) in 1925. They were living at 4 Astolat Avenue, Murrumbeena, Victoria from 1931. They are understood to have had two children.
- Margaret 'Madge' Esther Buckley (1889–7th July 1941) never married.
- Eileen Mary Buckley (1893–1964) married John William Le Masurier (1892–27th July 1939), a commercial traveller, in 1925. John enlisted in 1st to 7th Depot Units of Supply in Melbourne on 6th July 1915 (9564). He was described as a salesman or clerk, 5′ 9¼″ tall, weighing 149 lbs, with fair complexion, blue eyes, brown hair and his religious denomination was Church of England. He was assigned to E Company at Flemington on 14th July, D Company at Geelong on 16th August, Broadmeadows on 22nd November, C Company at Geelong next day and Broadmeadows Army Service Corps on 6th December. He rejoined 1st to 7th Depot Units of Supply on 20th January 1916. He embarked aboard HMAT A70 *Ballarat* on 18th February and was treated on board for a fractured shoulder blade from 21st February. He joined the Reinforcement Camp, Zeitoun on 23rd March and the Reinforcement Camp, Tel-el-Kebir on 17th April. He transferred to HQ Corps Troops and Infantry General Base Depot, Tel-el-Kebir on 23rd May and was attached to the Australian Record Section 26th-28th May. He mustered as an Australian Army Service Corps driver on 1st October at No.4 Camp, AASC Training Depot, Parkhouse Camp, Salisbury Plain. He was detached to Wareham 26th October–19th January 1917. John went to France on 20th February aboard SS *Arundel* from Folkestone and joined the Australian General Base Depot, Étaples next day. He joined 1st Anzac Entrenching Battalion on 3rd March. On 13th April he remustered as a private at his own request and joined 1st Australian Division Supply Column. He was attached to 1st Australian Division Train 23rd July–29th September and was granted leave to Britain 6th-20th December, rejoining his unit on 23rd December. John transferred to 1st Australian Division MT Company on 12th March 1918. He was granted leave to Nice 15th December–4th January 1919. On 6th May he arrived at Southampton and joined No.1 Group, Longbridge Deverill, Wiltshire. He returned to Australia aboard SS *Konig Friedrich August*, embarking at Devonport on 20th June and disembarking at Melbourne on 6th August. He was discharged on 28th September. John and Eileen were living at

Hawthorn is an inner suburb of Melbourne. First settled in the late 1830s, it and the cities of Camberwell and Kew were amalgamated in 1994 to form the City of Boroondara, now one of the most affluent suburbs.

3 Riley Street, Oakleigh, Victoria in 1927. Eileen was still living at 3 Riley Street in 1963. She died at Oakleigh East, Victoria. Eileen and John had at least two children:
  ◦ Gregory Vincent Le Masurier, an electrician, married Eida Jorgensen, a hairdresser, in 1951. He was a police constable in 1954, when they were living with his mother. They had moved to 38 Pamela Street, Mount Waverley, Victoria by 1963. He was the proprietor of the Evans Hotel, Dunolly, Victoria in 1977. By 1980 they were living at Upper Ross, Thuringowa, Queensland.
  ◦ Merlin Le Masurier (died 1986), a hairdresser, married Vincent Brian McMullan in 1954. They were living at 2 Sunnyside Road, Mount Waverley by 1963. They had four children – Johnathan (sic) McMullan (1962–63), Timothy Vincent McMullan, Joanne Maree McMullan and Geraldine Mary McMullan.
- Gerald Timothy Buckley (1895–4th October 1915) was a coach bodybuilder with Hoth Frazer, Victoria. He served for two years as a senior cadet and three years in 19th Battery, Field Artillery before enlisting as a driver in 12th Battery, 4th Field Artillery Brigade AIF at Melbourne on 7th July 1915 (4969) at Queens Road, Melbourne. Victoria. He was described as 5′ 6½″ tall, weighing 126 lbs, with fresh complexion, blue eyes, dark brown hair and his religious denomination was Roman Catholic. He joined the Field Artillery Reinforcements at Broadmeadows on 20th September. Gerald died of cerebro-meningitis at Alfred Hospital, Melbourne (Brighton General Cemetery, Caulfield South, Melbourne – RCB 114).
- Agnes Kathleen Buckley (1897–1980) never married.
- William Francis Buckley (1899–18th September 1953) was a munitions worker in Melbourne during the Great War (2316).
- Cyril Edmund Buckley (1902–26th May 1986), a railway employee, married Margaret Mary O'Leary (1902–91) in 1939. They were living at 7 Mary Avenue, Werribee, Victoria in 1942 and they were still there in 1980.

Maurice's paternal grandparents were Daniel Buckley and Margaret née O'Connell, both from Ireland. His maternal grandparents were Maurice Sexton and Ellen née Twomey. In addition to Agnes they had six other children:

- Catherine Cecelia Sexton (1861–1948) never married.
- Patrick Sexton (1864–28th February 1951) married Bridget Rea (c.1866–14th February 1951) in 1894 in Victoria. They both died at Mentone, Victoria. They had six children:
  ◦ Laura Mary Inez Sexton (1895–5th March 1978) never married.
  ◦ Sylvia Catherine Sexton (born 1897) married Martin Thomas Ramus (1895–1968) in 1923.
  ◦ Maurice Rea Sexton (1900–67) married Lena Alice Coleman (1900–79) in 1933 and Mary Iris Butterworth in 1957.

- Muriel Margaret Sexton (born 1902).
- Ellen Dorothea Sexton (1904–3rd October 1983) never married.
- Veronica May Sexton (born 1907) married Thomas Anthony Oliphant (1894–1977) in 1943.

- John Sexton (1865–1941).
- Jeremiah Sexton (6th December 1867–2nd December 1953) worked as a lithographer for ten years and as a dispenser for ten years at Melbourne Hospital. He served during the Second Boer War for a year and eighty-three days as a corporal in 3rd New South Wales Imperial Bushmen Regiment. He enlisted as George Sexton in No.2 Squadron, 1st Remount Unit at Melbourne on 15th September 1915 (452), described as a labourer, 5′ 6¼″ tall, weighing 137 lbs, with fresh complexion, blue eyes, grey hair and his religious denomination was Roman Catholic. His next of kin was his sister, Mrs Cliff Duckett, 92 Park Street, Royal Park, Melbourne. George embarked aboard HMAT A67 *Orsova* at Melbourne on 12th November, disembarking at Suez on 8th December. He was treated at 3rd Australian General Hospital, Abbassia from 3rd May 1916, having been kicked by a horse at Heliopolis. He was transferred to Montazah Convalescence Depot on 15th May. On 14th June he was discharged to Tel-el-Kebir for fourteen days light duties from 1st British Red Cross Hospital, Montazah and rejoined his unit next day. He joined the Details Camp at Moascar on 9th October. On 18th October he departed Suez aboard HMAT A44 *Vestalia* and disembarked in 3rd Military District on 21st November. He was discharged on 5th December. George enlisted in the Australian Flying Corps on 16th April 1917 (V64083) at Melbourne. He served with No.5 Australian General Hospital, Melbourne and was promoted acting corporal 5th July, corporal 1st August, lance sergeant 8th October and sergeant 29th October. He transferred to AFC Laverton on 28th October 1918. On 16th January 1919 he reverted to lance sergeant due to a reduction in establishment. He joined No.1 Home Training School, HQ Central Flying School on 18th March and was discharged on 31st December. He was enlisted temporarily in the Australian Air Corps on 1st January 1920 (36) and was discharged on 30th March 1921. He enlisted in the RAAF at Central Flying School, Laverton for six years on 31st March 1921 as a corporal aircraft hand general medical orderly (33), named George? (sic) Jeremiah Sexton. He gave his year of birth as 1870. He was posted from No.1 Flying Training School to No.1 Aircraft Depot, Point Cook on 1st July 1921 and attended the Central Training Depot, Liverpool 7th November–15th December. He was posted to No.1 Station HQ on 1st July 1922 and re-mustered as a trained nurse on 12th February 1923. He was admitted to Caulfield Repatriation Hospital on 24th August 1923 for a day and committed a crime (unspecified) on 29th January 1924. On 1st July 1925 he was posted to No.1 Flying Training School and re-engaged for another six years at Point Cook on 22nd December 1926 to commence on 31st March 1927. He was appointed provisional sergeant the same day but was discharged having reached the age for retirement on 6th December 1927.

- Maurice John Sexton (1870–19th July 1901).
- Mary Ellen Sexton (1872–1964) married Clifford Montague Duckett (10th May 1875–15th February 1948) in 1900. They were living at 92 Park Street, Royal Park, Melbourne by 1915. He was a salesman in 1937, by when they were living at Kamblea Grove, North Caulfield. He died there and she at Elsternwick, North Melbourne. They had four children:
    - Clifford Charles Duckett (1902–10 February 1925) married Beryl Vera Owens in 1924. Beryl married Allan Learmonth Stewart in 1927.
    - Francis Maurice Duckett (1905–87) married Gladys May Puddy (born 1907) in 1929.
    - Eric Sexton Duckett (31 October 1910–16 June 1976) married Violet Eastwood in 1935.
    - Beatrice Mary Duckett (1914–90) never married.

Maurice was educated at the Christian Brothers' School (later St Joseph's Technical College), Abbotsford, Victoria. He worked as a coach trimmer in the motor trade with the Auburn Carriage Company, Warrnambool, Victoria. He stated that he was employed by D White, Sturt Street, Melbourne when he enlisted.

Maurice had a medical at Warrnambool on 12th December 1914, was attested in 13th Light Horse Regiment AIF in Melbourne, Victoria on 18th December 1914 and was posted to the Depot, Broadmeadows Camp (107 & 633). He was described as 5' 7½" tall, weighing 140 lbs, with dark complexion, brown wavy hair and his religious denomination was Roman Catholic. He was posted to 1st Reinforcements, B Squadron, 13th Light Horse Regiment on 29th March 1915. He embarked aboard HMAT A40 *Ceramic* at Sydney on 25th June and disembarked at Suez, Egypt on 23rd July. The unit encamped at Heliopolis, Egypt. Maurice contracted venereal disease and was returned to Australia via Alexandria aboard HMAT A18 *Wiltshire* on 31st August, arriving in Melbourne on 25th September. He was admitted to Langwarrin Venereal Disease Hospital,

The Christian Brothers' School at Abbotsford was founded in 1893 as a primary school for boys. In its first year the school operated from a two-story brick building, which included a small chapel. By 1908 there were 450 pupils. About the same time A and B Companies, 12th Victorian Battalion, Australian Army Cadets were formed and continued into the 1970s. In 1930 the school was renamed St Joseph's Technical College, the second Catholic technical school established in Melbourne. A new wing was opened in 1941 to increase the number of pupils. However, student numbers declined and the school closed in 1990. In 2014 St Joseph's was named as one of the institutions in which abuse is alleged to have occurred or where an abuser had worked.

SS *Wiltshire* (10,390 tons) was built in 1912 by John Brown on Clydebank for the Federal Steam Navigation Co, London for the UK–Australia–New Zealand route. She was leased by the Commonwealth as HMAT A18 *Wiltshire* until 27th December 1917, when she was taken over by the British Admiralty. *Wiltshire* completed nine voyages from Australia, including the first convoy from Albany in October 1914. She was wrecked on 31st May 1922 in Rosalie Bay, Great Barrier Island, New Zealand. All 103 men aboard were saved.

Langwarrin Military Reserve was established in 1886 on an elevated location for the defence of Port Phillip and Melbourne. It was used mainly for volunteer encampments 1888–1910. When the Great War broke out, Langwarrin Internment Camp was established to detain up to 500 enemy aliens. Most lived in tents and sanitary arrangements were inadequate. Some internees even built huts at their own expense. Internees were paid to improve the camp by building fences, clearing ground and improving the water supply. By November 1915 there were 769 Germans, 104 Austrians and seventy-two Turks there but by December 1917 only 326 detainees remained at Langwarrin. In 1915 a military hospital for the treatment of venereal diseases was established and some internees worked there. Post-World War II the reserve was used occasionally for military training until 1974, when it came under the control of Balcombe Military Camp for training Army Reserve and school cadet units. In 1980 the reserve was leased to the Victorian Ministry of Conservation and in 1982 the State Government purchased it from the Commonwealth Government. All the buildings have been removed since (Australian War Memorial).

near Frankston, Melbourne. He went absent without leave on 18th January 1916, was declared a deserter on 21st January and was struck off strength on 20th March as an illegal absentee.

Maurice re-enlisted at Victoria Barracks, Sydney, New South Wales in B Company, 13th Battalion AIF as Gerald Sexton on 8th May 1916 (6594). The false name comprised one brother's Christian name and his mother's maiden name. He was described as a groom, 5′ 8½″ tall, weighing 140lbs, with fresh complexion, brown hair, hazel eyes and his religious denomination was Roman Catholic. His address was 74 Castlereagh Street, Sydney. He was posted to Showgrounds Camp, Sydney and joined 21st Reinforcements, 13th Battalion on 19th September. He sailed from Sydney on 7th October aboard HMAT A40 *Ceramic* arriving in Plymouth, Devon on 21st November. Maurice was immediately admitted to the Military Hospital, Devonport with a twisted right knee. He was transferred to 3rd Australian Auxiliary Hospital, Dartford on 28th November with synovitis right knee. On 9th December he was discharged from hospital and joined No.2 Command Depot, Weymouth. He transferred to Perham Down on 16th December and joined No.4 Camp, No.1 Command Depot, Perham

Down, Wiltshire from No.7 Camp on 19th December. He transferred to 4th Training Battalion, Codford, Wiltshire on 4th January 1917.

On 16th January Maurice went to France via Folkestone, Kent aboard SS *Princess Victoria*, joined 4th Australian Division Base Depot, Étaples next day and 13th Battalion on 21st January. He was admitted to 12th Australian Field Ambulance on 9th February, transferred to 4th Australian Field Ambulance with blistered feet and rejoined his unit on 24th February. Maurice was absent without leave from 1.30 p.m. until 6 p.m. on 7th June and from 5 p.m. on 15th June until 4 a.m. on 16th June, for which he was awarded twenty-eight days Field Punishment No. 2 and forfeited twenty days' pay. He was absent again on 10th September from 9.30 p.m. until 10.30 p.m. and was awarded ten days Field Punishment No. 2 and forfeited ten days' pay. He was granted leave 8th–24th December. Maurice was promoted lance corporal on 31st January 1918, temporary corporal on 19th April and corporal and lance sergeant on 27th June. He was wounded by shrapnel to the head and suffered shell concussion on 6th July. He was treated at 12th and 13th Australian Field Ambulances and returned to duty on 8th July, when he was appointed temporary sergeant.

3rd Australian Army Auxiliary Hospital was established at the Orchard Hospital in Dartford on 9th October 1916. It eventually had a capacity of 1,200 patients. Orchard Hospital opened in 1902 as a temporary hospital for smallpox patients. In 1910, with the decline of smallpox, it became a fever hospital but spent much of its time closed, being opened only for epidemics of scarlet fever and diphtheria. It was empty at the outbreak of war and became the Orchard Military Hospital until transferred for Australian use. A total of 56,441 patients were treated there. Many soldiers married local women. The Australian government presented the town with a German gun captured by the Australians, in appreciation of its hospitality during the war. The gun was scrapped during the Second World War (Australian War Memorial).

**Awarded the DCM for his actions on 8th August 1918 while in charge of a Lewis gun section – on four separate occasions his company was suddenly confronted by enemy machine gun fire and he brought his gun into action quickly and silenced the opposition. On one occasion, in some tall crops, he stood up in full view of the enemy firing from the hip until he had put the enemy machine gun out of action, LG 5th December 1918. His name was corrected in the London Gazette on 27th June 1919.** Promoted sergeant on 28th August. **Awarded the VC for his actions at Le Verguier, France on 18th September 1918, LG 14th December 1918. His name was corrected in the London Gazette on 8th August 1919.** Maurice was granted leave to Paris, France 18th October–9th November and 29th November–9th December. On 19th

December his mother initiated a change from his alias back to his real name. On 20th March 1919 he officially changed it back to Maurice Vincent Buckley under a Statutory Declaration at Hanzinelle, Belgium, witnessed by Lieutenant Colonel AS Allen, CO 13th Battalion.

Maurice left the Battalion on 21st April, arrived at Southampton on 30th April and joined No.4 Camp with 1916 personnel for return to Australia. The VC was presented by the King in the quadrangle at Buckingham Palace on 29th May. Maurice was treated at 1st Australian Dermatological Hospital, Bulford, Wiltshire for gonorrhoea and syphilis from 17th June. He went absent in London from 8.30 p.m. on 25th July until 8.45 p.m. on 1st August for which he was reprimanded and forfeited eight days' pay. He returned to 1st Australian Dermatological Hospital for more treatment 4th–30th August. On 29th

Maurice Buckley receives the VC from the King on 29th May 1919.

August he was found to be suffering from chronic gleet but was no longer infectious and was fit to travel on a troopship. A medical board at Sutton Veny, Wiltshire on 1st September found him fit for General Service and he joined No.2 Group next day. Maurice departed England aboard HMT *Raranga* on 8th September and arrived in Australia on 27th October. A medical board at Sturt Street, Melbourne that

1st Australian Dermatological Hospital was established at Abbassia, Egypt in 1915. In September 1916 it relocated to Bulford Camp on Salisbury Plain and became a specialist hospital for venereal diseases. At its peak the hospital could accommodate over 1,500 patients, some under guard. However, security was not tight and eventually criminal patients were treated at Lewes Prison, Sussex.

SS *Ratanga* (7,956 tons) was a refrigerated cargo ship launched on 21st December 1915 by Armstrong, Whitworth & Co Ltd for Shaw, Savill & Albion Co Ltd of Southampton. In 1950 she was broken up at Blyth by Hughes Bolckow Shipbreaking Co Ltd.

day found that he was suffering from shortness of breath and headaches. It was noted that he had been shell-shocked and had tachycardia effort syndrome. He was declared medically unfit and discharged on 11th December 1919.

Melbourne entrepreneur, John Wren, set Maurice up as a road contractor in Gippsland, Victoria. In February 1920 he was part of a delegation to Melbourne City Council seeking permission to hold the traditional St Patrick's Day March,

Mount St Evins Hospital was established in 1906 by the Sisters of Charity, adjacent to St Vincent's Hospital in Fitzroy.

The Buckley family grave in Brighton General Cemetery, Melbourne.

which several anti-Catholic and anti-Irish organisations had opposed. The Council voted in favour of the march, during which Maurice and thirteen other VC holders led 10,000 Catholic ex-service men and women.

On 15th January 1921, Maurice was working at Boolarra, near Morwell, Gippsland when a colleague bet him that he couldn't jump his horse over a set of railway gates. He cleared the gates on the first attempt but, when he tried to jump back over, his horse shied and he was thrown, hitting his head against the gates. He remounted and rode away without appearing to be hurt. However, that evening he was found unconscious beside the Gunyah Road, near Boolarra and was taken to Mount St Evins Private Hospital, 51 Victoria Parade, Fitzroy, Victoria by ambulance. There were signs that he might recover but he never regained consciousness and died there on 27th January. He was the first Australian VC to die after returning home. A requiem mass was held in St Patrick's Cathedral, Melbourne. He was buried in the family grave in Brighton General Cemetery, Melbourne on 28th January. The pallbearers were ten VC holders and the guard of honour comprised students of the Christian Brothers' School at Abbotsford, Victoria. He is commemorated in a number of other places:

- Australian Capital Territory
    - Buckley Court, Canberra.
    - Australian Victoria Cross Recipients plaque on the Victoria Cross Memorial, Campbell, dedicated on 24th July 2000.
    - Named on one of eleven plaques honouring 175 men from overseas awarded the VC for the Great War. The plaques were unveiled by the Senior Minister of State at the Foreign & Commonwealth Office and Minister for Faith and Communities, Baroness Warsi, at a reception at Lancaster House, London on 26th June 2014 attended by The Duke of Kent and relatives of the VC recipients. The Australian plaque is at the Australian War Memorial, Canberra.

Maurice Buckley's plaque at the Victoria Cross Memorial, Springvale Botanical Cemetery.

    - Named on the Roll of Honour at the Australian War Memorial.
    - Commemorative display in the Hall of Valour, Australian War Memorial, Canberra.
- Victoria
    - Victoria Cross Memorial, Springvale Botanical Cemetery, Melbourne dedicated on 10th November 2013.
    - Sexton Place, Wodonga on White Box Rise estate built on land formerly part of Bandiana Army Camp.
    - Buckley Street, Bittern, Melbourne on Victoria Cross Estate built in 1916–18.

- New South Wales
  - Victoria Cross Memorial, Queen Victoria Building, George Street, Sydney dedicated on 23rd February 1992 to commemorate the visit of Queen Elizabeth II and Prince Phillip on the occasion of the Sesquicentenary of the City of Sydney. Sir Roden Cutler VC AK KCMG, Edward Kenna VC and Keith Payne VC were in attendance.
  - Victoria Cross Recipients Wall, North Bondi War Memorial donated to Waverley on 27th November 2011 by The Returned & Services League of Australia.
  - Memorial Plaque at Armatree.
  - VC Memorial, Borella Road, Peards Complex, East Albury.
  - VC Memorial, Ingleburn RSL Club, Sydney.
- Communities and Local Government commemorative paving stones for the 145 VCs born in Australia, Belgium, Canada, China, Denmark, Egypt, France, Germany, India, Iraq, Japan, Nepal, Netherlands, Newfoundland, New Zealand, Pakistan, South Africa, Sri Lanka, Ukraine and United States of America were unveiled at the National Memorial Arboretum, Alrewas, Staffordshire by Prime Minister David Cameron MP and Sergeant Johnson Beharry VC on 5th March 2015.

In addition to the VC and DCM he was awarded the 1914–15 Star, British War Medal 1914–20 and Victory Medal 1914–19. In 1921 his mother loaned the medals to the Australian War Memorial. She sought return of the medals in 1927 because the museum was moving to Canberra but was persuaded to leave the VC 'a little longer'. The VC passed to Maurice's sister, Agnes, on the death of their mother in 1945. Agnes had the VC returned in 1952 because she wanted it displayed in Maurice's old school, which was celebrating its golden jubilee. The Director of the AWM requested Agnes to give the VC back in 1953 but it was not until 1958 that she agreed. In May 1975 she asked for the VC to be returned. The Director consulted Justice Starke who said that until 1953 the VC was not a gift but that the return in 1958 might have changed its status. Agnes was unmoved and requested directly and frequently for the return of her brother's VC and DCM. Agnes' legitimacy of ownership was questioned. Her older brother, Daniel, indicated that he would like the medals to remain at the AWM. Agnes was furious and sent her mother's will to prove her ownership. In March 1979 the acting Deputy Crown Solicitor advised that Agnes could not claim ownership until she proved the medals had belonged to her mother, despite that ownership being accepted by the AWM in 1921. Agnes wrote four times in March and April 1979 without receiving an answer and asked the Commonwealth Ombudsman for help. In July it was noted that there was no evidence that Maurice Buckley had left a will and therefore it could not be established that the mother had owned the medals. In August 1979 Agnes was asked for proof of her mother's ownership but she died in January 1980 and her executor pursued the matter no further. The VC is held in the Hall of Valour, Australian War Memorial, Treloar Crescent, Campbell, Australian Capital Territory.

## 240194 SERGEANT LAURENCE CALVERT
### 5th Battalion, The King's Own (Yorkshire Light Infantry)

Laurence Calvert was born on 16th February 1892 at 9 Selkirk Place, Dewsbury Road, Hunslet, West Riding of Yorkshire. He was registered as Lawrance (sic) at birth. His father, George Greenwood Calvert (9th April 1865–1895), was a copper plate worker or a tinner. He married Beatrice née Stevenson (1869–1922), on 19th December 1887. They were living at 3 South Terrace, Leeds in 1881, at 35 Algeria Street, Holbeck, Leeds in 1891, when she was a cap finisher, and at 24 Chandos Street, Holbeck, Leeds in 1901, when she was a tailor's machinist, living with her family and sister Ann. By 1911 she had moved to 11 Cross Princess Street, Holbeck and to 19 Beech Hill, Conisbrough, Yorkshire by 1914. Beatrice married Arthur Moody (1851–25th June 1932), a glass blower born at Chesterfield, Derbyshire, on 21st July 1920 at St Luke, Holbeck. He was living at 2 Normanton Terrace, Leeds and she at 12 Coupland Road, Leeds at the time. Arthur had married Sarah Frances Colbeck (1851–1919) on 19th November 1876 at St James's Church, Doncaster and they had four children – Charles William Moody 1878, Percy Moody 1882, Arthur Peter Moody 1884 and Albert Moody 1886. Laurence had a brother:

- Walter Stevenson Calvert (25th May 1888–1946) was an apprentice brass finisher for Messrs Haythorne Davis & Co until he enlisted in the Royal Navy on 18th September 1907. He was described as 5′ 3¼″ tall, weighing 118 lbs, with dark brown hair, brown eyes and dark complexion. He served aboard HMS *Victory* (18th September–29th October 1907, 21st April–31st May 1909, 4th April–29th May 1911 and 28th-30th March 1912), *Prince George* (30th October 1907–3rd February 1908), *Goliath* (4th February 1908–20th April 1909), *Canopus* (1st June–9th November 1909), *Aboukir* (10th November 1909–3rd April 1911), *Furious* (20th May–17th August 1911) and *Vindictive* (31st March–17th September 1912). He was aboard

Chandos Street, Holbeck, Leeds, where the family was living in 1901. A lady is sitting on the step of No.24 (Leodis).

HMS *Aboukir* when she escorted Queen Alexandra from Genoa, Italy to England when King Edward VII was dangerously ill at the end of April 1910. Walter served two periods of detention for seven and fourteen days, the latter for smuggling. He was discharged on 17th September 1912 'Services No Longer Required' and 'Not to be enlisted in the Royal Fleet Reserve after active service'. Walter was a miner living with his mother at 19 Beech Hill, Conisbrough when he enlisted in 8th York & Lancaster at Conisbrough on 2nd September 1914 (13795). He was described as 5′ 3″ tall, weighing 118 lbs, with dark complexion, brown eyes, dark brown hair and his religious denomination was Church of England. He was promoted lance corporal on 17th September and was posted to Barossa Barracks, Aldershot, Hampshire on 1st December. He was discharged medically unfit due to chronic lumbar pain on 18th January 1915.

HMS *Aboukir* (12,000 tons), a *Cressy* class armoured cruiser, was built between 1898 and 1900 at Govan on the Clyde and served mainly with the Mediterranean Fleet. She is seen here in Malta. She was armed with two 9.2″ Mk X guns, twelve 6″ Mk VII guns, twelve 12 Pounder QF guns, three 3 Pounder Hotchkiss guns and two 18″ Torpedo tubes. *Aboukir* went into reserve in 1912 and was recommissioned in the 7th Cruiser Squadron when war broke out. She had a reserve role in the Battle of the Heligoland Bight on 28th August 1914 and did not see any action. On 22nd September that year *Aboukir* was sunk by U-9, together with two sister ships, *Cressy* and *Hogue*. Losses from the three ships totalled sixty-two officers and 1,397 men and of these, 527 were aboard *Aboukir*.

On 8th June 1915 he re-enlisted in the Royal Navy (Tyneside Z/5199) as an ordinary seaman. He was stationed with the Royal Naval Division at Crystal Palace, London as an able seaman on 30th August and a leading seaman on 1st October. He was admitted to Croydon General Hospital with a gastric ulcer on 18th December and was discharged medically unfit for service on 6th April 1916. Walter married Lillian 'Lily' Gilliot (4 February 1898–30th August 1979), born at Castleford, Yorkshire, on 26th November 1917 at Denaby Main Parish Church. They were both living on Edlington Street, Denaby Main at the time, he at No.49 and she at No.3. In 1929 they were living at 7 Doncaster Road, Conisbrough and by 1930 at 22 Chambers Avenue, Conisbrough. By 1939 Walter was a general labourer and they were living at 18 Chambers Avenue, Conisbrough. Walter and Lily were Air Raid Precautions Wardens at the time. Walter's death was registered at Wharfedale, Yorkshire and Lily's at Halifax, Yorkshire. After Walter's death, Lily married three more times – see below the children. They had eight children, all registered at Doncaster:
- Carrie Calvert (15th September 1918–30th August 1985) married Sydney Holmes (16th June 1916–17th March 1996), born at Oxenhope, Yorkshire,

in 1937 at Keighley, Yorkshire. He was a tool and flat spring maker in 1939, when they were living at 9 Green Street, Keighley. They were living at 9 Murton Grove, Steeton, near Keighley at the time of her death there. They had two children – John Holmes 1938 and Sheila Holmes 1945.
- Mary Calvert (10th July 1920–24th May 2008) married John H Woodcock in 1945 at Keighley. They were living at 13 Yate Lane, Keighley in 1948 and at 1 Keighley Road, Keighley in 1957. John and Mary had two children – Christine M Woodcock 1946 and Linda J Woodcock 1951. Mary married Ernest Goss in 1965 at Bradford, Yorkshire. Mary died at Halifax, Yorkshire.
- Sarah Calvert (29th September 1922–28th June 1985) was a munitions worker during the Second World War. She married Herbert Sunderland (31st October 1918–3rd March 1995), born at Oxenhope, on 22nd January 1944 at Keighley. He worked on a poultry farm and served in the Royal Dragoon Guards during the Second World War (327554). Herbert and Sarah had four children – Graham W Sunderland 1946, Jean Sunderland 1948, Carole M Sunderland 1952 and Kathleen E Sunderland 1959. Herbert had married Doris Brown (6th June 1918–1991) in 1937 and they had a son, Eric Sunderland, in 1938. The marriage ended in divorce. Doris married Bernard Joseph Hornby (1909–50), born at Clayton-le-Moors, Lancashire, in June 1943 at Keighley. His father, Joseph Hornby (1886–22nd December 1917), went to France on 22nd June 1915 and was serving as a lance sergeant in 2/5th King's Own (Royal Lancaster Regiment) (17289) when he died of wounds (Bleuet Farm Cemetery, Belgium – II B 46). Bernard and Doris had three children, including Stephen Hornby (1945–2002). Bernard reportedly died in Penang, Malaysia. Bernard had married Kathleen Louisa Flynn (born 1906), born in Pembrokeshire, in 1933 at Blackburn, Lancashire. Bernard and Kathleen had a son, Anthony J Hornby, in 1939. The marriage ended in divorce. Kathleen married Thomas Pomfret in 1943 at Coventry, Warwickshire and Dennis Cohen in 1950 at Coventry. Doris married for a third time to John E Rickards in 1955 at Blackpool, Lancashire. She died at Chepstow, Monmouthshire.
- Annie Calvert (7th March 1925–12th January 2007) was a worsted spinner in 1939, living with her sister Carrie Holmes and family. She married Harold J Norton in 1944 at Keighley. They had a daughter, Norma Norton, in 1944. The marriage ended in divorce. Annie married Arthur Wheatcroft (27th November 1924–8th January 2010), born at Barnsley, in 1950, registered at Worth Valley, Yorkshire. They were living at 12 Denby Mount, Keighley in 1957 and at 6 Lindwell Grove, Greetland, Halifax in 1976. They had two children – Michael A Wheatcroft 1952 and Joanna E Wheatcroft 1961. Annie died at Calderdale, West Yorkshire. Harold married June T Stockdale (born c.1928) in 1953 and they had two children – Francis Norton 1954 and Mary T Norton 1955.

- John Henry Calvert (28th May 1927–7th August 2010) married Hilda Gallagher (1923–18th December 2010), born at Easington, Co Durham, in 1945 at Keighley. They had a son, Anthony 'Tony' Calvert, in 1946. John was living at Manorlands Hospice, Keighley at the time of his death there. Hilda was living at 11 Leesworth Court, Haworth Road, Cross Roads, Keighley at the time of her death there.
- Walter Calvert (8th July 1929–16th March 1992) married Mary O'Neill (30th April 1930–27th March 2011), born at Blackburn, Lancashire, in 1953 at Worth Valley. Mary was living with her mother at 29 St Thomas Street, Blackburn in 1939. They had six children – Jacqueline Calvert 1954, Susan M Calvert 1958, Laurence Calvert 1959, Lilian B Calvert 1961, Ian C Calvert 1962 and Judith A Calvert 1965.
- Lilian Calvert (1932–33).
- Beatrice Calvert (born 1934) married Ronald Hawksworth (23rd April 1925–2000), born at Barnsley, in 1950 at Worth Valley. They had two children – David Hawksworth 1955 and Karen Hawksworth 1957.

Lily Calvert married William Tubman (22nd July 1895–1947), born at Easington, Co Durham, in late 1946 at Keighley. William had married Jane Lilly Gallagher (late Robson, née Fishwick) (6th January 1886–31st December 1939), born at Ryhope Colliery, Sunderland, Co Durham, in 1928 at Easington. They had a son, William Tubman (1929–91), who married Renee Pearson (1931–98) in 1951 and they had six children – Glenn Tubman 1952, Susan A Tubman 1954, Keith W Tubman 1957, Gary F Tubman 1959, Patricia D Tubman 1961 and Katherine Tubman 1962. William senior and Jane were both incapacitated in 1939, living at 6 Hillhouse Lane, Keighley. Jane Fishwick had married Robert Jobson Robson (21st December 1883–29th February 1916), a coalminer, on 3rd June 1905 at Easington Register Office. He enlisted in the Durham Light Infantry (16787) at West Hartlepool on 3rd August 1914. He was described as 5′ 5″ tall, weighing 124 lbs, with fresh complexion, blue eyes, light brown hair and his religious denomination was Church of England. He was attested at the Depot on 31st August and was posted to 16th Battalion on 26th October. To France on 8th October 1915 to join B Company, 14th Battalion. Robert was killed in action in Belgium (Ypres (Menin Gate) Memorial, Belgium). Jane was awarded a pension of £1/2/6 per week from 11th September 1916. Robert and Jane had four children – John William Robson 1906, Margaret Isabella Robson 1910, Ann Robson 1912 and Mary Elizabeth Robson 1915. Jane Robson married Patrick Gallagher (1872–1925), born at Derryronane, Swinford, Co Mayo, Ireland, at Easington in 1917. They were living at 23 Rodridge Street, Station Town, Wingate in August 1918. Jane and Patrick had four children – Patrick Gallagher 1918, Norah Jane Gallagher 1921, Hilda Gallagher 1923 (she married John Henry Calvert in 1945 – see above) and Veronica Gallagher 1926.

Lily Tubman married William Woodward (14th March 1888–1969), born at Haydock, Lancashire, in 1954 at Worth Valley. William had married Ellen Foster (1890–1954) on 16th April 1910 at Billinge, Lancashire. He was a textile operator (wool finisher) in 1939, when they were living at 99 Main Street, Keighley. William and Ellen had twelve children – Frances A Woodward 1911, James Woodward 1912, John Woodward 1914, Eva Woodward 1915, Elizabeth A Woodward 1917, Della Woodward 1919, Ellen M Woodward 1921, Mary E Woodward 1923, Joyce SJ Woodward 1926, Audrey Woodward 1927, Winifred D Woodward 1928 and William Woodward 1929.

Lily Woodward married Albert Jebson (8th April 1898–1978), born at Rotherham, Yorkshire, in 1973 at Worth Valley. Albert was a miner at Newton Colliery, near Rotherham, living at 25 Fenton Street, Bradgate, Rotherham when he enlisted in 3rd York & Lancaster on 9th August 1918 at Barnsley. He was deemed to have enlisted on 2nd March 1916 (63461) and transferred to the Class Z Reserve on 11th January 1919. Albert had married Henrietta Morris (23rd September 1900–1973), born at Gainsborough, Lincolnshire, in 1922 at Rotherham. Albert was a general labourer and Henrietta was a drawer in a worsted mill in 1939, when they were living at 6B Cavendish Street, Keighley. He was also an Air Raid Precautions Warden and First Aid Responder at the time. Henrietta and Albert had five children – John C Jebson 1921, Laura Jebson 1923, Wilfred Jebson 1927, Herbert Ivor Jebson 1931 and Sandra L Jebson 1940.

Laurence's paternal grandfather, John William Calvert (29th October 1826–20th September 1881), born at Hunslet, married Eliza née Wood (29th March 1829–24th February 1892), born at Middleton, Yorkshire, at St George, Leeds on 17th March 1850. He was a master tinner in 1861, employing one man and one boy, and they were living at 17 Hunslet Moor End. They had moved to Chetwynd Terrace, Little Holbeck by 1866 and to 11 Milnes Street, Hunslet by 1871. In 1881 they were living with his son, Arthur. William died at Dewsbury Road, Hunslet. Eliza was living with her son, Oliver, and daughter, Mary, at 5 Mona Terrace, Hunslet in 1891, where she subsequently died. In addition to George they had six other children:

- Arthur Wood Calvert (1852–1931) was a tin/copper plate worker. He married Eliza Coultate (1852–), a domestic servant, in 1873 in Leeds. They were living at 3 South Terrace in 1881, at 88 Hunslet Lane in 1891 and at 78 Meadow Lane in 1901, all in Leeds. They had six children:
    - Henrietta Calvert (born 1874) was a dressmaker's assistant in 1891.
    - Wilfred Calvert (11th June 1876–1971) was an errand boy in 1891.
    - Lawson Coultate Calvert (1878–83).
    - Nellie Calvert (born 1883).
    - Arthur Coultate Calvert (22nd July 1885–1970) married Lily Stead in Hunslet in 1906. They had at least three children – George Calvert 1912, Daisy Calvert 1913 and Amy Calvert 1920.

- ○ Eveline Ann Calvert (27th December 1889–1983) married John W Mortimer in Leeds in 1914. They had a son, Eric Mortimer, in 1916.
- Walter Wood Calvert (born and died 1854).
- Herbert Wood Calvert (1855–56).
- William Calvert (born 22nd January 1860) was a copper plate worker living with his brother Arthur in 1881. He married Isabella Collinson (17th August 1863–30th September 1938) on 21st January 1887 at St Cuthbert, Hunslet Moor. They were living at Houghton Street, Hunslet in 1893 and at 49 Lodge Lane, Leeds in 1911. They had two children – Clarence Calvert (born and died 1891) and Frank Calvert (13th November 1892–25th March 1950).
- Oliver Wood Calvert (1868–17th May 1917) was a tin plate worker. He married Martha Drurey (11th June 1868–23rd March 1945) in 1897 at Hunslet. They were living at 3 Gaskell Street, Hunslet in 1901 and 1911. Martha was living with her daughter, Lily, a cashier bookkeeper, at Prospect Cottages, Pontefract Lane, Leeds in 1939. She was living at 21 Devon Street, Pontefract Lane at the time of her death there. They had two children – Doris Calvert (born 1897) and William Calvert (11th May 1900–1971), who served in the Army (195833) from 12th June 1918.
- Mary Berletta/Beretta Calvert (c.1870–November 1895) was a packer of drugs in 1891. She married Herbert 'Harry' Henry Burgon (1869–24th January 1937), a butcher, on 29th October 1894 at Christ Church, Leeds. Mary died following complications with the birth of their son, Herbert Henry Burgon (born and died 1895). Herbert married Edith Jane Ann Buckley (1877–19th January 1960) on 10th September 1900 at St Aidan, Leeds. They were living at 28 Strathmore View, Leeds in 1906 and at 43 Harehills Lane, Leeds in 1911. They were living at Cornergarth, Fitzroy Drive, Roundhay, Leeds at the time of his death there. Edith was living at 20 Oakwell Crescent, Leeds with her daughter, Edith and future son-in-law Harry Rippin, in 1939. She was living at Fairway, Lightridge Road, Fixby, Huddersfield at the time of her death at Park View Nursing Home, Bradford. Herbert and Edith had four children – Elizabeth 'Elsie' Hannah Beatrice Victoria Kennedy Burgon (1901–87), James Herbert Burgon (born 1902), Edith Kennedy Burgon (1906–91) and Leslie Burgon (1910–11).

His maternal grandfather, Robert Stevenson (1840–16th May 1879), born at Mexborough, Yorkshire, married Mary née Smith (c.1841–1914), born at Wakefield, Yorkshire, on 25th December 1863 at St Mary the Virgin, Hunslet. He was the publican at Sir Robert Peel Inn, 77 Dewsbury Road, Hunslet in 1871, and subsequently died there. Mary became the publican at the Inn following her husband's death. She was living with her family at 1 Fox Terrace, Hunslet in 1881. In addition to Beatrice, Mary and Robert had six other children all born at Hunslet:

- Walter Stevenson (born 30th March 1865) was a hop merchant's clerk living with his mother in 1881.
- Ann Stevenson (15th October 1866–1944) married Donald More Mackenzie (17th March 1866–27th May 1895), born at Wick, Caithness, Scotland, at Chorlton, Lancashire on 13th March 1890. They had two children – Agnes 'Aggie' MacKenzie (22nd September 1890–1974) and Mary MacKenzie (born 13th September 1892). Donald was a beerhouse keeper in 1891, when they were living at 46 Grey Street, Gorton, Manchester, Lancashire. He died at Chorlton. Ann was a tailor's machinist living with her sister, Beatrice, and her mother in 1901. In 1939 she was living with her daughter, Agnes, a costumier, at 2 Normanton Terrace, Leeds.

Sir Robert Peel Inn on Dewsbury Road, Hunslet, where Laurence's grandfather was the landlord in the 1870s. It closed in the late 1960s/early 1970s and has since been demolished (Leodis).

- William Stevenson (1st March 1868–later in 1868).
- William Stevenson (8th December 1870–1937) was a fitter when he married Margaret Anne Pickering (23rd January 1873–1946), born at Middlesbrough, Yorkshire, on 11th April 1898 at Hunslet Parish Church. By 1911 William was a printing machine fitter and they were living at 22 Methley Street, Meadow Road, Leeds. Margaret was still living there in 1939 with her son Walter. They had two children:
    - Mary Stevenson (born 1899).
    - Walter Stevenson (12th October 1902–1974), a joiner, married Margaret Ann Willans (11th February 1909–1970), a raincoat machinist in 1931.
- Agnes Baugh Stevenson (23rd May 1873–1930) married William Henry Clarkson (21st August 1873–13th August 1947), a salesman born at Holbeck, in 1896 at Hunslet. He was a representative for Singer Sewing Machines in 1911, when they were living at 30 Recreation Crescent, Holbeck. William subsequently died there. They had nine children including:

Laurence's maternal grandparents married at St Mary the Virgin in December 1863, although the building was not completed until the following year. The church was demolished in the early 1970s except for the spire, which was retained on the new church consecrated on 9th July 1975.

- Nora Clarkson (born 17th March 1897), a shirt cutter, married John Dean in 1916.
- Thomas Clarkson (1898–12th July 1916) served in 15th West Yorkshire (15/1898) and arrived in Egypt on 22nd December 1915. He was wounded on 1st July 1916 at Serre, France and subsequently died (Leeds (Holbeck) Cemetery – C 9200).
- Hilda Clarkson (2nd March 1900–1980) married Harold E Richardson at Hunslet in 1928. They had three children – Shirley Richardson 1932, Donald M Richardson 1935 and Doreen M Richardson 1944.
- Archer Clarkson (17th December 1901–1958) married Maud Bramley in Leeds in 1936. They had a son, Thomas H Clarkson, in 1936.
- Leslie Stevenson Clarkson (born 1907) married Maud D Liotard (born 1912) in Leeds in 1934. They had four children – David L Clarkson 1939, Paul R Clarkson 1941, Celeste M Clarkson 1944 and Nicholas A Clarkson 1948.
- Elsie Clarkson (born 21st December 1912) was a blouse and dress machinist in 1939.

• Robert Stevenson (11th December 1875–1962), a machine ruler, married Laura Taylor (1876–1919), born at Cleckheaton, Yorkshire, on 8th December 1897 at Hunslet Parish Church. He was an insurance agent in 1911, when they were living at 58 Woodview Road, Leeds. They had two children:
- Marjorie Bolingbroke Stevenson (10th January 1901–1999).
- Robert Bolingbroke Stevenson (1902–06).

Mary Stevenson married James Lowes (born c.1848) on 29th November 1881 at St Peter's, Hunslet Moor, Leeds. His fate is not known. She married Joseph Greaves (c.1839–1910), born at Holbeck, on 20th July 1887 at Hunslet. Joseph had married Susannah Stephenson (1836–86) on 9th November 1856 at St Peter's, Leeds and they had eleven children – George Greaves (1856–62), Matthew Greaves (1857), Sarah Ann Greaves (1861–62), Joshua Greaves (1863), Lavinia Greaves (1865), Eliza Ann Greaves (1866), Elizabeth Greaves (1868), Joseph Greaves (1870), George Edward Greaves (1875), Arthur Greaves (1877) and Walter Greaves (1880). Mary was the publican of the Rose and Crown and Blooming Rose public houses in Hunslet. They were living at 18 and 19 Burton Row, Hunslet in 1891 and at St Lawrence's Cottages, Ardwick-le-Street, Yorkshire in 1901. Mary was living with her daughter, Ann Mackenzie, and granddaughters Agnes and Mary Mackenzie at 25 Algeria Street, Leeds in 1911.

Laurence was educated at Rowland Road Board School, Dewsbury Road, Leeds and Cockburn Higher Grade School, Leeds. He worked as a van boy for the Midland Railway Co in Leeds and was later a pony driver (below ground) with Denaby & Cadeby Main Collieries Ltd, Mexborough. At that time he was boarding at 64 Clifton Street, Denaby Main, near Rotherham, Yorkshire with the family of

Cockburn Higher Grade School in Burton Road, named after Sir George Cockburn, Chairman of Leeds School Board, opened on 17th July 1902.

Michael and Rose Walsh. He subsequently worked at Maltby Colliery but returned to Cadeby Main shortly after the disastrous explosions there on 9th July 1912, in which ninety-one miners were killed.

Laurence enlisted in 5th Battalion, The King's Own (Yorkshire Light Infantry) on 17th April 1914 at Denaby (2141 later 80225 & 240194). The Battalion, part of the Territorial Force, proceeded on annual camp to Whitby, Yorkshire in late July and was recalled to Doncaster on 3rd or 4th August. The Battalion moved to Gainsborough and to York in February 1915. Laurence went to France with 1/5th King's Own Yorkshire Light Infantry, 148th Brigade, 49th Division, landing at Boulogne on 13th April 1915. He was wounded by a gunshot to the arm at Ypres in September and was evacuated to England for treatment at Brighton, Sussex. He returned to France in early 1916. The Battalion transferred to 187th Brigade, 62nd Division on 2nd February 1918 and was renamed 5th Battalion.

**Awarded the MM for his actions at Vaulx-Vaulxcourt on 2nd September 1918, LG 11th February 1919. Awarded the VC for his actions at Havrincourt, France on 12th September 1918, LG 15th November 1918.** When it was announced that he had been awarded the VC, his CO ordered a parade. Laurence was on the saluting dais as the whole unit, from the CO down, marched past him at the salute. After the war Laurence served in the Army of Occupation in Germany. He returned to England in 1919 and was admitted to hospital in Bristol, Gloucestershire. The VC was presented by the King at Buckingham Palace on 29th March 1919. Laurence was granted leave and travelled to Conisbrough, where he was presented with a gold watch by his colleagues at Denaby & Cadeby Main Collieries Ltd. He was also presented with a gold watch, £520, some War Bonds

Cadeby Main was sunk in order to work reserves of the Barnsley seam at a depth of 687m. The shafts were completed in February 1893 and production started later in the year. Up to 5,000 men worked there and at the related Denaby mine. The colliery closed in November 1986 and the surface plant was cleared the following year.

In the early hours of 9th July 1912 a series of explosions claimed thirty-five lives. Fortunately the King and Queen had been visiting the area and many men had taken a day off. As a result only 117 men reported for work on the night shift on 8th July, when there would normally have been about 450. Six hours later another explosion killed fifty-three colliery managers and members of the rescue team who were searching for survivors. Three more men died of their injuries later, bring the death toll to ninety-one. Amongst them was WH Pickering, Chief Government Inspector of Mines for Yorkshire and the North Midlands, and Charles Bury the colliery manager. The King and Queen went to the mine the following day to give support to the families. Edward Medals 1st Class (later replaced by the George Cross) were awarded to G Fisher and H Hulley, colliery deputies at Cadeby Colliery, and Edward Medals 2nd Class to JE Chambers Manager of Cortonwood Colliery, WH Prince a colliery contractor, Herbert Williamson the Mechanical Engineer at Denaby and Cadeby Collieries and Sergeant W Winch an instructor at the Wath Rescue Station. An investigation concluded that the cause of the explosion was a fire started some years before that had never been properly extinguished. Memorials to the dead were dedicated at cemeteries in Conisbrough and Denaby on 9th July 2012, exactly a century after the disaster.

The sinking of Denaby Main began in 1856 but appears to have been given up in 1860. It resumed in 1864. To counter the inflow of water, the shafts had to be lined with tubing and brick until the Barnsley seam was met at 409m. Coke ovens were built at the pithead and the colliery was linked to the railways. In 1956 the National Coal Board created an underground link to Cadeby Main and thereafter all coal from both mines came to the surface at Cadeby. In March 1968 the two collieries merged.

The Military Medal was awarded to other ranks of the British Army (later extended to other services) and Commonwealth countries for bravery on land. It was established on 25th March 1916 as the other ranks equivalent of the Military Cross, which was awarded to officers and warrant officers. The MM was the third level gallantry award, ranking below the DCM. Over 115,000 MMs were awarded during the Great War, as well as 5,700 bars and 180 second bars. Private Ernest Corey, a stretcher-bearer with 55th Battalion AIF, was awarded three bars. Over 15,000 MMs were awarded during the Second World War. It was discontinued in 1993, since when the MC has been awarded to all ranks within the British honours system.

The Belgian Order of Leopold II was established on 24th August 1900 by King Leopold II as King of the Congo Free State. In 1908, when Congo was handed over to Belgium, the Order was incorporated into the Belgian awards system. It is awarded for meritorious service and has become a long service order for the civil service. The order currently stands third after the Order of Leopold and the Order of the Crown in the Belgian honours hierarchy. The Order is issued in five classes and three medals. Chevalier or Knight is the lowest of the five classes.

and an illuminated address at the Large Hall, Conisbrough in April 1919. On 16th April he was presented with a chiming clock at Rowland Road School, Leeds by the Lord Mayor, Joseph Henry. **Awarded the Belgian Chevalier of the Order of Leopold II, LG 5th April 1919.**

Laurence was one of the VC Honour Guard at the burial of the Unknown Warrior at Westminster Abbey on 11th November 1920. He served in Ireland with the 2nd Battalion for a year and took part in operations against the Irish Republican Army. He returned to England on leave before departing for India with the 2nd Battalion in 1922. Laurence married Hélenè Marie Rose Crapoulet (26th September 1898–June 1974) on 6th March 1926 at Holy Trinity Church, Karachi, India (now Pakistan). She was the daughter of Marcel Crapoulet and was born at Puchevillers, France, where she met Laurence during the war. Her date of birth has also been recorded as 26th September 1899. They had five children:

- Helene Norah Victoria Calvert (August 1927–7th January 1928) born at Cherat, India (now Pakistan) and died at Peshawar, India (now Pakistan).
- Helene Marie Calvert (25th October 1929–30th August 1996), was baptised at St John's Church, Peshawar. She emigrated to New York, USA and married Jacques Bahbout (born 25th November 1930), born at Tanta, Egypt, in 1953 at Cambridge, Massachusetts. He worked for the United Nations. Helene travelled from New York to England aboard SS *Ile de France* to visit her parents, arriving at

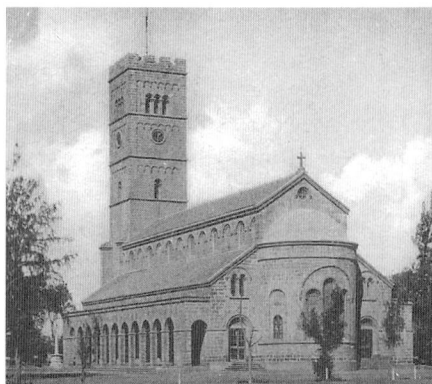

St John's Church, Peshawar, where Laurence's daughter, Helena, was baptised. It was constructed between 1851 and 1860 and is now the Cathedral Church of St John, part of the Anglican Diocese of Peshawar.

Laurence married Hélenè Crapoulet at Holy Trinity Church, Karachi in March 1926. It is now Holy Trinity Cathedral and the seat of the Church in Pakistan. It was built in 1855. As there were no lighthouses, the top of the tower had beacons to assist ships in Karachi Harbour. However, in 1904 it was discovered that the foundation was weak and the top two stories of the tower were removed to reduce its weight. During the Great War the tower was a signalling station. In 1970 the original pitched roof was replaced with a barrel vaulted roof.

Southampton, Hampshire on 26th March 1955. Jacques followed aboard SS *Ile de France*, arriving at Plymouth, Devon on 18th May 1955. They had two children, including Paul J Bahbout (born 1955 at Romford, Essex). The marriage ended in divorce. Helene married John 'Jack' M Crombie (15th November 1931–1983) in 1975 at Brentwood, Essex. Jacques married Alda Mohr in 1971 at Tonbridge, Kent.
* Laurence Calvert (21st July 1931–21st July 2013), born at Kanpur, Uttar Pradesh, India, worked for Ford Motor Co, Dagenham, Essex and lived at 79 St Andrew's Avenue, Hornchurch, Essex. He married June L Wilby née Smith (born 1935) in 1960 at Fulham, London, where she was born. June had married Dennis E Wilby (1924–2013), born at Burton-upon-Trent, Staffordshire, in 1954 at Fulham. The marriage ended in divorce and he emigrated to Canada. Laurence and June were living at 25 Windermere Avenue, Hornchurch by 1964. They had two children born at Romford, Essex:
    ○ Laurence Calvert (born 1961).
    ○ Pamela Calvert (born 1964) married David M Young in April 1990. They had three children.
* Peter Calvert (1st–10th April 1932) died of a cerebral haemorrhage in India.
* George Calvert (23rd October 1937–1st August 1999), born at Dagenham, Essex, worked for Ford Motor Co there. He married Margaret G Ferguson (born c.1934) in 1969 at Brentwood, Essex. He died at Rayleigh, Essex. They had two children:
    ○ Michael James Calvert (born 1973), born at Rochford, Essex.
    ○ David Colin Calvert (born 1975), born at Havering, Essex.

The family returned to England in 1928 for eight months leave, before rejoining the unit in India. Laurence served on the North West Frontier in 1930. He was discharged in England on 9th November 1932. They were living with Ann Wilding (born 1872) at 140 Castle Street, Woodbridge, Suffolk in 1939. They settled at 73 Oglethorpe Road, Dagenham, Essex. He worked as a messenger for National Provincial Bank (now National Westminster). He then became a commissionaire with a Bradford wholesale merchant before returning to the London area and worked at the head office of National Provincial Bank. He later transferred to the Dagenham branch, retiring about 1957.

During the Second World War, Laurence was a sergeant in B Company, 11th City of London (Essex) Battalion, Home Guard. The unit name was later changed to 11th City of London (Dagenham) Battalion based in Dagenham and Becontree. Laurence resigned through ill health and became a warden in the local Civil Defence.

Laurence attended a number of VC Reunions – the VC Garden Party at Buckingham Palace on 26th June 1920, the Victory Day Celebration Dinner & Reception at The Dorchester, London on 8th June 1946, the VC Centenary Celebrations at Hyde Park, London on 26th June 1956 and the 1st, 2nd and 3rd VC Association Reunions at the Café Royal, London on 24th July 1958, 7th July 1960 and 18th July 1962. The latter was the first of the combined VC and GC reunions. He was invited to attend King George VI's Coronation in 1937 but was unable to attend as he had pleurisy. He attended the funeral of AP Sullivan VC in the Guards' Chapel, Wellington Barracks, Birdcage Walk, London on 13th April 1937. In 1953 he and his wife attended the Coronation of Queen Elizabeth II. Laurence attended the bi-centennial celebrations of the King's Own Yorkshire Light Infantry in August 1955 and was presented to the Queen and Queen Mother, who were successive Colonels-in-Chief of the Regiment.

Laurence died at his home at 73 Oglethorpe Road, Dagenham, Essex on 7th July 1964 after a series of protracted illnesses. He was cremated at South Essex Crematorium, Corbets Tey, Upminster, Essex and his ashes were scattered in Rosebed 32, Garden of Remembrance, St Albans' Walk. A commemorative plaque in the Garden of Remembrance is no longer there but his name is in the Book of Remembrance. He is commemorated in a number of other places:

The Leeds Victoria Cross Memorial (Memorial to Valour).

- Leeds
    - Laurence Calvert Academy.
    - The Leeds Victoria Cross Memorial, outside Leeds City Art Gallery, Victoria Gardens, The Headrow, commemorates seventeen Leeds VC winners – AL Aaron, A Atkinson, WB Butler, L Calvert, H Daniels, W Edwards, DP Hirsch, C Hull, E McKenna, F McNess, A Mountain, J Pearson, A Poulter, JC Raynes, G Sanders, C Ward and J White.

The memorial in Coronation Park with Conisborough Castle in the background.

The Great War memorial in All Saints Church, Denaby Main, includes Laurence Calvert (Conisborough & Denaby Main Local History).

- ○ A Department for Communities and Local Government commemorative paving stone was dedicated at Cockburn School, Gipsy Lane, Beeston, Leeds, West Yorkshire on 12th November 2018.
- Conisbrough
  - ○ Memorial stone dedicated in Coronation Park on 9th September 2018.
  - ○ Calvert Way.
- Memorial Plaque, All Saints Church, Denaby Main, South Yorkshire.
- Calvert Mews, Barking and Dagenham, London, opened in 2010.

In addition to the VC and MM he was awarded the 1914–15 Star, British War Medal 1914–20, Victory Medal 1914–19 with MID Oakleaf, India General Service Medal 1909–1935 with clasp 'North West Frontier 1930–31', George VI Coronation Medal 1937, Elizabeth II Coronation Medal 1953 and the Belgian Order of Leopold. The VC was purchased by Lord Ashcroft at a private sale in 2004 and is held by the Michael Ashcroft Trust, the holding institution for the Lord Ashcroft Victoria Cross Collection, and is displayed in the Imperial War Museum's Lord Ashcroft Gallery.

The India General Service Medal 1909-1935 with the 'North West Frontier 1930–31' clasp. The Medal was approved on 1st January 1909, for issue to the British and Indian Armies for various minor military campaigns in India. It was extended in 1919 to include the RAF, and the 'Waziristan 1925' clasp was awarded only to RAF personnel. There were twelve clasps, including three for the North West Frontier – 1908, 1930–31 and 1935. Another three were for Waziristan – 1919–21, 1921–24 and 1925.

## LIEUTENANT DONALD JOHN DEAN
### 8th Battalion, The Queen's Own (Royal West Kent Regiment)

Donald Dean was born on 19th April 1897 at Herne Hill, Lambeth, London. His father, John Hambrook Dean (1865–7th June 1940), born at Sittingbourne, Kent, was living with his father at Whitehall, Sittingbourne at the time of the 1891 Census. He married Grace née Walduck (1868–25th November 1943), born at Harrow, Middlesex, in February 1891 at St Giles, London. John was a traveller in bricks in 1901, living at 7 Woodquest Avenue, Herne Hill, Lambeth, London. Grace was visiting her parents with her daughter, Elsie, at 20 Crook Log, Bexley, Dartford, Kent at the time of the 1901 Census. They were living at Waldene, Tunstall, Sittingbourne by 1911. Both John and Grace subsequently died there. Donald had four siblings:

- Elsie Muriel Dean (28th August 1893–7th October 1973), born at Wandsworth, London, married Charles William Turner (born c.1895), born in London, in 1918 at St Giles, London. She was living at Westerly, Gilham Lane, Forest Row, Sussex at the time of her death.
- Graham Smeed Dean (8th September 1895–6th March 1970), born at Herne Hill, Lambeth, enlisted in 2/4th East Kent Regiment (2802, 4491 & 241865), on the third attempt due to poor eyesight, on 11th November 1914 and was described as 5′ 8″ tall. He was posted to 3/4th Battalion on 25th April 1915. He

Evidence of settlement in Sittingbourne goes back to 2,000 BC. Following their invasion in AD 43, the Romans built Watling Street between Dover and London, which passed through Sittingbourne. They also established a port at Milton Regis and a number of villas have been discovered in the area. Sittingbourne was not mentioned in the Domesday Book in 1086 but Milton Regis was. After the murder of Thomas Becket, Archbishop of Canterbury, in 1170, Sittingbourne became a popular stop for pilgrims travelling to Canterbury and is mentioned in The Canterbury Tales. King Henry V stayed there on his way back from winning the Battle of Agincourt and Henry VIII in 1522 and 1532. In 1825 the future Queen Victoria stayed at the Rose Inn. With the coming of the railway in 1858, the town became a centre for brick and paper production for the rapidly expanding city of London and many Thames barges were built there to transport produce to the capital. The town suffered a number of air raids during the Great War.

transferred to a company of 2/4th East Kent, which, with companies from 2/4th Royal West Kent, 2/5th East Kent and 2/5th Royal West Kent, formed a Kent Composite Battalion under HQ 2/4th Royal West Kent. He embarked aboard HMT *Northland* at Devonport on 17th July for the Mediterranean Expeditionary Force and landed at Suvla Bay, Gallipoli on 10th August. On 25th August he was admitted to hospital and was transferred to the Military Hospital, Citadel, Cairo, Egypt on 1st September suffering from nervous shock. He was discharged to the Convalescence Depot, Abbassia on 18th September and rejoined his unit in Gallipoli on 7th October. On 25th November he was admitted to 2nd Welsh Field Ambulance with nervous debility and was transferred to Kasr-el-Aini Hospital, Cairo with neurosis on 2nd December. On 15th January 1916 he boarded HMHS *Salta* at Alexandria, arriving in England on 26th January. He was then transferred to 3/4th East Kent on 28th February, 3/5th East Kent on 17th May and 1/5th East Kent on 19th June, before embarking on a troopship bound for India. While aboard, on 1st July, he was sentenced to stand on deck for five days for refusing to obey an order the previous day. He received the same punishment for refusing to obey an order given by an NCO on 17th July. Graham joined Chak Lala Camp, Rawalpindi, India on 22nd July. He was admonished and put under stoppages of pay for losing a greatcoat by neglect on 21st October. On 20th January 1917 he transferred to Indian Expeditionary Force D and embarked at Karachi for Basrah, Mesopotamia on 23rd January, arriving on 28th January. He was wounded by gunshots to the left thigh, buttock and right hand on 15th February and was admitted to 135th Combined Field Ambulance. He was transferred to 133rd British General Hospital, Makina, Basrah and was discharged to 1st British Base Depot, Tamuna on 29th March. On 9th May he was admitted to 20th Combined Field Ambulance with inflamed parotid glands and was discharged from 133rd British General Hospital on 9th June. On 24th June he was admitted to 133rd British General Hospital with sandfly fever and was discharged on 2nd July. He rejoined his unit on 5th August but was admitted to 21st Combined Field Ambulance with heat effects on 21st August. He received five days extra fatigues for talking on parade on 5th September and was discharged from 20th Combined Field Ambulance on 7th September to rejoin his unit. He was admitted to 22nd Combined Field Ambulance with tonsillitis on 16th November and was discharged to his unit on 23rd November. On 3rd January 1918 he was awarded two extra guards for a minor offence while on sentry duty and on 7th February was awarded two days Field Punishment for being unshaven on guard mount. He was granted twenty-eight days leave in India, departing Basrah aboard AT *Varsova* on 10th June and returning aboard HT *Vasnu* from Bombay on 29th July. He disembarked at Basrah on 4th August and rejoining the unit on 26th August. He was admitted to 22nd Combined Field Ambulance with diarrhoea 4th-12th September. On 24th September he was attached as a cook to the Divisional Platoon School and rejoined his unit on 20th December. On 7th January 1919 he was attached to

the Expeditionary Force Canteen, Sharoban and rejoined the Battalion on 19th February. Graham embarked aboard SS *Egra* at Basrah on 12th March for return to Britain. He was demobilised on 6th May 1919. Graham married Henrietta Kate Walters (14th January 1897–19th January 1951), born at Strand, London, in 1927 at Woolwich, Kent. They lived at Wayside, 189 Shooters Hill, Woolwich, where they both subsequently died. They had two daughters:
  - Wendy Grace Walduck Dean (8th September 1928–18th November 1989), born at Wandsworth, London, married Leslie J White (16 March 1925–June 2004), in 1950 at Woolwich. Wendy died at Bexley, Kent.
  - Faith W Dean (born 1932), born at Woolwich, married James Ellis there in 1952. They had two sons – Stephen G Ellis 1955 and Mark A Ellis 1958.
- Harold Vincent Dean (4th October 1899–6th January 1988) worked in munitions when the Great War broke out and later trained as a ship's wireless operator. He subsequently served on cargo vessels and transports (952691) and was awarded the Mercantile Marine and British War Medals. He married Doris Margaret Glanfield Briggs (1st June 1902–July 1985) in 1927 at Dorking, Surrey. They were living at Denby Dene Courts, Hill Road, Haslemere, Surrey in 1939, when he was an Air Raid Precautions Warden. He was still living there at the time of his death. They had two children:
  - Christopher John Dean (28th November 1929–22nd July 1983), born at Milton, Kent, was at Fernden Preparatory School, Fernden Lane, Haslemere in 1939. He was living at 11 Courts Hill Road, Haslemere at the time of his death there.
  - Jennifer M Dean (born 1933), born at Hambledon, Surrey, is understood to have married Robert G Bishop in 1958 in Surrey. They had two children – Lyn J Bishop 1961 and Julie D Bishop 1965.
- Alan Walduck Dean (15th December 1905–13th September 1963), born at Sittingbourne, Kent, married Gertrude A Burger there in 1938. This was the second wedding, the first taking place in Vienna, Austria. It is believed that Gertrude was partly Jewish and the second marriage was to protect her against the Nazi anti-Jewish racial laws. With the political situation worsening, Alan returned to Vienna to collect Gerti's possessions. On 31st May 1939, while attempting to leave Germany at Aachen with socks stuffed with Gerti's jewellery, he was arrested and was returned to Vienna. Hoping that the local authorities would respect his military rank and decorations, Donald Dean flew out there. He had to smooth many diplomatic obstacles and pay a large sum to secure Alan's release. Alan was managing director of a lime works in 1939, living at Blean House, Swale, Kent and he was Chief Group Warden, Air Raid Precautions for Swale District Council. They later lived at Bursted Manor, Upper Hardres, Canterbury, Kent. He died at Brook Hospital, Greenwich, London.

Donald's paternal grandfather, George Hambrook Dean (29th April 1836–4th September 1924), born at Sittingbourne, Kent, went into partnership in the 1850s with his father-in-law, George Smeed, naming the business Smeed, Dean & Co Ltd. It became one of the largest brickmakers in England and had ninety-six sailing barges to transport bricks from Milton Creek, Sittingbourne to London. By the end of the 19th century the firm employed 1,200 people and was producing seventy million handmade bricks each year, including those used in the construction of Tower Bridge, King's Cross Station and Westminster Cathedral. George married Mary Ann née Smeed (c.1836–22nd May 1867), also born at Sittingbourne, on 30th August 1856 at Holy Trinity, Islington, London. By 1861 he was also a farmer of 110 acres, employing six men and a boy and living at Finch's, Sittingbourne. Mary died at Tunstall, Kent. George married Mary Fields (c.1836–80), born at Leverton, Lincolnshire, in 1869 at Newington, Kent. They were living at Whitehall, Sittingbourne by 1871. Mary died at Milton, Kent. George married Jane Mead (1843–29th January 1923), born at Snarestone, Leicestershire, in 1885 at Faringdon, Berkshire. By 1891 George was a JP and by 1911 was also a jam manufacturer. Both he and Jane died at Whitehall, Sittingbourne. George left effects valued at £184,929/2/6 (£11.3M in 2020). In addition to John they had six other children:

An advertisement for Smeed, Dean & Co products from the late 1920s.

Holy Trinity, Cloudesley Square, Islington was designed by Sir Charles Barry and was built in 1826-29. Barry also designed the Houses of Parliament. The church was neglected over the years and became redundant in the 1970s. In the 1980s it was leased to the Celestial Church of Christ, a Nigerian Pentecostal community, until 2018. The church is owned by the London Diocese of the Anglican Church and remains in poor condition. An English Heritage grant allowed for essential maintenance work but the money ran out. More funds will be required for a full restoration.

Adelaide Dock at Milton Creek with Smeed, Dean barges awaiting loading.

- Georgiana Smeed Dean (1858–1943), born at Tunstall, Kent, was a lady's maid for Mary Helen Burton, a Baptist minister's wife, at 80 Farleigh Road, Hackney, London in 1881.
- Mary Anne Smeed Dean (1859–8th December 1948), born at Milstead, Kent, married William Vinson Hudson (1858–6th April 1910), born at Hollingbourne, Kent, in 1882. They lived in Bexley, Kent at various times at The Elms, Cold Blow Farm and Manor Farm. William died at the Granville Hotel, Ramsgate, Kent. Mary was living at The Elms, Bexley at the time of her death, registered at Dartford, Kent. They had four children, all registered at Dartford:
    - Marion Ruth Hudson (22nd November 1883–1970) married Leonard Talman Ford (1880–1961), born at Hampstead, London, at Dartford in 1909.
    - Kathleen Hudson (5th October 1885–19th June 1966) married Gilbert Pearson Rogers (1875–1968), born at Ashton, Lancashire, at Dartford in 1907. Both their deaths were registered at Bromley, Kent.
    - Marjorie Hudson (1890–16th February 1926) never married.
    - Norman Hudson (29th April 1893–15th October 1971) lost a leg in the Great War and never married.
- Jessie Vincent Dean (1861–5th October 1932) married the Reverend John Doubleday (1849–11th January 1934), born at Spalding, Lincolnshire, at Pinchbeck, Lincolnshire, in 1884. He was a Baptist minister and they lived at Ingleside, Sittingbourne. They had nine children:
    - Hilda Jane Doubleday (1886–22nd June 1948) married Duncan Ebenezer McLean Ferguson in 1910.
    - Leslie Doubleday (later Sir Leslie) (4th September 1887–1975) married Nora Foster on 10th September 1912, registered at Tonbridge, and they had four children – Garth Leslie Doubleday (1913–2012) who served in the Royal Artillery in the Middle East in the Second World War, Gordon V Doubleday 1914, Phyllis N Doubleday 1915 and Barbara M Doubleday 1919. Leslie was a farmer and fruit grower. He applied for a commission in 4th East Kent on 20th October 1914 and was commissioned on 9th November. He was seconded for service with 71st Provisional Battalion, which was later absorbed by 69th Provisional Battalion, Lowestoft. Promoted lieutenant on 1st June 1916 and transferred to 2/1st West Kent Yeomanry, West Malling on 27th September. Promoted captain on 27th April 1918. He was wounded by a machine gun bullet in the right lung at Comines, Belgium on 29th September while attached to 10th Royal West Kent. He was evacuated to Britain on 16th October from Boulogne to Dover and was treated at Queen Alexandra Hospital, Millbank and Furness Auxiliary Hospital, Harrogate. A medical board at Millbank, London on 21st November found him unfit for General Service for four months and Home Service for two months. Medical boards at Millbank, London on 13th June and 26th September 1919

found he was twenty percent disabled and unfit for service for six months. Leslie was demobilised and disembodied from the Officers' Dispersal Unit, London on 13th June having served for eight months in Ireland and France as a company commander and three and half years in Britain. He returned to farming, living at Hempstead. Sittingbourne, Kent.
- Lilian Vincent Doubleday (born 1888).
- John Eric Doubleday (19th January 1890–1969) married Ethel L Burgess (1889–1959), born at East Ashford, at Eastry, Kent in 1913. They both died at Dover. They had three children – Kathleen E Doubleday 1914, Norman C Doubleday 1918 and Doubleday 1920.
- Georgiana/Georgina Smeed Doubleday (1st March 1891–18th February 1980) married Edwin Stephen Boulding (15th March 1889–1970) in 1920. They had three children – Eric S Boulding 1921, Keith J Boulding 1923 and Jessie S Boulding 1928.
- Jessie Margaret Doubleday (24th April 1894–22nd August 1977) married Alfred J Pettman in 1916.
- George 'Laddie' Hambrook Dean Doubleday (17th November 1895–11th February 1918) served in the Royal Naval Reserve. He was appointed probationary midshipman on 12th August 1912 and served as a cadet aboard P&O's SS *Beltana* from 29th November 1912 on emigration voyages to Sydney, Australia. He trained aboard HMS *Formidable* 14th February–13th March 1914 and was mobilised to HMS *Pembroke II* at Chatham on 8th August. He was assigned to HMS *Marmara* for training and was appointed acting sub lieutenant on 28th January 1916, with his rank of midshipman being confirmed on 22nd March. George applied to transfer to the RNAS on 19th July but could not be spared. He was promoted sub lieutenant on 28th March 1917, with seniority from 28th January. He was assigned to HMS *Westphalia* on 30th March, which had been requisitioned by the Admiralty on 21st October as a stores carrier at Long Hope, Scapa Flow, Rosyth and Sheerness. SS *Westphalia* was launched on Christmas Eve 1912 by Caledon Shipbuilding & Engineering Co, Dundee for the Leith, Hull & Hamburg Steam Packet Co. She operated between Grangemouth and Dundee and Hamburg, Germany. In March 1917 she was converted into a Q Ship, armed with a 4" Gun and two 14" Torpedoes. She was named variously *Cullist*, *Hayling*, *Jurassic* and *Prim*. The captain was Lieutenant Commander Salisbury H Simpson RN. On 13th July 1917 she was between the French and Irish coasts when a U-boat was sighted at ten kilometres. The U-boat fired thirty-eight rounds without hitting *Cullist*, then closed to 4,500m and fired another thirty rounds. At 2.07 p.m. *Cullist* returned fire and numerous hits were seen on the conning tower, gun and deck. The good shooting was largely due to George, who also assisted on the bridge during the action. There was an explosion aboard the U-boat and, three minutes

after commencing the engagement, she went down by the bows. As a result of this action, the captain was awarded the DSO. In addition the crew received two DSCs, including George (LG 29th August 1917), four DSMs and three MIDs. On 20th August *Cullist* was attacked by a U-boat, which fled after being fired upon. The ship received some damage and two stokers were injured. Another three DSMs were awarded for this action. On 28th September *Cullist* engaged

A 4″ naval gun on a merchant vessel converted to a Q-ship during the Great War. Two of the drop down panels that concealed it can be seen in the foreground and on the right.

a U-boat at 4,500m with thirteen rounds, of which eight were direct hits, causing the submarine to settle by the bow with nine metres of the stern out of the water. After fifteen seconds it disappeared. Soon afterwards another U-boat was spotted and was pursued but without result. On 17th November a U-boat opened fire at 7,300m and a shell glanced off *Cullist*'s side before bursting on the waterline. After disappearing into fog, the U-boat reappeared and continued to shell *Cullist* for fifty minutes. The decks and bridge were sprayed with shell splinters and water from near misses. The U-boat fired ninety-two rounds before *Cullist* returned fire from 4,100m with fourteen rounds, of which six were direct hits. The high gunnery efficiency was due entirely to George's zeal and energy (LG 22nd February 1918). Although badly damaged the U-boat turned away, dived and escaped. George was appointed acting lieutenant on 28th January 1918. On 11th February *Cullist* was torpedoed and sunk by *U-97* (Kapitänleutnant Hans von Mohl) in the Irish Sea with the loss of forty-three of her seventy crew, including George (Portsmouth Naval Memorial).

George 'Laddie' Hambrook Dean Doubleday is remembered on the war memorial in St John the Baptist Church, Tunstall, Kent.

- ○ Stuart Mead Doubleday (3rd January 1897–27th November 1959).
- ○ Marion Bessie Doubleday (26th December 1897–1982) married William E Carey (24th November 1890–1971), born in Croydon, Surrey, in 1927 at Milton, Kent.

- Esther Smeed Dean (1862–63) was a twin with Sarah.
- Sarah Smeed Dean (1862–63) was a twin with Esther.
- George Smeed Dean (1864–12th November 1906) was an engineer's apprentice in 1881. He married Sarah Annie Elizabeth Acworth (1864–7th February 1944) at Chatham, Kent in 1890, where she was born. They lived at Gore Court Lodge, Tunstall, where he subsequently died. By 1911 Sarah was a fruit grower, living with her daughter, Doris, and two of her sisters at Gore Court Lodge. She was living at 28 Park Crescent, Chatham, Kent at the time of her death there. They had two children:
    - Doris Queenie Dean (4th April 1897–19th August 1987) married James SA Worboys/Warboys in 1920.
    - George Smeed Dean (26th October 1900–1969) married Mabel Gladys Taylor (born 1904) in 1922.

His maternal grandfather, Thomas Henry Walduck (31st March 1826–8th March 1909), born in London, was an apprentice to Joseph Masters, a stationer, in January 1840. By 1851 he was a printer. He married Susannah Beck (died 1858), in 1851 in London. He married Elizabeth née Smith (c.1841–1st January 1910) on 11th April 1861 at Harrow Parish Church, Middlesex, by when he was a hotel proprietor. They were living at Walduck's Hotel, 93 & 95 Southampton Row, St George, Bloomsbury, London by 1881. By 1901 they had moved to 20 Crook Log, Bexley, Dartford, Kent. Thomas and Elizabeth both died at Lorne Villa, Bexley Heath, Kent leaving effects valued at £26,878/0/3 (£3.25M in 2020). Elizabeth's death was registered at East Preston, Sussex. In addition to Grace, Thomas had five other children from his two marriages:

- Thomas Henry Walduck (1852–57), born and died at Holborn.
- Clara Walduck (1862–8th July 1914) married Thomas Richard Edwards (27th February 1857–30th May 1926), born at Llanddewi Rhydderch, near Abergavenny, Monmouthshire, in 1887 at St Giles, London. He trained at the Baptist College, Pontypool and was accepted for missionary work with the Baptist Missionary Society on 8th July 1879. He worked at Barisal, Bengal, India (now Bangladesh) and also instructed preachers at Serampore College. He retired in 1907 and by 1911 they were living at White House, Eastwood, Leigh-on-Sea, Essex, where he established a Baptist cause. Clare subsequently died there. Thomas was living at Summerland, Eastwood in 1917 and later that year at Lucerne, Page Heath Lane, Bickley, Kent. He returned to North Bengal in 1919 but had to relinquish his missionary activities in 1921 and returned to Britain. Clara and Thomas had had six children by 1911, three of whom were deceased. It is believed that most of them were born in Bengal, India but at least one was born in England. Those known are:
    - Frank Walduck Edwards (6th November 1888–25th July 1889), born at Serampore.

- ○ Rose Edwards (27th November 1889–10th March 1892).
- ○ May Edwards (born c.1891).
- ○ Spenser Ernest Edwards (15th August 1896–9th March 1917), born at Lorne Villa, Bexleyheath, Kent, was educated at Taunton School, where he was a corporal in the OTC. He left school on 1st July 1915 and enlisted in the Inns of Court OTC at 10 Stone Buildings, Lincoln's Inn, London on 5th July (4624). He was described as 5′ 7½″ tall and weighed 117 lbs. He was discharged on 22nd September at Berkhamsted on appointment to a commission in 3/4th Battalion, The Buffs (East Kent Regiment) on 23rd September. Spenser joined 1/4th Buffs in India on 27th August 1916. He embarked aboard HMHS *Dover Castle* at Bombay, India on 26th October and disembarked at Southampton on 2nd December for six months' medical leave, which was due to end on 26th April 1917. However, he died at Lambeth, London on 9th March 1917 and is buried in Brookwood Cemetery, Surrey (C178924).
- ○ Cyril Walduck Edwards (20th August 1902–16th December 1982).
• Herbert Henry Walduck (3rd August 1863–6th February 1948) gained his Certificate of Competency as Second Mate in the Merchant Service on 26th July 1883. He married Ellen Louisa Smith (c.1866–23rd June 1932) in 1893 at St Giles, London. Herbert was a company director in 1914. They were living at 17a Lambolle Road, Hampstead, London at the time of her death there. He was living at Convent Cottage, Broadway Road, Sidmouth, Devon in 1939 and at Heatherby, Sidmouth, Devon at the time of his death there, leaving effects valued at £34,582/12/9 (£1.4M in 2020). They had two children:
  - ○ Constance Ellen Walduck (13th May 1894–June 1982) married Charles Clive Herd (30th April 1879–1976), born at Derby, Derbyshire, at Hampstead in 1924. They both died on the Isle of Wight. They had a daughter – Gabrielle CP Herd, born in 1925 at Kensington, London.
  - ○ Ronald Henry Walduck (1900–21st July 1927), born in Hendon, Middlesex and died at Smallburgh, Norfolk.
• Jessie Walduck (1865–9th May 1932) was the manageress of Walduck's (Premier) Hotel, 91–95 Southampton Row, Bloomsbury, London in 1901. She never married and was living at Lucerne, Ufton Road, Milton Regis, Kent at the time of her death there.
• Harold Walduck (13th December 1872–27th July 1958) married Sarah Alicia Walduck (sic) (5th January 1874–23rd September 1952), born

The Premier Hotel at 150 Southampton Row, Bloomsbury, close to the British Museum. The building is still there.

at Ballarat, Victoria, Australia, on 27th November 1900 in Bloomsbury, London. Harold was the proprietor of Walduck's Hotel in 1901. The marriage ended in divorce. Sarah was living at Lower Woodside House, Hatfield, Hertfordshire in 1939 with her sons, Harold and Hugh, plus Hugh's wife, Enid. Sarah was living at Ashdown, Bullstrode Park, Gerrards Cross, Buckinghamshire at the time of her death. Harold married Norah 'Noni' Drury White (28th October 1893–29th March 1975), born at Crook and Billy Row, Co Durham, in 1935 at Pancras, London. He was chairman of Imperial London Hotels in 1939, when they were living at Holley Cottage, Wall End, Elstree, Hertfordshire. They were living at St Annes, Fourth Avenue, Frinton-on-Sea, Essex at the time of his death there, leaving effects valued at £104,201/10/4 (£2.5M in 2020). Norah was living at 1 Hanover Terrace, London at the time of her death there. Harold had six children from his first marriage:

- Amy Margaret Walduck (1st April 1904–1970), born at St Giles, London, married Kenneth Dudley Foster (23rd July 1899–1972), born at West Bromwich, Staffordshire, in 1928 at Marylebone, London. They had three children – Alicia J Foster 1929, David K Foster 1931 and Norman J D Foster 1938. His death was registered at Bridgnorth and hers at Wellington, both in Shropshire.
- Harold Norman Walduck (9th February 1906–9th July 1964).
- Evelyn Grace Walduck (16th May 1907–1990).
- Dorothy Irene Walduck (born 25th September 1909) married Berners Plestow A Vallance (born 1904), born at Guildford, Surrey, at Hatfield, Hertfordshire, in 1933.
- Enid Joyce Walduck (19th January 1912–1997) married John Edmund S Sawyer (1905–62), born at Fulham, London, at Hatfield in 1936. He died at Amersham, Buckinghamshire. They had three daughters – Diana J Sawyer 1937, Elizabeth G Sawyer 1939 and Pamela A Sawyer 1945.
- Hugh Stanley Walduck (16th March 1916–11th April 1975) married Enid Rosalind Tudehope (25th September 1917–December 2005) at Westminster, London in 1939. They had three children – Thomas H Walduck 1943, Stephen H Walduck 1947 and Victoria L Walduck 1950. He died at Hatfield.

Donald was educated privately by Mrs Hilda Miriam Boulton at Smith's Farm, Appledore, Ashford, Kent, together with his brothers, Graham and Harold, and his cousin, Margaret Jessie Doubleday. Later he is believed to have attended Quernmore House School, London Lane, Bromley, Kent. He was a keen Scout and a member of 1st Sittingbourne Troop. He worked for the family brick-making firm and at the outbreak of war he joined the Kent Special Constabulary, being too young to join the Army initially. He enlisted in 28th Battalion, London Regiment (Artists' Rifles) on 19th April 1915 (3692), adding a year to his age, and paying the Artists' Rifles joining fee of £1/5/-. At first he lived with his uncle, Harold Walduck, at

Quernmore House School for boys was founded in 1880 in Holwood Road, off Bromley High Street. By the turn of the century it had moved to Plaistow Lodge, a large mansion built in 1770, in the northwest of the town at Kinnaird Park on London Lane. On the outbreak of the Great War the school's infirmary was used as an auxiliary hospital for convalescence under the Kent/52 Voluntary Aid Detachment. After the Second World War the school was taken over by the County Council as Quernmore Secondary School. In 1986 it became the Parish Church of England Primary School, which dates back to 1716. The original 1770 building was Grade II* listed in 1955.

the Premier Hotel, Russell Square while training in the area with the 3rd Battalion. He moved to Richmond Park in early May and later to High Beech, near Epping Forest. On 11th August Donald proceeded to Rouen, France to join 1/28th London at St Omer. The Battalion was under GHQ Troops to provide ceremonial guards as well as posts on all roads leading into the town to check the identity of all entering or leaving. Donald once checked the pass of the Prince of Wales. The Battalion also ran an officers' training unit at Blendecques near St Omer that eventually trained 10,256 junior officers. Donald and a comrade were made acting corporals and put in charge of prisoners from a detention camp for sanitary work in the Hesdin area. He also did one turn of duty in the trenches at Ploegsteert at a time when both sides had made an unspoken agreement not to throw grenades at each other as the trenches were so close.

Donald attended a six weeks' intensive course at the cadet school and was commissioned in 11th Battalion, Queen's Own (Royal West Kent Regiment) on 4th October 1916. He joined the Battalion just after it had been badly mauled at Eaucourt l'Abbaye on the Somme. Of the twenty cadets in his division at cadet school, he was the only one alive eight weeks after they were commissioned. He took command of 16 Platoon in D Company, some of whom were hard-bitten men from Wapping and he had trouble controlling them at first. One day the Battalion was paraded in marching order after two jars of rum had been stolen from the QM. Platoon commanders were to check their men's water bottles. The first man Dean checked had a bottle full of rum. Looks were exchanged but no words. Dean declared to the CO that no rum was found and thereafter there was a bond of understanding with his men. The Battalion moved soon afterwards to Reninghelst, near Ypres. He was appointed Battalion Machine Gun Officer and later Patrol Officer.

On the night of 31st October/1st November, newly arrived Second Lieutenant John Oswald Knight was sent out on a patrol. Knight failed to return and Donald went out with a sergeant to try to find him, without success. Knight had been seriously wounded and died in captivity later (Oosttaverne Wood Cemetery, Belgium – V G 25). Donald led a patrol at St Eloi on 7th March 1917 to ascertain if the German lines were still occupied. They were and he dived into a shell hole for cover but was struck by grenade fragments in the leg, neck and left arm. He was evacuated to England, having been operated on in a hospital at Boulogne, but the splinter in his neck remained, despite efforts to remove it in France and at King Edward VII's Hospital in London. It was not removed until six years later in Chatham. He convalesced at the home of Sir Henry and Lady Samuelson, Hatchford Park, Cobham, Surrey. Having been passed for General Service by a medical board, he joined the 3rd Battalion at Fort Horsted, Chatham.

Donald returned to France towards the end of the Battle of Messines in June 1917, during which 11th Battalion had suffered heavy casualties. He was wounded three more times, including on one occasion being gassed and blinded temporarily. In the attack on Tower Hamlets on 20th September he commanded D Company. He was hit by grenade splinters in the left forearm but continued and was later hit by a burst of machine gun fire in the left forearm again and left thigh. Another bullet entered his trouser pocket, passed through a purse, buckling several coins, and stopped against his flask. According to Donald the coins and flask saved his marital prospects. He was carried back on a stretcher by two German prisoners. He was sheltered in a dugout that collapsed under shellfire, dislocating his jaw and breaking his nose. He was dug out but a man near him was killed. He was eventually evacuated to a hospital at Étaples and then to the Prince of Wales's Hospital in the Great Western Railway Hotel, Marylebone Road, London. He was granted a month's sick leave by a medical board and joined the 3rd Battalion at Rochester. While recovering he attended a Vickers Machine Gun course at the Machine Gun School, Grantham. He led a draft returning to France from Southampton to Le Havre, then returned to Chatham. Donald was eventually passed by a medical board and returned to France around the time of his 21st birthday in April 1918.

Donald was promoted lieutenant on 4th April and joined 8th Battalion from the base at Étaples on 22nd April (11th Battalion had been disbanded by then). He temporarily commanded a company as an acting captain until a more senior officer arrived and took over. In May the Battalion moved to the Lens sector and he was involved in many fights in the cellars and sewers there. He had become war weary and was not happy in the 8th Battalion because most of his friends had been killed or wounded. He applied for a transfer to the Machine Gun Corps before the VC action but felt he had to withdraw it and stay with the unit thereafter. **Awarded the VC for his actions northwest of Lens, France on 24th-26th September 1918, LG 14th December 1918.** He was recommended for the VC by his CO, Lieutenant Colonel Arthur Cecil Corfe DSO (1877–1949). At the end of September the Battalion moved to the Cambrai sector and Donald captured a machine gun post at Awoingt. He picked up a German automatic pistol and kept it for forty years before handing it over to the police. On 10th October the Battalion was in divisional reserve but received an occasional heavy long-range shell. Donald ordered his men to dig in. As he supervised the work, he was the only man totally exposed as a heavy shell burst in the company area. He was hit by splinters in the right hip and left thigh, the only casualty in the Battalion that day. He was evacuated to England and was treated at the Cambridge Military Hospital, Aldershot. He was released on sick leave over Christmas and during it was informed by his uncle, John Doubleday, who was living next door, that he been awarded the VC. Donald was posted to the 3rd Battalion in late January 1919 on light duties and was demobilised from Crystal Palace.

Donald's CO, Arthur Cecil Corfe, had a remarkable life. He was born a New Zealander, but played rugby union for Queensland and made an international appearance for Australia against Great Britain during the Lions Tour in 1899. He served in 3rd Queensland Contingent and 10th New Zealand Contingent in the Boer War and was later a major in the South African Defence Force and ADC to General Smuts. After the Great War he became a member of the League of Nations Commission for the repatriation of Greeks and Bulgarians. He is seen here with the Queensland rugby union team of 1899, standing second from right.

The VC was presented by the King in the ballroom of Buckingham Palace on 15th February 1919. Donald is reputed to have been mentioned-in-despatches but this has not been traced in the London Gazette. After the investiture Donald returned home and was presented with a silver casket by the Sittingbourne, Milton and Milton Rural District Council. He relinquished his commission on 31st July 1920.

Donald rejoined the family brick firm. Initially his grandfather objected to paying him £3 per week and Donald threatened to take a Government training course as a forestry officer in one of the colonies instead. He got the £3. He worked for the company until his retirement in 1972 and was the last director of Smeed, Dean and Co Ltd. After retiring he opened the Dolphin Yard Sailing Barge Museum at Sittingbourne. Donald married Marjorie Emily Wood (2nd March 1902–29th October 1988), born at Faversham, Kent, in June 1923 at St Michael's Church, Sittingbourne. They lived at Woodcourt, 1 Park Avenue, Sittingbourne, Kent. Her

Dolphin Yard Sailing Barge Museum.

death was registered at Swale, Kent and she is buried with her husband. She left effects valued at £842,691 (£2.4M in 2020). They had three children:

- Laurence John Dean (25th February–11th April 1924).
- Michael John Dean (12th January 1929–25th August 1985) was at boarding school at Chesterton, Melville Road, Falmouth, Cornwall in 1939. He was living at Grove End, Tunstall, Sittingbourne at the time of his death.
- Susan V Dean (born 1932) married Peter St John Charles Bavin (1926–1st May 1996), born at Chepstow, Monmouthshire, in 1955 at Sittingbourne. He was commissioned in the King's Shropshire Light Infantry on 13th October 1945 and was promoted war substantive lieutenant on 13th April 1946. He last appears in the Army List in December 1947. They had three sons – Nicholas J Bavin 1960, Stephen PC Bavin 1961 and David Andrew Bavin 1967.

Marjorie's father, Walter Rayner Wood (1877–17th February 1961), born at Milton Regis, Kent, was a commercial traveller in dog and game foods. He married Alice Emily née Geering (1876–1917), born at Borden, Kent, in 1900 at Milton, Kent. They were living at 8 Belmont Terrace, Faversham, Kent in 1901 and at 42 Park Road, Sittingbourne in 1911. Walter married Florence May Pullin (born 14th May 1890), born at Weston-super-Mare, Somerset, in 1927 at Fulham, London. They were living at 22 Gore Court Road, Sittingbourne in 1939, by when he was a commercial traveller for a biscuit manufacturer. Walter was living at Denbrae, Gore Court Road, Sittingbourne at the time of his death there.

42 Park Road, Sittingbourne, where Marjorie's family was living in 1911 (Zoopla).

St George's Memorial Church in Ypres commemorates the British and Commonwealth troops, who died in the battles in the Ypres Salient during the Great War. The church was built following an appeal by The Ypres League and its President, Field Marshal Sir John French, Earl of Ypres. The land was donated by the town and the church was designed by Sir Reginald Bloomfield. Field Marshal Lord Plumer laid the foundation stone on 24th July 1927 and the church was consecrated by the Bishop of Fulham on 24th March 1929. There are many plaques and memorials to regiments, associations and individuals within.

Donald was commissioned in 4th Battalion, The Buffs (East Kent Regiment) TA on 27th August 1920. He was promoted captain on 28th July 1921, brevet major on 1st January 1927 and major on 1st April 1930. He attended the Territorial Army Senior Officers' Course at Sheerness, Kent in 1932 and was promoted lieutenant colonel on 20th March 1936 to command 4th Battalion at Dibgate Camp, Kent. **Awarded the Efficiency Decoration (Territorial), LG 19th June 1936.**

He was involved in the building of St George's Memorial Church, Ypres in 1927 and arranged for a commemorative plaque to the Royal West Kent Regiment to be placed there. The Friends of St George's was founded in 1955, when he became its Vice-Chairman and held the position until 1979.

When mobilisation was ordered, 4th Battalion assembled at Canterbury. Detachments guarded vulnerable points in Kent, including all the railway tunnels between Canterbury and Folkestone and Dover. The Battalion also took in many new recruits and trained them. The Battalion moved to Aldershot to join the rest of the Brigade there. A few days later Dean was invited to tea with GOC 44th Home Counties Division, Major General Edmund 'Snowey' Osborne CB DSO, who told him that he was recommended for a staff post in the War Office as he wanted no TA COs, just Regulars, in the Division. Dean was very unhappy about this but had no choice other than to hand over command. He had no contact with 4th Buffs again until 1946.

On 1st November 1939 Donald formed and commanded No.5 Group, Auxiliary Military Pioneer Corps at No.4 Centre, Clacton (a Butlin's holiday camp). He transferred to the Auxiliary Military Pioneer Corps on 9th November (21378).

Donald crossed to France via Calais to report to the Director of Labour at GHQ in Arras for orders. No.5 Group embarked at Southampton for Cherbourg on 3rd December, then moved to Doullens on 5th December. Donald was also appointed OC Troops Doullens on 20th December. At one time No.5 Group had fifteen companies under command, more than brigade strength. Donald found that he was younger than almost all his officers and that a number needed to be weeded out for various reasons. Most men were older reservists (one asked Donald if he could still draw his old age pension and his Army pay) or young soldiers with very little training.

Butlin's holiday camp at Clacton opened on 11th June 1938. During the Second World War all Butlin's camps were requisitioned. Clacton was originally planned as a prisoner of war camp but was used to train the Pioneer Corps instead. It reopened as a holiday camp in 1946 and closed in 1983. It reopened for a short time as a theme park but was then sold and redeveloped for housing.

Equipment and vehicles were in short supply. The Group also lacked clothing and boots. The C-in-C, Lord Gort VC, saw two of Donald's men in Arras smothered in chalk, having been enlarging the tunnels under the town. Gort enquired who the men belonged to and why their CO allowed them to be seen as such in public. Dean replied 'that I entirely agreed that it was a disgrace that British soldiers should be seen in public in such a condition but to rectify it I was faced with three alternatives – first to keep a proportion of my men off duty and in bed while their only uniforms were washed, second to confine such men to barracks until their present uniforms were worn out and new ones issued or third to issue all pioneers with a suit of denims or a second uniform, which I had been pressing for weeks quite unsuccessfully'. As a result a second uniform was granted for all AMPC personnel in the BEF.

Initially there were many disciplinary problems in the Group and Donald preferred to deal with them 'in-house'. He secured the use of a disused civilian prison in Doullens and staffed it from his own resources. After a few months conduct was so vastly improved that he closed the prison. A French officer advised him to open a brothel to prevent the spread of venereal disease. This he did and installed a madam who had experience of dealing with the British in the Great War. Donald arranged for weekly medical inspections for the girls and there were no cases of VD reported. The brothel was so well run that the Germans took it over later. At this time only a quarter of Pioneers were armed and most had had no skill at arms training. Dean set up training for every man and eventually all 4,000 were trained to fire a rifle. He also set up a school of instruction for prospective NCOs and refresher courses for the existing ones. On 2nd November he was introduced to the King, who was on a visit to GHQ. The Group had little communications equipment and relied on the French civilian telephone system. In Doullens the French operators gave preference to French callers until Dean instructed his interpreter to buy the largest box of chocolates he could find in Paris. This was sent to the 'charming young lady operator with the golden voice, and her colleagues'. Thereafter the telephone exchange worked very well for them.

When the German invasion commenced on 10th May 1940, the Group suffered numerous air attacks and was often sent to investigate reports of enemy parachute landings. During the retreat, Donald broke into an abandoned canteen at Avesne and loaded up his vehicle with cigarettes for his troops. No.5 Group concentrated at St Pol on 19th May and was ordered to make its way to Boulogne as quickly as possible. Next day Donald and his QM issued food from abandoned dumps to refugees. He organised a rapid defence to repulse the first enemy troops approaching the town and then persuaded a French train driver to take his men to Boulogne, while others made their way there by lorry. The train journey was very slow and had to be at night. They were bombed frequently but got to Wimereux, close to Boulogne early on the 21st.

Donald arrived in Boulogne at 4.00 a.m. on 23rd May, only thirty minutes before the first German tanks. He confiscated the weapons of men being evacuated to arm his own troops. With 250 men he set off to hold the crossings over the River Canche. However, a bridge had not been blown and the enemy were already across. Having blunted the advance they returned to Boulogne to find that the Guards had arrived to defend the town. Donald's pioneers held eight roadblocks and reinforced 2nd Welsh Guards. He set one roadblock alight with a punctured petrol tank to stop a tank. While covering the withdrawal of the Guards he drove to the quay but his car was riddled with bullets as he crossed a bridge near the harbour mouth. He lost another car the day before when it was hit by bomb splinters.

The enemy penetrated into the town and heavy street fighting took place. Two of Donald's roadblocks were overrun and captured before he could withdraw them. He pulled his men back to the Gare Maritime and manned barricades abandoned by the Guards as they fell back to board destroyers for evacuation. Donald was knocked unconscious by an explosion but regained consciousness when his clothing caught fire. He was originally reported to have been killed in action. The next day he persuaded the captain of the destroyer HMS *Vimiera* to delay sailing for twenty minutes while he searched for stragglers. This was the last ship to leave Boulogne. **He was mentioned in a War Office despatch, LG 26th July 1940.**

HMS *Vimiera*, a V-Class destroyer, was built as part of the 1917-18 programme by Swan, Hunter & Wighan Richardson at Wallsend on the Tyne. She was laid down in October 1916, launched on 22nd June 1917 and was completed on 19th September. One of her early missions was to return delegates to the Soviet Union during the first phase of negotiations for the Anglo-Soviet Trade Agreement. Before the Second World War *Vimiera* was converted to an escort destroyer with enhanced anti-aircraft and anti-submarine capability. In January 1940 she joined the Nore Command for coastal convoy escort duties in the North Sea and English Channel. In April 1940 she transferred to the command of C-in-C Dover to support operations in France, including providing anti-aircraft defence around Dunkirk and naval gunfire support. On 19th May she rescued survivors from HMS *Whitley* and in the following days took reinforcements to Boulogne and evacuated wounded and medical staff from there. In the actions around Boulogne and Calais, *Vimiera* sustained substantial damage. She was the last ship to leave Boulogne before it fell to German forces. She went in for repair on 25th May 1940 and was consequently not involved in the Dunkirk evacuation. *Vimiera* redeployed to the North Sea to defend East Coast convoys. On 9th January 1942 she was sunk by a mine in the Thames estuary off East Spile Buoy with the loss of ninety-six of her crew.

The Group survivors were sent to Aldershot initially and reformed on 25th May at Caister, having suffered 500 casualties out of 1,100. The Group returned to No. 4 Centre, Clacton, Essex on 4th June. Donald recommended twenty of his officers and men for decorations or mentions and most were granted. However, he was unhappy that the COs of 2nd Irish and Welsh Guards, together with the Brigade commander, were awarded DSOs, whereas his pioneers, who were fighting in Boulogne before the Guards arrived and were still fighting after they departed, having fought alongside them and covered their withdrawal and embarkation, received little recognition. Donald sent a message to CO 2nd Welsh Guards that he could collect the weapons left by his Battalion on Boulogne harbour, that had been so useful in continuing the fight after the Guards departed. He received no thanks for this. The Group moved to Buntingford, Hertfordshire on 24th June to support XI Corps. The work largely involved airfield construction, maintenance after bombing, camp construction and stores depot work. Donald moved his family nearby to get them away from Kent. The house they stayed in was narrowly missed by delayed action bombs.

On 21st March 1942, HQ No.5 Group embarked aboard MS *Sobieski* at Glasgow without any of its companies. The convoy departed Greenock on 23rd March and arrived off Freetown, Sierra Leone on 6th April. Donald did not go ashore and the convoy departed again on 9th April. It arrived at Durban, South Africa on 22nd April and departed again on 28th April. After putting to sea the senior officers were briefed on the destination and plans. All other ranks were not briefed until 2nd May. No.5 Group took part in the landings near Diego Suarez (now Antsiranana) in the north of Madagascar on 5th May (Operation Ironclad). The aim was to prevent Madagascan ports being used by the Japanese Navy, particularly its submarines. Next day he took change of all working parties on Blue Beach and later controlled all civilian labour. About 2,000 native prisoners of war were also employed until it was pointed out that under the Geneva Convention they could not handle offensive materials. Donald solved this by having them discharged from the French Army and re-employing them as civilian labourers. As a result, he ended up with 3,000 labourers and 500 wives etc, known as 'Dean Force'. At the end of July an East African Military Labour Group HQ arrived and relieved HQ 5 Group. He embarked at Diego Suarez with 121 Force on HMT *Dilwara* on 21st August and arrived at Mombasa, Kenya on 26th August. At the end of August, Donald was an umpire on Exercise Touchstone, a practice for the defence of Mombasa and a rehearsal for the next landings on Madagascar.

*Dilwara* left Mombasa on 5th September in convoy with 121 Force to capture Majunga (now Mahajanga) on the west coast of Madagascar, held by French Vichy forces. Donald supervised the landing of No.5 Group on Green Beach on 10th September (Operation Stream Line Jane). He left Majunga for Tananarive (French name for the capital of Madagascar, Antananarivo) with other heads of service and accompanied by his batman, Private O'Connor, on 25th September, arriving on 27th September. There he set about organising native labour for the RASC and

MS *Dilwara* (12,598 tons) was built at Barclay Curle & Co shipyards, Glasgow, Scotland for the British India Steam Navigation Co and was launched on 17th October 1935. During her career she was a troopship, an education ship and a budget cruise ship. She was purchased in 1960 by China Navigation Co, Hong Kong and renamed *Kuala Lumpur*. She was refitted as a cruise ship and was also used seasonally to carry Muslim pilgrims from Singapore and Malaysia to Jeddah. On cruises she carried 198 first class passengers but on pilgrim voyages this rose to 242 first class and 1,669 third class. She was scrapped in December 1971.

RAOC. On 2nd October he was ordered to inaugurate and command a prisoner of war camp for French officers and later another camp for Malgache and Senegalese troops. Donald handed over command of No.5 Group on 17th October and sailed aboard SS *Ocean Pride* with 121 Force when it departed next day. The ship arrived at Durban on 24th October, sailed the next day, arrived at Cape Town on 27th October, departed there on 2nd November and arrived at Liverpool, Lancashire on 30th November.

Donald took command of No.48 Group in the Chester area on 1st January 1943. He took command of No.19 Group on 17th April 1943 and the HQ moved to Ayrshire, Scotland in preparation for embarkation with Force X. However, four days later they were transferred to Force Y. Dean went to the War Office and discovered that they were destined to land in Sicily. The Group HQ moved to Aldershot and left there for Liverpool, where the HQ and four companies embarked on RMS *Franconia* in late June. The other four companies were aboard another transport. They landed at Algiers briefly and then went on to Malta but were not allowed ashore. The Group landed at Augusta harbour in southeast Sicily and later moved by sea to Catania. In addition to British companies, there were two Indian, a Basuto and a Bechuana pioneer companies in Donald's command.

The Group HQ embarked aboard SS *Ville d'Oran* at Syracuse at the end of October but did not sail until 5th November and landed at Taranto, Italy on 7th November. Next day they departed by train for Naples, the journey taking two days, and joined the road party there. Donald was appointed Acting Assistant Director of Labour for X Corps and had under command up to twelve pioneer companies, including Italians, Basutos, Bechuanas, Mauritians, Seychellois and Swazis. British pioneers were being withdrawn in preparation for the Normandy landings. Group HQ was established at Capua. Much of the work involved man-packing supplies up to the front lines in the mountains, even after two mule companies were formed. On the return journeys wounded were carried out. Donald often accompanied the carrying parties. In five months the Group had up to 500 casualties. At the end of 1943 the Group moved to Sessa, living under canvas in snowy conditions.

Donald was appointed Assistant Director of Labour in HQ V Corps on the Adriatic side of Italy in March 1944. He was based at Paglieta before moving to the San Vito area and on 16th June to Campobasso. He was granted leave in Egypt on 2nd July with seven other war worn officers. They flew to Alexandria and had a flying day trip to Beirut then on to Cairo. A week was spent there and another at Alexandria. On 14th August, Donald and his team left V Corps to form twelve companies of Italian pioneers under Eighth Army, each with a British cadre. **He was mentioned in a War Office despatch for his work with X Corps, LG 24th August 1944.** He was also appointed Labour Adviser to 55 Area and 71 Sub-Area. On 19th September they moved to Arezzo and took over more companies from No.39 Group.

On 1st December Donald was appointed Deputy Director of Labour No.1 District, with its HQ at Foligno, and was appointed acting colonel on 4th December. His HQ moved to Perugia on 1st January 1945. Most British pioneers had long since gone back to Britain for the campaign in northwest Europe and most Indians had been withdrawn for operations in Burma. As a result, great reliance was placed on Italians and on average he had 42,000 civilian employees. Promoted colonel on 11th April. On 4th May he moved his HQ to Forli, southeast of Bologna, and after the end of the war to Padua. On 13th June he handed over and travelled to Naples, arriving on 16th June. After a medical, he sailed from there aboard MV *Carnarvon Castle*, arriving at Southampton on 25th June. Next day he went to 'somewhere near Aldershot' and was released from service.

Donald was appointed Honorary Colonel of 4th Queen's Own Buffs (The Royal Kent Regiment) on 1st August 1946. He kept this appointment until 1964, by when The Buffs (Royal East Kent Regiment) had amalgamated with The Queen's Own Royal West Kent Regiment to form The Queen's Own Buffs, The Royal Kent Regiment.

The Order of the Dannebrog was instituted in 1671 by Danish King Christian V. Originally membership was limited to fifty noble or royal members, who formed the White Knights to distinguish them from the Blue Knights, members of the Order of the Elephant. In 1808 the Order was divided into four classes, with the Grand Commander class reserved for royalty with close ties to the Danish Royal House. From 1951 women could also be members of the Order. Today the Order honours servants of the Danish state for meritorious civil or military service, for contribution to the arts, sciences or business life and for working for Danish interests.

The Most Excellent Order of the British Empire was established on 4th June 1917 by George V to fill a gap in the honours system. It comprises five classes both civil and military. The two most senior classes make the recipient a knight or dame. The Officer (OBE) is the fourth highest class of the Order, above the Member (MBE). The order was created in particular to honour those who had served in a variety of non-combatant roles during the Great War. The affiliated British Empire Medal was awarded until 1993 but was reinstituted in 2012. The British monarch is Sovereign of the Order and appoints all other members on the advice of the government of the United Kingdom and some Commonwealth countries. The next senior member is the Grand Master, the last of whom was Prince Philip, who was appointed in 1953 and held it until his death in 2021. The Order is limited to 300 Knights and Dames Grand Cross (GBE), 845 Knights and Dames Commander (CBE & DBE) and 8,960 Commanders (CBE). There is no limit on the total number of OBEs and MBEs but no more than 858 OBEs and 1,464 MBEs may be appointed each year. Although the order was initially to recognise meritorious service, it was also awarded for gallantry, in particular when the actions fell short of the standard for the George Medal. In 1974 the gallantry aspect was replaced by the Queen's Gallantry Medal.

**Appointed Commander of the Danish Order of Dannebrog by the King of Denmark, who was Colonel-in-Chief of The Buffs.** Donald transferred to the TA Reserve of Officers on 13th February 1951. **Awarded four clasps to the Efficiency Decoration (Territorial), LG 16th March 1951.**

Donald was a member of the Kent Territorial and Auxiliary Forces Association and was appointed an **Officer of the Order of the British Empire (Civil Division) for his services, LG 10th June 1961**. He was appointed a Justice of the Peace in 1951 and Deputy Lieutenant, Kent on 22nd July 1957, LG 26th July 1957. Donald attended the Ypres Veteran's Annual Shell-Hole Supper at Wemyss Barracks, Canterbury in 1962. His efforts were instrumental in bringing Sittingbourne and Ypres together and they were officially twinned in 1964. He was a Freemason (Saint Michael Lodge No.1273 and Sacdingbirna Lodge No.6728). Donald was also:

President of:
- Sittingbourne Branch, Royal British Legion and was awarded the Legion's highest award, National Certificate of Appreciation, in August 1983.
- Sittingbourne Horticultural Society.
- 11th Battalion, The Queen's Own Buffs Association, Sandwich, Kent.

Chairman of the Sittingbourne Branch of the Regimental Association, The Queen's Own Buffs, The Royal Kent Regiment. His wife was Chairwoman of the Ladies Guild of the Association.

Regimental representative on the Army Benevolent Fund Steering Committee.

Member of Tunstall Parish Council.

Churchwarden at Tunstall for forty-six years.

Queen Margrethe II (born 16th April 1940) became heir presumptive to her father, King Frederick IX of Denmark in 1953, when a constitutional amendment allowed women to inherit the throne. Her education included a year at North Foreland Lodge in Hampshire, England. She studied prehistoric archaeology at Girton College, Cambridge 1960–61, political science at Aarhus University 1961–62, attended the Sorbonne in 1963 and the London School of Economics in 1965. Princess Margrethe married a French diplomat, Henri de Laborde de Monpezat, in 1967 and they were married for over fifty years until his death in 2018. They had two children – Crown Prince Frederik in 1968 and Joachim the following year. Margrethe succeeded her father on his death on 14th January 1972 and became the first female monarch of Denmark since Margrethe I, who ruled the Scandinavian kingdoms 1375–1412. In addition to her royal duties, Margrethe is a talented painter and her illustrations (under the pseudonym Ingahild Grathmer) were used in the Danish edition of Tolkien's, *The Lord of the Rings*. She is also fluent in five languages and is an accomplished costume designer, having designed costumes for the Royal
Danish Ballet and some of her own clothes. Queen Margrethe is Colonel-in-Chief of the British Army's Princess of Wales's Royal Regiment (PWRR), following a family tradition. The PWRR is the successor to the East and West Sussex, East and West Kent, Middlesex and Hampshire Regiments.

On 6th April 1970, Donald was one of '10 VCs on a VC10' on the inaugural flight of the Super Vickers VC 10 from London to Nairobi by East African Airlines. The ten VCs, five each from both World Wars selected by drawing names out of a hat, were guests of the company for a nine-day holiday in Kenya, Tanzania and Uganda. In Kenya the schedule included Nairobi, Nyeri, Treetops, where Princess Elizabeth succeeded to the throne, Tsavo National Park and Mombasa. On 13th April the party flew over Ngorongoro Crater, the Serengeti and Lake Victoria to Uganda. In Kampala they were hosted by General Idi Amin and travelled up the Nile to Murchison Falls. Back in Nairobi they visited State House to meet President Kenyatta before flying back to Heathrow.

On 4th May 1974, Donald attended the Presentation of Colours to 1st, 2nd and 3rd Battalions, The Queen's Regiment and 5th Volunteer Battalion by Queen Margarethe II of Denmark, Allied Colonel-in-Chief, at Armoury House, London. Also present were ECT Wilson VC, Mrs Rachel Roupell, widow of GRP Roupell VC and Mrs Grace Hilary Edwards, widow of FJ Edwards VC.

Donald attended all but one VC reunion between 1920 and 1981:

- VC Garden Party at Buckingham Palace on 26th June 1920.
- VC Dinner at the Royal Gallery of the House of Lords, London on 9th November 1929.
- Victory Day Celebration Dinner & Reception at The Dorchester, London on 8th June 1946.

St John the Baptist Church is situated in the village of Tunstall, a small village in which shops and pubs have been prohibited since the Middle Ages. There is no mention of a church there in the Domesday Book but there is evidence that there was one in Saxon times. The oldest part of the present building dates to c.1250 and the chancel is built in Caen stone. The nave was rebuilt c.1350 and the north and south aisles, tower and south porch were added. The south chancel chapel was added early in the 15th century and had been extended by 1655. An extensive restoration was carried out between 1848 and 1856. More recently the Hales or Lady Chapel has been restored, the organ has been replaced, the bells have been recast and an extension built. One of the rectors at the church, Simon de Meopham, became Archbishop of Canterbury in 1327 (Tony Grant).

- VC Centenary Celebrations at Hyde Park, London on 26th June 1956.
- 1st–5th and 7th–12th VC & GC Association Reunions in London on 24th July 1958, 7th July 1960, 18th July 1962, 16th July 1964, 14th July 1966, 18th June 1970, 14th July 1972, 23rd May 1974, 22nd April 1976, 11th May 1978 and 18th May 1981. All were held at the Café Royal except for those in 1970 at the Connaught Rooms, Covent Garden and 1981 at the Savoy Hotel.

Donald died at his home on 9th December 1985. His funeral was held at St John the Baptist Church, Tunstall, Kent on 16th December, followed by cremation at

Dean Road, Sittingbourne (Memorials to Valour).

Donald's ashes are buried in the family grave in the churchyard of St John the Baptist Church, Tunstall (Tony Grant).

The British War Medal was instituted on 26th July 1919 for all ranks who served for twenty-eight days in an operational theatre between 5th August 1914 and 11th November 1918, or who died on active service before completing twenty-eight days. Eligibility was extended in 1919–20 to mine-clearing at sea and operations in North and South Russia, eastern Baltic, Siberia, Black Sea and Caspian Sea. Many veterans were awarded the 1914–15 Star, British War Medal and Victory Medal. They became known as Pip, Squeak and Wilfred after a strip cartoon published in the Daily Mirror from 1919 to 1956.

The King George VI Coronation Medal was awarded to the Royal Family, selected officers of state, officials, servants of the Royal Household, ministers, government and local government officials, mayors, public servants, members of the armed forces and police in Britain, the colonies and Dominions. A total of 90,279 medals were awarded.

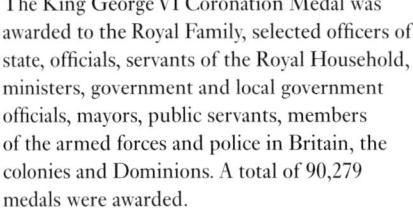

The Queen Elizabeth II Silver Jubilee Medal was created in 1977 to mark the 25th anniversary of the Queen's accession in the United Kingdom, Canada, Australia and New Zealand. Until 1977 the United Kingdom authorities decided on a total number for coronation and jubilee medals, which were then allocated to Empire, Dominion and Commonwealth countries. From 1977 the award was at the discretion of each national government – 30,000 in Britain, 1,507 in New Zealand, 6,870 in Australia and 30,000 in Canada.

Charing Crematorium, Kent. His ashes were interred in the family grave at St John the Baptist Church, Tunstall. He was the last surviving British soldier VC of the Great War. He is commemorated in a number of other places:

- Dean Road, Sittingbourne, Kent.
- Memorial stone at Swale VC Garden, Crescent Hall, Central Avenue, Sittingbourne, Kent, dedicated in May 1995.
- A Department for Communities and Local Government commemorative paving stone was dedicated at Sittingbourne War Memorial, Crescent Hall, Central Avenue, Sittingbourne, Kent on 9th November 2014.
- Memorial paving stone unveiled outside Freemason's Hall, Covent Garden, London on 25th April 2017 by the Duke of Kent.
- Memorial plaque in St George's Church, Ypres, Belgium.

In addition to the VC he was awarded the Officer of the Order of the British Empire (Civil Division), 1914–15 Star, British War Medal 1914–20, Victory Medal 1914–19 with Mentioned-in-Despatches Oakleaf, 1939–45 Star, Italy Star, Defence Medal, War Medal 1939–45 with Mentioned-in-Despatches Oakleaf, George VI Coronation Medal 1937, Elizabeth II Coronation Medal 1953, Elizabeth II Silver Jubilee Medal 1977, Efficiency Decoration (Territorial) with four clasps and the Danish Order of the Dannebrog. The current location of the VC is not known.

### 43247 CORPORAL DAVID FERGUSON HUNTER
### 1/5th (City of Glasgow) Battalion, The Highland Light Infantry

David Hunter was born on 28th November 1891 at Quarry Row, Kingseat, Dunfermline, Fife, Scotland. His father, Peter Hunter (28th June 1862–4th March 1933), born at The Square, Alloa, Clackmannanshire, was a coal miner at Dean Colliery in 1883, living at Kingseat, Dunfermline. He married Maria née Ferguson (c.1865–28th December 1938), born at Brechin, Forfarshire, on 31st December 1883 at James Street, Dunfermline. She was a weaver and was living at 29 Queen Street, Dunfermline. They were living at Kingseat in 1883, at 10 Brucefield Avenue, Dunfermline in 1896 and at 27 Main Street, Kingseat in 1901. By 1918 he was employed by the Fife Electric Power Company's generating station at Townhill. Maria ran a small confectionery business from home. They both died at Main Street, Kingseat. David was the fourth of twelve children but six died in infancy. The ten known siblings were all born at Kingseat:

- Mary Hunter (born and died 1884.)
- Robert Hunter (born 1st July 1885) was a coal miner. He served in the Machine Gun Corps, attached to the Black Watch, during the Great War.
- Thomas Ferguson Hunter (24th May 1887–November 1968), a coalminer, married Euphemia Wilson (4th June 1886–25th January 1980), born in Glasgow, Lanarkshire, on 31st December 1907 at Main Street, Kingseat. He was living at 43 Bank Street, Lochgelly when he enlisted in the Army Service Corps, Motor Transport on 6th February 1915 (M2/048368) and joined at Grove Park on 15th February He was described as a motor driver and/or barman, 5′ 8¼″ tall and weighing 134 lbs. He embarked on SS *Atlanta* at Southampton on 14th March, disembarked at Rouen next day and was attached to 1/2nd (47th) London Division Ammunition Park. He was granted leave to Britain 27th December

Settlement in the Dunfermline area dates back to Neolithic times. Malcolm III established Dunfermline as the seat of royal power in the mid-11th century and the town effectively became the capital of Scotland until the 1430s. A new church, inaugurated around 1072, evolved into an abbey in 1128. At the peak of its power the Abbey controlled four burghs, three courts of regality and large tracts of land from Moray to Berwickshire. A number of British monarchs were born in Dunfermline Palace including:

David II, son of Robert the Bruce in 1324.
James I (reigned 1406-37) in 1394.
Charles I of Scotland, England and Ireland (reigned 1625-49) in 1600.

Seven Scottish Kings are buried at Dunfermline, the last being Robert the Bruce in 1329, although his heart was taken to Melrose Abbey. Despite much of the Abbey being destroyed by Edward I in 1303, there are substantial remains, which are Category A listed. The Reformation meant a reduction in Dunfermline's ecclesiastical importance. The Union of the Crowns ended the town's royal connections when James VI moved the Scottish Court to London in 1603. In May 1624 a fire destroyed about three-quarters of the medieval burgh. The decline in Dunfermline's fortunes continued until the agricultural and industrial revolutions, with increasing demand for lime, salt and coal. As the mines moved inland, numerous wooden wagon ways were constructed to move minerals, particularly coal, to the coast. Later the lines were converted to railways. After the Second World War industries such as linen and coal mining declined and eventually closed. The entrepreneur and philanthropist, Andrew Carnegie, who was born in Dunfermline in 1835, gifted to the town a free library, public swimming baths and Pittencrieff Park. In 1888 two Dunfermline men, John Reid and Robert Lockhart, demonstrated golf in America for the first time. Reid established America's first golf club, St Andrews, at Yonkers, New York, and Andrew Carnegie was one of the first members. John MacLaren Erskine VC (1894-1917) was also born in Dunfermline. His story appears in the second book in this series, *Victoria Crosses on the Western Front, April 1915-June 1916*.

1915–3rd January 1916 and 18th-28th January 1917, by when he was serving with 47th Ammunition Sub Park as a lorry driver. He was granted the Good Conduct Badge on 6th February 1917 and leave to Britain 3rd-17th March 1918. On 13th March 1918 he was transferred to 47th Division MT Company and was granted leave to Britain 21st November–5th December. On 10th February 1919 he was appointed unpaid acting lance corporal in 382nd MT Company. He was serving in 57th Division MT Company on 19th May and returned to Britain on 22nd May, where he was demobilised on 21st June 1919. They emigrated to the USA, arriving at Boston, Massachusetts on 1st September 1923. They were living at West Run Road, Munhall, Pennsylvania on 27th April 1942, when he was working at the Illinois Steel Corporation, described as 5′ 8″ tall, weighing 134 lbs, with light complexion, gray eyes, grey hair and his right wrist was crooked. They both died in California. They had three daughters, all born in Scotland – Janet W Hunter (born 9th April 1909), Maria Ferguson Hunter (born 31st May 1911) and Euphemia W Hunter (born 30th October 1920).

- Peter Hunter (5th July 1889–21st December 1891).
- Maria Hunter (1893–97).
- Helen Hunter (c.1895–97).
- James Hunter (29th April 1898–19th March 1981) was rejected by a military medical board and was employed as a hairdresser in Lochgelly at the time. He married Blanche Beveredge (1898–10th July 1935), born at Dundee, Forfarshire, on 24th December 1919 at Main Street, Kingseat. They emigrated to Brisbane, Queensland, Australia aboard TSS *Jervis Bay*, arriving on 16th January 1928. He was a hairdresser living with his family on Kew Road, Graceville, Brisbane in 1931. James was living with his daughter on Verney Road, Graceville in 1943, both working as hairdressers. James and Blanche had two children:
    - Ella Hunter (30th October 1920–1st December 2001), born at Kingseat, Dunfermline, married Victor Ronald Mabin (24th April 1917–10th September 1989), born in Brisbane, on 12th May 1945. He joined the Australian Army on 22nd October 1939 at Sherwood, Queensland (QX591) and served in Africa and Papua New Guinea. He was discharged as a lieutenant on 28th December 1944. He was a carrier in 1949, when they were living on Verney Road, Graceville. By 1958 he was a contractor and they were living on Moggill Road, Moggill. By 1972 he was a salesman and they were living at 60 Simpsons Road, Barden. By 1977 he was a newsagent and they were living at 10 Blaxland Road, Dalby, where they both subsequently died. They had three children – Victor James Mabin, Margaret Blanche Mabin and Barbara Joyce Mabin (1956–77).
    - Gordon James 'Jock' Hunter (1st May 1930–3rd July 2000), born in Brisbane, married June Rose Reiser on 14th September 1951. He was a public servant in 1963, when they were living at 166 Drayton Street, Dalby. They had moved to Jandowae Road, Dalby by 1972 and to Alambie, Dalby by 1977. Gordon was still living there in 1980 but June was a shop assistant living at 77 Perth Street, Toowoomba, Queensland. They had five children – David James Hunter 1952, Kay Joyce Hunter 1955, Sandra Ann Hunter 1959, Trudy Yvette Hunter 1966 and Andrew Gilbert Hunter 1969.
- Janet 'Nettie' Hunter (20th February 1901–10th October 1984), a housekeeper, married Hugh Malcolm (2nd November 1896–9th January 1980), a coal miner, on 21st January 1921 at Halbeath, Dunfermline. He died at Victoria Hospital, Kirkcaldy and she at 81 Golfdrum Street, Dunfermline. They had three children:
    - James Malcolm (27th June 1922–2005), a coal miner, married Marion Paterson Cowan (1921–2001), a weaver, on 4th April 1947 at North Church, Kelty, Fife. She was living at 143 Centre Street, Kelty. She died at Dunfermline and he at Cowdenbeath. They had a son, Hugh Malcolm (1950–2018).
    - Maria Ferguson Malcolm (27th April 1925–2005) married William Knowles (1923–2007), a coal miner, on 16th July 1948 at Townhill Church of

Scotland Church, Dunfermline. He was living at 49 Woodhead Street, High Valleyfield, Fife. They had two daughters – Janice Ann Knowles 1951 and Margaret Blair Knowles 1958.
    ◦ Peter Malcolm (born 30th August 1932), an insurance agent, married Margaret Mitchell Davidson (born 1932), a despatch clerk born at Lochore, on 3rd July 1954 at Co-operative Hall, Kelty, Fife. She was living at 166 Oakfield Street, Kelty. They had a daughter, Linda Margaret Malcolm, in 1956.
- Margaret Hunter (born 21st March 1906).
- Robina Ferguson Hunter (1908–10).

David's paternal grandfather, Robert Hunter (c.1841–9th December 1915), born at Dunfermline, Fife, was a coal miner. He married Helen née Whyte (c.1840–8th June 1899), also born at Dunfermline, on 17th December 1860 at Alloa, Clackmannanshire. They were living at 2 Porch Row, Dunfermline in 1881. They both died at Kingseat, Dunfermline. In addition to Peter they had five other children:

- Robert Hunter (born 16th May 1861) was a coal miner in 1881. He married Jessie Hay (born c.1862) on 24th July 1883 at Dunfermline. She was reportedly born in Kent, England, possibly as Janet/Jannet Hay, registered at North Aylesford. She was living with her mother at her maternal grandparents' home at Wemyss, Fife in 1871 and with her mother and siblings at Buckhaven, Fife in 1881, by when she was a net worker. Jessie had a son named Robert on 30th December 1882. Robert and Jessie were living at Windygates, Fife in 1901. They had ten children – Alexander Hunter (15th May 1884), Peter Hunter (3rd June 1886–4th October 1939), Margaret Jane Hunter (20th January 1889), James Hunter (29th December 1891), Helen Hunter (21st May 1894), David Hunter (16th September 1896), Jessie Hunter (16th December 1897), George Hunter (30th November 1900–13th August 1963), Henry McBeath Hunter (24th October 1903) and Janet Hunter (24th April 1906).
- James Hunter (born 10th June 1868) was a coal miner in 1881. He married Helen Gray (born c.1873), a pithead worker (sic), on 31st December 1894 at The Manse of Beath, Fife. They were living at Brick Row, Dunfermline in 1911. They had seven children:
    ◦ Robert Hunter (born c.1895).
    ◦ Helen Whyte Hunter (born 24th September 1896) married James Miller in Dunfermline in 1921.
    ◦ John Whitehall (registered as Whitehill) Gray Hunter (1st February 1898–18th July 1946) emigrated to Canada and spent a short time in the Canadian Army early in the Second World War. He was involved in mining at Newcastle, Alberta and died at Drumheller, Strathmore, Alberta.
    ◦ Alice Sanderson Hunter (31st December 1899–1961) never married.

- ○ James Hunter (born 18th November 1901).
- ○ Peter Hunter (born c.1903).
- ○ Janet Whyte Hunter (born 27th March 1909) married James Traynor in Dunfermline in 1929.
- George Hunter (born c.1875).
- Janet Hunter (born 1878).
- Helen Hunter (born 1880).

His maternal grandfather, Thomas Ferguson (born c.1839), born at Dundee, Forfarshire, married Mary Ann née Grieve (born c.1838), also born at Dundee. He was a linen handloom weaver in 1861, when they were living at 3 Dundee Loan, Forfar, Angus. In 1881 they were living at Goat, Damside Street, Dunfermline. Thomas later became a bricklayer. In addition to Maria they had eight other children:

The development and growth of Dundee began with William the Lion's charter in the late 12th century. The town became a Royal Burgh in 1292. It was occupied by English forces for several years until recaptured by Robert the Bruce in 1312. In 1548 it was burned to the ground by the English and again by Parliamentarian forces in 1651. The town played a major role in the Jacobite cause when the Stuart standard was raised there in 1689. The Jacobite claimant, James VIII & III (The Old Pretender), made a public entry into the town in January 1716.

The economy in mediaeval times centred on exporting raw wool. Finished textiles followed in the 15th century and the textile industry was industrialised in the 18th century. In the early 19th century the Dundee mills converted from linen to jute, which dominated industry to the end of the century and caused rapid urban expansion. At its height Dundee had sixty-two jute mills employing 50,000 workers. Supporting industries, notably whaling, maritime and shipbuilding, expanded commensurately. Up to 200 ships per year were built there, including Captain Robert Falcon Scott's Antarctic research vessel RRS *Discovery*, which is displayed at Discovery Point in the city. Other significant industries were James Keiller & Sons' marmalade factory and the publisher DC Thomson. It was said that Dundee was built on three Js – Jute, Jam and Journalism. The jute industry declined in the early 20th century and was eventually replaced by light engineering and microelectronics. The town saw one of the worst rail disasters in British history when the Tay Rail Bridge collapsed in a storm in December 1879, with the loss of seventy-five lives. Winston Churchill was the local MP 1908–22. The city is the birthplace of a number of notable people including:

Adam Duncan, 1st Viscount Duncan of Camperdown (1731–1804), defeated the Dutch fleet off Camperdown in October 1797, one of the most significant naval actions in history.

Margaret Taylor Naysmith Fenwick (1919–92), the first female leader of a national trade union.

- Maryann Ferguson (born 1858), born at Dundee, was a factory worker in 1881.
- Thomas Ferguson (born 1861) was a dyer in 1881.
- David Ferguson (born c.1862) was a miner in 1881.
- James Ferguson (born c.1866), born at Dunfermline, Fife, was a miner in 1881.
- Robina Ferguson (born c.1868).
- Daniel Ferguson (born 1870).
- Jessie Ferguson (born c.1874).
- Robert Ferguson (born 1877).

Damside Street, Dunfermline, where David's maternal grandparents were living in 1881.

David was educated at St Leonard's School, Dunfermline 9th February–29th November 1897 and Halbeath School, Dunfermline. He was a coach painter briefly before becoming a coal miner at Aitken Colliery. He moved to Dean Colliery to work alongside his father. David was also a church organist. He enlisted in 7th Argyll & Sutherland Highlanders, Territorial Force in 1910.

David Hunter married Isabella Wilson (1st April 1891–23rd June 1937), a rubber worker, born at 30 Pittencrieff Street, Dunfermline, on 27th June 1913 at Milton Green, Dunfermline. They were living at 35 Forth Street, Dunfermline in 1918.

Aitken Colliery opened in 1896 and was named after Fife Coal Company's chairman, Thomas Aitken of Livingston. At the time it was said to be the largest coal mine in Scotland. It had two shafts, one of 370m and the other of 183m, linked to Lindsay Colliery. The mine was nationalised in 1947 and closed in 1963. The site has since been obliterated by opencast mining. The average workforce was 1,250 with a peak of 1,431 in 1956 (Scottish Mining Museum).

Isabella died at 40 Haig Crescent, Dunfermline. They had six children, all born at 35 Forth Street:

- Agnes 'Nan' Reid Hunter (11th August 1914–17th November 2010) was a rubber worker. She married Charles Archibald (2nd September 1913–19th February 1995), an assistant flesher born at 14 Natal Place, Dunfermline, on 12th August 1936 at United Hall, Queen Anne Street, Dunfermline. He was later a butcher. He died at Falkirk, Stirlingshire and she at Grangemouth, Stirlingshire. They had at least one son:
    - David Ferguson Archibald (10th September 1946–7th May 2006) married Pamela Margaret Murphy (born 1949) in 1970 at Falkirk, where she was born, and they lived at 89 Kerse Road, Grangemouth.
- Maria 'Rea' Ferguson Hunter (5th August 1916–9th March 1999) was a rubber worker before enlisting in the Auxiliary Territorial Service and was promoted corporal. She married Corporal Russell Whyte RAF (1917–83), born at Gateside House, Saline, Fife, on 29th May 1943 at The Abbey, Dunfermline. After leaving the RAF, Russell was a security officer and they lived at 2 Henderson Place, Saline. They both died at Dunfermline. They had at least one son:
    - Alan Charles Whyte (born 1946) married Norma L Carter (born 1947) in 1966 at Lincoln, England, where she was born. They had three children – Samantha Michelle Whyte 1967, Kevin Whyte 1977 and Gavin Whyte 1978.
- James Wilson Hunter (27th October 1919–8th December 1984) was serving in the Dunfermline Territorials with his father in 1938. He served in the Royal Signals during the Second World War and spent three and a half years as a prisoner of war of the Japanese. He married Mary Hogg Duncan (1920–73), a factory worker born at Muiravonside, on 7th March 1941 at Cairneymount Church, Maddiston, Stirlingshire. James became a telecommunications line inspector. He married Anne Campbell Corrieri née Legge (1926–2020), born at Cowdenbeath, Fife, in 1974. They lived at 4 McCane Place, Dunfermline. Anne had married Antonio Corrieri (1920–69), born at Kelty, Fife, in 1949 at Dunfermline. They were living at 89 Nethertown Broad Street, Dunfermline in 1960. James died at 7 Whirlbut Crescent, Dunfermline. James and Mary had a son:
    - David James Hunter (born 1941), who played football for Morton and was involved in developing youth players with Dunfermline Athletic Football Club.
- David Meldrum Hunter, a twin with Elwin (19th November 1923–2006), was serving as a bugler in the Dunfermline Territorials with his father in 1938 and was employed at Carnegie Baths. He served in the Royal Navy during the Second World War. David married Mary Ferris in 1946. He married Cecilia Baird late Wilson née Collins (15th July 1922–10th August 2007), born at Abbeyhill, Midlothian, in 1959. She had married Hugh Wilson at Kirkliston in 1942. He was serving as a RAFVR pilot officer (wireless operator/air gunner) (178769)

with 90 Squadron RAF when he was killed on a raid against the Opel factory in Rüsselsheim am Main, Germany on 25th/26th August 1944 (Durnbach War Cemetery, Bayern, Germany – 6 A 2). Cecilia married James Baird (24th June 1924–10th July 2006), born in Edinburgh, Midlothian, in 1949 at Haymarket, Edinburgh. James and Cecilia had two children, including James Baird in 1948. The marriage ended in divorce and James married Ethel Roberts.
* Elwin Walter Catt Hunter, a twin with David (19th November 1923–29th March 2016) was serving as a trumpeter in the Dunfermline Territorials with his father in 1938. He was employed by Smith & Guthrie, Dunfermline and also played accordion in a local band. He served in the Royal Artillery during the Second World War. Elwin married Charlotte Bell (c.1928–26th October 2008) on 16th February 1952 at Dunfermline. They were living at 9 Kersie Road, Throsk, Stirlingshire in 1966 and at 38 Kersie Road by 1968. Elwin was appointed a director of Throsk Community Enterprises Ltd in 2009. He died at Allan Lodge Care Home, Bridge of Allan, Stirlingshire. They had two sons:
  ○ Ian Hunter was a Chartered Accountant and a member of the Chartered Institute of Taxation. He worked briefly for HM Revenue & Customs before joining the Edinburgh office of Arthur Young McClelland Moores & Co (later Ernst & Young LLP) in 1976 and became a partner in the firm in May 1986. He retired in June 2011 and continued as a consultant to the firm until June 2012. He was appointed a director of Dunfermline Athletic FC.
  ○ Graham Hunter.
* Thomas Hunter (born 12th February 1930) was serving as a sergeant in 1st Seaforth Highlanders at Casemates Barracks, Gibraltar when he married Maria Dorita Seoane Lopez (c.1936–2001), a driver born at La Linea, Spain, there on 10th August 1957. They had four children:
  ○ David Thomas Hunter (born 2nd July 1958) born at Münster, West Germany.
  ○ Dorita Hunter (born 21st January 1960), born at British Military Hospital Münster, was a recruitment consultant at Seacot, Leith Links, Edinburgh, Midlothian. She married Gavin John Stewart Orr (born 16th February 1960), a solicitor, in February 1988 at the Church of St Andrew and St George, Edinburgh. They had two children.
  ○ Esmeralda Iris Hunter (born 20th October 1961), born at RAF Hospital, Changi, Singapore, married Mehrdad Mortazavi (born 1960) at Bonnyrigg and Lasswade in 1984. He was appointed a director of Lochrin Autos (Edinburgh) Ltd on

Casemates Barracks in Gibraltar, where David's son, Thomas, was based in 1957.

20th February 2002. She graduated BA Commerce and served as a director and company secretary of Lochrin Autos. They had a daughter, Nastasha Mortazavi, in 1987.
  ○ Paul Luis/Lewis Hunter (born 22nd September 1962), also born at RAF Hospital, Changi, was Secretary of Lochrin Autos 13th February 1998–18th October 1999.

Isabella's father, James Wilson (born c.1850), was the son of a wine and spirit merchant, who ran a public house in Nicholson Street, Edinburgh. It was adjacent to a building used by travelling circuses and James developed a consuming desire to perform in the circus. His father eventually agreed and James was taken on as a potential flying trapeze artist at the age of eight by Pablo Fanque. James toured with several different circuses throughout Britain, Europe and the United States. He married Agnes née Reid (born c.1861), a provision saleswoman, living at 7 West Russell Street, Glasgow, Lanarkshire, on 2nd June 1884 at St Peter's Church, Braid Street, Glasgow. By then he was a photographer and they lived at 5 Wemyss Place, Glasgow. He was a brewery cellarman in 1891 and later a clerk. They later lived at 14 Johnston Crescent, Dunfermline. In 1918 he was district agent for the *Dundee Courier*, living at Milton Green, Dunfermline.

David enlisted in 1/1st Highland Cyclist Battalion (1420) in August or September 1914. He is understood to have transferred to the Royal Engineers before going to France in 1916 but there are no details of this on his medal index card. He was wounded soon after arrival and spent six weeks in hospital. David was promoted corporal before transferring to 1/5th Highland Light Infantry (43247) in mid-September 1918. **Awarded the VC for his actions at Moeuvres, France on 16th-20th September 1918, LG 23rd October 1918.**

David was appointed acting sergeant soon after the VC action. Amongst many letters of congratulations was one from Harry (later Sir Harry) Lauder, the famous Scottish comedian and singer: *I just wish to be one of the thousands of your countrymen who would like to congratulate you on your courage. You certainly have covered your regiment with undying glory. The days of Wallace and Bruce are not dead, and shall never die while men like you and your comrades stand*

Pablo Fanque, born William Darby (1810–71) in Norwich, England, an equestrian performer and circus proprietor, was the first non-white British circus owner. He is best known for being mentioned in The Beatles song *Being for the Benefit of Mr Kite* on the *Sgt Pepper's Lonely Hearts Club Band* album in 1967.

Harry Lauder (1870–1950) was a Scottish singer and comedian, who achieved international success. Winston Churchill said he 'rendered measureless service to the Scottish race and to the British Empire' Among his most popular songs were *Roamin' in the Gloamin*, *I Love a Lassie* and *The End of the Road*. By 1911 he was the highest paid performer in the world and became the first British artist to sell a million records. He raised enormous amounts of money during the Great War, for which he was knighted in 1919. He wrote *The End of the Road* after the death of his son in action on 28th December 1916. Captain John Lauder was serving with 1/8th Argyll and Sutherland Highlanders and is buried in Ovillers Military Cemetery, near Albert, France (I A 6) (The Scotsman).

*and defend the best cause the world has ever known. Yours in admiration, Harry Lauder, to one of the lamps of civilisation.*

David arrived home on leave on 2nd November. The VC was presented by the King in the ballroom at Buckingham Palace on 16th November. David was presented with a gold watch and a wallet containing War Bonds to the value of £250 by Provost Norval at the Cooperative Hall in Dunfermline on 16th December. His wife was presented with a gold watch and their daughters each received a gold locket. The front of the watch presented to David carried the Dunfermline Coat of Arms and the back was engraved with his initials and *Presented to Sergt David Ferguson Hunter, VC, by the citizens of Dunfermline in recognition of his heroism at Moeuvres on 17th September 1918.* David was discharged from the Army in January 1919. He returned to work at Dean Colliery, Kingseat as a miner and later moved to a mine at Steelend. He was forced to give up mining following an accident and worked as a country postman 1924–51. **Awarded the Imperial Service Medal for twenty-seven years' service with the Post Office, LG 18th December 1951.** David returned to the mines as a storekeeper for five years at Comrie Colliery before retiring.

David served in the Territorial Army with 7th Argyll and Sutherland Highlanders. In October 1938 he was serving

David Hunter when he was a postman.

The Imperial Service Medal was established on 8th August 1902 by King Edward VII for presentation to selected civil servants who completed at least twenty-five years service on retirement. Originally the medal was a seven-pointed star or a laurel wreath for women, in the same pattern as the Imperial Service Order. In 1920 it was changed to its current form of a circular silver medal.

The sinking of Comrie Colliery commenced in 1936 and production started in 1939. It was owned by Fife Coal Company until nationalisation in 1947. There were two shafts, each 130m deep. Important features included forced-fan ventilation, fully mechanised underground transport and skip-winding for raising the coal. The skips came from Germany and, just one week before the outbreak of war, the German engineers were called home with the installation unfinished. The average workforce was 1,245 with a peak of 1,498 in 1963. The colliery closed in 1986 and, with the exception of a few buildings, it was demolished in 1989. A smokeless fuel plant was established in 1964 and by 1983 three-quarters of the mine's output was sold to the South of Scotland Electricity Board.

in 229th Anti-Aircraft Battery, Elgin Street, Dunfermline and retired in 1939, having been awarded the Efficiency Medal. Isabella died in 1937 and David married Elizabeth 'Betsy' Anne Donald Young née Stephen (7th December 1890–23rd December 1970), a school cleaner born at Cross-Roads, Durris, Kincardineshire, on 9th June 1939 at Saline Parish Church, near Dunfermline. She was living at Loch House, Saline at the time. They lived at 40 Haig Crescent, Dunfermline. Betsy had married David Young in 1916 at St Clement, Angus and they had two daughters. She died at Oaklea, Saline, Fife.

Betsy's mother was Mary Ann Imray Stephen (4th July 1870–7th May 1953), a domestic servant born at Backdykes, Durris, Kincardineshire. She married Alexander Milne (13th January 1866–20th July 1952), an agricultural labourer

The Efficiency Medal was instituted on 23rd September 1930 for award to part-time warrant officers, NCOs and men after twelve years efficient service on the active list of the Militia and Territorial Army of the United Kingdom and other auxiliary military forces throughout the Empire. War service counted two-fold. It equates to the Efficiency Decoration for commissioned officers. In the United Kingdom the medal bears a subsidiary title on a scroll bar attached to the medal suspender, 'MILITIA, 'TERRITORIAL' or 'T. & A.V.R' to denote service in the Militia (Supplementary Reserve 1930–51), Territorial Army (1930–67 & 1982–99) or Territorial & Army Volunteer Reserve (1967–82). Clasps were awarded for subsequent completion of further periods of six years efficient service. The medal superseded the Volunteer Long Service Medal, Volunteer Long Service Medal for India and the Colonies, Colonial Auxiliary Forces Long Service Medal, Militia Long Service Medal, Special Reserve Long Service and Good Conduct Medal and the Territorial Efficiency Medal. In the United Kingdom, the medal was superseded by the Volunteer Reserves Service Medal in 1999. In the Commonwealth, the Efficiency Medal was gradually superseded by national medals, although New Zealand continues to award the Efficiency Medal (New Zealand).

born at Culsalmond, Aberdeenshire, on 4th August 1893 at St Paul's, Waverley Hall, Aberdeen. In 1901 they were living at House Bridgefoot, Aberdeenshire. Alexander died at 26 Cornhill Road, Aberdeen and Mary at Woodend Hospital, Northfield Lodge, Aberdeen. They had four children, the first three born at Rayne, Aberdeenshire:

A church was established in Saline before 1249 but the oldest known church building dates from around 1640. That building was demolished after completion of the current church in 1811. Major alterations were made in 1819, 1905 and 1972.

 * Isabella Milne (born 1897) was a twin with Mary.
 * Mary Milne (born 1897) was a twin with Isabella.
 * Jessie Milne (1900–74) never married.
 * William Alexander Milne (28th December 1905–8th June 1963), born at Bridge of Dun, Angus and died at Leith, Midlothian, was a prison warder at Aberdeen, Barlinnie in Glasgow and Perth 1930–61. He married Margret Ann Williamson (5th August 1909–1st March 1989), born at Duncansclate, Burra, Shetland Islands, on 28th December 1931 at Aberdeen. He died at Leith, Midlothian and she at Perth Royal Infirmary.

David became a Freemason and was a Member of the Union Lodge (No.250 Scottish Constitution) Dunfermline, Fife, Initiated on 3rd January 1919, Passed on 6th February and Raised on 3rd May. He was introduced to the King and Queen and the Duke and Duchess of York when they visited Dunfermline on 13th July 1923. David joined the Home Guard during the Second World War, although he does not appear to have qualified for any medals.

On 29th September 1957, he and William Angus VC led a protest march in Blythswood Square, Glasgow demanding the retention of the Highland Light Infantry following the decision to disband it and merge with the Royal Scots Fusiliers. They were joined by 8,000 former members of the Regiment and were watched by 90,000 people. Both VCs made a speech but, despite the protest, the two regiments amalgamated in 1959 to form the Royal Highland Fusiliers.

In January 1962 his twenty-seven year old Morris car failed the roadworthiness test. He needed a car to ferry his wife around

David Hunter (centre) and William Angus at the protest march in Blythswood Square, Glasgow on 29th September 1957.

but did not have the money to purchase a new vehicle. He decided to sell his VC rather than seek charity or take out a loan. His Regiment offered to buy the medal but a car dealer heard of his plight and presented Hunter with a new car instead. Hunter thanked the Regiment for its generous offer and promised to bequeath his decoration to it when he died and this was honoured.

David attended a number of VC reunions – the VC Garden Party at Buckingham Palace on 26th June 1920, the VC Dinner at the Royal Gallery of the House of Lords, London on 9th November 1929, the Victory Day Celebration Dinner & Reception at The Dorchester, London on 8th June 1946, the VC Centenary Celebrations at Hyde Park, London on 26th June 1956 and the first four VC (& GC from 1962) Association Reunions at the Café Royal, London on 24th July 1958, 7th July 1960, 18th July 1962 and 16th July 1964.

David Hunter died following a heart attack at Northern Hospital, Dunfermline on 12th February 1965. The Royal Highland Fusiliers provided a piper and a guard of honour at his funeral on 15th February. John Carmichael VC and John Hamilton VC were amongst the mourners. He is buried in Dunfermline Cemetery, Halbeath Road, Fife (Eastern Division, Grave 7510). His family could not agree on a headstone so none was placed over his grave. On 12th August 2004 a headstone was dedicated in a ceremony organised by the Royal Highland Fusiliers, Mrs Mary Fairbairn of Abercorn Memorials, Edinburgh, and Union Lodge Dunfermline No.250. David is commemorated in a number of other places:

- A bust, commissioned by the Imperial War Museum, London to represent all Scots who were awarded the VC in the Great War, was created by the sculptor Jacob Epstein. It was first displayed at the Royal Academy and later in the

The Dunfermline Poor House at Leys Park was built in 1843. In 1904 it became a hospital and in 1909 a fever hospital. With the creation of the National Health Service in 1948 it came under the West Fife Hospital Board and became the Northern Hospital. It closed in 1985 and since 1988 has been a nursing home. It is a Category B listed building.

130  Victoria Crosses on the Western Front – Battles of the Hindenburg Line

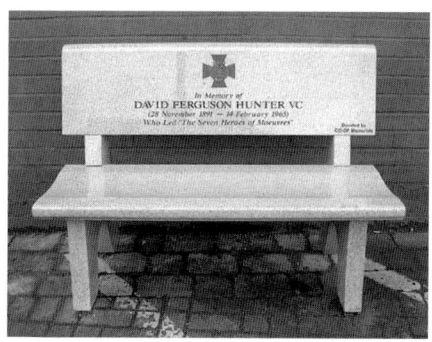

The Memorial bench at Dunfermline Athletic Football Club, East End Park (Memorials to Valour).

David Hunter's gravestone in Dunfermline Cemetery (Memorials to Valour).

Imperial War Museum in the mid-1990s as part of an exhibition commemorating the VC and GC.
- In 1919 the Imperial War Museum commissioned A Neville Lewis to paint a portrait of Hunter in full uniform, kit and VC ribbon. The portrait is still owned by the Imperial War Museum.
- Memorial bench at Dunfermline Athletic Football Club, East End Park, Dunfermline dedicated in March 2017.
- A Department for Communities and Local Government commemorative paving stone was dedicated at East End Park, Dunfermline, Fife on 16th September 2018.
- A bagpipe tune, *The Seven Heroes of Moeuvres*, composed by T Menzies Rodger, was first published in *Logan's Collection of Highland Bagpipe Music* about 1925.

The Royal Highland Fusiliers Museum on Sauchiehall Street, Glasgow.

In addition to the VC he was awarded the British War Medal 1914–20, Victory Medal 1914–19, Imperial Service Medal, George VI Coronation Medal 1937, Elizabeth II Coronation Medal 1953 and Efficiency Medal with 'Territorial' clasp. His medals were presented to the Royal Highland Fusiliers on 2nd April 1965 by his widow. The VC is held by the Royal Highland Fusiliers Museum, 518 Sauchiehall Street, Glasgow.

## 24/213 SERGEANT HENRY JOHN LAURENT
### 2nd Battalion, New Zealand Rifle Brigade

Henry 'Harry' Laurent was born on 15th April 1895 at Tarata, Taranaki, New Zealand. His father, John Martin Laurent (9th February 1867–25th January 1951), a farmer, married Mary Martha née Knofflock (20th February 1876–24th June 1959), born at Inglewood, Taranaki, on 5th January 1895. They were living at Lake Road, Hawera when Harry enlisted. Mary was living with her son, Vivian, at 77 Buckland Avenue, Auckland in 1954. Both John and Mary died in Auckland. Harry had six siblings:

- Eileen Gertrude Martha Laurent (10th October 1896–14th September 1996) married Alexander Hamilton Notman (October 1893–17th November 1954), born in Edinburgh, Scotland, on 12th November 1924. He was a farmer,

The Taranaki region in the west of North Island is dominated by the stratovolcano Mount Taranaki (2,518m), which last erupted in the mid-18th century. Captain James Cook initially named it Mount Egmont after the Earl of Egmont, First Lord of the Admiralty. It very closely resembles Mount Fuji in Japan and was used as the backdrop for the film *The Last Samurai* (2003). The region is exceptionally fertile due to generous rainfall and rich volcanic soil and, as a result, dairy farming predominates. There are also oil and gas reserves, which provide most of New Zealand's gas supply. The area was occupied by Māori tribes from the 13th century and the first contact with Europeans was about 1823. In 1828 Richard Barrett set up a trading post at Ngamotu (now New Plymouth) and settlement began in 1841. European expansion led to conflict when the Māori refused to sell their land. War broke out at Waitara in March 1860 and an uneasy truce negotiated a year later was broken in April 1863 as tensions over land boiled over again. In the Second Taranaki War the army systematically took possession of Māori land and laid waste to villages and cultivations. Behind the advancing troops a line of redoubts was built and settlers built their homes and developed farms. Māori resistance in the area continued until 1869. The confiscations were subsequently acknowledged by the New Zealand Government to be unjust and illegal. Sir Harry Albert Atkinson KCMG (1831–92), Premier of New Zealand four times, was born in Broxton, Cheshire, England and emigrated to New Zealand. He and his brother bought farmland in Taranaki.

working for J Savage, of Ohangai, South Taranaki, when he enlisted in C Company, 1st Battalion, Trentham Regiment, New Zealand Rifle Brigade at Trentham on 28th May 1915 (23/859). He was described as 5' 8" tall, weighing 156 lbs, with fair complexion, blue eyes, light coloured hair and his religious denomination was Presbyterian. He sailed for Suez, Egypt, disembarking on 15th November. He embarked aboard HT *Arcadian* for France on 6th April 1916. On 1st April 1917 he was admitted to hospital with diphtheria. He was admitted to 3rd New Zealand Field Ambulance on 1st November with tonsillitis and transferred to the New Zealand Stationary Hospital next day and to 7th General Hospital on 3rd November. He joined the Base Depot, Étaples on 12th November and rejoined the Battalion on 14th December. Alexander was granted leave in Britain 26th February–13th March 1918. He returned to Britain on 26th December. On 1st February 1919 he embarked aboard SS *Hororata* and was discharged in New Zealand on 12th April 1919. Eileen and Alexander lived at Hawera, South Taranaki and he was a factory manager at Tokaora. Eileen was living at 1 Douglas Street, Waitotara, Taranaki in 1981. They had a son:

High Street, Hawera c.1920 with its distinctive water tower constructed 1912–14. The town currently has a population of about 12,500 and is near the coast of the South Taranaki Bight. A military base was established there in 1866 and the town grew up around it in the early 1870s. The railway arrived in August 1881.

  ○ Bruce Alexander Notman (c.1928–14th March 2014) married Colleen Anne Rae in 1953. He was an engineer in 1954, when they were living at 9 Clifford Street, Hawera and they were still there in 1981. They had at least two children – Debbie Notman and Geoffrey Bruce Notman.
* Maude Constance Elizabeth Laurent (25th April 1898–31st August 1954) married James Wilson (1900–78) in 1937. He was an agent in 1938, when they were living at 26 Clifton Road, Auckland. They had moved to 5 Cadman Avenue, Onehunga by 1946 and to 586 Great South Road, Tamaki by 1949, when he was a mechanic. She died at Greenlane Hospital, Auckland.
* Vivian Allen Laurent (25th August 1899–29th June 1978) was a land agent. He married Gladys Elizabeth Mary Harrison (11th December 1901–4th December 1989), born at Opunake, South Taranaki, on 14th June 1922 at St Mary's Church, Hawera, South Taranaki. He was a cheese factory manager in 1946, when they were living at Netherton, Auckland. He was living on his own at 77 Buckland Avenue, Auckland in 1949. They filed for divorce in the High Court of Auckland

in 1954. Gladys was living with her son, Raymond, at 78a Hinemoa Street, Waikato after the separation and had moved to 27 Bretton Terrace, Waikato by 1957. He died at Greenlane, Auckland. Gladys died at Hamilton. They are buried side by side in Hamilton Park Cemetery, Waikato. They had two children:
  - Elaine Gladys Laurent (23rd December 1923–7th September 2000) was living with her parents in 1946. She married Ernest Gordon Smith (9th March 1921–10th January 1985). He was a confectioner in 1963, when they were living at 23 Allen Street, Morrinsville, Waikato. By 1969 he was a milk bar proprietor and they were living at 15 Osborne Avenue, Morrinsville. Later he was a clerk at Morrinsville and was buried there at Piako Cemetery. They had two children – Leonie Margaret Smith and Raymond Gordon Smith (1952–2008).
  - Raymond John Laurent was a driver in 1949 living at Netherton. He married Marie Isabelle Duthie (12th March 1929–19th October 2016) in April 1953 at St Peter's Cathedral, Hamilton, Waikato. He was a pilot in 1954, when they were living at 78a Hinemoa Street, Waikato. They had three children.
- Newton Laurent (23rd February 1901–18th December 1903).
- Florence Evelyn Laurent (16th November 1903–20 August 1989) married John Edward Pennell (April 1899–31st October 1976) in 1926 and they lived at Takanini, Auckland. He was a cheesemaker in 1942, when they were living at Tawhiti Road, Hawera. They had retired to 111 Ferguson Drive, Thames-Coromandel by 1972. They had a stillborn son in 1927.
- Reginald Martin Laurent (24th May 1910–1st May 1983) married Marjorie Frances Smith (1910–8th January 1991). He was a cheesemaker working for the Co-operative Dairy Co Ltd, Te Kowhai in 1940. He was an executive in 1972, when they were living at 70 Insoll Avenue, Waikato. They had retired to 16 Egmont Street, Waikato by 1981. They had two sons:
  - Martin Roger Laurent.
  - Clinton Reginald Laurent (born July 1948) qualified as a doctor and emigrated to England. He married Carol A Williams in 1975 at St Marylebone, London. He was appointed Director of Global Demographics Ltd, Harrogate, Yorkshire, England on 9th January 2014. They had at least one child – Clara Theau Laurent (1976).

Harry's paternal grandfather, Rudolphe Marie Martin Joseph de St Laurent (25th April 1826–19th July 1919), born in Normandy, France, was a major in the French Army. He married Elizabeth Lucy Scott (14th October 1837–10th June 1921), born at Newcastle upon Tyne, Northumberland, in New Zealand on 1st August 1857. He was naturalised on 17th January 1902. In addition to John they had eleven other children:

- Rudolph Richard Laurent (11th October 1858–17th July 1911) married Delia Rowan/Roughin (c.1860–17th November 1944) on 19th January 1887 at

Wellington. He died in Auckland Hospital. She moved to St Kilda, Victoria, Australia and was living at 56 Mitford Street in 1922, at 77 Argyle Street in 1931 and at 90 Grey Street in 1936. She had moved into St Joseph's Retirement Home, 112B St Georges Road, Northcote, Victoria by 1942. They had five children – Isobel Grace Laurent (1888–2nd April 1928), Leonard Richard Laurent (1889–1955), John Herbert Laurent (31st August 1891–28th April 1965), Rowan Laurent (1892–1910) and Delia Laurent (1896–1972).

- William James Laurent (31st October 1860–30th May 1926) married Mathilde Nicoline Wilde (10th July 1864–18th July 1951), born in Denmark, on 5th September 1886. He was a farmer in November 1916 when they were living at Normanby, Taranaki. He died at Hawera and she at New Plymouth, Taranaki. They had fourteen children:
  - Mathilda Katherine Annie Laurent (9th December 1888–24th October 1966) married August Julius Schneebeli (c.1882–1959) in 1910. They had at least four children – Julia Emalie Mathilda Schneebeli 1911, Frieda Schneebeli 1913, Hugh August Schneebeli 1917 and Ross Julius Schneebeli 1919.
  - Frederick 'Wilfred' Rudolph Karl Laurent (10th January 1889–25th October 1972), a farmer, married Elsie Ann Stinson (1889–1965) in 1913. They had at least three children – Thelma Mavis Laurent 1914, Albert Vernon Laurent 1916 and Delcie Yvonne Laurent.
  - Rose Elizabeth Christina Laurent (17th February 1890–17th June 1967) married Fred Cavendish Starck (1886–28th November 1970) in 1914. They had a daughter – Doris Joy Starck, who married as Whitcombe.
  - Violet Sophia Laurent (21st February 1891–16th August 1938).
  - Harold George Laurent (18th April 1892–25th March 1976) married Coralie Hilda Goddard (1888–1966) in 1917. They had at least two children – Beulah Ellen Laurent 1920 and Cedric George Laurent. Beulah married as Morgan. It is understood that Harold later married Dorothy, as she was his wife when he died.
  - Marie Emma Laurent (1893–1986) married John Gardiner in 1929.
  - Arthur William Laurent (1894–12th July 1970), a piano tuner, married Gertrude Barton (1892–27th February 1983) in 1918. They had a son, Ian Leslie Laurent.
  - Daisy Octavia Laurent (1895–1947).
  - William 'Bill' John Laurent (14th October 1896–20th September 1970). He was a joiner working for Joseph Quinn and living at 83 Glover Road, Hawera when he enlisted in B Company, 23rd Reinforcements on 9th October 1916 (39832). He was serving as a cadet in 11th Regiment Territorials and was described as 5′ 6″ tall, weighing 134 lbs with dark complexion, blue eyes, dark hair and his religious denomination was Methodist. He joined at Trentham on 13th November. He forfeited two days' pay for overstaying his leave 2nd–

4th March 1917. He embarked on HMNZT 79 *Ruapehu* on 14th March, disembarked at Devonport on 21st May and joined the Wellington Company, 4th Reserve Battalion, Sling Camp, Bulford next day. William went to France on 22nd June and joined the New Zealand Infantry & General Base Depot, Étaples next day. He was posted to 11th Company, 3rd Wellington on 9th July. He was wounded on 6th August and was admitted to 4th New Zealand Field Ambulance until discharged to duty on 8th August and rejoined his unit on 17th August. He was wounded by a gunshot to the left thigh and arm on 4th October and was admitted to 3rd New Zealand Field Ambulance and No.3 Australian Casualty Clearing Station. On 6th October he was transferred to 11th General Hospital, Camiers and was evacuated to Britain aboard HMHS *Panama* on 11th October, where he was admitted to No.1 New Zealand General Hospital, Brockenhurst on 14th October. He was transferred to the New Zealand Convalescence Hospital, Hornchurch on 19 October and joined the New Zealand Command Depot, Codford on 28th November. He was on leave until 14th December. He forfeited two days' pay and was fined two days' pay for being absent without leave from Codford from 11.45 p.m. on 22nd February until 7.30 p.m. on 23rd February 1918. William transferred to 3rd Reserve Battalion, Wellington Regiment, 4th New Zealand Infantry Reserve Brigade, Sling Camp, Bulford on 4th March and departed for France on 8th May He joined the New Zealand Infantry & General Base Depot, Étaples on 10th May, No.1 New Zealand Entrenching Battalion on 12th May and transferred to 11th Company, 1st Wellington on 20th July. He was detached to the New Zealand Division Lewis Gun School 11th-24th August and Third Army School 4th-7th October. He was admitted to 2nd New Zealand Field Ambulance with a gunshot wound to the buttock on 8th November and was transferred to 9th (USA) General Hospital, Rouen on 11th November and to 2nd Convalescence Hospital on 13th November. He was attached to the New Zealand Infantry & General Base Depot, Étaples 3rd-21st January 1919 and transferred to Sling Camp, Bulford on 17th February. He embarked at Tilbury aboard HMNZT 82 *Pakeha* on 12th April, disembarked at Wellington on 30th May and was discharged on 27th June 1919. William married Edith Florence Cullen (11th July 1904–9th March 1990) on 18th October 1924. They had three children – Sydney Gordon Spencer Laurent (13th October 1925–3rd July 2011), Brian Rex Laurent (9th January 1927–7th August 2015) and Sylvia Joy Laurent (24th June 1928–21st June 2001). Edith is believed to have left Bill and had a relationship with Patrick Brendan McCarthy (9th September 1906–27th July 1990). They had a daughter, Kay Jocelyn McCarthy (1935–2004). When Bill died his next-of-kin was Mrs MA Laurent, 53 Te Awa Avenue, Napier.

- Herbert Leslie Laurent (11th March 1898–28th November 1971) enlisted on 13th March 1918 (81134). He was described as a farm hand, 5′ 5½″ tall,

weighing 141 lbs, with fair complexion, grey eyes, brown hair and his religious denomination was Church of England. He was posted to F Company, 41st Reinforcements on 22nd May and embarked at Wellington aboard HMNZT 108 *Ulimaroa* on 27th July. He disembarked in London on 4th October and joined the New Zealand Rifle Brigade Reserve Depot, Brocton on 4th October. On 31st January 1919 items lost through no negligence of his own were replaced at public expense. He was admitted to 2nd New Zealand Hospital, Walton-on-Thames with appendicitis on 10th February. He was discharged on leave on 12th June to report to Sling Camp, Bulford, Wiltshire on 26th June. Herbert embarked at London on SS *Mamari* on 3rd July, disembarked at Auckland on 20th August and was discharged on 17th September 1919. He was involved in a motorcycle accident in June 1921, lost the sight in his right eye and had poor vision in the left eye particularly at night. He married Doris Irene Julian (2nd January 1911–2001) in 1937. Herbert attested for service on 17th February 1942 (2/13/1421 and 501255) and entered camp at Trentham on 18th March. He was living at 39 Vogel Street, Hawera at the time and was described as a store barman at the Central Hotel, Hawera, 5′ 5½″ tall, weighing 165 lbs, with fresh complexion, grey eyes, grey hair and his religious denomination was Church of England. He transferred to Wanganui on 14th April and was granted sick leave from 18th April. A medical board graded him IV Permanently Unfit on 24th April and he was discharged at Wellington on 16th July 1942 with defective vision. Herbert was living at 35 Vogel Street, Hawera when he died.
   - Ernest Morton Laurent (7th April 1899–4th October 1982), was a retired piano tuner when he died. He married Hazel Lilian Mildred Beryl Morris (born 1904) in 1924 and they had two sons – Clive William Laurent and Lyall Morris Laurent.
   - May Isobel Laurent (1st May 1900–29th November 1972) married Sofus Poulsen (c.1893–1956) in 1921. He was naturalised in 1925.
   - Elsie Laurent (10th June 1903–30th May 1980).
   - Cyril Henry Laurent (1st August 1907–21st December 1997) married Jane Elizabeth Claridge (1900–15th December 1971) in 1932.
- Edward Antony Laurent (15th November 1863–8th January 1921) married Emma Allen (1st February 1880–1st August 1963) in 1896. They had eleven children:
   - Bertrand Harold Laurent (born 1st October 1896) was a farm hand, working for his father at Eltham, when he enlisted in 3rd Wellington Infantry Regiment NZEF (30381) at Featherston on 21st August 1916. He had served previously in 11th Taranaki Rifles. He was described as 5′ 10½″ tall, weighing 161 lbs with dark complexion, grey eyes, dark brown hair and his religious denomination was Presbyterian. His next of kin was his father living at Mangawhero Road, Eltham. Bertrand was posted to H Company, 20th Reinforcements on 24th August and embarked aboard HMNZT

71 *Port Lyttleton* at Wellington on 7th December. He disembarked at Devonport on 18th February 1917 and joined D Company, 5th Reserve Battalion Rifle Brigade, Sling Camp, Bulford, Wiltshire next day. He joined 4th New Zealand Brigade, Codford, Wiltshire on 30th March and was taken on strength of 3rd Wellington. He embarked for France on 28th May. In 31st May he was admitted to No.53 Casualty Clearing Station with mumps and transferred to 7th General Hospital, St Omer on 1st June. He was discharged to the Base Depot on 19th June and rejoined the Battalion on 24th June. He was promoted lance corporal on 9th September. On 4th October he was wounded by a gunshot to the right leg and was treated at 3rd New Zealand Field Ambulance and No.44 Casualty Clearing Station. On 6th October he was admitted to 18th General Hospital, Camiers and embarked for England aboard HMHS *Newhaven* on 20th October, where he was admitted to the Military Hospital Hampstead. He was transferred to No.2 New Zealand Hospital, Walton-on-Thames on 23rd November and was granted leave 28th November–14th December while at the Convalescence Depot, Hornchurch. Bertrand was on the attached strength of the New Zealand Command Depot, Codford on 3rd January 1918 and was granted leave until 18th January. He joined 4th Reserve Battalion, Wellington Regiment, Sling Camp, Bulford on 14th February. On 25th February he forfeited two days' pay. He was on a Lewis gun course at Hayling Island 2nd-26th April and was appointed temporary corporal on 17th May. He was promoted corporal on 28th November and was sent on another Lewis gun course at Hayling Island on 6th January 1919. On 15th January he was admitted to VAD Hospital 32, Hayling Island with bronchial catarrah and was transferred to No.2 New Zealand Hospital, Walton-on-Thames on 1st February. He was granted leave 19th March–1st April, then reported to Sling Camp. Bertrand was promoted sergeant on 5th April and married Catherine Alice Johnson (9th September 1898–24th September 1984) at St Mary's Church, Walton-on-Thames on 23rd July. She was living at 4 Dale Road, Walton-on-Thames, close to the VAD Hospital. He joined C Group at Torquay on 25th August and embarked aboard HMNZT 94 *Arawa* there on 5th October. He disembarked at Auckland on 15th November and was discharged at Wellington on 14th December 1919. Catherine followed him to New Zealand. She returned to England with her children aboard SS *Ionic* in 1926, arriving at Southampton, Hampshire. Bertrand and Catherine were living at 2 Lovelace Gardens, Walton-on-Thames in 1936. He was boarding at 2 Dudley Road, Walton-on-Thames in 1937 and in 1939 Catherine was living with her children at 9 Cottimore Avenue, Walton-on-Thames. At that time Eunice was an assistant in a draper's shop and Trevor was an apprentice aircraft fitter. Bertrand was not with the family. Catherine was living at Springcroft, 58 Springfield Road, St Leonards-on-Sea, Sussex,

The building of Sling Camp commenced in 1903, but it expanded rapidly once war broke out. By 1916 it had been taken over by New Zealand forces and comprised four main sections – Auckland, Wellington, Otago, and Canterbury Lines. Its main purpose was to train reinforcements and recovering casualties. At the end of the war,

there were 4,600 New Zealand troops there and it became a repatriation centre. The men were eager to return home, but no troopships were available due to overuse during the war and strikes. Eventually the men rioted in frustration and in the aftermath they were put to work carving an enormous Kiwi into the chalk hillside in February and March 1919. Although Sling Camp was removed in the 1920s, the Bulford Kiwi remains to this day. It covers 6,100 m2 and is 130m long. In the post-war years the Kiwi Polish Co maintained it and during the Second World War it was covered over to prevent it being used by enemy aircraft as a navigation marker. In 1948 local Boy Scouts removed the covering and added fresh chalk. Military units then took over the maintenance including the author's own unit, 249th Signal Squadron (AMF(L)), in the 1980s and 90s.

    England at the time of her death there. They had four children, all born in New Zealand and all married in England – Eunice R Laurent (1920–84), Errol Anthony Laurent (1922–2004), Trevor Malcolm Laurent (1924–2000) and Basil J Laurent.
- Muriel Adele Laurent (1897–30th July 1977) married Frederick York Wilson in 1929. They had a daughter, Adele Diane Davies.
- Rudolphe Edward Laurent (January 1899–19th June 1946) married Barbara Maud Taylor (c.1898–1968) in 1925.
- Victoria Marjory Laurent (December 1899–14th May 1900).
- Cecil Laurent (1901–69) married Marguerite Ellen Fake (born 1904) in 1924.
- Albert Victor Laurent (1904–2nd December 1965), was a driver living at Morrisville when he died. He married Kathleen Mary Oxenham (born 1906) in 1927. They had at least two sons – Allen Jack Laurent and Thomas Anthony Laurent.
- Clarence Allen Laurent (born 1909) married Mona Annie Moore (born 1911) in 1938.
- Beryl Olive Laurent (1911–72).
- Valentine Joffre Laurent (1915–2008).
- Laurel Zoe Laurent (12th January 1916–28th February 2004) married Henry Ernest McGlade (born 1916) in 1935.
- June Laurent (born 1918).
• Leonard Francois Laurent (20th October 1864–2nd September 1952) married Anne Sophia London (22nd October 1872–19th December 1957) on 2nd January 1897. They had three children:

- Lenore Frances Lillian Laurent (1901–44) married Reginald Bernasconi Butcher (born 1903) in 1926.
- Florence Iris de St Laurent (1903–78) married Albert James Lydhlam/Lidhlam May (17th February 1896–24th June 1957) in 1924. Albert enlisted at Featherston Camp on 6th March 1916 in the Waikato Mounted Rifles (10862). He was described as a farmer, 5′ 4½″ tall, weighing 128 lbs, with dark complexion, hazel eyes, dark brown hair and his religious denomination was Roman Catholic. His next of kin was his mother, Mrs R May, Massey Street, West Town, New Plymouth. He was serving in the Mounted Territorials and transferred to the New Zealand Cyclist Company on 4th April. He embarked on HMNZT 52 *Makoia* on 6th May and disembarked at Suez, Egypt on 22nd June. He embarked aboard HT *Tunisian* at Alexandria for France on 10th July. He was awarded seven days Field Punishment No.2 for threatening Military Police at Estaires on 30th September. Albert was granted leave to Britain 12th–26th August 1917. On 30th January 1918 the three New Zealand Cyclist Companies became XXII Corps Cyclist Battalion. He was in hospital 7th–12th February and was granted leave in Britain 2nd–20th March. However, he overstayed his leave until 8 a.m. on 21st March for which he was awarded three days Field Punishment No.2, forfeited two days' pay and was placed at the end of the leave roster. He was wounded by a gunshot to the temple on 26th April and was admitted to 63rd Field Ambulance. He was treated at No.2 Canadian Casualty Clearing Station next day and moved by 33 Ambulance Train to 22nd General Hospital, Camiers. On 29th April he was transferred to 6th Convalescence Depot, Camiers and was discharged to the New Zealand Infantry & General Base Depot on 1st May. On 5th May he was admitted to 24th General Hospital with the same wound and was transferred to 6th Convalescence Depot on 30th May. He was discharged to the New Zealand Infantry & General Base Depot on 2nd June, transferred to No.3 New

The New Zealand Prime Minister, William Massey, inspecting the New Zealand Cyclist Corps at Oissy in northern France on 3rd July 1918. The Corps was created in March 1916 with recruits training to join the Mounted Rifles. Intended as mobile infantry, when the cyclists arrived in France in July 1916 they had little to do due to the stationary nature of trench warfare. As a result they spent much of the war controlling traffic, laying cables and repairing trenches. In early 1918 the New Zealand Cyclist Corps did fight as infantry, taking part in the Battle of the Lys in April and offensive actions in the Second Battle of the Marne in July and August (New Zealand History).

Zealand Entrenching Battalion on 16th June and rejoined XXII Corps Cyclist Battalion on 16th August. The unit became the New Zealand Cyclist Battalion in September. On 16th January 1919 Albert was admitted to 1/2nd London Field Ambulance with impetigo and rejoined his unit on 5th February. He embarked aboard SS *Rimutaka* at Plymouth on 5th April, disembarked in New Zealand on 29th May and was discharged on 25th June 1919.
- Raymond Gerald Paris Laurent (1907–71).

- George Robert Laurent (4th June 1869–26th August 1933) married Edith Emily Smith (3rd October 1879–11th December 1959). They had eleven children – Myrtle May Laurent (1903–16), Manu Inez Laurent (1905–34), Rudolphe William Laurent (1907–77), Inez Adele Laurent (1908–2001), George Laurent (1910–11), Allan Laurent (1912–91), Leonard George Laurent (1913–88), Edith Esme Laurent (1916–69), Bernardt Laurent (1917–85), Thelma Laurent (born 1918) and Myrtle Amonica Laurent (born 1920), who married Harold James Kelly in 1940.
- Mary Katherine Laurent (13th July 1871–10th February 1873).
- Madeline Anne Marie Laurent (17th August 1873–6th December 1963) married Carr Fenning Dowman (13th June 1874–17th September 1945) on 7th July 1903. They had four children:
  - Rudolphe William Carr 'Bill' Dowman (1904–2000) married Evelyn Ada Roberts in 1928.
  - Avis Madeline Sarah Jane Dowman (1st June 1906–27th July 1907).
  - Violet Goldsmith Dowman (born 1911) married Nelson Gordon in 1934.
  - Dorothy Emma Eveline Noreen Mary Dowman (born 1917).
- Elizabeth Lucy Martin Laurent (21st March 1875–28th December 1963) married Frederick George Smith (18th August 1873–5th April 1945). They had four children:
  - Eleanor Catherine Collister Smith (1st January 1899–26th July 1985) married William John Bethell (18th March 1898–13th July 1969), born in Birmingham, England, on 21st October 1925 at Whitley Memorial Church, New Plymouth. They had five children – Helen Lucy Bethell 1927, Nolia Winifred Bethell 1930, Enid Norma Joy Bethell 1933, David John Bethell 1935 and Margaret Eleanor Bethell 1942. They lived at 92 Campbell Street, Palmerston North and by 1969 had moved to 27 Elstree Avenue, Glen Innes. William joined the Junior Cadets in 1910 and the Senior Cadets, Territorial Force in 1917. He was a farm manager for WG Bethell when he enlisted in E Company, 41st Reinforcements on 13th March 1918 (81074). He was called up on 22nd May and entered camp next day. His next of kin was his mother, Mrs Nellie Bethell, Post Office, Mangorei, Taranaki. William embarked aboard HMNZT 108 *Ulimaroa* at Wellington on 27th July, disembarked in London and joined 3rd Reserve Battalion, Wellington Regiment, Sling

Camp, Bulford, Wiltshire on 4th October. He was admitted to Tidworth Military Hospital with rubella on 29th November and was discharged on 10th December. He embarked aboard HMAT D34 *Port Hacking* at Liverpool on 4th July 1919, disembarked in New Zealand on 20th August and was discharged on 18th September 1919. William had a military medical on 24th June 1940 and was described as 6′ 3¾″ tall, weighing 189 lbs, with fair complexion, grey eyes and dark hair. He was found to be Grade II temporarily unfit for Home Defence. He enlisted in 10th Company, National Military Reserve on 17th September 1940 (2/22/131 and 550161). He was mobilised with 14th Battalion, National Reserve, entered camp on 14th January 1942 and transferred to 2nd Battalion, Taranaki Regiment on 29th January. He was classified Grade I by a medical board on 1st October and was appointed temporary lance corporal on 25th November. He was on sick leave 17th–21st May 1943 and transferred to the RNZAF on 9th June but was not selected and returned to the Base Depot on 11th June, where he joined the Camp Staff Linton on 1st July. Appointed temporary corporal Camp Police on 1st September and was also employed variously as a storeman, men's mess kitchen hand and on general duties with the Camp QM. He reverted to the ranks on 6th July 1944 and transferred to 5th Motor Transport Workshops as a bodybuilder on 2nd October. He transferred to the strength of Workshops, Trentham on 1st April 1945 but remained at Showgrounds. He was fined 10/- for exceeding the speed limit on 4th May. On 31st May he transferred to Ordnance No.2 Sub Depot, Palmerston North and to 35th Army Troops Salvage Company on 11 December. He was appointed temporary lance corporal on 7th January 1946 and was on sick leave at home 4th–16th July. Appointed temporary corporal on 14th August and transferred to the Interim Army on 11th September. He joined the Construction Company RNZE on 31st January 1947 and was appointed temporary sergeant on 3rd March. He was discharged on 31st March 1948 and enlisted in the New Zealand Regular Force at Petone on 1st April for one year as a sapper on probation (32321). He was a qualified carpenter and welder. Promoted sergeant on 1st September. He was attached to 10th Coastal Regiment RNZA on a number of occasions. His service was extended for two years on 1st April 1949, one year on 1st April 1951, three years on 1st April 1952 and one year on 1st April 1955, 1956 and 1957. On 3rd December 1950 he lacerated his left thumb while sharpening scissors at Linton Camp and was treated at Palmerston North Hospital. He returned to duty on 18th December. He was admitted to Palmerston North Hospital 1st–15th August, 27th–29th August and 10th–12th September 1951 with septic arthritis in the right wrist caused by a nail wound on 1st August. He was granted sick leave 15th–27th August, was convalescent at home 29th August–10th September and was on sick leave again until 3rd January 1952.

On 12th March he applied for the post of range warden due to his injured wrist and was transferred from the RNZE to the New Zealand Regiment on 24th June for employment as a range warden at HQ Linton. He lost his spectacles while fighting a fire in Block 1, Linton Camp on 18th February 1953, when another hose swept them away. On 18th December he claimed replacement British War and Victory Medals which had been lost in a house fire at Inglewood in 1927. He was to be involved in the royal visit and needed to wear the medals. The British War Medal was issued in January 1954 but he had no entitlement to the Victory Medal as he had never served in an operational theatre. He was admitted to Palmerston North Hospital for a haemorrhoidectomy on 10th August 1954 and was on sick leave until 12th September. A medical examination on 3rd February 1955 graded him for Home Service only, as did all medicals thereafter. He reverted to corporal/acting sergeant on 1st April 1957 and was discharged on 12th May 1958.
- George Frederick Smith (born 8th May 1900).
- Robert Cecil Smith (10th June 1901–1978) married Delina Miriam Poletti (c.1903–47) in 1929.
- Godfrey Lance Smith (born 12th July 1902) married Amelia Frances Batter in 1927.

• Charles Frederick Laurent (13th June 1877–15th November 1966) married Annie Parrish (19th October 1891–October 1985) on 26th December 1911. They had at least two children:
- Grace Elizabeth Annie Laurent (1912–99) married Albert Jones in 1932.
- Ruth Mavis Margaret Laurent (5th April 1914–1976) married William Henry Ellis Reynolds in 1935.

• Wilhelmina Jane Laurent (17th August 1879–7th March 1966) married Frank Lambert (11th March 1876–15th October 1958) on 24th October 1901 at Tarata, Taranaki. They had nine children:
- William Archie Lambert (30th January 1903–24th January 1970) married Gertrude Dodunski (born 1906) in 1929.
- Elizabeth Flora 'Cissie' Lambert (10th February 1904–26th September 1973) married James Thomson Humphrey (1900–67), born at Dennistoun, Scotland, in 1930.
- Beatrice 'Trixie' Victoria Lambert (13th July 1905–2nd April 1986) married Stephen Arthur Couchman (c.1891–1968) in 1928.
- Violet Frances Minnie Lambert (born and died 1908).
- Minnie Vera Violet Katherine Lambert (1909–27th August 1935) married Ivo Spiers Southcombe (1909–68) in 1933. Ivo married Gwendolyn Isabel O'Mahony in 1938.
- Herman Joseph Lambert (4th July 1910–14th April 1983) married Sylvia May Heal in 1933.
- Frances Mavis Lambert (17th September 1912–2003).

- Rudolph Isaac Lambert (7th May 1914–13th August 1980).
- Alexander George Leslie Lambert (31st December 1919–13th August 1982).
• Sarah Evelyn Laurent (4th November 1883–30th August 1982) married Herbert Luke Hogg (1875–August 1961), an engineer born at Stockton, Co Durham, England, on 26th January 1902. They had six children:
    - Evelyn Louisa Elizabeth Hogg (1903–28) married Albert Roy Schon in 1923. Albert married Violet Rebecca Morris (c.1902–49) in 1930.
    - John Etienne Hogg (31st July 1904–11th June 1964) married Vera Lillian Hawkey (1907–55) in 1926.
    - Florence Adeline Annie Hogg (9th September 1905–1988) married Selwyn Alfred Marryatt (1903–58) in 1926.
    - Charles Lorenza Hogg (1907–83) married Ivy Ellen Colbourne in 1928.
    - Oswald Benson Hogg (17th April 1909–14th November 1998) married Jean May Macintosh (born 1915) in 1935.
    - Raymond Claude Hogg (born 1913).

The marriage ended in divorce. Herbert married May Florence Dive (1889–9th September 1965) in 1929. They were living at 82 Karaka Street, Castlecliff, Taranaki in 1957. Sarah had a relationship with John Clayton Rowe (6th March 1889–25th June 1978). He was a carpenter, described as 6′ tall, of slight build, with sallow complexion, fair hair and grey eyes. He was issued with a warrant by the police in 1927 for failing to comply with the terms of a maintenance order for the support of his two children in the sum of £8/17/-. The debt was cleared on 11th January 1928. John and Sarah (recorded as Mrs Hogg) were living at Smart Road, Fitzroy, Taranaki in 1928. By 1946 they were living as man and wife at 19 Dawson Street, Taranaki. By 1963 he was a foreman and they were living at 1 Ferner Avenue, Mount Albert, Auckland. Sarah and John had two children – Clayton McDonald Rowe (2nd March 1924–1998) and Marcia Jewell Rowe (1925–30th June 2002). John had married Ellen 'Dolly' Myrtle Feakins (5th January 1891–31st March 1983) on 17th May 1910 at Lepperton, New Plymouth. He was living at Lepperton in 1919. They either divorced or he deserted Ellen, who never remarried and lived the rest of her life at 28 Newton Street, New Plymouth. John and Dolly had seven children – Nellie Margaret Hellier Rowe (1910–97), Noel John Rowe (1911–91), James McDonald Rowe (1913–16)), Norman Bernard Rowe (born 1916), Dermot James Rowe (born 1917), Kenneth Victor Rowe (1918–94) and Monica Noeline Rowe (1921–83).

His maternal grandfather, August Friedrich 'Fred' Knofflock (1850–15th September 1924), born at Lauenberg, Pommern, Germany married Wilhemine 'Minnie' Louise Charlotte née Bohl (1852–5th December 1945), born at Felstrom, Lauenberg, on 5th December 1872 at Bresin, Lauenberg. They emigrated to New Zealand in May 1874 because of religious persecution. On arrival at Wellington, they transferred to SS *Taranaki* for onward travel to New Plymouth and settled at Inglewood. He

Lauenburg (now Lębork) in northwest Poland was founded on the site of a Polish settlement dating back to the 10th century. It was Germanized to Lewin and then Lewinburg by the Teutonic Knights after annexation from Poland in 1310. In 1440 the town joined the Prussian Confederation. In the Thirteen Years War, which broke out in 1454, Lauenburg remained loyal to the Prussian Confederation and not the Teutonic Order. Troops from the Polish city of Gdańsk (Danzig) reoccupied Lauenburg in 1459 and were replaced by Teutonic Knights the following year. After the Teutonic Knights were defeated, Lębork passed to Poland. The Protestant Reformation
was introduced in 1519 and the Counter-Reformation was largely ineffective in the Lutheran town. Lębork was occupied by the Swedes in the Northern Wars and it passed to Brandenburg–Prussia in 1657. Swedish troops burnt it down before retreating. In 1701, Lauenburg became a Prussian territory under the sovereignty of the Polish Crown and in the 1773 Treaty of Warsaw full sovereignty was granted to Prussia. Lauenburg developed as an industrial centre after 1852, when it was connected to Danzig and Stettin (Szczecin) by rail. The town became part of Germany in 1871. New German settlers came to the town, but Poles still lived there and maintained their language, culture and identity. Poland regained independence in 1918 but the town remained in Germany and many Poles moved to Poland. When the Nazis took power, Poles and Jews were persecuted and this intensified after the outbreak of the Second World War, when a concentration camp was established at Lauenburg. The town was occupied by the Red Army on 10th March 1945 and most of the Old Town was burned in the subsequent Soviet rampage. As Lębork, the town came under Polish administration in the post-war Potsdam Agreement. Germans were immediately expelled or allowed to leave voluntarily in the 1950s and were replaced by Polish citizens.

farmed on Bristol Road and she became the local midwife despite never mastering English. He was naturalised on 17th November 1881. He died at New Plymouth and she at Hamilton, Waikato. In addition to Mary they had thirteen other children:

- Auguste Berth 'Bertha' Knofflock (21st January 1872–11th February 1956), born at Kattschow, Lauenberg and died in Auckland. She married James Gordon Hendry (2nd January 1871–6th December 1948), a baker born in London, England, in New Zealand in 1891. They were living in New Plymouth in 1896. Bertha and James had four children:
  ○ James David Hendry (born 24th October 1891) married Lucy Evelyn/Eveleen Barriball (24th March 1894–24th July 1971) on 16th July 1913 at Hamilton. James was a driver in 1914, when they were living at Clemow Road, Fitzroy, Taranaki. They had two children – Rowe-Allan James Hendry (22nd March 1914–4th November 1991) and Gwendolyne/Gwendoline Lorraine Hendry (30th June 1916–2001). James and Lucy divorced in 1923. Lucy married James Pakurangi Alley (July 1888–24th May 1953), born at Thames, New Zealand, in 1930. He had married Stella Inglis (born July 1898) and had a daughter, Patricia. Lucy later married John Frederick

Munro (11th March 1897–26th December 1976), a blacksmith. They were living at 24 Kensington Avenue, Balmoral, Auckland at the time of her death there.
- Frederick Hendry (born and died 1892).
- Rowe Allen Gordon Hendry (7th September 1893–22nd April 1963) married Ella Louisa Willis on 4th September 1915 and they had at least two children – Norma Mary Ella Hendry 1916 and Victor Raymond Hendry 1918. He worked for the Post Office and they lived at 32 Calliope Road, Devonport, Auckland. Rowe enlisted on 16th June 1917 at Hamilton, New Plymouth (62204). He was described as a clerk with the Post & Telegraph Department, 5′ 4½″ tall, weighing 129 lbs, with dark complexion, blue eyes, dark hair and his religious denomination was Church of England. He was serving with the Post & Telegraph Corps as a sergeant at the time. He joined 33rd Specialist Company at Trentham on 26th July and transferred to 36th Reinforcements as a corporal on 25th August. He transferred to D Company, 37th Reinforcements on 3rd January 1918, 39th Reinforcements on 16th February and Instructional Staff as a corporal on 28th February. He transferred to D Company, 40th Reinforcements on 5th April, to D Company, 39th Reinforcements on 28th April, to 43rd Reinforcements on 5th June, to 45th Reinforcements on 22nd June, to 46th Reinforcements on 5th July, to E Company, 46th Reinforcements on 28th August and A Company, 48th Reinforcements on 13th September. He was sent on leave without pay until further orders when the training camps were demobilised on 18th November 1918. Discharged on 13th February 1919. Rowe and Ella were living at 38 Union Street, Palmerston North when he enlisted at Palmerston North on 17th December 1940 (816125). He was described as a postal supervisor, 5′ 5¾″ tall, weighing 136 lbs, with bright complexion, blue eyes and brown hair. He was found fit for garrison duties in the tropics. He gave his date of birth as 7th September 1893 and his wife was living Ella Louisa Hendry, 38 Union Street, Palmerston North. Rowe joined 12th Company, National Military Reserve on New Zealand Temporary Service at Palmerston North. He entered camp on 19th January 1942 and was serving with 3rd Battalion, Wellington West Coast Regiment on 22nd April. James transferred to the Home Guard on 12th August and was discharged in Wellington on 4th October 1942 to 165 Cook Street, Palmerston North.
- Isabella Ida Lena/Iderlena Hendry (1895–4th March 1927) married Arthur Edward de Cudray Tronson (2nd March 1889–3rd November 1962), born at Waipawa, at Hamilton on 15th July 1913. It is assumed that they divorced as Isabella married John Arthur Vernon Irving (1872–1928) on 24th August 1920. Arthur married Genevieve Ethel Tronson and had a son, Melville Leslie Tronson, with Genevieve in 1920. Melville was living at 33 Valley Road, Mount Eden, Auckland in November 1962. Arthur attested at

Trentham on 20th January 1916 and was discharged from Featherston on 26th February medically unfit for service with a broken wrist. He attested again on 28th September and enlisted on 17th October (38616). He was described as a carpenter, working for M McRay at Te Kuiti, 5′ 7½″ tall, weighing 156 lbs, with dark complexion, blue eyes, brown hair and his religious denomination was Church of England. His next of kin was his wife living at 87 Apu Crescent, Lyall Bay, Wellington until they divorced and he nominated his brother living at 30 Marine Parade, Napier. He declared one dependent child and previous service in the Ranfurly Rifles, Napier. He was posted to J Company, 22nd Reinforcements on 17th October and was promoted corporal on 2nd November and sergeant on 20th December. Arthur absented himself without leave from 22nd January until apprehended by the military police on 8th March in Christchurch. He reverted to private on 21st March and transferred to J Company, 24th Reinforcements on 3rd April. A District Court Martial at Trentham on 28th May found him not guilty of desertion but of absence and of losing clothing and equipment by neglect. He was sentenced to eighty-four days detention and stoppage of pay. He embarked on HMNZT 86 *Maunganui* at Wellington on 12th June and was released from detention aboard on 19th July. He disembarked at Devonport on 16th August and joined D Company, 5th Reserve Battalion, New Zealand Rifle Brigade at Tidworth. He was admitted to 3rd New Zealand General Hospital, Codford from Sling Camp with a sprained ankle on 13th September and was discharged to the New Zealand Command Depot, Codford on 22nd October. He was re-admitted to 3rd New Zealand General Hospital with haemorrhoids on 14th November, transferred to the Venereal Disease Section next day and forfeited a day's pay for failing to attend a vaccination treatment on 27th December. Arthur was discharged from the VD Section on 8th January 1918 and joined the New Zealand Command Depot, Codford on 15th January. He was admitted to 3rd New Zealand General Hospital with haemorrhoids again 22nd–26th January. He was admitted to 1st New Zealand General Hospital, Brockenhurst on 29th January and was discharged to leave on 27th March to report to Torquay on 4th April. He forfeited three days' pay and was confined to barracks for three days for being absent from 4 p.m. on 17th April until 3.15 p.m. on 19th April. He was classified medically unfit on 20th April, embarked at Liverpool on HMNZT 100 *Ulimaroa* on 1st May and disembarked in New Zealand on 14th June. Arthur was granted sick leave 15th–21st June and was discharged no longer physically fit for war service due to chronic constipation on 12th July 1918.

Bertha and James divorced. She married Harry Hopkinson (c.1873–12th April 1950), a blacksmith, in 1903. They were living at Mahoe Street, Waikato in 1935. Harry had married Clara Jonette Jacobsen (22nd June 1878–19th May 1902) on

23rd May 1895 and they had four children – Ellen Marjorie Hopkinson (1897–1975), Charles Henry Hopkinson (1898–1959), Alice Hopkinson (born and died 1899) and Alfred Hopkinson (born and died 1901). James Hendry married Elizabeth Kirk (born 1881) in 1904 at Christchurch and they had a daughter, Tesla Alice Hendry, in 1905.

- Otto Herman Knofflock (10th January 1874–15th October 1962), a farmer born at Perlin, Lauenberg, married Rose Evelyn Parsons (23rd June 1879–7th November 1972), born at Barrow-in-Furness, Lancashire, England, on 11th December 1901. They were the first couple to be married in the newly built Wesleyan Church, Tataraimaka. They lived at Westown, where he was later a nurseryman for Duncan & Davies Ltd. He died at New Plymouth. They had five children:
  - Norman William Knofflock (2nd October 1902–27th December 1998) was a farmer living at Urenui. He married Dorothy Joan Oxenham in 1937.
  - Edith Evelyn Knofflock (1st January 1903–18th September 1991) was a nurse in a private hospital at Hawera and was also a dressmaker. She later set up the Selfit School of Dressmaking in Douglas Street. She never married.
  - Nora Mary Knofflock (8th February 1905–3rd February 1979) never married.
  - Matilda Wilhemine Knofflock (16th August 1906–10th September 1984) married Claude Hellier in 1933.
  - Edward Otto Knofflock (10th May 1908–6th October 1998) married Frances Rose Field (c.1910–69) in 1934.
- Matilda Wilhemina Eliza 'Tilly' Knofflock (20th April 1878–11th May 1910), born at Inglewood, married William Hancox (15th July 1874–21st October 1916), born at Invercargill, on 10th December 1900. Matilda died at Stratford Hospital, Inglewood. They had three sons:
  - Ernest Edward Hancox (21st June 1901–13th April 1978).
  - Harry William James Hancox (17th July 1905–1st May 1983).
  - Frederick George Alfred Hancox (7th May 1907–23rd September 1969) served as a driver in the New Zealand Army Service Corps (42271).

William married Jessie Moffett (21st June 1888–26th October 1972) on 4th January 1911 at Stratford. They had two children – William Harold Hancox (1912–88) and Clifford Arnold John Hancox (1915–85). Jessie married Carl Woisin (1886–1925) in February 1921 and they had four children – twins Clara Phillis Woisin (1921–2010) and Jessie Woisin (1921–2012), Nellie Doreen Woisin (1923–90) and William Woisin (born and died 1925). Carl had married Ethel Williams (1895–1920) in 1915 and they had four children – Vernon Carl Woisin (21st August 1916–17th August 1942), Ella Ruby Woisin (1917–2008), Ina Merle Woisin (1918–2010) and Doris Ethel Woisin (1920–89). Vernon served as a lance corporal in the New Zealand Infantry (24385) and was a prisoner of war aboard the Italian ship *Nino Bixio* when she was torpedoed by the submarine, HMS *Turbulent*, off Greece. Of the 3,200 prisoners of war aboard, about 200 died

(118 New Zealanders) including Vernon (Phaleron War Cemetery, Greece – 13 B 4). The ship was towed to Pylos, Greece and beached. Ironically, after the war *Nino Bixio* made several trips to New Zealand.
- Robert Wilhelm/William 'Bob' Knofflock (18th May 1879–4th June 1963) was a labourer in 1914, living at Eltham. He married Annie Brew (8th June 1898–11th October 1985) in 1920. They had two daughters – Dorothy Joan Knofflock 1922 and Patricia Nancy Knofflock 1926.
- Edward 'Richard Ted' Knofflock (23rd October 1880–27th July 1968) was a labourer living at Whangamomona in 1954.
- Ernst Reinhold 'Ernie' Knofflock (28th June 1881–22nd October 1963) was a bushman, working for Mr McKenner at Whangamomona, New Plymouth, when he enlisted in B Company, 10th Reinforcements at Trentham on 15th November 1915 (10/3927). He gave his name as Ernest and his date of birth as 28th July 1883. He was described as 5′ 10″ tall, weighing 180 lbs, with fair complexion, blue eyes, reddish brown hair and his religious denomination was Anglican. He embarked on 5th March 1916, disembarked at Suez, Egypt on 10th April and embarked aboard HMT *Kildonan Castle* at Port Said for France on 13th April. He joined the New Zealand Infantry and General Base Depot, Étaples on 24th April and 11th Taranaki Company, 1st Wellington on 24th May. He was awarded twenty-one days' Field Punishment No.2 for neglecting to obey an order on 9th December. He was awarded twenty-eight days' Field Punishment No.2 and forfeited three days' pay for being absent without leave from 9 p.m. on 26th February to 9 p.m. on 28th February 1917. Ernest was granted leave to Britain 16th–28th October. He was detached to 3rd Canadian Tunnelling Company on 9th November. On 15th January 1918 he was admitted to 3rd East Lancashire Field Ambulance with scabies and rejoined the Battalion on 10th February. He was admitted to No.63 Casualty Clearing Station on 13th February and 55th General Hospital, Boulogne with boils on the knee and leg on 5th March. He was transferred to 12th Convalescence Depot on 12th March, to the Base Depot on 26th April and rejoined the Battalion on 11th May. Ernest was wounded by a gunshot to the chest on 17th May and was admitted to 1st New Zealand Field Ambulance. He was transferred to No.56 Casualty Clearing Station on 18th May and 10th General Hospital, Rouen on 19th May. On 21st May he was evacuated to Britain aboard HMHS *St David* and was admitted to the New Zealand General Hospital, Brockenhurst on 23rd May. A medical board on 4th July classified him unfit for service. He was discharged on 12th July to report to the New Zealand Discharge Depot, Torquay on 25th July. He was confined to barracks for seven days for being absent without leave from 11 p.m. on 16th July to 6.30 p.m. on 17th July. He was confined to barracks for seven days for being absent without leave from 8 p.m. on 25th July to 11.15 a.m. on 26th July. He was awarded seven days' detention, but was not held in custody, for being absent from defaulters' parade 1.30–9.30 p.m. on 17th and 18th August. He embarked on RMS *Remuera*

at Liverpool on 7th September and was admitted to the isolation hospital aboard on 14th October. His pay was deducted by £-/4/11 for losing a pair of puttees on 18th October. He disembarked in New Zealand on 22nd October. He forfeited eight days' pay for absenting himself without leave from 10 p.m. on 24th December until 10.30 a.m. on 31st December. On 21st January 1919 he was discharged at Wellington no longer physically fit for war service due to a gunshot wound and syphilis. He was living in retirement on Moa Street, Inglewood in 1954 and died at New Plymouth.

- Theodore Bernhardt/Bernard 'Teeda' Knofflock (1st August 1883–22nd January 1961), a farmer, married Ethel May Rowe (1st March 1888–10th March 1974) on 24th August 1910. In retirement they lived at Junction Road, Inglewood. They had three children:
    - Elma 'Alma' May Knofflock (1st December 1912–14th June 1994) married Richard Charles Watson in 1933.
    - Sylvia Alice Knofflock (27th April 1920–25th October 2006) married as Charteris.
    - Roy Vincent Knofflock (26th November 1926–2000).
- Frederick August 'Fred' Knofflock (7th September 1884–16th September 1954) married Ivy Annie Miles (4th December 1889–2nd August 1972) in 1912. They were living at Lincoln Road, Inglewood in 1941. She was living with her son Keith and his wife in 1972. Ivy and Frederick had five children:
    - Violet Annie Knofflock (12th November 1914–10th February 2004) married Gordon Joseph Sattler in 1937.
    - Gordon Charles Knofflock (14th March 1916–30th November 1941) was serving in 21st Battalion, New Zealand Infantry (62834) when he was killed in action at Sidi Rezegh, Libya (Knightsbridge War Cemetery, Acroma, Libya – 6 D 5).
    - Mary Norah Knofflock (born 1918).
    - Margaret Joan Knofflock (1920–27th September 2015).
    - Keith Alfred Knofflock (31st August 1923–2003), a herd tester, married Joan Barbara Adlam (11th November 1930–21st October 1974). They lived at 26 James Street, Inglewood.
- Carl Wilhelm Knofflock (8th May 1886–10th August 1975) was a labourer working for Mr Hickey at Opunake when he enlisted in the New Zealand Medical Corps at Hawera on 20th March 1917 as Carl Lewis Knofflock (3/3786). His date of birth in various documents in his service record is given as 28th May 1885 and 1888. He had six months previous service in the Volunteers and was described as 5' 9½" tall, weighing 175 lbs, with fresh complexion, blue eyes, fair hair and his religious denomination was Church of England. He transferred to Featherston on 20th October, Awapuni on 9th November and Trentham on 17th December. Carl embarked aboard HMNZT 99 *Athenic* with 33rd Reinforcements on 31st December and disembarked at Glasgow on 25th February 1918. He joined the

Medical Corps Reserve Battalion at Sling Camp, Bulford on 26th February, the Reserve Depot, Ewshott on 28th February and was attached to the New Zealand Medical HQ, London on 23rd April. He rejoined the Depot at Ewshott on 5th May and was promoted lance corporal on 16th June. When he went to France on 26th September he reverted to the ranks. He joined the New Zealand Infantry and General Base Depot, Étaples on 29th September, 3rd Entrenching Battalion on 1st October and 1st New Zealand Field Ambulance on 3rd October. He joined 2nd New Zealand Field Ambulance on 15th February 1919, returned to Britain on 11th March and joined at Codford on 17th March. He transferred to Sling Camp on 14th May and embarked aboard SS *Briton* at Tilbury on 17th June. Carl disembarked in New Zealand on 24th July and was discharged on 20th August 1919. He married Eileen Venus Robertson (8th May 1904–7th October 1989) on 30th March 1929. They lived at Rimu Street, Inglewood. He was a resident at Rangimarie Home, Taranaki in 1972 and subsequently died there. They had four children including – Terence 'Terry' Caleb Knofflock (1927–99), Ross David Knofflock (25th May 1934–1977) and D'Arcy Baden Knofflock (born 26th January 1941).

- Emma Louisa 'Em' Knofflock (28th July 1887–1st April 1987) married Noble King (25th August 1884–26th June 1939), a cabinetmaker, on 26th January 1910. They were living at James Street, Inglewood in 1914 and at 28 Elliott Street, Inglewood by 1928. They had four children:
  - Cecil Noble King (2nd July 1910–19th January 1911).
  - Victor Roy King (6th September 1911–18th December 1982).
  - Lionel Stanley King (9th January 1914–4th March 1993) married Nancy Isabel Wilton in 1940.
  - Iris May King (15th May 1916–23rd September 1992) married Victor Lennard Reynolds (born 1917) in 1940.
- Edith 'Edie' Elizabeth Knofflock (25th April 1890–9th June 1966) married William Sutton McSweeney (1889–3rd August 1952), a butcher born at Opunake, in 1913. They were living at Ruataniwha Street, Waipukurau, Hawke's Bay in 1935 and 41 South Street, Palmerston North, Manawatu-Wanganui by 1946. They had at least four children:
  - Lyna Frances McSweeney (1914–91) married Herbert Cecil Bodell (born 1911) in 1935.
  - William Ian Hamilton McSweeney (1915–89).
  - Frederick William McSweeney (1916–62) married Joan Leslie Fowler (born 1918) in 1939.
  - Elma Edith McSweeney (1916–83) married Lloyd William Lean (born 1907) in 1937.
- Wilhelm Albert Knofflock (1st April–2nd October 1892).
- Richard 'Dick' Albert Knofflock (24th September 1894–28th June 1983) was a farm hand in 1914, living at Bristol Road, Inglewood.

Harry was educated at Hawera District High School, Tarata, Taranaki and worked in a cheese factory. He enlisted in the Taranaki Rifles, a Territorial unit, on 1st March 1911. He enlisted in the NZEF on 28th May 1915, described as an engineer, 5′ 5½″ tall, weighing 140 lbs, with fair complexion, blue eyes, auburn hair and his religious denomination was Presbyterian. He was posted to A Company, 2nd Battalion, Trentham Regiment and sailed for Egypt aboard HMNZT 33 *Navua* on 9th October with 2nd Battalion, 3rd New Zealand (Rifle) Brigade. He disembarked on 18th November. He moved to Ismailia on 17th January 1916 and was admitted to the New Zealand General Hospital, Abbassia on 28th January with an auricular haemorrhage and rejoined the Battalion at Ismailia on 20th March. He embarked at Alexandria for France on 6th April and was wounded on 1st October on the Somme. He was admitted to XV Corps Main Dressing Station and No.38 Casualty Clearing Station and was transferred to No.1 Canadian General Hospital, Étaples the following day. He was transferred to 3rd Convalescence Depot, Étaples on 13th October, to the New Zealand Infantry & General Base Depot on 16th October and rejoined the Battalion on 22nd October.

Harry was detached to 2nd Anzac Reinforcement Camp on 9th October 1917 and rejoined the unit on 20th October. He was promoted lance corporal 21st October, corporal 6th November and sergeant on 24th November. He was granted leave in England 16th–31st January 1918 and was detached to IV Corps Bombing School 5th–25th July. **Awarded the VC for his actions at Gouzeaucourt, France on 12th September 1918, LG 15th November 1918.** He was nominated by the GOC for officer training and was posted to No.13 Officer Cadet Battalion, Newmarket on 22nd October, joining on 8th November. He was granted leave 18th December–6th January 1919. On 14th February 1919 Harry was commissioned and transferred to B Group, Codford on 17th February. He was granted leave until 3rd March, which included the VC investiture by the King in the ballroom of Buckingham Palace on 26th February. Harry had a medical for leaving the service at Codford on 2nd April. He embarked at Plymouth for return to New Zealand aboard HMNZT 110 *Ruahine* on 19th May, disembarked on 8th July and was granted twenty-eight days leave. When he returned

SS *Navua* (2,930 tons) was built by David J Dunlop at Port Glasgow for the Union Steamship Co of Dunedin, New Zealand in 1904 for the Pacific Island service. During the Great War she sailed as HMNZT 33, 44, 53, 63, 78 from New Zealand to Egypt and Britain between October 1915 and April 1917. In 1920 she returned to civilian traffic and carried out one trans-Pacific voyage. On 31st December 1924 *Navua* was withdrawn from service and laid up at Port Chalmers. In 1927 she was sold to Khedivial Mail Steam Ship & Graving Dock Co, London and was renamed *Roda*. In September 1932 she was scrapped in Egypt.

SS *Ruahine* (10,758 tons) was built by W Denny & Bros, Dumbarton for the New Zealand Shipping Co in 1909. During the Great War she sailed as HMNZT 92 and 110 from New Zealand to Britain between August 1917 and October 1918. In 1949 she was sold to Grimaldi Bros (Ragruppamento Armatore Fratelli Grimaldi), Naples, Italy and, after extensive rebuilding and being renamed *Auriga*, carried emigrants to South America. She was scrapped at Savona in March 1957.

to Hawera he received a civic reception and was presented with a gold watch and chain by the Mayor from local contributions. Harry and the Mayor planted oak trees in the Tower Gardens to commemorate peace. Harry was discharged from the NZEF on 5th August 1919 and was absorbed into the New Zealand Rifle Brigade, Territorial Force. He was on the Reserve of Officers 1st March 1920–31st July 1924. His address at the time was Hastings Road, Matapu, Hawera.

Harry married Ethel Montgomery 'Monty' Homewood (12th March 1903–7th September 1986), born in Chelsea, London, England, on 20th July 1921 at St Mary's Anglican Church, Hawera. They were living at 73 Gladstone Street, Hawera in March 1925, at 12 Vogel Street, Hawera in December 1943 and at 302 Riverslea Road North, Hastings, Hawkes Bay in 1973. They had three sons:

- John Rudolph Laurent (3rd March 1923–14th September 2007) married Denise Maitland Romans (25th April 1923–26th March 2007), born at Balclutha, on 12th May 1948 at Timaru. They lived at Havelock North. He was a watchmaker in 1978, when they were living at 308W St Aubyn Street, Hastings, Hawke's Bay. They had four children, including Paul John Laurent, who was a watchmaker living with his parents in 1978.
- Peter Alroy Laurent married Gwendolyn Steel née Williams (31st October 1921–6th March 1986) in 1948. He was a contractor in 1954, when they were living at Kaeo, Hobson and later at Awanui Road, Kaitaia, Hobson. He was a company director in 1962, when they were living at 101 Matthews Avenue, Kaitaia. They

Biographies 153

73 Gladstone Street, Hawera (First National).

12 Vogel Street, Hawera (First National).

divorced in 1978. By 1981 he was living at Stratford Drive, Cable Bay, Bay of Islands. Gwendolyn had married Malcolm Joseph Steel (23rd October 1912–26th August 1944) on 20th July 1940 at Auckland and they lived at Remuera, Auckland. Malcolm was serving as a pilot (flying officer) in the Royal New Zealand Air Force in 101 Squadron RAF (424533) when he was killed in action (Choloy War Cemetery, Meurthe-et-Moselle, France – 1 D 3). Gwendolyn had five children from her two marriages. It is believed that Peter later married Jacqui and they lived at Manganui, Taranaki. Peter was a director of Mahimahi Contractors Ltd 6th April 1992–8th June 2001.
- Lloyd Aston Laurent married Euphemia Florence and they were living at 306N St Aubyn Street, Hastings in 1978. He was a salesman in 1981, when they were living at 2/1304 Southland Road, Hastings.

Monty's father, Frederick Arthur Homewood (18th June 1873–30th November 1943), born at Hever, Kent, England, married Rosa Margaritha née Bohny (c.1874–1927), born at Frutigen, Berne, Switzerland, in 1899 at Tunbridge Wells, Kent.

Frutigen has probably been settled since the Bronze Age. By 1260 the scattered farmers of the valley had formed a political and business association. In 1400, the expanding city-state of Bern annexed the valley but the association was powerful enough to force Bern to make concessions and residents were freed from taxes or to provide labour for local lords. The valley held these freedoms until 1854. The village church of St Quirinus was first mentioned in 1228 and was built over older churches of the 8th or 9th century. It was rebuilt in 1421 and the current church was built on its ruins after a fire in 1727. Frutigen resisted the Protestant Reformation but adopted it after the Interlaken uprising was suppressed. The agricultural economy began to shift in 1850 as lace and watch factories moved into the valley. The railway came in 1901.

They were living at 78 London Road, Southborough, Kent in 1901 when he was a miller's traveller. They had moved to 6 Brookdene Road, Plumstead, London by 1911 when he was a baker. Rosa died at Brighton, Sussex and Frederick at Paddington, London. In addition to Monty they had five other children:

London Road, Southborough, Kent, where Harry's parents-in-law were living in 1901.

- Margaret Rose Homewood (14th April 1901–1950), born at Tunbridge Wells, married Archibald Wilson Swales (13th April 1895–9th April 1959) on 11th August 1924 at St Andrew's Parish Church, Willesden, Middlesex. He was a cashier and general clerk living at 66 Grange Road, Leigh-on-Sea, Essex and she was living at 58 Huddlestone Road, Willesden Green at the time. Archibald was a clerk and shorthand typist at the time of the 1939 Register, when they were living at 94 Grange Road, Southend-on-Sea, Essex. He was also with the Auxiliary Fire Service at that time. He was living at 38 Pembury Road, Westcliffe-on-Sea, Essex at the time of his death at Westcliffe Hospital. They had a daughter:
    - Joan Margaret Swales (born 1925) married Victor G Webb at Southend in 1946. They had four children – Howard G Swales 1947, Nigel R Swales 1948, Gerald T Swales 1958 and Simon A Swales 1963.
- Lena Madeline Homewood (born 1908), born at Bexleyheath, Kent, married Thomas E Morgan in 1932 at Hendon, Middlesex.
- Arthur G Homewood (born 1911).
- Eileen E Homewood (born 1914).
- Doreen Violet Homewood (9th January 1917–July 1994) married Raymond William Laurence Ranford (23rd December 1915–6th April 2006) in 1940 at Uxbridge, Middlesex. He was an aircraft fitter in 1939, when they were living at 2 Myrtle Avenue, Ruislip, Middlesex. They had moved to 43 The Ridgeway, Ruislip by 1953. They had two children:
    - Denise A Ranford (born 29th February 1948) married Mark AH Jarvis in 1975 at Hillingdon.
    - Laurence A Ranford (born 1949).

Frederick married Bessie Victoria Jordan née Roper (c.1880–29th November 1963), born at Bridport, Dorset, in 1935 at Willesden, London. She was a domestic servant in 1901 at 76a East Street, Bridport. He was a carpenter and joiner in 1939, when they were living at 65 Park Road, Paddington, London and were still there at the time of his death at Paddington Hospital, Harrow Road, London. Bessie was living at 30 Pembridge Square, Bayswater, London at the time of her death at Edgware General Hospital, Hendon, Middlesex. Her date of birth was recorded as 1st December 1886 in the 1939 Register but her age at death was registered as only seventy-three in 1963. Bessie had married Edwin Tom Jordan (born 1883), a surveyor's assistant born at Winchester, Hampshire, on 25th December 1905 at Holy Trinity Church, Kilburn, London. He was living at 40 Glengall Street, London at the time. By 1911 he was an agricultural auctioneer and they were living at 4 Quex Road, Kilburn. Edwin and Bessie had a son, Denis Jordan (26th July 1910–21st March 1971), who married Betty I Collier in 1936.

Harry had a variety of jobs. He took up farming and was a grocer's assistant when he applied to join the Permanent Staff in March 1925 but does not appear to have been accepted or he failed to take up the offer. He was a commercial traveller for Levin & Co when he was recalled for service in the Reserve of Officers Supplementary List 1st September 1939–31st July 1941. He was appointed temporary major on 1st August 1941 to command the Manaia Battalion, Group No.8A, Home Guard. He was appointed temporary lieutenant colonel on 1st December as Group 8A Director. Harry returned to the Reserve of Officers, Supplementary List 30th November 1942–30th November 1943. He was then posted to 1st Battalion, Taranaki Regiment and was seconded as OC No. 47 Squadron Air Training Corps, Hawera 1st December 1943–23rd August 1945. He ceased active service in August 1945 as a lieutenant colonel and was posted to the Retired List of Officers from the Wellington West Coast and Taranaki Regiment on 30th May 1949.

He was a Freemason, being Initiated into Taranaki Lodge No. 240, which met at Hawera, on 16th April 1942. He was installed as Worshipful Master in 1950. In 1966 he became a Joining Member of Heretaunga Lodge No. 73, meeting at Hastings. Harry attended a number of VC Reunions – the VC Centenary Celebrations at Hyde Park, London on 26th June 1956 and the 3rd, 6th, 7th, 8th and 9th VC & GC Association Reunions on 18th July 1962, 19th July 1968, 18th June 1970, 14th July 1972 and 23rd May 1974 at the Café Royal, London, except 1970, which was at the Connaught Rooms, Covent Garden. He also attended a number of VC reunions in New Zealand – VC Dinner in Wellington on 9th November 1929 and a VC commemoration dinner at La Scala, Dunedin on 29th January 1956, hosted by the Governor-General, Lieutenant General Sir Willoughby Norrie and Lady Norrie, at

Harry in later life.

St Matthew's Church is one of Hastings' oldest buildings and has Category One designation from the Historic Places Trust. The wooden nave was built in 1886 and the reinforced concrete sections were added in 1915. The church was damaged in the 1931 earthquake but was restored and the tower height was reduced.

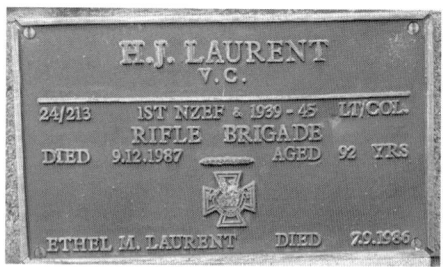

Harry and Ethel's memorial plaque in Hawera Cemetery.

The statues to Harry Laurent VC (left) and John Grant VC (right) in Victoria Cross Gardens, Hawera opened on 15th September 2018.

which ten VCs were present (Bassett, Crichton, Elliott, Frickleton, Grant, Hinton, Holbrook, Hulme, Laurent and Upham).

Harry died at his son's home at Southland Road, Hastings, Hawke's Bay on 9th December 1987. At the time he was the oldest surviving New Zealand VC holder of the Great War. His funeral was held at St Matthew's Church, Hastings on 14th December. His ashes are interred in the Memorial Wall at Hawera Cemetery. He is commemorated in a number of other places:

- Hawera
    - Laurent VC Street named in 1936.
    - Statue in Victoria Cross Gardens.
    - Plaque on a commemorative oak tree he planted in 1919 on Water Tower Grounds, Albion Street.
- Laurent Barracks, Linton Military Camp, near Palmerston North.
- Laurent Place, Greenmeadows, Napier.
- An obelisk surmounted with a sundial in the centre of the War Memorial Wall, Caroline Bay, Timaru bears the names of eleven New Zealand VCs.

Harry's oak tree plaque.

- Victoria Cross memorial dedicated by the Reverend Keith Elliott VC outside the Headquarters of the Dunedin Branch of the Returned Services Association and unveiled by Governor General Sir Charles Willoughby Moke Norrie GCMG GCVO CB DSO MC on 29th January 1956, the centenary of the institution of the VC by Queen Victoria. The memorial was later transferred to Anzac Square in front of the railway station. It was moved again to near Dunedin Cenotaph in Queen's Gardens and rededicated on 11th November 2001.

The Victoria Cross memorial near Dunedin Cenotaph.

- Named on one of eleven plaques honouring 175 men from overseas awarded the VC for the Great War. The plaques were unveiled by the Senior Minister of State at the Foreign & Commonwealth Office and Minister for Faith and Communities, Baroness Warsi, at a reception at Lancaster House, London on 26th June 2014 attended by The Duke of Kent and relatives of the VC recipients. The New Zealand plaque was unveiled on 7th May 2015 at a ceremony attended by Defence Minister Gerry Brownlee and Defence Force Chief Lieutenant General Tim Keating. Corporal Willie Apiata VC read the names of the sixteen men on the plaque, which is displayed in the grounds of Parliament in Wellington.

The 60c stamp featuring Harry Laurent.

- An issue of twenty-two 60c stamps by New Zealand Post entitled 'Victoria Cross – the New Zealand Story' honouring New Zealand's twenty-two Victoria Cross holders was issued on 14th April 2011.
- Communities and Local Government commemorative paving stones for the 145 VCs born in Australia, Belgium, Canada, China, Denmark, Egypt, France, Germany, India, Iraq, Japan, Nepal, Netherlands, Newfoundland, New Zealand, Pakistan, South Africa, Sri Lanka, Ukraine and United States of America were unveiled at the National Memorial Arboretum, Alrewas, Staffordshire by Prime Minister David Cameron MP and Sergeant Johnson Beharry VC on 5th March 2015.

Harry's commemorative paving stone at the National Memorial Arboretum, Alrewas.

The New Zealand War Service Medal was awarded to members of New Zealand armed forces, National Military Reserve, Home Guard, Merchant Navy and Naval Auxiliary Patrol Service. Qualification was twenty-eight days' full-time aggregated service or six months' part-time aggregated service between 3rd September 1939 and 2nd September 1945. Service ended by death, wounds or honourable discharge automatically qualified for the medal, About 238,000 medals were issued.

In addition to the VC he was awarded the 1914–15 Star, British War Medal 1914–20, Victory Medal 1914–19, War Medal 1939–45, New Zealand War Service Medal 1939–45, George VI Coronation Medal 1937, Elizabeth II Coronation Medal 1953 and Elizabeth II Silver Jubilee Medal 1977. The VC is held by the National Army Museum, State Highway One, Waiouru, New Zealand.

On 2nd December 2007, ninety-six medals were stolen from Queen Elizabeth II Army Memorial Museum (now the National Army Museum), by James Joseph Kapa and Ronald van Wakeren, including nine VCs (Andrew, Elliott, Frickleton, Grant, Hinton, Hulme, Judson, Laurent and Upham) and two GCs. A $300,000 reward was offered by medal collector, Lord Michael Ashcroft, and Nelson businessman, Tom Sturgess. The collection was recovered on 16th February 2008 and the medals were returned to the Museum in October. Kapa was jailed for six years and van Wakeren for eleven years for this and other crimes. Upgrades to security at the Museum cost NZ$1.4M.

National Army Museum, Waiouru.

## 58062 LANCE CORPORAL LEONARD ALLAN LEWIS
### 6th Battalion, The Northamptonshire Regiment

Allan Leonard Lewis, as he was known in the family, was born on 28th February 1895 at Wood Villa, Brilley, Whitney-on-Wye, Herefordshire. His name is also seen as Alan Leonard Lewis. His father, George Lewis (29th August 1867–1939), born at Brilley, married Annie Elizabeth née Gidley (18th May 1868–1952), a domestic servant born at Lyme Regis, Dorset, on 10th May 1893 at the Register Office, Kington, Herefordshire. George was a jobbing carpenter on the Whitney Estate in 1901 and 1911, when they were living at Wyeside, Whitney-on-Wye. She was living with her son, Albert, and grandson, Donald Lewis (born 1922), at Wyeside Cottage, Kington in 1939. Allan had eight siblings:

- Frank Lewis (8th March 1894–1971) was a wagoner on a farm run by John and Gladys Ethel Lloyd at Bryngwyn, Breconshire in 1911. He served in India with 1/1st Brecknockshire Battalion (Territorial Force), The South Wales Borderers during the Great War. He married Elizabeth 'Bessie' Lewis (23rd May 1898–1959), born at Dorstone, Herefordshire, on 4th June 1920. He was a cowman and a hay worker on a farm in 1939, when they were living at Castleton Barn, Priory Wood, Clifford, Herefordshire. They had five children:
    - Allan Leonard Lewis (18th February 1922–17th August 1982) was named after his uncle. He joined the Royal Navy and served as a chief petty officer (yeoman of signals) aboard HMS *Rodney* and other ships. He married Harriet Price Merryman (born 19th August 1923) in July 1944 at Ross, Herefordshire. Harriet was living with her parents at Yew Tree Cottages, Dore and Bredwardine, Herefordshire in 1939. Allan and Harriet were living at Queenswood, Dinmore

Whitney-on-Wye in Herefordshire on the River Wye, is a mile east of the English/Welsh border. At the time of the 2011 Census it had a population of just 117. The church shown here, dedicated to Saints Peter and Paul, is mentioned in the Domesday Book. During the 1830 Captain Swing Riots, dispossessed farm labourers in Whitney threatened arson and machine breaking to try to obtain a living wage.

Hill, Leominster, Herefordshire at the time of his death there. They had three children – Nigel Lewis 1949, Graham Lewis 1958 and Sharon Lewis 1964.
- Ivy G Lewis (20th January 1924–2017) married Trevor J Harvey in 1946 at Bristol, Gloucestershire. They had two children – Leslie D Harvey 1947 and Barbara Harvey 1949.
- Mary Lewis (born 17th November 1926) married Gerald F Mason in April 1947 at Radnor West, Radnorshire.
- Joyce Lewis (3rd March 1928–1st December 2010) married George 'Dovey' Wilfred Lewis (sic) (10th December 1915–24th February 2003), born at Boughrood, Radnorshire, on 31st December 1949. He served as a lance corporal in the South Wales Borderers during the Second World War (3908610) and was taken prisoner by the Germans. He was held at Stalag XI-A (also known as Stalag 341), Altengrabow, Saxony-Anhalt (Prisoner 142465) but escaped, survived for eighteen months and weighed less than eighty pounds when he was finally rescued. George ran the George Hotel, Brecon with his sister, Blanche, and later a taxi business from his mother's pub, the Boat, at Boughrood. George became the landlord of the Hollybush Inn, near Hay-on-Wye, Herefordshire about 1955. He died at Bronllys Hospital, Brecon. Joyce was living at 38 The Meadows, Hay when she died at Hereford County Hospital. They had five children – Michael Walter Lewis 1951, Dawn Marie Lewis 1953, Andrew Paul Lewis 1955, Jane Lewis 1962 and Sally Ann Lewis 1965.
- Leslie Lewis (1st August 1930–2003) was raised by his mother's brother, Samuel Lewis, a colliery hewer, and his wife, Flossie, at 25 Central Road, Abercarn, Monmouthshire, because his mother suffered post-natal depression. Leslie married Alma Jean Watson (28th September 1930–17th April 2016) in 1955 at Bedwellty, Monmouthshire. They had three children – Patricia Lewis 1956, Deborah Lewis 1961 and Julie J Lewis 1962.

- Lucy Helen Lewis (15th October 1897–21st November 1938) married Henry James Lott (20th December 1888–8th December 1952), a licensed victualler, born at Regent's Park Barracks, London, in 1930. He was a turner when he enlisted in the Highland Light Infantry on 20th July 1906 at Bury St Edmunds, Suffolk (10201) having previously served in 3rd and 1st Volunteer Battalions, Suffolk Regiment. He was described as 5′ 9¼″ tall, weighing 121 lbs, with fresh complexion, brown eyes, light brown hair and his religious denomination was Roman Catholic. He joined at Hamilton on 23rd July and gained 3rd class army education on 4th September. He transferred to 7th (The Princess Royal's) Dragoon Guards (7051) at Canterbury, Kent on 15th October 1906, to be with his older brother. He gained 2nd class army education on 2nd May 1907. He was in hospital in Canterbury with influenza 6th-11th January 1908 and with an abscess 11th-17th July. On 11th September he was found fit for service in

Egypt and embarked on 17th September. He was in hospital in Cairo with gonorrhoea 7th September–13th October 1909. On 30th September 1910 he was found fit for service in India, embarked aboard HT *Longola* on 3rd October and disembarked on 12th October. Henry was promoted lance corporal on 21st February 1912 and extended his service to complete twelve years on 25th June. He passed the Army Signalling and Field Telephony course at Poona 3rd August–31st October. On 27th March 1913 he gained 1st class army education at Trimulgherry, Deccan and in May was at Secunderabad. Promoted corporal on 10th August 1914, embarked at Bombay on 16th September and disembarked at Marseille, France on 13th October, where he was attached to the Signal Troop, HQ 9th Cavalry Brigade. Promoted lance sergeant 5th April 1915, returned to the Regiment on 22nd April and was appointed acting sergeant on 9th October. On 30th January 1916 Henry was commissioned in the Durham Light Infantry and joined 14th Battalion on 9th February. He was wounded by a gunshot in the right arm and shoulder on 4th June near Ypres, Belgium. He was treated at 18th Field Ambulance and No.10 Casualty Clearing Station next day and transferred to 20th General Hospital, Étaples. On 23rd July he was evacuated to Britain aboard HMHS *Dieppe* from Calais to Dover and was treated at 5th Northern General Hospital in Leicester, 1st Northern General Hospital in Newcastle upon Tyne and Brighton Military Hospital. A medical board at 5th Northern General Hospital on 29th September found he was unfit for any service for six weeks and he was granted leave until 11th November. A medical board at 2nd Eastern General Hospital, Brighton on 16th November found he was unfit for any service for two months and he was granted another two month's leave to 15th January 1917. Henry was Mentioned in Despatches, LG 4th January 1917. A medical board on 19th January found him unfit for General Service for six weeks and Home Service for one month but fit for light duty and he joined 3rd Battalion on 21st January. Three more medical boards, on 19th February, 9th March and 10th April, found him unfit for General Service but fit for light duty. Wound pensions of £50 were granted annually from 4th June 1917 until 3rd June 1921. Promoted lieutenant on 30th July. A medical board on 31st July found him unfit for General Service for six months but fit for Home Service and he returned to 3rd Battalion. A medical board on 16th November found him unfit for General Service for two months but fit for Home Service and he was to resume duty with 68th Recruiting Area, Newcastle upon Tyne. A medical board on 23rd January 1918 found him permanently unfit for military service in all categories and he was placed on the Half Pay List on account of ill-health caused by wounds on 15th February. A medical board on 14th March 1919 found him permanently unfit in all categories and he was employed at the Ministry of Pensions, Area HQ, Market Street, Omagh, Ireland. A medical board on 17th March 1920 found him fit for General Service and he was restored to the establishment on 16th April, with effect from 17th March. He was serving with the Ministry of Pensions, Grand Central Hotel, Belfast, Ireland at the time. He was posted to 1st Battalion (Details) at Tidworth, Hampshire but a medical board at the Military Hospital, Newcastle upon Tyne on 29th July 1920 found him to be forty percent disabled. A medical board there on 13th December 1921 found him to be thirty percent disabled. He was serving with 2nd Battalion when he attended a special medical board at York on 27th March 1922, which found him permanently unfit for General Service. He was transferred to the Half Pay List on account of ill health on 10th May 1922. A medical board at West Block, Tothill Street, Westminster, London on 20th May found him permanently unfit for General Service. On 13th June half pay was extended to 9th May 1925. However, on 20th August he requested to be retired with a gratuity in lieu of retired pay, in order to set up a small business. He was retired on 9th September with a gratuity of £450 being paid next day. He was living at Sussex Hotel, Eastbourne and became a licensed victualler at The Terminus Hotel, 33 Terminus Road, Eastbourne, Sussex. Lucy and Henry were still living there at the time of her death at St Mary Hospital, Eastbourne. Henry married Alice Hill (born 27th September 1888), a widow, in 1946. Alice was living with James and Mabel Joy, probably her sister and brother-in-law, in Guildford, Surrey in 1939. Henry was still at the Terminus Hotel at the time of his death at St Mary Hospital, Eastbourne. Alice was living at 34 Melbourne Road, Eastbourne when she died there on 1st/2nd November 1965. Lucy had four children, including two before she married:

- Donald Lewis (on 21st February 1922) born at Croydon, Surrey, was a gardener/handyman in 1939, living with his maternal grandparents at Wyeside Cottage, Kington, Herefordshire. He married Ivy Parrington (born 1927) in 1950. They had a daughter, Mary Elizabeth Lewis in 1950.
- Beryl Lewis (6th May 1925–13th February 2020), born at Birmingham, Warwickshire, was raised by her aunt, Ivy Lennard née Lewis (see below). She was known as Beryl Stead, possibly the surname of her natural father. Beryl had two children – Vivian/Vivienne S Stead 1944 and Sheila M Berridge (sic) 1948. She married Albert Roy Berridge (13th September 1917–January 1989), born at Edmonton, Middlesex, in 1949 at Swindon, Wiltshire. They were living

The Terminus Hotel in Eastbourne, where Allan's sister, Lucy, and husband were living in 1952.

at Great Western House, Great Western Road, Gloucester in 1950 and 46 Birchall Avenue, Matson, Gloucester by 1956. His death was registered at Bristol, Avon and she died at Gloucestershire Royal Hospital, Gloucester. They had three daughters – Pamela D Berridge 1951, Beryl A Berridge 1958 and Fiona Helen Berridge 1966. Albert had married Gwynneth Chapman (1918–83), born at Cymbran, Monmouthshire, in 1937 at Edmonton. She was living at 21 Bayford Avenue, Birmingham in 1939 and was an Air Raid Precautions Warden at the time. They were living at 2 Gordon Road, Stroud Green, Hornsey, London in 1946. They had two children – John Berridge 1940 and Sybil J Berridge 1943. The marriage ended in divorce. Gwynneth had a daughter, Diane M Jameison (sic) in 1946, and married Stanley John Jameison (1914–61), born in London, in 1949 at Wood Green, Middlesex. He was an assistant in a fried fish shop in 1939 and was living with his siblings at 62 East Walk, East Barnet, Hertfordshire. Stanley and Gwynneth were living at 2 Gordon Road, Stroud Green, Hornsey in 1952. He died at 16 Southsea House, Darlington Gardens, Harold Hill, Romford, Essex. Gwynneth married Frederick James Brine (1914–95), born at Edmonton, in 1964 at Romford. He was a light lorry driver in 1939, living with his father and siblings at 99 Riversdale Road, Islington, London. Gwynneth was living at 176 Albany Road, Hornchurch, Essex at the time of her death there. Frederick's death was registered at Havering, Essex.
  - Peter H Lott (born 1931) married Jean P Brown in 1953. They had a son, James A Lott, in 1955.
  - John A Lott (born 1933) married Susan E Longley (born 1936), born at Solihull, Warwickshire, in 1961. They had a son, Paul J Lott, in 1961. Susan married George J Woodley in 1975.
- Edith Maud Lewis (1st April 1900–1978) married William Rice Weale (22nd January 1895–1978) in 1922 at Builth Wells. He was a hackney cab driver in 1939, when they were living at Corner House, High Street, Builth Wells. They had two children:
  - Dorothy Megan Weale (20th December 1923–1976) was a shop assistant in 1939, living with her parents. She never married.
  - Sylvia Fortune Weale (3rd July 1926–6th November 2008) married Erwin FF Hoeft in 1951 at Builth Wells.
- Annie Lilian 'Lily' Lewis (2nd January 1903–1983) married John Richard George Morris (24th October 1906–1971), born in Liverpool, Lancashire, in 1932. He was a carpenter and joiner in 1939, when they were living at Coopers Hall Cottage, Dore and Bredwardine, Herefordshire. He was also serving in the Auxiliary Fire Service. They had a daughter, Valerie Rose Morris (1933–27th November 2011), who married Peter Brian Wilding (born 1939) in 1966.
- Ivy Beatrice Lewis (29th August 1905–October 1985) married Bindabun Lennard (1st July 1903–1978), born at Llanganten, Brecknockshire, in 1926

at Builth Wells. They raised Ivy's niece, Beryl Lewis. He was an ammunition worker in 1939, when they were living at Wyeside Cottage, Kington, next door to his parents-in-law. They had a son:
  ○ Denzil Lennard (born 1932) married Maureen S Pratt in 1957 at Warwick. They had three children – Andrew C Lennard 1960, Sandra J Lennard 1961 and Jeanette AE Lennard 1963.
* Stanley George Lewis (29th November 1907–13th January 2000) married Elsie Mary Hewlett (30th April 1906–June 1992), born at Monmouth, in 1938. He was a carpenter in 1939, when they were living at The Grove, Kington.
* Hector Lewis (13th July 1910–5th February 1992) married Mary Agnes Halsey (3rd September 1912–January 1981), born at Chichester, Sussex, in 1935 at Builth, Brecknockshire. He was a railway porter (heavy) in 1939, when they were living at Top Flat, Grove House, Chichester. He was also an Air Raid Precautions Warden on the railways. He was living at 47 Parklands Road, Chichester at the time of his death there. They had two children – John Lewis 1941 and Roger J Lewis 1943.
* Albert Edward 'Robin' Lewis (4th January 1913–5th April 1985) was a general labourer in 1939, living with his mother at Wyeside Cottage, Kington. He served in the British Army during the Second World War and married Ida Myfanwy Williams (7th July 1915–1994), born at Rhayader, Radnorshire, in 1942 at St Asaph, Flintshire. They were living at 3 Kyrle Pope Court, Sudbury Avenue, Hereford at the time of his death there.

Allan's paternal grandfather, Thomas Tatham Lewis (c.1833–24th July 1886), a carpenter born at Brilley, married Eleanor 'Ellen' née Wilton (November 1832–1919), also born at Brilley, in 1857. They were living at Merthyr, Brilley in 1861 and at Brilley Wood, Brilley in 1871 and 1881. Thomas died at Staunton-on-Wye, Herefordshire. Ellen was living with her daughter, Ellen and family, in 1901. Her death was registered at Kington, Herefordshire. In addition to George they had five other children:

* Thomas Lewis (born 1858) was not with the family in 1871 and may have died young.
* Henry Lewis (13th May 1861–1932) was a carpenter in 1881, living with his parents, and was later a farmer. He married Esther Colley (1866–1936) in 1884. They were living at Whitburn, Brilley in 1901 and at Crossway Farm, Brilley in 1911. They had eleven children, three of whom did not survive infancy:
  ○ Beatrice Lewis (born 1885).
  ○ Thomas Henry Lewis (born 1888) is believed to have married Ellen Capps in 1915.
  ○ John Lewis (1892–1932) a twin with Herbert.
  ○ Herbert Lewis (born 1892) a twin with John.

- Florence 'Florrie' Esther Lewis (9th September 1897–1964).
- Ethel Blanche Lewis (28th September 1898–1904).
- Reginald Walter Lewis (22nd November 1899–19th April 1951).
- William James Lewis (18th August 1901–1962).
- Frederick George Lewis (born 24th October 1905).
* Eleanor 'Ellen' Hannah Lewis (14th August 1864–1946) married Frank Morris (6th August 1863–1944), an estate labourer born at Huntington, Herefordshire, in 1895. They were living at Brilley Wood in 1901, 1911 and 1939, by when he was an estate carter. They had at least four children:
  - Frank Morris (3rd January 1896–2nd August 1971) enlisted in the Army Service Corps (T4/065247) as a driver at Hereford on 22nd February 1915 and joined at Aldershot on 25th February. He was described as an agricultural labourer, 5′ 5″ tall and weighing 126 lbs. He went to France to join 3rd Company, 41st Division Train, embarking at Southampton on 3rd May 1916 and disembarking at Le Havre next day. He was treated at 140th Field Ambulance for impetigo on 29th December, transferred to 138th Field Ambulance with scabies on 1st January 1917 and was discharged through the Divisional Rest Station to his unit the same day. On 3rd January he was admitted to a casualty clearing station with scabies and transferred to 4th Stationary Hospital the next day. He rejoined his unit on 20th January. He was again admitted to 138th Field Ambulance with impetigo on 6th February and returned to duty on 16th February. Awarded the good conduct badge on 22nd February. He served with the Division in Italy from 12th November and was granted home leave 2nd-16th February 1918. He was also granted home leave 25th January–8th February 1919. Frank transferred to 17th Army Auxiliary (H) Company on 6th May. He returned to Britain on 23rd June and was serving with 310 Company when he joined No.1 Dispersal Unit, Prees Heath on 25th June. He transferred to the Class Z Reserve on 23rd July 1919.
  - Thomas Leonard Morris (23rd September 1897–10th April 1971).
  - Elizabeth Ellen Morris (8th April 1899–1977) married Edgar H Beddoes (1st October 1898–1971) in 1922.
  - Catherine Evelyn Morris (born 1907).
* Charles Lewis (8th September 1870–1935) was a patient at the Hereford County and City Lunatic Asylum, Burghill, near Hereford in 1911.
* Leonard Lewis (4th December 1873–20th March 1949) was a signalman for the Midland Railway Company. He married Hannah 'Annie' McClure (4th September 1874–1969), born at Fiskerton, Nottinghamshire, in 1898 at Southwell, Nottinghamshire. They were living at 71 Randolph Road, Normanton, Derbyshire in 1901. He was visiting his sister, Ellen and her family, at the time of the 1911 Census, whilst Hannah was living with her children at 11 Cameron Road, Derby. They were living at 169 Edleston Road, Crewe, Cheshire at the time of his death there. They had two children:

The construction of the Hereford County and City Lunatic Asylum at Burghill commenced in 1868 and the facility opened in August 1871. Within the one hundred acres of gardens were a farm and several cottages. The asylum had separate blocks for men and women, each housing 200 patients. It was extended in the early 20th century and was renamed Burghill Mental Hospital in the 1930s. In 1948 it joined the National Health Service and was renamed St Mary's Hospital. It closed in 1994 and the main building has since been demolished.

- Dorothy Kathleen Lewis (born 1899) married Frederick J Williams in 1926.
- Sidney Leonard Lewis (27th July 1902–1975) married Gladys R Litchfield (born 1904) in 1927.

His maternal grandfather, Frank Boswell (1844–82), was born at Oxford, Oxfordshire and was baptised on 4th November 1844 at St Michael, Oxford. He was a photographer, living with Mary Gidley (born c.1846), born in Devonshire, and their daughter Annie Elizabeth at Church Street, Lyme Regis, Dorset in 1871. No marriage record had been found and it is not known what became of Mary after 1877. By 1881 Frank was living with Emily Moore (born 20th February 1858 and believed to have died in 1937), born at Charmouth, Dorset, at 20 Market Place, Frome, Somerset. She was recorded as his wife in that year's census but again no marriage record has been found. In addition to Annie, Frank had six other children from his two relationships:

- Alice Boswell (1867–2nd December 1927), born at Lyme Regis, Dorset, was adopted by William (1822–1906) and Elizabeth Mansfield before 1871. William, who was born at Uplyme, Devon, married Elizabeth Baker Saunders (1822–1916), born at Falmouth, Cornwall, on 19th May 1846 at Lyme Regis. In 1871 William was a cabinetmaker and auctioneer, and they were living at Broadway House, Silver Street, Lyme Regis. In 1891 Alice's brother, Frank, and sister, Mary, were boarding there with William and Elizabeth. By 1901, William, Elizabeth and Alice were living at Pilot House, Uplyme, Devon. At the time of the 1911 Census, Alice and Elizabeth were visiting Felix Davis, a nurseryman, and his family at 12 Church Street, Lyme Regis. Alice never married and died at Box House, Axminster.
- Lucy Boswell (16th September 1873–16th April 1966) was a pupil teacher at St Michael's School, Tamar Street. Wantage, Berkshire, run by the Sisters of Mercy, in 1891. She married Frederick George Lloyd (c.1871–28th May 1928), an organist born at Wyken, Shropshire, on 31st March 1900 at the Parish Church,

Hampton Hill, Middlesex. They were living at Woodside, Rickmansworth, Hertfordshire in 1901 and at Burleigh, Parsonage Road, Rickmansworth in 1928, where he died. Lucy was living as a retired teacher at High Street, Frome in 1939 and at The Green, Rode, Somerset at the time of her death at Mendip Hospital, Wells, Somerset. They are believed to have had a daughter:
    - Margaret Lucy Lloyd (9th April 1907–November 1992), born at Amersham, Buckinghamshire. She married David L Watts at Salisbury, Wiltshire in 1936. They divorced and she married Thomas N Hughes at Salisbury in 1949. David married Phyllis M Green née Marchant at Salisbury in 1948. Thomas had married Susie Frances Stanbridge (1903–47) at Amersham in 1930. Margaret died at Bournemouth, Dorset.
- Frank Boswell (7th March 1875–13th January 1961) was a cabinetmaker in 1891, living at the home of William Mansfield, also a cabinetmaker, at Broadway House, Silver Street, Lyme Regis. He married Emily White (17th February 1870–22nd June 1951), born at Lyndhurst, Hampshire, in 1899 at New Forest, Hampshire. They were living at 7 Sherborne Lane, Lyme Regis in 1901. They were still there in 1911 by when he was a cabinetmaker and dealer. By 1918 they were living at 6 Sherborne Lane, where Emily subsequently died. Frank was living at Eagle House, Sherborne Lane, Lyme Regis at the time of his death at The Cottage Hospital, Lyme Regis. They had two sons, both cabinetmakers:
    - Frank Boswell (10th February 1900–1976) enlisted in 4th Reserve Battalion, Dorsetshire Regiment on 11th February 1918 and was called up to join the Depot, Dorchester on 19th March (31607). He was described as 5′ 5″ tall, weighing 118 lbs, with fresh complexion, brown hair, brown eyes and his religious denomination was Church of England. His next of kin was his mother. He transferred to 2/1st North Somerset Yeomanry (23266) on 26th March and was serving with the unit as a signaller in September and October 1918. On 3rd March 1919 he was compulsorily transferred to 1/8th (Cyclist) Battalion, Essex Regiment (61032) and was serving at Galway, Ireland when he was transferred to the Dispersal Station, Fovant, Wiltshire on 10th November. He transferred to the Class Z Reserve on demobilisation on 10th December 1919.
    - Rupert Bruce Boswell (5th January 1903–1978).
- Mary Boswell (born 1877) was living with her sister, Alice, and brother, Frank, at the home of William and Elizabeth Mansfield at Broadway House, Silver Street, Lyme Regis in 1891. By 1901 she was a general servant for the Reverend William Thomas Wellacott and his family at the Vicarage, Bradworthy, Devon.
- Harry Moore (20th March 1879–6th November 1964), born at Frome, was baptised as Henry Boswell on 10th September 1882 at Christ Church, Frome. He was living with his widowed maternal grandmother, Elizabeth Moore, a milk seller, at Rose Cottage, The Street, Charmouth, Dorset in 1891. He was living at Smithers Cottage, Epsom, Surrey when his brother, William, enlisted in

September 1900. Harry married Charlotte Chick (13th November 1872–1943), born at Broadwinsor, Dorset, in 1900 at Beaminster, Dorset. She was living with her grandmother, Mary Chick (1825–1911) and her husband Edmund Halson/Hallson (1816–87) at Wall Lane Gate House, Burstock, Dorset in 1881. In 1891 she was a nursemaid living with the family of William and Florence Armitage at 60 Hendford, Yeovil, Somerset. In 1911 he was a carpenter and she was a dressmaker living at Broadwindsor, Beaminster. They were living at Farleigh Glen, Dewlands Road, Verwood, Dorset in 1939. Charlotte's death was registered at Blandford, Dorset. Harry was living at White Cottage, West Woodyates, Salisbury, Wiltshire at the time of his death at Newbridge Hospital, Salisbury. They had two daughters – Ivy Elizabeth Boswell 1902 and Emily May Boswell 1904.

- William Moore (born 1882) was baptised as William Boswell on 10th September 1882 at Christ Church, Frome and was living with his maternal grandmother in 1891. He was a carpenter when he enlisted in the Royal Field Artillery as William Boswell at Dorchester on 4th September 1900 (12475). He was described as 5′ 9¾″ tall, weighing 134 lbs, with fresh complexion, blue eyes and fair hair. His next of kin was his brother, Harry. His place of birth was given as Surrey. He joined No.4 Depot Battery RFA, Newport, Monmouthshire on 8th September. He was discharged on 26th January 1901 at his own request on payment of £10. His intended residence was Francis Road, Bournemouth. He was unmarried and boarding with Edgar Arthur Baker, grocer's assistant, his wife Amelia and their daughter Edith at Charmouth, Francis Road, Bournemouth at the time of the 1901 Census. He re-enlisted in the Royal Engineers (75686) as William Moore on 11th April 1912 but nothing more is known of his service. A William Moore served in the Royal Engineers (87494) 3rd May 1915–31st May 1919. The service records were partially damaged by fire in the Second World War but significant differences with the William Boswell/Moore born at Frome in 1882 are apparent and it is believed that they are not the same person.

Emily Moore was living with Frederick Smith (born c.1847), an optician and watchmaker born at Weymouth, Dorset, at 23 Oxford Street, Southampton, Hampshire in 1891. She was living with her children at 19 Myrtle Terrace, South Stoneham in 1901 and was recorded as a widow. She was living alone at 371 Portswood Road, Southampton in 1911 and was recorded as a spinster. Emily had three more children:

- Edgar Moore (20th September 1889–28th February 1962) was born at 23 Oxford Street, Southampton, and his father was Frederick Smith. Edgar enlisted in the Royal Navy on 6th March 1908 (L208), described as 5′ 8″ tall, with light brown hair, grey eyes, fair complexion and tattoo spots on his left forearm. He was discharged the following day. He married Mary Ann Clark (2nd March 1893–13th May 1958), born at Heavitree, Exeter, Devon, on 28th January 1911 at Southampton. He was a dock labourer in 1911, when they were living with

his father-in-law at 83 York Street, Northam, Southampton. He was a hydraulic crane driver in 1939 when they were living at 42 Kent Street, Southampton. He died at 86 Dimond Road, Southampton. They had four children – Alfred Edgar Moore 1911, Dorothy Eva Moore 1914, Ivy Mary Moore 1916 and Emily Elizabeth Moore 1919.
- Percy Charles Moore (25th September 1890–30th December 1961) served during the Great War. He married Alice Emily Kneller (16th October 1903–1987) in 1926 at Southampton, where they were both born. He was a builder's labourer in 1939, when they were living at 521 Portswood Road, Southampton. He enlisted in 207th Heavy Anti-Aircraft Training Regiment on 13th March 1941 (1782044) at Devizes, Wiltshire. He served in 9th Anti-Aircraft Regiment RA from 9th June and 107th Heavy Anti-Aircraft Regiment RA from 31st August, in the northwest of England. He was with 124th Heavy Anti-Aircraft Regiment from 4th April 1943 and transferred to the Class Z (T) Reserve on 21st January 1946. He was discharged as being overage in 1954. They had two children – Dora Moore 1926 and Rosemary R Moore 1937.
- Basil Moore (14th October 1893–1954), born at South Stoneham, Hampshire, married Rita Edith Johnson (17th September 1902–1987), born at Alverstoke, Hampshire, in 1922 at South Stoneham. He was a scaler at a shipyard in 1939, when they were living at 155 Bluebell Road, Southampton. They had a son, Jack Moore (born 21st August 1923).

Allan was educated at Whitney-on-Wye School until 1908. He worked as a farm labourer for Mr Tom Prosser at Wern Farm, Brilley and by 1911 he was a cowman for Mr Arthur Price at Penhenallt Farm near Hay. He moved to South Wales and was employed as a gardener for Mr J Picton at Truscod, Llandeilo Graban. Later he became a bus conductor before qualifying as a motorbus driver for the Great Western Railway's Neath to Pontardawe route in Glamorgan. He was living at 17 Creswell Road, Neath, Glamorgan at the time.

The former Whitney-on-Wye School is now a private dwelling.

A rather battered photograph of Allan and his tent mates at Grove Park, London, while undergoing training with the ASC (SF Hoeft).

Longleat is the seat of the Marquess of Bath and today is known for its Elizabethan country house and safari park. The surrounding 1,000 acres of parkland was landscaped by Capability Brown and there is also farmland and woodland that includes a holiday village. It was the first stately home to open to the public in 1949 and the safari park, which opened in 1966, was the first outside Africa. The house was built over twelve years for Sir John Thynne after the original house, the dissolved Longleat Priory, was destroyed by fire in 1567. Modifications were made later by Sir Christopher Wren and others. The Thynn (sic) family held the title of Viscount Weymouth from 1682 and the title of Marquess of Bath since 1789. During the Great War the house became a Red Cross hospital. During the Second World War the Royal School for Daughters of Officers of the Army was evacuated there and an American hospital was constructed in the grounds. The Longleat hedge maze, with 2,720m of paths, is the longest in the world.

Allan enlisted in the Army Service Corps (Mechanical Transport) in March 1915 (M2/104722) and went to France on 17th September. He was evacuated to Britain in early 1917 with jaundice and was treated at the Red Cross Hospital, Longleat House, Wiltshire. Whilst there, Lord and Lady Bath and their daughter, Kathleen, appear

The Vis-en-Artois Memorial bears the names of 9,843 men from Great Britain, Ireland and South Africa who died between 8th August and 11th November 1918 in the Advance to Victory 'in Picardy and Artois, between the Somme and Loos', who have no known grave. The Canadian, Australian and New Zealand missing are commemorated on other memorials. The memorial was designed by JR Truelove, with sculpture by Ernest Gillick, and was unveiled by the Secretary of State for War, Thomas Shaw, on 4th August 1930.

to have taken an interest in him. He transferred to the Northamptonshire Regiment (58062) and served with the 2nd (Home Service) Garrison Battalion at Sheerness, Kent and at the School of Instruction in France. He was subsequently posted to the 6th Battalion and promoted lance corporal. **Awarded the VC for his actions at Ronssoy, near Lempire, France on 18th September 1918, LG 31st January 1919.**

Allan was killed by flying shrapnel in the head while he tried to get his men under cover during an enemy barrage at Doleful Post, near Lempire, France on 21st September 1918. His body was buried by an Australian soldier on 30th September, who removed Allan's pay book and sent it to his mother. The grave could not be identified after the war and he is commemorated on Panel 7 of the Vis-en-Artois Memorial, France. The VC was presented to his parents by the King in the ballroom at Buckingham Palace on 10th April 1919. Allan is commemorated in a number of other places:

- Herefordshire
    - Plaque and a tree in St Peter and St Paul's Churchyard, Whitney-on-Wye.
    - Whitney-on-Wye War Memorial, St Peter and St Paul's Church.
    - Brilley War Memorial in St Mary's Churchyard.
    - A Department for Communities and Local Government commemorative paving stone was dedicated at Lady Arbour, Hereford Cathedral, 5 College Cloisters, Cathedral Close, Hereford on 22nd September 2018.
    - A plaque at Hereford Cathedral was unveiled on 21st September 2018.
    - Statue in Old Market, Hereford dedicated on 21st September 2018.
- Neath, South Wales
    - Allan Leonard Lewis VC Pub, Orchard Street.
    - Plaque at the railway station.

The Whitney-on-Wye War Memorial outside St Peter and St Paul's Church. Allan's initials are shown incorrectly as AE.

Brilley War Memorial.

Allan Lewis' statue in Old Market, Hereford.

The Allan Leonard Lewis VC pub in Neath opened in October 2017 having previously been a Conservative club.

The Ring of Remembrance (L'Anneau de la Mémoire), designed by Philippe Prost, was inaugurated on 11th November 2014 by French President Hollande, Nord-Pas-de-Calais région président, Daniel Percheron, and German Minister of Defense, Ursula von der Leyen. The inspiration is a human ring holding hands, a sign of fellowship and unity among countries that were enemies. It commemorates 576,606 soldiers of forty nations who died in Nord-Pas-de-Calais in the Great War. It is co-located with the largest French national cemetery of Notre-Dame-de-Lorette, which can be seen in the background. The Ring is a 345m ellipse, including a raised section of sixty-one metres. Although the ring is a symbol of peace in Europe, the overhang reminds visitors that peace is not guaranteed and conflict can return at any time. Within the Ring are 500 stainless steel panels facing inwards arranged like the pages of a book. Each is three metres tall and has c.1,200 names listed alphabetically by surname regardless of nationality, gender, religion or rank. The first name is 'A' and the last is 'Zschiesche'. The 500th panel is blank for newly discovered names. There are four panels of Smiths alone.

The 1914–15 Star was instituted in December 1918 for personnel who served in any theatre between 5th August 1914 and 31st December 1915. Those awarded the 1914 Star, Africa General Service Medal and Khedive's Sudan Medal 1910 were ineligible to receive it. The 1914–15 Star was awarded with the British War and Victory Medals, the trio known as Pip, Squeak and Wilfred after comic strip characters. 2,366,000 medals were awarded to members of the British, Dominion and Empire forces.

- A Great Western Railway Intercity Express Train was named after Lance Corporal Allan Leonard Lewis VC and Flight Sub-Lieutenant Harold Day DSC on 9th November 2018 at Paddington Station, London to mark the 100th anniversary of the end of the Great War. It features the names of all 2,545 men who worked for GWR and died during the war. One hundred of them have their details displayed.
- Named on the Great Western Railway Roll of Honour under the clock arch at Paddington Station, London.
- Named on The Ring of Remembrance (Ring of Memory) at Ablain-Saint-Nazaire, France, inaugurated on 11th November 2014.

In addition to the VC he was awarded the 1914–15 Star, British War Medal 1914–20 and Victory Medal 1914–19. The location of the medals is not known and they may still be with the family.

## 355014 LANCE SERGEANT WILLIAM HERBERT WARING
### 25th (Montgomery & Welsh Horse Yeomanry) Battalion, The Royal Welsh Fusiliers

William Waring was born on 13th October 1885 at Brewery Yard, Raven Street, Welshpool, Montgomeryshire, Wales. His father, Richard Waring (15th May 1852–1926), was a gardener in 1873. He is reputed to have served as a corporal, possibly in the 24th (The 2nd Warwickshire) Regiment of Foot in the Zulu War in South Africa in 1879, where he lost his left leg. However, no service record has been found to support this, although he did lose his left leg at some time. He married Ann/Annie Elizabeth née Jones (c.1850–1929), born at Shrewsbury, Shropshire, on 26th May 1872 at Welshpool Register Office. She was a dairymaid in 1871, working for William and Martha  Jones, farmers of 256 acres at Llewynolin, Montgomery, Montgomeryshire. Richard was a nail maker in 1881, when the family was living at Brewery Yard, Welshpool, Montgomery. They had moved to 8 Raven Street, Welshpool by 1891, to 2 Newills

Montgomeryshire Imperial Yeomanry passing through Welshpool. The town was historically in Montgomeryshire but since 1974 has been in Powys. It is on the River Severn a few miles from the English border. It was known as Pool until 1835 when the name changed to Welshpool to distinguish it from Poole in Dorset. The churches date back to the 5th and 6th centuries and were reputedly founded by St Cynfelin (also known as Matu). The town was devastated by Owain Glyndŵr in 1400 at the start of his rebellion against Henry IV.

Row, Welshpool by 1901 and 21 Rock Terrace, Welshpool by 1911, when he was a fishmonger. His death was registered at Forden, Montgomeryshire and hers at Oswestry, Shropshire. William had nine siblings:

- John Thomas Waring (1873–1918), born in Welshpool, was a general labourer in 1891 and a butcher's journeyman in 1901, when he was still living with his parents. He married Sarah Jane Griffiths (1857–21st December 1935) in 1903. She was a general domestic servant at the Checkers Inn, Broad Street, Montgomery in 1901. John and Sarah were living at 1 Quarry Place, Welshpool in 1911, by when he was a farm labourer. He was diagnosed with a pyloric obstruction in 1914 and was advised to use a stomach tube at Shrewsbury Hospital. He was a butcher when he enlisted in 2/7th Royal Welch Fusiliers on 23rd August 1915 (20129) having previously served in 4th South Wales Borderers. He was described as 5′ 8″ tall and weighed 140 lbs. He was posted to No.1 Supernumerary Company and was a factory guard on 10th December, being employed at Towyn and Penrhyndeudraeth, Merionethshire. He suffered dilatation of the stomach, was unable to use his stomach tube and his condition worsened. A medical board at Shrewsbury on 13th December found him unfit for General and Home Service but able to carry out light duties. He was advised to have an operation at Shrewsbury Hospital, but this does not appear to have been carried out. He was discharged at Towyn, medically unfit for further military service on 14th January 1916. John's death was registered at Forden and Sarah was living at Mill Cottage, Marton Chirbury, Shropshire at the time of her death there.
- Richard Waring (26th September 1874–14th July 1952), born at West Derby, Lancashire, married Jane Alice Parkinson (15th January 1872–1948), born at Preston, Lancashire, in 1895 at Oswestry. He was a journeyman baker in 1901, when they were living at Croeswilmot Cottage, Weston Lane, Oswestry. By 1911

he was the licensee of the Bear Hotel, Salop Road, Oswestry and was still there in 1919. In 1939 he was a bread baker and cake confectionery and they were living at Croes Wylan Cottage, Weston Lane, Oswestry. They had a daughter:
- Margaret Alice Waring (3rd April 1896–8th February 1980) married Thomas Hinton in 1917. She was living with her mother at the time of the 1939 Register. She was living at Springfield, Drawbriggs Lane, Appleby-in-Westmorland, Cumbria at the time of her death there. Margaret and Thomas had two children – Ronald Hinton (1918–98) and Jean Hinton (born 1922).

- Elizabeth Margaret Waring (1876–91).
- Sarah Ann 'Annie' Waring (16th January 1878–11th January 1941) married William James Sapple (30th September 1876–1959), a timberman and carrier, in 1904. He enlisted in 4th Battalion, South Wales Borderers (Militia) (1976) at Welshpool on 30th August 1893 and had a medical at Brecon on 1st September. He was described as a miller employed by H Gregory, almost 5' 6" tall, weighing 108 lbs, with fresh complexion, blue eyes, brown hair and his religious denomination was Church of England. William attended annual training from 1894 and transferred to the Militia Reserve on 3rd June 1897. He re-engaged in the Militia Reserve on 14th June 1899 and was embodied for permanent service abroad with the Regular Force on 3rd March 1900. He embarked for South Africa on 16th March and disembarked in England and returned to the Militia on 20th August 1902. He was awarded the Queen's South Africa Medal with three clasps (Cape Colony, Orange Free State and Johannesburg). William was disembodied next day and was discharged on the termination of his engagement on 29th August 1903. Sarah and William were living at 34 Higher West Street, Weaste, Salford, Lancashire in 1911. He enlisted in No.5 Supernumerary Company, 8th Manchester on 25th January 1915 at Ardwick, Manchester (1222), described as 5' 11½" tall, weighing 168 lbs and his religious denomination was Church of England. He had once contracted malaria. He transferred to 317th Protection Company, Royal Defence Corps on 29th April 1916 (16505) and to 313th Protection Company RDC on 28th September 1917. He was promoted lance corporal on 4th May 1918 and from 11th September his medical classification was B2. William had a medical at Knockaloe, Isle of Man

The Royal Defence Corps was formed by Royal Warrant on 17th March 1916, to carry out duties connected with the local defence of the United Kingdom, including those hitherto performed by the Supernumerary Territorial Force Companies, as well as those allotted to the Observer Companies now in process of formation. Administration of the RDC for the whole country was the responsibility of the City of London TF Association. By April 1918 about 27,000 men were serving in the RDC and of these 14,000 were guarding prisoner of war camps.

on 4th February 1919 and was disembodied on demobilisation on 7th February. He was a timber porter in the docks in 1939, when they were still living at 34 Higher West Street. He was described as a dock labourer at the time of his wife's death at The Grove, Llandrinio, Montgomeryshire. They had a son:
    * William George Sapple (6th August 1906–1957), born at Salford, Lancashire, was a sheet metal worker in 1939, living with his parents. He married Gladys May Pryce (born 1919), a clerk, on 9th June 1941 at Llandrinio Parish Church, Montgomeryshire. At the time he was living at 26 Alexandra Road, Peel Green, Eccles, Lancashire and she at The Grove, Llandrinio. His death was registered at Barton, Lancashire. They had four children – David G Sapple 1942, Susan A Sapple 1945, Shirley Sapple 1950 and Sylvia P Sapple 1953.
* David Waring (1879–80).
* Sydness Waring (1881–90).
* Charles Waring (1883–1907), born in Welshpool was a butcher's journeyman in 1901. He married Mary Ann Jones (born 1882) in 1906. She was living with her parents at 3 Clifton Street, Welshpool in 1911. They had a daughter:
    * Winifred Alice Waring (17th May 1907–14th March 1967) married Edwin Thomas Hough (4th May 1908–1966), born at Cannock, Staffordshire, in 1932. Edwin was living with his grandparents at White Pump Cottage, Wheaton Aston, Staffordshire in 1911. He was a waggoner on a farm in 1939, when they were living at White Abbey Cottage, Atcham, Shropshire. His death was registered at Lichfield, Staffordshire. Winifred was living at 239 Wimblebury Road, Heath Hayes, Cannock at the time of her death at the General Infirmary, Stafford. It is believed that they had three children but only one, Edwin Raymond Hough (1942–2007), is confirmed. The others may be Sylvia J Hough 1934 and Eileen M Hough 1937.
* Frederick Waring (13th May 1889–1st December 1972) enlisted in B Squadron, Montgomeryshire Yeomanry (1076) at Welshpool on 16th April 1908, with service reckoning from 1st April. He gave his age as twenty-two, his trade as poultry dresser and claimed previous service with the Imperial Yeomanry from 18th May 1903. He attended annual training 27th May–10th June 1908, 27th May–10th June 1909, 26th May–9th June 1910, 23rd May–6th June 1911, 23rd May–6th June 1912 and 22nd May–5th June 1913. Frederick was a feather (poultry) dealer in 1911, working for Mr Bushell at Welshpool. He married Alice Mary Pugh (26th March 1886–16th February 1978), born at Machynlleth, Montgomeryshire, in 1911. They lived at 8 Canal Road, Four Crosses, Llanymynech. Frederick was embodied on 5th August 1914 and was posted to 2/1st Montgomeryshire Yeomanry on 11th June 1915. He was discharged at Southwold on 14th January 1916 medically unfit for further military service due to rheumatism in the left leg, which began at Hailsham on 25th December 1914. It eventually affected both legs. He was described as twenty-five years and eight months old, 5′ 10½″

tall, with fair complexion, grey eyes, dark hair and his trade was poultry dresser. He was awarded the Territorial Force Efficiency Medal. Frederick re-enlisted in the Montgomeryshire Yeomanry on 3rd April 1916 (3495) but was so affected by rheumatism that he was graded medically C3 and was unable to do anything but very light work. He was a farm produce merchant in 1939, when they were living at Nantcribbau, Forden. They had a daughter:
  ○ Myfanwy Elizabeth Waring (11th March 1912–October 1994) married John Torrence (6th April 1905–April 1972) at Stockport, Cheshire in 1933. He was working for the government in 1939, when they were living at 5 Walnut Tree Road, Stockport. They had seven children – Gordon John Torrence 1932, Freda A Torrence 1934, Donald G Torrence 1935, Jean Hazel Torrence 1937, Kenneth D Torrence 1939, Dorothy M Torrence 1941 and Pamela R Torrence 1945. Myfanwy married Simon Francis in Rochdale, Lancashire in 1981.
• George Waring (1892–23rd December 1935) was a feather (poultry) dealer in 1911, living with his parents. He was discharged from 1/7th Royal Welsh Fusiliers on 18th June 1915 (696) due to being medically unfit caused by idiocy, which commenced in October 1914. His address was 21 Rock Terrace, Welshpool. He married Sarah Annie Brown (9th April 1894–3rd March 1980) in 1917 at Llanfyllin, Montgomeryshire. She was a servant in 1911 working for Robert Henry Sockett, a chemist's assistant, at Hampton House, Llandysilio, Montgomeryshire. George subsequently served in the Army Service Corps (M/337854) and was discharged on 2nd March 1919. They were living at Grove House, Llandrinio, Montgomeryshire at the time of his death there. Sarah was a farm produce merchant in 1939, living with her daughter at Grove House. They had a daughter, Beryl Waring (born 1929), who married as Stedman.

William's paternal grandfather, John Waring (c.1824–66), was a nailer living with his parents in 1841. He married Elizabeth née Roberts (c.1826–1906) in 1848 at Montgomery. She was working for farmers Richard and Mary Wilcox at Forden in 1841. John was a police officer in 1851, when they were living at High Street, Welshpool. By 1861 he was a nail maker and they were living on Raven Street, Welshpool. Elizabeth was still living there in 1871. Her death was registered at West Derby, Lancashire. In addition to Richard they had another son:

• David Waring (1861–1924) married Louisa Griffith (1862–14th October 1935) in 1882 at West Derby, Lancashire, where she was born. He was a grocer's assistant in 1891,

High Street, Welshpool, where William's paternal grandparents were living in 1851.

when they were living at 8 Lark Hill Lane, West Derby. By 1901 he was a cab driver and they were living at 9 Valley Road, Walton on the Hill, Lancashire. His mother was living with them. By 1911 they had moved to 194 Whitefield Road, Liverpool. They had fifteen children:
- Louisa Waring (1882–14th February 1910) was a telephone operator in 1901.
- Frederick Arnold Waring (21st February 1884–1961) was an apprentice dental mechanic in 1901.
- Edith Elizabeth Waring (1885–1960) never married.
- Albert Ewart Waring (1887–1965) married Florence Mildred Firth (1889–1935) in 1916 at West Derby. They had a son, Alan F. Firth in 1921. Albert enlisted in the Western Telegraph Battalion, Royal Engineers TF (546) as an airline sapper in Liverpool on 30th May 1911. He was a lineman living at 194 Whitefield Road, Everton and was described as 5′ 5¼″ tall with previous service in 1st Volunteer Battalion, King's Liverpool Regiment. He attended summer camps at Holmscales 30th July–13th August 1911, at Kirkham 4th-18th August 1912 and at Rhyl 20th July–3rd August 1913. Promoted lance corporal on 5th June 1913. He was embodied on 5th August 1914 and went to France on 26th October with Western Army Troops Signal Company RE TF. Appointed acting second corporal on 3rd May 1915 with W6 Airline Section. He returned to Britain on 21st May 1916 and was discharged time expired after five years on 30th May 1916 at Watton, Norfolk. Albert married Margaret Maxwell in Liverpool in 1941.
- Matthew David Waring (1888–3rd July 1892).
- Stanley Waring (born 3rd December 1890) married Sarah Elizabeth née Slinger (1894–1944) at West Derby in 1916. He enlisted in the Canadian Engineers, Canadian Expeditionary Force (2011074) at Montréal, Canada on 4th June 1918. He was a locomotive fireman living at 38 Shakespeare Street, Liverpool, England, described as 5′ 6½″ tall, weighing 145 lbs, with dark complexion, brown eyes, brown hair and his religious denomination was Church of England. On medical examination he had an enlarged left testicle but insufficient to cause rejection for service. Embarked on SS *Saturnia* on 29th June and disembarked in England on 22nd July. He was taken on the strength of 2nd Canadian Engineers Railway Battalion at Seaford and transferred to 3rd Canadian Engineers Railway Battalion there on 6th August. He was treated at No.14 Canadian General Hospital, Eastbourne, Sussex for influenza 31st October–18th November 1918 and was discharged to the Canadian Engineers Training Depot. Stanley was appointed paid acting corporal on 5th December and reverted to sapper at his own request on 21st January 1919. He transferred to the Canadian Engineers Training Depot on 13th June, to H Wing at Witley, Surrey on 16th June and was struck off strength to R Wing on 3rd July. He was discharged in England from No.2 Canadian Discharge Depot on 21st August 1919. Stanley and

Sarah had six children – Harold Waring 1917, Stanley Waring 1920, Leslie Waring 1925, twins Albert and Edith M Waring 1928 and George W Waring 1934.
- Eveline May Waring (born 1893) married Albert Williams in 1920.
- Mary Clarice Waring (27th October 1894–1978) married Edward Cecil Spilsbury (born 1890) in 1922. Edward served in the Royal Field Artillery (808 & 676590) as a corporal and went to France on 29th September 1915. Mary married John Jenkinson in 1939.
- Harold Waring (born 1896).
- Eric Charles Whitley Waring (born and died 1898).
- John Ernest Waring (15th July 1899–1982).
- Catherine Maud Waring (1901–7th August 1901).
- David Reginald Waring (1902–68) married Florence M McLean (23rd July 1900–1979) in 1926. They had three children – Sydney D Waring 1927, Robert G Waring 1930 and Edna M Waring 1936.
- Arthur Waring (1904–18th December 1904).
- Thomas George Waring (born 1906) married Elizabeth A Thompson in 1934.

His maternal grandfather, Thomas Jones (born c.1819), a tailor, married Margaret Jones (born c.1818). They were living at 10 Powell's Row, Welshpool in 1851 and were still there in 1881. In addition to Ann they had three other children:

- William Jones (born c.1854).
- Charles Jones (born 1857).
- John Jones (born 1865).

William was educated at Christ Church (Church of England) Infants' School, Welshpool and at Berriew Road Boys' National School, Welshpool. He was a general labourer working on the Elan Valley reservoir scheme in Radnorshire in 1901, boarding with six others with John and Sarah Collingworth, 35 Elan Village, Llanwrthwl, Brecon. He was later employed by Mr H Bushell, a poultry dealer in Welshpool and was living with his parents in 1911. William was a member of the Welshpool Lodge of the Order of Druids. He played amateur football for Welshpool Reserves in November 1906 and scored two goals in a 5–0 win over Royal Welsh Warehouse of Newtown in the Montgomeryshire League. He was playing for Montgomery by 1909 and was in the winning team in the final of the Montgomeryshire Challenge Cup. He was playing for the same team in 1911 with two of his brothers, when they lost in the semi-final. He later played for Llanfyllin and fullback for Welshpool in the Shropshire League in 1912. In 1913 he played for Oswestry United in the Lancashire Combination League.

The Elan Valley reservoirs were created by damming the Elan and Claerwen rivers. They were built by Birmingham Corporation Water Department to provide clean water for the rapidly expanding industrial city. Water from the reservoirs is transported to Frankley Reservoir in Birmingham through the 117 kms long Elan aqueduct. No pumping is required because the Elan Valley reservoirs are fifty-two metres higher. The purpose-built Elan Village was home to thousands of navvies and some families while they built the first four dams (Caban-coch, Garreg-ddu, Pen-y-garreg and Craig-goch) between 1893 and 1904. The project was officially opened by King Edward VII and Queen Alexandra on 21st July 1904. The fifth dam (Claerwen) was not completed until 1952 and was opened by Queen Elizabeth II in one of her first official engagements. Building materials, up to 1,000 tons daily, were brought in on the Elan Valley Railway, which had been lifted by 1916. Access to Elan Village was strictly controlled to maintain order and health. All newly arrived workers were deloused and examined for infectious diseases. A man and wife shared each terraced house with up to eight single men. Facilities included a school, hospital, isolation hospital for infectious cases, bath house, library, public hall, shop, canteen and a pub that sold beer to men only. Electricity for the village was provided by hydro-generators. It would be a century later before small-scale hydro-generation was again introduced. The small Nant-y-Gro dam was constructed early in the project to supply water to the navvies' village. When construction was completed it became redundant. In 1942 Barnes Wallis used it to prove his theory that an underwater explosion against a dam wall would create sufficient hydrostatic pressure to breach it. The test was successful and the remains of the breached dam can still be seen, although partly obscured by trees. Wallis went on to develop the Upkeep bouncing bombs that were used in May 1943 to breach the Möhne and Eder dams in Germany.

William enlisted in the Montgomeryshire Imperial Yeomanry on 14th September 1903 (1452) and served until 13th September 1907. He rejoined on 28th November 1907. The unit title changed to the Montgomeryshire Yeomanry (Dragoons) on the formation of the Territorial Force on 1st April 1908. He rejoined B Squadron at Welshpool on 30th April 1908, with effect from 1st April, and attended annual training for two weeks every year in May and June from 1908 to 1913. He was promoted corporal on 23rd May 1911 and sergeant on 22nd May 1913. William was awarded a silver watch as the best shot in his squadron in 1913 and a silver cup as a member of the best troop in the squadron in May 1914. The unit was mobilised on 5th August 1914 at Llandrindod Wells, Montgomeryshire and as 1/1st Montgomeryshire Yeomanry moved to Holt Hall, near Sheringham, Norfolk. Winter billets were occupied at Cromer and the unit was dismounted in November. He re-engaged for the duration of the war on 22nd December 1915. On 3rd March 1916 he embarked aboard HMT *Arcadian* at Devonport, Devon and disembarked

The Montgomeryshire Yeomanry formed in 1803 for home defence and internal security duties during the Napoleonic Wars. Originally named the Montgomeryshire Volunteer Legion, it consisted of four combined cavalry and infantry troops. The infantry element was short lived and the unit was renamed the Montgomeryshire Yeomanry Cavalry. Further troops were added in 1813 and 1819. Along with many other Yeomanry regiments, the Montgomeryshire was disbanded in 1828 when government funding was withdrawn. However, this was restored in 1831 and the Regiment reformed with its four original troops. Others were added and disbanded at various times. Regimental HQ was established at Welshpool and in 1893 the six troops were reorganised

into three squadrons. During the Second Boer War the Imperial Yeomanry was created and the Montgomeryshire Yeomanry raised 31st and 49th (Montgomeryshire) Companies, which landed in South Africa on 6th April 1900 and served with other Welsh Yeomanry companies in 9th Battalion, Imperial Yeomanry. Two more companies (88th (Welsh Yeomanry) and 89th (Montgomeryshire) Companies) were raised for the second contingent and the four companies comprised the whole of 9th Battalion. The concept of the Imperial Yeomanry as mounted infantry was successful. Before the war ended, Yeomanry regiments at home were converted into Imperial Yeomanry, with an establishment of an HQ, four squadrons and a machine gun section. This included the Montgomeryshire Imperial Yeomanry, which raised an additional squadron. The Imperial Yeomanry were subsumed into the Territorial Force in 1908 and the unit was officially titled the Montgomeryshire Yeomanry (Dragoons). When war was declared on 4th August 1914, the Montgomeryshire Yeomanry mobilised as part of the South Wales Mounted Brigade and became 1/1st Montgomeryshire Yeomanry. It moved to Thetford, Norfolk and in November 1915 the Brigade was dismounted. In March 1916 it was sent to Egypt and the South Wales Mounted Brigade was absorbed into 4th Dismounted Brigade. In March 1917 the units were re-roled as infantry. 1/1st Montgomeryshire Yeomanry and the Welsh Horse Yeomanry amalgamated to form 25th (Montgomery and Welsh Horse Yeomanry) Battalion, Royal Welsh Fusiliers in 231st Brigade, 74th (Yeomanry) Division. In May 1918 the Division moved to France. 2/1st Montgomeryshire Yeomanry formed in September 1914. It was converted to a cyclist unit in October 1916 and spent the entire war in Britain. 3/1st Montgomeryshire Yeomanry formed in June 1915 and later converted to infantry. The unit disbanded in January 1917, with personnel transferring to 2/1st Montgomeryshire Yeomanry or 4th (Reserve) Battalion, Royal Welsh Fusiliers. Post-war a squadron combined with a company of 1st Herefordshire Regiment to form 332nd (Radnorshire) Field Battery (Howitzers) at Llandrindod Wells. The remainder of the Regiment formed two companies in 7th (Merioneth and Montgomeryshire) Battalion, Royal Welsh Fusiliers in March 1920.

at Alexandria, Egypt on 13th March. 1/1st Montgomeryshire Yeomanry, as part of the South Wales Mounted Brigade, joined with the Welsh Border Mounted Brigade to form 4th Dismounted Brigade in the Western Frontier Force on 20th March.

On 4th March 1917 the 1/1st Montgomeryshire Yeomanry and 1/1st Welsh Horse amalgamated at Helmia, Egypt to form 25th (Montgomeryshire and Welsh Horse Yeomanry) Battalion, The Royal Welsh Fusiliers in 231st Brigade, 74th Division although William's service record shows that he joined the Battalion on

SS *Ortona* was built by Vickers, Sons & Maxim Ltd at Barrow-in-Furness in 1899 for the Pacific Steam Navigation Co. She was the last Pacific Steam ship built for the London-Australia route. Her maiden voyage departed London on 24th November 1899. On 8th May 1906 *Ortona* was sold to the Royal Mail Steam Packet Co. In April 1909 she transferred to the Royal Mail West Indies service and in 1910 was converted by Harland & Wolff in Belfast into a 320-capacity cruise ship (8,939 tons). She was renamed RMS *Arcadian* on 21st September 1910 as all the Company's liners had names beginning with

A. Her first world cruise commenced in January 1912 and at the time she was the largest dedicated cruise ship in the world. During the voyage Sir Robert Baden-Powell, founder of the Scout Movement, met Olave St Claire Soames aboard and they were married that October. In February 1915, *Arcadian* was hired by the Admiralty. On 7th April 1915 General Sir Ian Hamilton used the ship and HMS *Queen Elizabeth* as his headquarters during the opening phase of the Gallipoli campaign. On 15th April 1917 *Arcadian* was steaming from Thessaloniki to Alexandria with 1,335 troops and crew aboard. About forty kilometres northeast of the Greek island of Milos she was torpedoed by UC-74 and sank within six minutes with the loss of 279 lives (State Library of Queensland).

16th December 1916 (355014). He reverted to private at his own request on 21st March 1917 but was appointed paid acting sergeant on 31st October and acting company quartermaster sergeant on 24th November. He again reverted to private at own request on 29th November. **Awarded the MM for his actions at Beit Ur el-Foqa, Palestine on 29th-30th November during the Third Battle of Gaza, LG 4th February 1918.** Hill 1750 and the village were taken at dawn after a short fight but the Turks realised the weakness of the British force and drove it out again. Promoted corporal on 2nd December, acting sergeant on 7th January 1918 and paid lance sergeant on 9th March. He reverted to lance sergeant on 13th April.

William, seated on the right, with a group of soldiers from a number of other cap badges. He is wearing the ribbon of the Territorial Efficiency Medal; the only VC recipient to be awarded both medals.

William embarked at Alexandria on 29th April and disembarked in France with the Battalion on 7th May. Granted fourteen days leave in Britain from 18th August. **Awarded the VC for his actions at Ronssoy, France on 18th September 1918, LG 31st January 1919.** He was treated for his wounds at a field ambulance and casualty clearing stations before being admitted to a general hospital at Le Havre, where he died on 8th October 1918. He is buried in Ste Marie Cemetery, Le Havre (62 V 1 3). The posthumous VC was presented to his parents by the King in the ballroom at Buckingham Palace on 8th March 1919. He is commemorated in a number of other places:

Beit Ur el-Foqa (today Beit Ur al Fauqa) is about eight kilometres west of Ramallah. Archaeology dates back to the Late Bronze Age and the site was the ancient town of Bethoron, which dominated an important ancient route. In the nearby ravines the Roman Twelfth Legion was destroyed in 66 AD in the First Jewish-Roman War. After the Jewish Revolt had been crushed in 70 AD, the Romans built a fortress in the village to guard the road to Jerusalem. Later in the Roman period Beit Ur el-Foqa lost its importance. It was known as Bethoron Superior or Vetus Betor in the Crusader era. Palestine was incorporated into the Ottoman Empire in 1517 and the village is recorded in the census of 1596. By the time of the British Mandate 1922 Census the village had a population of 147, rising to 210 by 1945. After the 1948 Arab-Israeli War, Beit Ur al-Fauqa became part of Jordan. However, since the 1967 Six-Day War the village has been under Israeli occupation as part of the West Bank. Over 200 acres of land from the village has since been confiscated to construct the Israeli settlement of Beit Horon.

Welshpool War Memorial in St Mary's Churchyard. William's name is on the first panel to the right of the column (Memorials to Valour).

William Waring's grave in Ste Marie Cemetery, Le Havre (Memorials to Valour).

- Waring Court, Barracks Field Estate, Hightown, Wrexham.
- Welshpool War Memorial in St Mary's Churchyard.
- Name on the family grave in the Welsh Baptist Church Burial Ground of Christ Church Churchyard, Welshpool.

On the left is the North Wales Heroes' Memorial. Above the archway the room is lined with wood panels listing 8,500 people from the region who died on active service during the First World War. The University College of North Wales, Bangor (now Bangor University) is in the top right of the picture. Prime Minister David Lloyd George was a patron and students at Bangor University helped with fund-raising for the Memorial. It was opened by the Prince of Wales (later Edward VIII) on 1st November 1923.

The Waring family grave in the Welsh Baptist Church Burial Ground of Christ Church Churchyard. William is commemorated on the third block from the bottom.

The Territorial Force Efficiency Medal was established in 1908 for long service by NCOs and men in the Territorial Force. It replaced the Volunteer Long Service Medal and Imperial Yeomanry Long Service Medal. Minimum qualification was twelve years, including twelve annual training camps. Previous service in other part-time forces counted towards the award and war service counted double. Bars were awarded for further periods of twelve years.

- Memorial in Welshpool Town Hall unveiled in 2015, including a replica set of medals.
- North Wales Heroes' Memorial, Bangor.
- A Department for Communities and Local Government commemorative paving stone was dedicated at Welshpool Town Hall, Hall Street, Welshpool, Powys, Wales on 5th December 2015.

Biographies 185

Welshpool Town Hall.

William's parents and other relatives outside Buckingham Palace after the investiture on 8th March 1919. His father is wearing his son's VC and TFEM on his right breast.

In addition to the VC and MM he was awarded the British War Medal 1914–20, Victory Medal 1914–19 and Territorial Force Efficiency Medal. His mother left the medals to Welshpool Town Council in June 1929. The VC was loaned to the Royal Welch Fusiliers Museum for one year to celebrate the tercentenary of the Regiment before being returned to Welshpool Town Council, Triangle House, Union Street, Welshpool, Powys. Replica medals are displayed at the Town Hall.

William's commemorative paving stone at Welshpool Town Hall (Memorials to Valour).

## SECOND LIEUTENANT WILLIAM ALLISON WHITE
### 38th Battalion, Machine Gun Corps

William White was born on 19th October 1894 at 5 Lavender Walk, Mitcham, Surrey. His father, Samuel White (1869–14th June 1943), born at Barrow-in-Furness, Lancashire, was a house decorator. He married Eliza née Maloney (1864–27th April 1943), born at Portadown, Co Down, Ireland, in 1892 at Croydon, Surrey. They were living at 49 Martell Road, West Dulwich, London in 1911 and later moved to Mizpah, 38 Princes Terrace, Brighton, Sussex. Samuel was a building contractor when his son, William, applied for a commission in November 1916. Eliza died at Mizpah and Samuel at the Royal Sussex County Hospital. William had two sisters:

- Martha Louisa White (15th September 1893–12th June 1980), born at Mitcham, Surrey, was an apprentice dressmaker in 1911. She emigrated to New South Wales, Australia in 1914. She married Herbert Myer Myers (17th August 1887–12th July 1975), a telegraphist born in Sydney, in 1917 at Waverley, NSW. They had a number of addresses in NSW: 31 Arden Street, Coogee 1930; Eden Monaro 1933; Uralla (as postmaster) 1936; Cook 1943; Grayndler 1949; Watson 1958; 6 Tenth Street, Kingsford-Smith 1968; and 122 Mandarin Street, Villawood, NSW 1972. Herbert died at Glenfield Masonic Homes (later The Frank Whiddon Masonic Homes of New South Wales), 81 Belmont Road, Glenfield. Martha was living at 5/13 Kennedy Parade, Seven Hills, Lalor Park, Chifley, NSW in 1977. She died at Wingham Court Nursing Home (later The Whiddon Group Wingham Residential Aged Care), 12 Primrose Street, Wingham. They had five children:
    - Alison Jack Myers (7th January 1918–21st March 1962), born at Tarlo, Henderson Street, Bondi, was an engineer. He married Joyce Russell Stevens (born 31st August 1916) in 1941 at Sydney. They lived at 82 Rothschild Avenue, Redfern. He was a garage proprietor in 1949, by when they were living at 2 Collins Street, Redfern, and they had moved to 73 Rothschild

William with his parents and sisters, Martha on the left, and Charlotte on the right.

Avenue, Rosebury by 1954. Jack was racing at Catalina Racing Circuit, Katoomba, when he was thrown from his car in a crash and suffered fatal injuries, including a compound fracture of the skull. Joyce was a director of a firm in 1972, when she was living at 7/41 Bath Street, Monterey. They had two children.

- Eric Geoffrey Myers (28th June 1919–12th December 2006), born at Bondi, was a motor mechanic when he enlisted in the RAAF on 15th July 1940 at Mascot, NSW (32334). He was a flight sergeant serving with No.5 Repair and Servicing Unit when he was discharged on 27th November 1945. He married Pansy Robinson (born 24th October 1913) on 19th March 1943 at St John's Anglican Church, South Townsville, Queensland. By 1949 he was a butcher living at 149 Bundock Street, Townsville and they were still there in 1980. He was living at Aitkenvale, Queensland at the time of his death there. They had two children.
- Harold William Myers (May 1921–26th April 2001) enlisted as a telegraphist in the Royal Australian Navy on 18th May 1942 (S/V156) and was serving aboard HMAS *Rushcutter* when he was discharged on 10th May 1946. He married Joyce Swilks (born c.1930) in 1950 at Uralla, NSW, where she was born. They lived at 58 Second Avenue,

Mitcham dates back to pre-Roman days. Many finds from the Anglo-Saxon graveyard are in the British Museum. The Church of St Peter & St Paul, which was rebuilt 1819-21, retains the original Saxon tower. Sir Walter Raleigh had a residence there. It became known for its lavender fields and in 1749 John Potter and William Moore founded a company to make and market toiletries made from local herbs and flowers. In the industrial age works grew up along the banks of the Wandle to make snuff and work copper, iron, flour and produce dyes. The area became the centre for English calico printing by 1750. The Surrey Iron Railway became the world's first public railway in 1803. More industries were set up, despite the failure of the railway, and the population doubled between 1900 and 1910. Mitcham has the world's oldest cricket club.

38 Princes Terrace, Brighton where William's parents lived later in life.

Berala before moving to 11 Wellington Road, Birrong, Sefton, Blaxland by 1972. Harold died at Toukley, NSW. They had two children.
- Noel Myers (18th December 1924–12th January 2008) was an instrument maker and later an electrician, working for the State Electricity Commission, Victoria. He married Mary Eva Bellis (14th June 1924–12th April 2007) on 19th April 1947 at Wangaratta, Victoria, where she was born. They were living at Woodcourt Road, Berowra, NSW in 1949, at 26 Pollock Avenue, Traralgon, Victoria in 1954, at 71 Hampton Street, Moe, Victoria in 1963, High Street, Wycheproof, Victoria in 1968 and at 3 Heather Grove, Ringwood, Victoria in 1972. By then he was a district assistant secretary. They both died at Melbourne, Victoria. They had two children, including Kenneth Noel Myers (11th June 1954–1971), born at Box Hill, Victoria. He was a promising road racing cyclist until he was run down and killed.
- Samuel Alick Myers (31st August 1926–4th July 2015), born at Roslyn Private Hospital, Forest Road, Arncliffe, NSW, was a toolmaker. He married Gweneth Audrey Roots (born 1928) on 5th November 1949 at Wesley Chapel, Sydney. He was a foreman by 1963, when they were living at 122 Mandarin Street, Villawood. By 1977 he was a director and they were living at 9 Birrawa Street, Greystanes, before moving to Lot 27, Lake Russell Drive, Avocado Heights. Sam died at Coffs Harbour. They had four children, including Stephen John Myers.

• Charlotte Mary White (29th September 1895–10th February 1979), born at Croydon, Surrey, also emigrated to New South Wales, Australia in 1914. She married William Richmond Rae (20th November 1890–17th August 1951), a fireman born at Double Row, Eglinton Irons Works, Kilwinning, Ayrshire, Scotland, in 1916 at Waverley. They were living at Blue Gum, Helensburgh in 1930 before moving to Boomerang Street there. Charlotte was living at 23 Coward Street, Watson, near Mascot in 1958 and at 11/25 Roosevelt Avenue, Banks, NSW in 1977. They had four children including:
- Flora Rae (25th April 1925–10th February 2008), born at Mascot, married Arthur William Lawrence (1931–19th October 1995) at Randwick in 1947. He was a storekeeper in 1949, when they were living at 1 Westmoreland Street, Glebe. By 1954 he was a nursing attendant and they were living at 6 Boomerang Street, Helensburgh. By 1958 he was a grocer and they were living at 104 Banksia Avenue, Engadine. He was a cleaner by 1968, when they were living at 5 Ischia Street, Cronulla. He died at Albion Park and she at Bowral.
- William Richmond Rae (c.1930–2nd December 2014) was a fitter machinist, living with his sister, Jean, and her husband, in 1954. He died at Rose Bay, Sydney.
- Jean Eliza Rae (died 16th June 1982) married Reginald Lindsay Herbert (1914–19th February 2009) at Waverley in 1938. He was a storeman in 1954,

when they were living at 14 Walker Avenue, Grayndler. They had moved to 23 Coward Street, Watson, near Mascot by 1958. He was later an attendant. She died at Watson and he at Thames Holt Retirement Village, Sutherland. They had a son.

William's paternal grandfather, William White (1844–1909), born at Whitehaven, Cumberland, married Martha née Underwood (1844–83), born at Egremont, Cumberland, at Cockermouth, Cumberland in 1863. William was a mariner in 1881, when they were living at 11 Kendal Cottages, Barrow-in-Furness, Lancashire. Martha probably died from complications with the birth of their daughter, Annie. William married Mary Ann Davies (born c.1845), born at Latton, Wiltshire, at

Barrow-in-Furness in Cumbria was historically part of Lancashire. It became a municipal borough in 1867 and merged with Dalton-in-Furness Urban District in 1974. There is evidence of Neolithic settlement in the area and a Viking community in the early 9th century. Furness Abbey was built on the orders of King Stephen in 1123. The monks discovered iron ore deposits, and the proceeds from mining and smelting, together with agriculture and fisheries, meant that by the 15th century the Abbey was the second richest and most powerful Cistercian abbey in England. After being twice invaded by the Scots in 1316 and 1322, Edward III allowed the Abbey to build a motte and bailey castle on Piel Island. In the early 1840s there were only thirty-two dwellings in Barrow but this was about to change. The iron prospector Henry Schneider arrived in 1839 and he discovered large deposits of haematite. He and others opened the Furness Railway in 1846 to transport iron ore and slate to the coast. With locally available coal in abundance, factories opened to smelt and export steel. By 1876, the Barrow Hematite Steel Co's works were the world's largest. Docks were built between 1863 and 1881. By 1881 Barrow's population had swollen to 47,259. James Ramsden founded the Barrow and Calcutta Jute Co in 1870 and its jute mill employed 2,000 women at its peak. The availability of steel led to the development of shipbuilding. The first ship built was the *Jane Roper*, launched in 1852, and the first steamship, the *Duke of Devonshire* (3,000 tons), was launched in 1873. Shipbuilding increased and on 18th February 1871 the Barrow Shipbuilding Co was incorporated. It was taken over by the Sheffield steel firm, Vickers, in 1897, by when it was the largest employer in Barrow. The shipyard was heavily engaged in constructing warships, particularly for the Royal Navy, but also for export, such as *Mikasa*, the Japanese flagship during the 1905 Russo-Japanese War. The Royal Navy's first submarine, *Holland I*, was built in 1901. Shipbuilding was given a significant boost during the Great War and the town's population reached an estimated peak of 82,000. During the Second World War, Barrow's industry became a target for the Luftwaffe. The town suffered most in April–May 1941. In total eighty-three people were killed and 11,000 houses were damaged. Iron and steel making and mining declined after the Second World War and had ended by 1983, leaving the Vickers shipyard as the main employer. The BAE Systems shipyard there is still the UK's largest by workforce. Gas was discovered in Morecambe Bay in the 1980s and is processed in south Barrow. In the early 21st century, four offshore wind farms were constructed with over 160 turbines providing sufficient power for half a million homes. Amongst the famous people originating from, or living in, Barrow are Emlyn Hughes (1947–2004), the Liverpool and England football captain, and Dame Stella Rimington (born 1935), Director General of MI5 1992–96.

Barrow-in-Furness in 1887. They were living at 3 Harrogate Street, Barrow-in-Furness in 1891, by when he was a fireman in a shipyard. By 1901 they were living at 8 Forman's Cottages, Barrow-in-Furness and he was once again a mariner. In addition to Samuel, William and Martha had eight other children:

- Edward White (1864–75), born at Whitehaven and died at Ulverston.
- William White (1865–20th February 1947) was a railway labourer and later a bridge painter. He married his aunt, Rebecca Roberts née White (1849–1920) on 1st April 1889 at Barrow-in-Furness Register Office. She had married Samuel Roberts (October 1840–April 1882), an ostler, on 3rd November 1867 at St James, Whitehaven. William and Rebecca were living at 31 Hall Street, Barrow-in-Furness in 1891 and 1901. By 1911 they were living at 54 Risedale Road, Barrow-in-Furness. He was living later at 59 Smeaton Street, Barrow-in-Furness. He died at North Lonsdale Hospital, Barrow-in-Furness. Rebecca had seven children from her two marriages:
    - William Roberts (1868–1920) was a shipyard labourer in 1891.
    - Richard White Roberts (1870–1944) was an ironworks labourer in 1891.
    - Sarah Ann Roberts (1874–1953) was a weaver in a jute mill in 1891. She married John Mallinson in 1900.
    - Rebecca Dixon Roberts (1878–1946) married Thomas Wilson in 1898. They had at least one daughter, Rebecca Roberts Wilson, in 1905.
    - Agnes Roberts (born 1880).
    - Isabella Roberts (born 1884), father unknown.
    - Albert Edward White (1889–1947).
- Allison Collier White (1871–1927), born at Ulverston, was a general duties water main layer with Barrow-in-Furness Corporation. He married Mary Jane Roberts (1872–1934), born at Whitehaven, in 1891. They were living at 43 Parker Street, Barrow-in-Furness in 1911. They had four children:
    - William Edward White (1892–17th May 1963) was a water main joiner in 1911.
    - Samuel White (1893–7th February 1963) was a gas labourer in 1911. He was a gas fitter when he enlisted at Liverpool in 10th (Scottish) Battalion, The King's (Liverpool Regiment) on 5th January 1916, described as 5′ 7″ tall. He went to France on 14th July. Samuel transferred to 13th Battalion on 16th September, the Depot in Britain on 18th October and 3rd Battalion on 30th April 1917. He was compulsorily transferred to the Royal Army Medical Corps (144238) on 1st August 1918. He was demobilised and transferred to the Class Z Army Reserve on 9th March 1919, with sixty percent disability due to gunshot wounds to the face and left hand. He was awarded a pension of £-/16/6 per week to be reviewed after a year.
    - Mary Jane White (born c.1899).
    - Martha Underwood White (20th August 1902–1975) never married.

- Mary White (born 1874).
- Henry White (c.1876–87) was born at Barrow-in-Furness.
- Martha White (1878–8th April 1957) married George Henry Cuss (1877–1957), born at Cricklade, Wiltshire, at Barrow-in-Furness in 1902. He enlisted in the Wiltshire Regiment (4120) in 1894 and was a Corporation lamplighter in 1911, when they were living at 5 Lindal Street, Barrow-in-Furness before moving to 49 Fenton Street. He served in the Great War in the Devonshire Regiment (12945) and Wiltshire Regiment (47557) and went to France on 28th July 1915. Martha died at Roose Hospital, Barrow-in-Furness. They had four daughters:
    - Elsie Cuss (born 1903) married Nathan Howard (1898–1968) in 1933. They had two daughters – Joyce I Howard 1934 and Jeanne E Howard 1936.
    - Irene Cuss (born 1905) married Albert E Phillips in 1936.
    - Mary Cuss (1908–56) married William L Rutherford (1904–68) in 1933. They had a daughter, Audrey Rutherford, in 1936.
    - Martha Cuss (born 1915) married Percy Wright in 1937.
- Robert White (19th February 1881–1883), born at 11 Kendal Cottages, Barrow-in-Furness.
- Annie White (1883–17th June 1954) married Robert James Drake (1881–1946), born at Wareham, Dorset, at Salisbury, Wiltshire in 1914. Robert had married Rosa 'Rosie' Margaret Hargrave (23rd February 1879–1914), born at Tarrant Gunville, Dorset, on 23rd December 1901 at Swanage, Dorset. Robert was a coal carter in 1911, when they were living at 2 Albert Place, Castle Street, Salisbury. Annie was living at 4 Ashfield Road, Salisbury at the time of her death there. Robert had eight children from his two marriages, all registered in Salisbury:
    - Eleanor Kathleen Drake (born 27th July 1904) married James Harrison at Amesbury, Wiltshire in 1928.
    - Robert James Drake (12th November 1906–1970) married Kathleen V R Beavan/Beaven (born 1912) in 1937.
    - Henry Francis Charles Drake (1910–57) married Elsie Phillimore (born 1905), born at Amesbury, in 1931. They had three children – Heather M Drake 1932, Geraldine R Drake 1933 and Roland Drake 1934.
    - Allison Collier Drake (21st November 1915–2000) married Ellen B Downes (born 1919) in 1939. They had a son, Anthony R Drake, in 1944.
    - Ernest Roger Drake (1920–30th November 1939) was serving in 4th Wiltshire (5569848) when he died (Salisbury (London Road) Cemetery – M 379).

William's cousin, Ernest, is buried in Salisbury (London Road) Cemetery.

- Sylvia Marjorie J Drake (30th March 1921–1984) married Herbert C Hatcher in 1945. She died at Blackburn, Lancashire. They had five children – Monica Hatcher 1947, Maureen Hatcher 1948, David Hatcher 1950, Barbara Hatcher 1952 and Brenda Hatcher 1953.
- Victor Frederick G Drake (13th September 1924–1983) married Freda D Hallums (born 1925) at Southend, Essex in 1946. They had three children – Geoffrey R Drake 1947, Jean M Drake 1951 and Graham V Drake 1960.
- Alexander W Drake (1930–31).

The building of Salter's Hill School commenced in 1878. It opened on 12th April 1880 and was designed for 600 children aged from seven to fourteen. It was extended to accommodate 1,200 children in 1904-05. In 1933-34 the intake changed to seven to eleven years old and was divided into separate Boys' and Girls' Schools. The Boys' School was closed during the Second World War. In 1951 the name of the school changed to Kingswood.

His maternal grandparents were Edward Maloney and Margaret née McEvoy. William was educated at Salter's Hill School, West Norwood, London and at the Municipal Technical School, Barrow-in-Furness. He was an apprentice with Vickers at Barrow-in-Furness, working on the first rigid airship, HMA1, the *Mayfly*. On 22nd February 1910 William enlisted in D Company, 4th Battalion, The King's Own (Royal Lancaster) Regiment) TF (1292). He was promoted corporal in 1912 and sergeant on 3rd August 1914, when he was appointed Battalion Machine Gun Sergeant. At Slough, Berkshire on 10th and 15th October he was charged with neglect of duty as a NCO by not seeing that his billet was clean, but was admonished

The Barrow-in-Furness School of Science and Art operated privately from 1877 until taken over by the Council in 1891. The foundation stone for a new Barrow Corporation Technical School in Abbey Road was laid on 26th May 1900 and the school was officially opened on 25th August 1903. The School expanded to create a new Central College of Further Education, which moved to a new building in Howard Street in 1954. The Technical School split from the College in 1964 and moved to a new building in Thorncliffe Road in 1970, as a result of the original building becoming dilapidated. However, it was redeveloped in the early 2000s and was named the Nan Tait Centre in honour of Agnes 'Nan' Tait, who was the Mayor of the Borough of Barrow-in-Furness 1959-60. The building is now Grade II listed and is a cultural, exhibition and arts centre.

In 1871 James Ramsden formed the Iron Shipbuilding Co, but soon changed its name to Barrow Shipbuilding Co. In 1897 the Sheffield firm of Vickers & Sons bought the Barrow Shipbuilding Co and its subsidiary, the Maxim Nordenfelt Guns & Ammunition Co, and became Vickers, Sons & Maxim Ltd. The shipyard at Barrow became the Naval Construction & Armaments Co. In 1911 the company was renamed Vickers Ltd and in 1927 became Vickers Armstrong Ltd after merging with Armstrong Whitworth, whose shipyard was on the Tyne. In 1955 the shipbuilding division changed to Vickers Armstrong Shipbuilders Ltd and in 1968 to Vickers Ltd Shipbuilding Group. The shipbuilding group was nationalised in 1977 and was subsumed into British Shipbuilders. The former Vickers yard at Barrow was the first of the British Shipbuilders group to return to the private sector, when it was sold in March 1986 to an employee-led company, VSEL Consortium. In 1995 VSEL was taken over by GEC and became Marconi Marine (VSEL). With the merger of British Aerospace and GEC's defence business, VSEL passed to BAE Systems and in 2003 became an independent division, BAE Systems Submarines, renamed BAE Systems Submarine Solutions in 2007.

on both occasions. He was discharged on the termination of his engagement in the TF on 21st February 1916.

William enlisted in the Machine Gun Corps as a staff sergeant instructor at the Machine Gun School at Grantham on 22nd February 1916 (29863). He was posted as an instructor to No.2 Company, No.1 Cadet Battalion MGC at Bisley Camp, Surrey on 28th September. His application for a commission on 12th January 1917 describes him as a marine engineer (war and mercantile boilers, marine gun mountings etc), although he stated he was a plater in his attestation papers. He commenced training at No.1 Cadet Battalion MGC on 1st March. William was commissioned on 26th June 1917 and went to France on 10th August, where he joined the Base Depot. He joined 176th Company MGC (38th Division) on 18th August. He was admitted to 128th Field Ambulance with pyrexia of unknown origin on 29th September and was treated at 11th Corps Rest Station 4th-6th October before rejoining the unit. He was granted leave to Britain 18th December–2nd January 1918. William was slightly wounded on 3rd March 1918 but remained at duty. He was admitted to 130th (St John) Field Ambulance with pyrexia of unknown origin on 6th June, transferred to No.3 Casualty Clearing Station and 3rd General Hospital, Le Tréport on 8th June, joined the Base Depot, Camiers on 21st June and rejoined his unit on 27th June. William was granted leave in England 25th August–10th September. **Awarded the VC for his actions at Gouzeaucourt, France on 18th September 1918, LG 15th November 1918.** The VC was presented by the King at Buckingham Palace on 27th March 1919.

William received a gunshot wound to the hand on 7th October and was admitted to 129th Field Ambulance. He was transferred to No.18 Casualty Clearing Station on 9th October and to 20th General Hospital, Camiers next day. On 13th October he was evacuated to Britain aboard HMHS *Liege*. A medical board on 16th October found him unfit for General and Home Service for six months and for two months for light duty. He was granted leave until 10th March 1919. William was promoted lieutenant on 26th December 1918. A medical board on 17th February 1919 again found him unfit for General and Home Service for six months but fit for light duty and recommended three weeks leave. A medical board on 4th April found him fit for General Service and he rejoined his unit.

William volunteered for the North Russia Relief Force in Archangel in 1919 with fellow VCs HEM Douglas, GWStG Grogan, MSS Moore, J Sherwood-Kelly and AM Toye. When some White Russian troops switched sides to join the Bolsheviks, he was taken prisoner and sentenced to death, although some sources state that this occurred in Ireland, when he was captured by the IRA. He managed to escape by climbing over a high wall but sustained a severe head injury that caused him to suffer occasional blank periods for the rest of his life. He served in Cork, Limerick and Tipperary in Ireland until being demobilised on 18th November 1920. He relinquished his commission on 6th January 1921, retaining the rank of lieutenant.

His Majesty's Airship No.1 was designed and built by Vickers, Sons & Maxim at Barrow, as an aerial scout airship for the Royal Navy. It was the first British rigid airship and was constructed to compete with the German airship programme. Officially it was HMA *Hermione* because the naval contingent at Barrow were attached to HMS *Hermione*, a cruiser moored locally, but was known to the crew as *Mayfly*. The airship was 156m long, fourteen metres in diameter, capable of 74 kph for 24 hours, with a ceiling of 460m, while carrying a crew of twenty. Mooring was to be to a mast, a practice that the British were the first to adopt and *Mayfly* was the first rigid airship to be fitted with the mooring equipment in the nose. On 24th September 1911 it was moved from its shed in Cavendish Dock to conduct full trials but broke in two as a result of being subjected to strong winds before its first flight. Churchill later referred to it as the Won't Fly but, despite never having flown, the brief career of *Mayfly* provided valuable technical experience for airship designers.

William was living at 49 Martell Road, West Dulwich, London in 1920. He married Violet Victoria Price (20th August 1898–20th April 1956) in Cardiff, Glamorgan in 1921, where she was born. They lived at 8 St George's Bungalows, Hildenborough, Kent. Violet and her daughter, Daphne, were living with her mother at the time of the 1939 Register at 114 Mardy Street, Cardiff. She died at Pembury Hospital, Kent. They had two children:

- Daphne Victoria White (born 7th January 1923), born at Islington, London, married Lieutenant Royston James, Wiltshire Regiment, in 1946 at Maidstone, Kent. He enlisted in the Wiltshire Regiment and was promoted through the ranks to warrant officer class 2 (company sergeant major). He was granted an Emergency Commission on 20th October 1942 (257314) and was promoted lieutenant on

20th April 1943, captain (Short Service Commission) on 20th September 1948 and major on 20th October 1955. He was granted a Regular Commission as a lieutenant (quartermaster) on 14th June 1956. Royston transferred to the Duke of Edinburgh's Royal Regiment in June 1959 when the Wiltshire and Royal Berkshire Regiments amalgamated. He retired, having attained the retirement age on 29th September 1967.
- Geoffrey Allison White (born 1927), born at Cardiff, served in the Kenya Police Force and was an assistant superintendent. He was awarded the Colonial Police Medal (LG 1st January 1963) and was appointed Regional Commissioner of Police for North Eastern Kenya on 1st June 1963. He married Carole R Morton (born 1949) in 1972 at Cardiff, where she was born. They lived at 22 Allison Court, 136 Oxford Road, Reading, Berkshire and had a son, Neil Geoffrey White, in 1973.

Violet's father, George Edward Price (1854–1928), born at Oldbury, Worcestershire, married Elizabeth Charlotte née Mitchell (13th November 1857–1943), at Cardiff, Glamorgan in 1886, where she was born. He was a warehouseman in 1891, when they were living at 31 Plantagenet Street, Cardiff. He was a flour miller in 1901, when they were living at 101 Tudor Road, Cardiff, Glamorgan. They were still living there in 1911, by when he was a warehouseman again. Elizabeth was living with her daughters, Blanche, Lilian, Dora and Violet, and her granddaughter, Daphne White, at 114 Mardy Street, Cardiff in 1939. In addition to Violet they had nine other children including:

- Blanche Elizabeth Price (28th August 1887–October 1973) was a servant in 1911 at the home of William and Clara Taylor, cartage contractor, 66 Richards Street, Cathays, Cardiff. She never married and was living with her mother in 1939.
- Thomas Alexander Price (1888–26th November 1967) was a miller's warehouseman in 1911. He married Agnes née O'Keefe late Humphreys in 1924. She had married Henry Humphreys on 8th February 1902 at St Peter's, Cardiff. He treated her cruelly and she left him in June 1910, obtaining a maintenance order against him. In March 1912 they met in the street and Henry assaulted her, resulting in him being fined at the police court. Henry was watched by a private detective in 1914, who found that he was living with Mrs Florence Shell as his wife at Brecon Street, Cardiff. Florence had two girls. Agnes was a barmaid, living at the Cambrian Hotel, St Mary Street, Cardiff, when she took him to court to seek a divorce, which was granted and she also gained custody of their child with costs awarded against Henry. Thomas was living at 80 St Isan Road, Heath, Cardiff at the time of his death there.
- Lilian Gertrude Price (14th October 1890–1980) was a draper's assistant in 1911 and she married William Jones in 1917. William died before 1939, when Lilian was living with her mother at 114 Mardy Street, Cardiff and was working as a bookkeeping clerk/cashier.

- Gladys May Price (born 1893) was a music shop assistant in 1911.
- Dora Elizabeth/Edith Price (4th March 1895–1984) was a music shop assistant in 1911. She never married and was living with her mother in 1939. She died at Southend-on-Sea.
- George Edward Price (born 1903) was a twin with William.
- William Henry Price (born 1903) was a twin with George.

William became a Freemason and was a member of St Luke's Lodge No.144. He unveiled a memorial at St Luke's, West Norwood, London on 6th November 1921. On 10th May 1925 he attended the unveiling of the Machine Gun Corps Memorial. William was a company director by August 1934. That month he was charged at Bromley, Kent with being drunk and incapable of taking care of himself in Kelsey Lane, Beckenham, Kent on 28th August. He pleaded not guilty to being drunk but guilty of not being able to look after himself due to occasional blank periods resulting from the head injury he received in 1919. The case was dismissed with payment of costs and a warning by the chairman, Mr WA Waring, to be very careful in future. William's address at the time was Village Way, Beckenham, Kent.

He was called up in August 1939 for the Royal Artillery from the TA Reserve of Officers Class II as a captain. He was appointed senior gun control officer on 2nd September for service in anti-aircraft batteries in southern England. Later he served with the Royal Navy and the Intelligence Corps 1944–45. He relinquished his commission having exceeded the age limit on 17th November 1945, retaining

The Machine Gun Corps Memorial (The Boy David) was originally next to Grosvenor Place near Hyde Park Corner. It was unveiled on 10th May 1925 by Prince Arthur, Duke of Connaught. Four former members of the Corps who received the VC (Arthur Cross, Reginald Graham, Allan Ker and William White) were in attendance and laid a wreath. The memorial was controversial, as it included the Biblical quotation, *Saul has slain his thousands but David his tens of thousands* (1 Samuel 18:7). Some interpreted this as glorifying war. However, Derwent Wood, who sculptured the statue, wanted to depict the true nature of war. As a RAMC orderly from 1915, he had witnessed its full horrors and had designed masks for soldiers with facial disfigurements. The Machine Gun Corps had a short life from October 1915 until 1922. During that time, 11,500 officers and 159,000 other ranks served in the Corps. Of these 51,049 (30%) became casualties (2,791 killed and 48,258 wounded, missing or prisoners of war). This high casualty rate was due to the exposed positions from which it had to fight and led to its nickname, 'The Suicide Club'. In 1945 the memorial was dismantled because of roadworks and was not rededicated in its present location until 1963. It was Grade II listed in 1970, upgraded to Grade II* in 2014. The memorial is on the north side of the traffic island at Hyde Park Corner close to Wellington Arch and the Royal Artillery, New Zealand and Australian War Memorials (David Dixon).

the rank of captain. He was appointed training officer of a British Legion Village in October 1947 and was a research mechanic by 1956.

William attended a number of VC reunions – the VC Garden Party at Buckingham Palace on 26th June 1920, the VC Dinner at the Royal Gallery of the House of Lords on 9th November 1929, the Victory Day Celebration Dinner & Reception at The Dorchester, London on 8th June 1946, the VC Centenary Celebrations at Hyde Park, London on 26th June 1956 and the 1st-5th and 7th-9th VC & GC Association Reunions at the Café Royal, London on 24th July 1958, 7th July 1960, 18th July 1962, 16th July 1964, 14th July 1966, 18th June 1970 (Connaught Rooms, Covent Garden), 14th July 1972 and 23rd May 1974.

On 6th April 1970, William was one of '10 VCs on a VC10' on the inaugural flight of the Super Vickers VC 10 from London to Nairobi by East African Airlines. The ten VCs, five each from both World Wars selected by drawing names out of a hat, were guests of the company for a nine-day holiday in Kenya, Tanzania and Uganda. In Kenya the schedule included Nairobi, Nyeri, Treetops, where Princess Elizabeth succeeded to the throne, Tsavo National Park and Mombasa. On 13th April the party flew over Ngorongoro Crater, the Serengeti and Lake Victoria to Uganda. In Kampala they were hosted by General Idi Amin and travelled up the Nile to Murchison Falls. Back in Nairobi they visited State House to meet President Kenyatta before flying back to Heathrow.

William died at the Priory Nursing Home, Wellington, Shropshire on 13th September 1974. He was cremated at Emstrey Crematorium, Shrewsbury, Shropshire on 20th September 1974. His ashes were buried in the family grave at St John's Churchyard, Hildenborough, Kent (Grave 506). He is commemorated in a number of other places:

* Memorial paving stone unveiled outside Freemason's Hall, Covent Garden, London on 25th April 2017 by the Duke of Kent KG.
* A Department for Communities and Local Government commemorative paving stone was dedicated at Mitcham War Memorial, Lower Green West, Merton, London on 18th September 2018.

Violet and William's grave in St John's Churchyard, Hildenborough.

Freemason's Hall, Covent Garden, London.

William's unique medal group, owned by Lord Ashcroft and displayed in the Imperial War Museum.

The Territorial Force War Medal 1914–19 was established in April 1920 for members of the Territorial Force and Territorial Force Nursing Service who volunteered for service overseas. They award criteria were:

- To have been serving on 4th August 1914 or have completed four years service with the Force before 4th August 1914 and rejoined on or before 30th September 1914.
- Undertook on or before 30th September 1914 to serve outside the United Kingdom.
- Served outside the United Kingdom between 5th August 1914 and 11th November 1918.
- Did not qualify for the 1914 Star or 1914–15 Star.

A total of 33,944 Territorial Force War Medals were awarded, including 227 to nurses of the Territorial Force Nursing Service.

In addition to the VC he was awarded the British War Medal 1914–20, Victory Medal 1914–19 with Mentioned-in-Despatches Oakleaf, Territorial Force War Medal 1914–19, Defence Medal, War Medal 1939–45, George VI Coronation Medal 1937, Elizabeth II Coronation Medal 1953, Efficiency Decoration (Territorial) and Territorial Efficiency Medal. The medals were sold for £9,500 by Sotheby's on 2nd July 1980. They were listed for £20,000 by Giuseppe Miceli on 1st July 1984 and 1st December 1988. On 1st August 1993, they were purchased for £18,000 at Dix Noonan Webb by Lord Ashcroft. The medals are held by the Michael Ashcroft Trust, the holding institution for the Lord Ashcroft Victoria Cross Collection, and are displayed in the Imperial War Museum's Lord Ashcroft Gallery. William's VC was one of eighteen displayed by the Michael Ashcroft Trust at the Rugby Football Union Museum, Twickenham, London 16th-20th September 2008 in conjunction with a charity rugby match between 'England Old 'Uns' and 'Rest of the World Old 'Uns' there on 20th September. The proceeds were donated to the charity, 'Help for Heroes'.

Biographies 199

## 3244A PRIVATE JAMES PARK WOODS
### 48th Australian Infantry Battalion AIF

James Woods was born on 2nd January 1886 at Finniss Street, Gawler, South Australia. He was known as Jim. He gave his age as twenty-five years and nine months when he enlisted in September 1916 and he is recorded as seventy-three years old when he died on his headstone, both of which indicate the birth was in 1890/91. However, the birth was registered at Port Gawler in 1886 (Book 367, P.14). 1. His father, also James Park Woods (c.1841–14th October 1917), born at Two Wells, SA, was a blacksmith, who served his apprenticeship at James Martin & Co's works. James senior married Esther Scott late Rankin née Johnston (12th January 1853–12th March 1893), born at Mount Crawford, Clare, SA, on 2nd November 1878 at Redhill, Daly, SA. Her name is also seen as Ester.

Murray Street in Gawler at the time of the 1897 Queen Victoria Diamond Jubilee celebrations. Gawler is the oldest country town on the Australian mainland in South Australia and was named after the second Governor, George Gawler. It is about forty kilometres north of the state capital, Adelaide, close to the major wine producing district of the Barossa Valley. In recent years it has been subsumed in Adelaide's growth and is now an outer northern suburb. Gawler prospered initially through the discovery of copper nearby. Later industries included flour milling and engineering, in particular the works of James Martin & Co, which manufactured agricultural, mining and ore processing machinery and smelters for the mines of Broken Hill and the Western Australian goldfields. It also produced steam locomotives and rolling stock. May Bros & Co also manufactured mining and agricultural machinery.

She had married Neil Rankin (1843–30th October 1877) on 6th January 1871 at Mount Rufus Congregational Church, Kapunda, SA. James junior had thirteen siblings from his mother's two marriages:

- Elizabeth Mary Rankin (born 17th October 1871).
- Ann Rankin (born c.1872).
- Margaret Ann Rankin (4th April 1874–31st January 1946) married John Barnard (c.1870–December 1913) on 8th September 1892 at St George's Anglican Church, Gawler, SA. Margaret married John Jackson Massicks (c.1865–23rd September 1936) on 2nd November 1918 at St John's Church, Halifax Street, Adelaide. They both died at Whyalla, SA. Margaret had five children from her first marriage:
  - Isabel Barnard (25th December 1894–31st January 1896).
  - Eleanor 'Queenie' Barnard (20th August 1896–5th September 1961) married Patrick 'Peter' Glancey (23rd May 1888–4th June 1937), a hairdresser born at 14 Arthur Street, Cowdenbeath, Fife, Scotland, on 25th January 1916 at the Registry Office, Adelaide. They were living at Whyalla, SA at the time of his death. They had five children – John Glancey (23rd-29th May 1916), Helen Margaret Glancey (3rd March 1918–29th March 1958), Eleanor Georgina Glancey (26th April 1920–1st July 1992), John Andrew Glancey (1st May 1925–30th October 1970) and Patrick Gavin Arthur Glancey (1930–25th August 2008). Queenie married Robert Henry 'Harry' Stafford Thompson (14th September 1880–21st December 1958), born at Port MacDonnell, SA, on 1st October 1938. He was found guilty of unlawful gaming at Whyalla on 17th April 1947 and was fined £4 with costs of 10/-.
  - Elsie Barnard (3rd September 1898–12th December 1899).
  - John Henry Barnard (13th November 1901–27th October 1964) married Grace Emily Smith (1908–3rd September 1973) on 26th May 1926 at Whyalla, SA. They had three children – Thomas John Barnard 1926, Harold Arthur Barnard 1927 and another son c.1932.
  - Richard 'Barnie' Arthur Barnard (14th January 1909–28th July 1954), a foreman, married Barbara Wilsdon (3rd September 1917–30th July 1977), born at Hummock Hill, Flinders, SA, on 17th September 1936 at the Presbyterian Church, Goodwood, SA. They were living at 56 Whitehead Street, Whyalla in 1941 and later at 86 Broadbent Terrace there. They had

On 11th April 1890 the first locomotive built in South Australia rolls out of James Martin & Co's workshop. The VC's father served his apprenticeship with this firm.

three children – Roberta Barnard 1937, Lola Barnard c.1940 and Robert John Barnard 1948. Barbara married Stuart Anderson (born c.1910) and they had two children – Charmaine Mary Anderson 1959 and David Anderson (died c.1962).
- Peter Bell Rankin (1st September 1875–10th January 1933), born at Frome, SA, married Ellen May (surname unknown) (born c.1880) c.1910. They were living at King Street, Prospect, SA at the time of his death. Ellen may have married again but an Ellen May Rankin was living on her own at 30 Leader Street, Goodwood, Boothby, SA in 1939 and 1941.
- John Duncan Rankin (12th June 1877–21st April 1878).
- William John 'Jock' Woods (12th September 1879–23rd June 1957) married Emily Selina Heading (26th July 1883–3rd June 1974) on 24th June 1911 at her father's residence at Campbelltown, SA. They moved to Hindmarsh, SA and then to Claremont, Western Australia, before returning to SA and settling at Payneham. They had two daughters:
  - Iris Emily Woods (12th June 1912–16th April 2000) married Lancelot Webster (4th July 1911–24th July 2004) on 13th July 1940 at the Methodist Church, Klemzig. She died at Aldgate, SA and he at Mount Barker, SA. They had a daughter c.1942.
  - Avis Anne Woods (9th July 1917–26th October 2003) married Wilfred Henry Heading (26th October 1912–2nd February 2005), born at Kilkenny, Hindmarsh, SA, on 29th November 1941. They had five children.
- Annie Jane Woods (3rd January 1881–30th January 1961) married John Condon on 13th August 1910 (1882–9th January 1961) at Adelaide. They lived at 120 Irish Harp Road, Prospect, SA. They both died at Blair Athol, Port Adelaide. They had three children:
  - James Patrick Condon (17th July 1911–4th December 1977) was a teacher, living with his parents, when he married Laurel Dardanella Clarke (20th February 1916–17th October 1992), born at Wirrabara, SA, on 7th January 1939 in Adelaide. He died at Hampstead Gardens, Port Adelaide and she at Henley Beach, Charles Sturt City, SA. They had four children, including Barrie James Condon (c.1939–2016).
  - Helen Veronica Condon (born 1914) was a clerk in 1939.
  - Adrian John Condon (8th September 1917–30th August 1988) was a clerk in 1939. He enlisted in the RAAF at Prospect, SA on 29th April 1940 and was discharged as a warrant officer from 218th Squadron RAAF on 19th October 1945. Adrian married Pamela Isabel (1930–21st January 1996). He was a farmer in 1977, when they were living at Kalang Road, Bellingen, NSW.
- Harold James Woods (10th July 1882–11th October 1968) married Gertrude Lucette Thorning (1888–27th August 1971) in 1911 in Sydney, NSW. They had children, including Winifred Woods, born on 23rd April 1915 in Queensland.

- Sylvanus Samuel Woods (31st May 1884–16th March 1960) was a labourer when he enlisted in C Company, 10th Battalion AIF on 19th August 1914 at Morphetville, SA (119). He was described as 5′ 4″ tall, weighing 146 lbs, with dark complexion, grey eyes, brown hair and his religious denomination was Church of England. Sylvanus departed Adelaide aboard HMAT A12 *Saldanha* for the Middle East on 21st October 1914. He was a driver when he was admitted to No.2 Australian General Hospital, Mena House, Cairo with influenza on 18th February 1915. He was taken on strength of the Mediterranean Expeditionary Force on 2nd March and was based at No.4 Camp, Mex, Alexandria from 26th May. Promoted lance corporal on 1st October and transferred to Transport Details at Maadi on 3rd November. Promoted corporal on 19th January 1916, backdated to 1st September 1915. He sailed for France from Alexandria aboard HMT *Maryland* on 26th March, arriving at Marseille on 2nd April. He was taken ill with a septic foot on 20th May, was admitted to 3rd Australian Field Ambulance on 24th May and rejoined the unit on 30th May. Appointed temporary sergeant on 16th June 1917 and was attached to the Transport School 1st-11th September. Promoted sergeant on 13th September, backdated to 28th August, and was granted leave in Britain 4th-21st December. Sylvanus received multiple gunshot wounds to the chest and right arm (brachial plexus) on 2nd June 1918 and was admitted to 3rd Australian Field Ambulance next day. He was transferred to No.15 Casualty Clearing Station and 53rd General Hospital on 3rd June and was evacuated to England aboard HMHS *Pieter de Coninck*, for admission to the General Military Hospital, Edmonton, Middlesex on 13th June. He was transferred to 3rd Australian Auxiliary Hospital, Dartford, Kent on 24th June and was found unfit for all service for six months on 29th June. He was granted leave 9th-23rd July, then reported to No.2 Command Depot, Weymouth. He embarked aboard HT *Arawa* at Liverpool on 15th September and disembarked in Australia on 18th November. He was granted seven days leave and was then admitted to No.15 Australian General Hospital, Torrens Park on 26th November and to No.7 Australian General Hospital on 5th December. He claimed that he was suffering from various pains but nothing unusual was found and he returned to Torrens Park on 6th December. A medical board on 13th December found he had good movement in the shoulder and fingers and disability was only slight. Sylvanus was discharged medically unfit on 10th February 1919. He was paid a war pension for 25% incapacity until 25th September. He married Isabella Alice Probert (3rd August 1896–22nd January 1980), born at Broken Hill, New South Wales, on 14th May 1919 at Holy Trinity Church, Adelaide. He was employed by the Irrigation Department at Jervois and other settlements as a stableman, stickman, labourer and ganger from 31st March 1919 until 1923, when he was unemployed. He was employed by South Australia Railways, Southern Division from 2nd September 1925 in various jobs and locations. He suffered a broken jaw in an accident and pleurisy and pneumonia in 1937 and was off work for twelve weeks. He also suffered from arthritis in the wounded shoulder and the disability

was classified as permanent in 1938. As a result, his war pension was restored at half the previous rate from 27th February 1938. Sylvanus and Isabella lived at various addresses in Port Augusta, Adelaide, Glenelg and Bowden. In May 1952 he applied for treatment for hypertension and coronary sclerosis but, as the conditions were not attributable to his war service, the claim was rejected. He died at Port Pirie, SA. Isabella lived at various addresses in York, Port Germein, Glenelg, Colonel Light Gardens and Seaview Downs. She died at Illoura Nursing Home, Beulah Road, Norwood, Adelaide. They had five children:
- John 'Jack' Harold Woods (1st March 1920–29th July 1998) was charged, with others, on 28th January 1937 with disorderly conduct at Wanbi, SA and was fined £-/5/- with costs of £1. He enlisted in the Australian Army on 31st October 1939 at Renmark, SA (SX763), giving his date of birth as 1st March 1919. He served in 2/33rd Infantry Battalion and was discharged as a corporal from the Australian Army Service Corps, 2nd AIF Depot on 10th March 1945. He died at Victor Harbour, SA.
- William Roy Samuel Woods (8th November 1921–8th March 1969) married Rita Ellen Thompson (6th September 1923–1st August 2011), born at Glanville, Port Adelaide, in Adelaide c.1944. They lived at 10 First Avenue, Woodville Gardens, SA. William is believed to have served in the Second World War and post war in the Australian Army. He died at the Repatriation General Hospital, Daws Road, Daw Park, SA. They had seven children – Carolynn Anne Woods (1947–2013), Bruce Woods, Helen Lorna Woods (1952–2014), Susan Woods, Jan Woods, Diane Woods and Jillian Woods. Rita married as Merritt c.1970 at Adelaide. She died at Pennington, SA and her ashes were buried with her first husband.
- Samuel David Woods (25th May 1926–8th September 1974) enlisted in the RAAF on 28th May 1945 at Renmark, SA (154715) and was discharged as a leading aircraftman from 3 Transport and Movement Office on 17th May 1946. He died at Colonel Light Gardens, SA.
- James Lawrence 'Laurie' Woods (3rd March 1928–15th September 2008) was charged with Ronald Gordon Jones, both aged fourteen, at Renmark, SA with larceny from Ernest John Whenan on 30th October 1942. The charge was dismissed under the Offenders Probation Act on a bond of £1 compensation each. Laurie enlisted in the Royal Australian Navy in 1951 at Adelaide (R45047) and served aboard HMAS *Lonsdale*. He was discharged in 1957. He married Margaret Ann Bates (21st March 1922–23rd July 2015) on 18th December 1956 at Yass, NSW. He was a metal worker in 1958 and they were living at 104 Concord Road, Concord, NSW, before moving to 12 Dora Street, Blacktown, NSW in 1963. By 1980 he was a rubber worker. His ashes were scattered at sea from HMAS *Melbourne* at Shark Bay, WA. They had two daughters – Suellen Mary Woods and Joanne Dora Woods.
- Isabella Annie Woods (born 14th May 1930).

- Margaretta 'Rita' Esther Woods (born 1st February 1888) was a teacher at Gawler Primary School until 1915. She married Douglas Blakeley Thomas (5th August 1891–10th September 1956), born at Rose Park, SA, on 8th August 1916 at Norwood, SA. He was an accountant in 1917, when they were living at The Laurels, corner of Shenton and Devon Roads, Claremont, SA. By 1941 he was an agent and they were living at 39 Cremorne Street, New Parkside, SA. Living with them was Jill Blakeley Thomas (died 2005), a typist, but her relationship is not clear. She married Mervyn Nugent Archdall (died 2003) in 1946. Rita and Douglas had a son:
    ○ Walter John Douglas Thomas (19th June 1917–14th July 2006), born at Claremont, was a salesman. He enlisted in the Australian Army on 10th

Newry, now in Northern Ireland, was founded in 1144 alongside a Cistercian monstery but there are settlements in the area dating back to the Bronze Age. It developed as a market town and became a port in 1742 when it was linked to Lough Neagh by canal. It has a cathedral and is the seat of the Roman Catholic Diocese of Dromore. In the 820s the Danes plundered the area before attacking Armagh. In 1162 the monastery was attacked and raided by Irish clans but this was followed by a safe period after a number of Norman motte-and-bailey castles were built in and around Newry. Newry abbey was converted to a collegiate church in 1543 and was surrendered to the Crown in 1548. It was one of the richest and largest in Ireland. During the 1689 Raid on Newry, Williamite forces repulsed an attack by the Jacobites. Newry was the scene of several violent incidents during the Troubles including multiple murders, bombings and mortar attacks. Newry is the birthplace of Patrick Anthony Jennings OBE (born 12th June 1945) the Newry Town, Watford, Tottenham Hotspur, Arsenal and Northern Ireland goalkeeper. He gained a record 119 caps for Northern Ireland and made over 1,000 top level club appearances. He won the FA Cup with Spurs and Arsenal and, despite being a goalkeeper, he scored in the 1967 FA Charity Shield. The city is also the birthplace of Ronan Patrick Rafferty (born 13th January 1964), the golfer who led the 1989 European Tour Order of Merit and qualified for the 1989 Ryder Cup team.

July 1942 at Plympton, SA (SX22503) and was discharged as a sergeant at 4 Australian Army Ordnance Depot on 6th February 1946. He married Gwenyth Mildred Ferguson (14th November 1916–7th July 1988), born at Parkside, SA. They had a son, Ian Blakeley Thomas (1950–2016).
- Thomas Frederick Woods (26th August 1889–1958) died at Sunset Hospital, Dalkeith, WA.
- Mary 'Mamie' Hardie Woods (7th November 1891–5th February 1973) married Albert Roy Graham (5th December 1891–1st May 1956), born at Thebarton, Hindmarsh, SA, at Prospect on 14th March 1913. They had two children – Hilda Myrtle Graham 1913 and Howard Hardie Graham 1916. Mamie married William Hatherley (born c.1893).
- Newton Joshua Woods (12th March–18th June 1893).

James' paternal grandfather, Samuel Woods (c.1816–17th June 1856), born at Newry, Ireland, married Jane née Mullen (c.1817–25th March 1893) at Newry in 1838, where she was also born. They both died at Gawler, South Australia. In addition to James they had eight other children:

- Maria Elizabeth Woods (1st May 1839–10th June 1920) married Joshua Finch (24th July 1834–15th February 1920), born at Clerkenwell, London, England, on 11th August 1858 at St George's Church, Gawler. They had twelve children:
    - John Joshua Finch (1st July 1859–2nd April 1889).
    - Samuel Finch (4th April 1861–8th December 1950).
    - Annie Maria Finch (29th March 1863–29th June 1941) never married.
    - Ada Lucy Finch (17th May 1865–22nd June 1937) never married.
    - Newton Cutler Finch (29th June 1867–19th June 1933) married Ada Quarton (1878–1955) in 1901. They had two children – Herbert Newton Finch 1905 and Laura Evelyn Finch 1909.
    - Elliott Raymond Finch (31st August 1869–26th August 1935).
    - Harold William Finch (17th December 1871–30th March 1872).
    - Emma Leticia Finch (26th January 1873–23rd September 1964) married Edwin Weston (1869–1944) in 1906. They had two sons – Ronald Edwin Weston 1913 and Horace Raymond Weston 1916.
    - Jane Ethel Finch (11th April 1875–12th May 1961).
    - Howard William Finch (20th August 1877–25th March 1950) married Amy Laura (died 1964) in 1909. They had a daughter, Dorothy Finch, in 1912.
    - Horace James Finch (16th October 1879–16th November 1964) married Nellie May in 1911. They had two daughters – Ellice Mary Finch 1913 and Joyce Nellie Finch 1915.
    - Oswald Harold Finch (15th June 1884–26th May 1918) married Alice Ethel (died 1941) in 1912. They had a son, Noel Oswald Finch, in 1915.

- Mary Sarah Woods (c.1843–11th January 1927) married John Mossop (1846–20th September 1919), born at Western Cape, South Africa, on 31st October 1874 at Gawler, SA. He died at Hindmarsh and she at Norwood, SA. They had four children:
  - Louisa Jane Mossop (6th February 1877–23rd June 1881).
  - John Garland Mossop (25th March 1879–12th May 1957) married Hilda Helen Maud Martin (1879–1966) in 1908. They had four children – Madeline Laura Mossop 1909, Hylda Doreen Mossop 1910, John Norton Mossop 1914 and Kenneth Winston Mossop 1920.
  - Nellie Maria Mossop (4th August 1880–29th June 1962) married David Bowyer Peter in 1908. They had two children – James Garland Peter 1909 and Duncan Peter 1914.
  - Maria Elizabeth Mossop (28th July 1882–1952) married Frank Gaen in 1916. They had two daughters – Ellen Jeanette Gaen 1919 and Mary Gertrude Gaen 1920.
- Anna Woods (30th June 1845–11th March 1913) never married.
- William John Woods (4th May 1847–4th April 1899) married Caroline Amelia Drought (c.1846–6th November 1942), born in Ireland, on 18th February 1873 at Trinity Church, Adelaide. She was the daughter of Dr Frederick Drought MRCS (Dublin) (1788–1866) and Maria Armstrong (1823–99) of Dublin. Frederick married Maria on 11th December 1854, just one week before she sailed to Australia with her six children aboard the Barque *Rienzi* on 18th December, arriving at Adelaide, SA via Melbourne, Victoria in April 1855. Frederick did not accompany them and died on 23rd July 1866 at Richmond, Fairview, Dublin. It is believed that the marriage was to satisfy immigration requirements that precluded unmarried mothers travelling to South Australia. William died at Harrington Street, Prospect, SA and Caroline at Parkside Mental Hospital, SA. They had a daughter:
  - Murielle Theodosia Woods (11th August 1886–6th January 1918) married Alexander Alfred Allen (1892–1946) in 1915. They had a son, Alexander Rex Allen, in 1916. Alexander senior married Gladys Rose (died 1960) in 1924.
- Samuel Woods (8th April 1849–2nd September 1924) married Elizabeth Gray (4th May 1855–30th December 1902), born at Ballarat, Victoria, on 17th April 1876 at Moonta, SA. She died at Yorketown, SA. Samuel married Alice Honor Moodie née Eames (4th October 1858–2nd August 1922), born at Lyndoch, SA, on 13th December 1910 at Fullarton, SA. Alice had married Sinclair Simpson Moodie (12th May 1838–30th July 1892), born at Edinburgh, Midlothian, Scotland, as his second wife on 21st May 1884 at Adelaide. Sinclair and Alice had two children – Olive Margaret Eames Moodie (1883–1949) and Leslie Bruce Eames Moodie (1890–1959). Alice died at Adelaide and Samuel at Payneham, SA. Samuel and Elizabeth had eight children:

- Frederick Arthur Woods (2nd January 1878–28th November 1956) married Mary Gertrude in 1902. They had four children – Doreen Gray Woods 1903, Gwendolen May Woods 1905, Lyall Alexander Woods 1908 and Harrold Allan Woods 1910.
- Walter Edgar Woods (1st April 1880–1st November 1971) married Ethel Maud Mary (1879–1941) in 1906. They had three children – Nelly Hooper Woods 1907, Ronald Walter Woods 1911 and Ethel Mary Woods 1913.
- Leopold Woods (23rd March 1883–8th August 1971) married Mary Jane in 1908. They had two sons – Milton Dennison Woods 1909 and Rupert Allen Woods 1914.
- Florence Jane Woods (5th July 1885–1966) married Cyril Victor Moyle Besanko (19th July 1886–6th October 1940) in 1912. They had two children – Benjamin Geoffry Moyle Besanko 1915 and Maxine Elaine Besanko 1921. Cyril enlisted in 4th Battalion AIF on 17th August 1914 at Randwick, NSW and was allocated the number 6. He was described as an electrician, 5′ 7½″ tall, weighing 150 lbs, with mid complexion, grey eyes, brown hair and his religious denomination was Methodist. He was assigned to the Signal Section, embarked with the Battalion on 20th October and disembarked in Egypt on 2nd December. The Battalion landed at Gallipoli on 25th April 1915 and Cyril was promoted lance corporal on 30th July. He received a gunshot wound to the foot on 9th August and was evacuated aboard HMHS *Devanha*. He was admitted to No.2 Australian General Hospital, Ghezirah, Alexandria, Egypt on 12th August, transferred to Mena House on 15th August and to the Sultan's Palace Convalescence Hospital, Montazah on 25th August for seven days' light duty at Mustapha. He joined the Overseas Base on 25th September and embarked for Mudros on HMT *Borda* on 18th October. Cyril rejoined the Battalion on 30th October and was promoted corporal on 2nd November. He disembarked at Alexandria from HT *Simla* on 29th December and was promoted sergeant on 20th February 1916. He embarked aboard HT *Simla* at Alexandria on 23rd March and disembarked at Marseille on 30th March. He was admitted to 1st Australian Field Ambulance on 16th May and was transferred to No.1 Australian Casualty Clearing Station, Estaires next day with gonorrhoea. He was transferred to 9th Stationary Hospital, Le Havre by 7 Ambulance Train on 20th May and by 2 Hospital Train to 18th General Hospital, Dannes-Camiers on 30th June. Cyril was discharged to 1st Australian Division Base Depot, Étaples on 1st July and rejoined the Battalion on 19th July. He was wounded by gunshots to the chest and right arm at Pozières on 23rd July and was admitted to 1/2nd South Midland Field Ambulance and No.44 Casualty Clearing Station. He was transferred by 24 Ambulance Train on 24th July to 12th General Hospital and was evacuated to England for admission to 1st Southern General Hospital, Edgbaston, Birmingham on 1st August.

He was transferred to 1st Auxiliary Hospital, Harefield on 28th September and was granted leave 4th-19th October, then reported to No.2 Command Depot, Weymouth. He was awarded the MM, LG 27th October 1916. Cyril returned to Australia aboard HMAT A18 *Wiltshire*, departing Portland on 12th December and disembarking on 3rd January 1917. He was awarded the DCM – although severely wounded himself, he rescued a wounded man under very heavy fire, LG 1st January 1917. He was discharged medically unfit on 4th April 1917. His address was 2 Royal Avenue, Hyde Park, SA.

Sergeant Cyril Victor Moyle Besanko DCM MM.

- Stuart Woods (1st December 1887–3rd May 1959) married Elizabeth Sophia (died 1957) in 1913. They had two children – Doris Elizabeth Woods 1916 and Malcolm Stuart Woods 1919.
- Claude Woods (27th May 1890–7th March 1966) married Gertie Cecilia Heinrich (1893–1957) in 1914. They had three daughters – Maimie Woods 1915, Fay Grey Woods 1917 and Roma Elaine Woods 1919.
- Malcolm Edward Woods (4th May 1893–6th August 1916) enlisted at Adelaide on 3rd August 1915 in 12th Reinforcements, 16th Battalion AIF (B4441). He was described as a store assistant, 5′ 4½″ tall, weighing 120 lbs, with fair complexion, blue eyes, brown hair and his religious denomination was Methodist. He embarked on RMS *Malwa* at Adelaide on 2nd December and transferred to 48th Battalion at Tel-el-Kebir on 9th March 1916 (3777). He embarked at Alexandria on 2nd June and disembarked at Marseille on 9th June. Malcolm was reported wounded and missing on 6th August 1916,

The Villers-Bretonneux Australian National Memorial commemorates 10,773 soldiers of the Australian Imperial Force who died in France in the Great War and who have no known grave. The location was chosen due to the important role played by the AIF in the Second Battle of Villers-Bretonneux in April 1918. It was designed by Sir Edwin Lutyens after previous designs proved too expensive. The memorial was unveiled on 22nd July 1938 by King George VI, whose speech was broadcast directly in Australia.

but on 4th May 1917 a court of enquiry revised this to missing and killed in action (Villers-Bretonneux Memorial, France).
  - May Elizabeth Woods (23rd April 1896–1992) married Herbert Kaibel (1889–1961) in 1920. They had two children – Margaret Kathleen Kaibel 1921 and Roland Kaibel 1923.
- Thomas Barnard Woods (4th February 1851–21st October 1905) married Caroline Randall (1852–3rd October 1926) on 23rd August 1871 at High Street, Gawler. He died at Two Wells and she at 31 Clifton Street, Hawthorn, SA. They had twelve children:
  - Maud Jane Woods (5th December 1871–26th March 1872).
  - Frank Horace Woods (1873–16th April 1917) married Agnes Janet (died 1950) in 1900. They had eight children – Horace Leonard Woods 1901, Kingsley Bruce Woods 1903, Gertrude Caroline Agnes Woods 1906, Constance Rosa Woods 1908, William Thomas Woods 1910, twins Bessie Florence Woods and Elizabeth Florence Woods 1912 and Hilda Jean Piercy Woods 1916.
  - Samuel Bruce Woods (31st January 1875–1920).
  - Charles William Woods (21st April 1877–3rd May 1952).
  - Hilda Annie Woods (30th January 1879–1968) married Leopold George Garfield Gladstone Wright (1884–1955) in 1908. They had four children – Bernard Thomas Wright 1910, Murray George Wright 1913, Harry Dudley Wright 1917 and Muriel Jean Wright 1919.
  - Eustace Hubert Bernard Woods (17th June 1881–30th June 1966) married Jessie in 1903. They had a daughter, Gladys Woods, in 1904.
  - Margaretta Mabel Woods (11th December 1883–1st July 1943).
  - Albert Randall Woods (17th March 1886–29th August 1967) married Amy Elizabeth (1955) in 1937.
  - Newton Ernest Woods (6th May 1888–12th March 1892).
  - Thomas Cecil Woods (25th July 1891–13th February 1981).
  - Harry Joshua Woods (13th March 1893–28th July 1916) enlisted in the AIF at Oaklands, SA on 30th December 1914 (1849) and was posted to the Infantry Base Depot. He was described as a machinist, 5′ 8¼″ tall, weighing 142 lbs, with fair complexion, grey eyes, brown hair and his religious denomination was Methodist. He transferred to 4th Reinforcements, 10th Battalion on 1st February 1915 and embarked on HMAT A17 *Port Lincoln* at Adelaide on 1st April. He joined the Battalion at Gallipoli on 5th June. He was treated at 2nd Australian Field Ambulance Beach Dressing Station and Anzac Casualty Clearing Station for diarrhoea on 23rd August and was transferred to Mudros later that day. He embarked on RMS *Aquitania* on 18th September and was admitted to the Fulham Military Hospital on 26th September with dysentery. Harry was absent without leave in London 27th-28th November for which he was awarded four days' detention and

forfeited two days' pay. He returned to Egypt on 3rd February 1916 and was attached to 6th Field Company AE on 19th February before rejoining the Battalion at Serapeum on 7th March. He embarked aboard RMS *Saxonia* at Alexandria on 27th March and disembarked at Marseille on 3rd April. On 13th June he was promoted lance corporal. Harry was wounded on 22nd July, died six days later and was buried in Gordon Dump Cemetery, Ovillers-la-Boisselle, France (I A 4) by the Reverend RA Harris. His mother, who was living on Queen Street, Gawler, was granted a pension of £2 per fortnight from 27th October.

Harry Joshua Woods' grave in Gordon Dump Cemetery.

○ Arthur Norman Woods (born 23rd July 1895) married Veronica in 1924. They had a daughter, Patricia Woods, in 1926.

- Jane Elizabeth Woods (4th January 1853–6th June 1926) never married and died at Kingswood, Adelaide.
- Margaret/Margaretta Woods (21st April 1856–31st August 1941) married James Robertson (28th December 1850–7th May 1931), born at Newcastle upon Tyne, Northumberland, England, on 3rd February 1876 at the Wesleyan Church, Gawler. He died at his son's residence at 29 Woodfield Avenue, Fullarton, SA and Margaretta at Bridgewater, SA. They had five children:
  ○ Gertrude Annie Robertson (3rd February 1877–1960) married Herbert Ernest Poole (died 1969) in 1905.
  ○ James Bolton Robertson (16th April 1879–24th October 1935).
  ○ Clarence Tertius Robertson (5th October 1883–7th July 1970) married Amy Millicent Evelyn Fiveash (1883–1973) in 1905. They had a son, Roland Fiveash Robertson, in 1908.
  ○ Margaretta 'Greta' Woods Robertson (2nd April 1891–27th May 1988) married Archie Hannaford McPhie in 1918. They had two children – John Milroy McPhie 1919 and Jean Elsbeth McPhie 1924.
  ○ Jean Elise Robertson (10th January 1894–13th August 1982) married Donald Phillip Tullie Wollaston (1895–1995) in 1920. They had three children – Elise Margarette Woolaston 1922, unnamed born and died 1925 and Romola Jean Woolaston 1927.

His maternal grandfather, John Johnston (18th June 1815–16th September 1894), born at Polmont, Stirlingshire, Scotland, married Elizabeth née Hardie (January 1831–1912), on 11th April 1852 at Falkirk, Stirlingshire, where she was born. John died at Redhill, SA and Elizabeth at Adelaide. In addition to Esther they had five other children:

- John Murray Johnston (9th December 1854–26th April 1935), a twin with Thomas, born at Reedy Creek, SA, married Rosina Matilda Creak (1860–16th July 1928), born at Carlton, Victoria, on 12th August 1880. He was a carpenter in 1909, when they were living at Waterloo Road, Northcote, Victoria. She died there and he at Cheltenham, Victoria. They had nine children:
    - Albert Murray Johnston (1881–1964) married Elizabeth Annie Kimpton in 1946.
    - Hollist Benjamin Creak Johnston (1883–1965) married Ethel May Prior (1886–1946) in 1910. They had two daughters – Shirley Hollist Johnston 1912 and Mary May Johnston 1917.
    - Clarence John Lee Johnston (1885–1964) married Margaret Wilson McDougall (1886–1949) in 1915. They had two children – Jean Alberta

Polmont overlooks the Firth of Forth. The Romans built two temporary marching camps there and the Antonine Wall passes close by. The village was originally part of Falkirk but became an independent parish in 1724. During the Second World War Polish forces had a signals training school in the since demolished St Margaret's School.

Falkirk was historically within the county of Stirlingshire in the Forth Valley, about thirty kilometres northwest of Edinburgh. Falkirk Old Parish Church is on the site of the medieval church, which may date from the 7th century. At the Battle of Falkirk on 22nd July 1298, King Edward I of England defeated William Wallace. At the Battle of Falkirk Muir on 17th January 1746, the Jacobites defeated a government army. The nearby Carron Co works made beams for James Watt's steam engine in 1765, carronades for the Royal Navy and later pillar-boxes for the Post Office. The town is at the junction of the Forth and Clyde (1790) and Union Canals (1822) and became a centre of heavy industry, particularly iron and steel. During the 19th century Falkirk became the first town in Great Britain to have fully automated street lighting. The town is the birthplace of James Walker (1781-1862), the civil engineer who worked with his uncle on the construction of London's West India and East India Docks. The first engineering work in his own right was Commercial Road, connecting West India Docks to the City. He worked on the Surrey Commercial Docks from 1810 onwards. In 1821 he built his first lighthouse and went on to build another twenty-one, including Start Point, Maplin Sands, Wolf Rock, Whitby, Bishop Rock and the Needles on the Isle of Wight. Walker succeeded Thomas Telford as President of the Institution of Civil Engineers 1834-45. He was also chief engineer within Trinity House and consulting engineer to the Board of Admiralty. His other projects included Vauxhall Bridge, various railways and canals, consulting engineer for three towers of the Houses of Parliament (Clock, Victoria and Central) and the breakwaters in Alderney and Jersey to provide Royal Navy anchorages.

Johnston 1915 and Robert Nicholson Johnston 1918. He married Lydia Maude Hirst (1896–1989) in 1951.
- ○ Myrtle Rose Johnston (born 1887).
- ○ Elma Beatrice Johnston (1891–1970) married Walter John Murphy in 1929.
- ○ Leslie Charles Johnston (born 1893).
- ○ Lionel Hardie Johnston (1894–1977).
- ○ Stanley Thomas Johnston (6th November 1897–8th July 1980) married Ivy Margaret Shewan (1898–1927) in 1925 and Clara Veronica Doris Hilton in 1930.
- ○ Frank Herbert Johnston (1899–1925).
- Thomas Hardie Johnston (9th December 1854–13th October 1856) was a twin with John.
- Margaret Parr Carlaw Johnston (14th October 1856–13th January 1918) married Charles James Lang (10th August 1843–4th July 1885), born at Oatlands, Tasmania, on 13th June 1877 at Redhill. Charles had married Mary Anne Radford (17th January 1834–25th September 1875), born in Manchester, Lancashire, England, on 22nd September 1863 at Adelaide. Charles and Mary had a son, James Lang, in 1865. Charles died on the railway about seventy-five kilometres west of Bordertown, SA. Margaret married Walter Frederick Miles (2nd October 1858–3rd April 1904), born at Kent Town, SA, on 9th July 1885 at Port Pirie, SA. Walter died at Fitzroy, Victoria and Margaret at Melbourne Hospital, Victoria. Margaret and Walter had four children:
  - ○ Herbert Vernon Miles (1886–1953) married Clarice Holly Coulter (c.1891–1960) in 1944.
  - ○ Arthur Bernard Miles (19th February 1888–7th August 1960) married Violet Hughes (1891–1960) in 1914. They had a son, Walter Raymond Miles in 1916.
  - ○ Ernest Arnold 'Owey' Miles (26th November 1889–18th May 1970) married Clarice Violet Turner (1889–1958) in 1916.
  - ○ Leslie George Miles (7th May 1891–1956) married Pearl Amy Chibnall (1893–1978) in 1920.
- Thomas Hardie Johnston (4th June 1860–16th December 1895), born at North Rhine, Angaston, SA, married Evangeline Brooks (died 20th November 1928) on 2nd August 1881 at Redhill, SA. Evangeline married Samuel Tucker (c.1853–26th December 1923) in 1913 at Adelaide. Thomas and Evangeline had nine children:
  - ○ Lawrence Hardie Johnston (23rd March 1883–23rd May 1965).
  - ○ Edgar Rufus Johnston (10th November 1884–26th March 1885).
  - ○ Gertrude May Johnston (25th December 1885–1959) is believed to have married John Barr Orr (1895–1982), born at Warrington, Lancashire, England, at Daly, SA in 1917.
  - ○ Florence Maggie Johnston (3rd April 1887–29th December 1944).
  - ○ Ida Johnston (1st August 1888–1974) is believed to have married William John Ernest Eimbrodt (died 1919) in 1912. They had two daughters –

Gertrude Ida Eimbrodt 1913 and Gwen Eimbrodt 1915. Ida is understood to have married William Charles Packham (1899–1972) in 1921. They had three children – Dorothy Jean Packham 1922, Marjorie Joan Packham 1924 and William Ross Packham 1927.
- Alice Pearl Johnston (27th February 1890–1971).
- Hilda Grace Johnston (16th May 1891–19th July 1973) is believed to have married as Boundy.
- Frederick Roy Johnston (21st January 1894–14th April 1940) enlisted in 10th Battalion AIF at Morphetville, SA on 18th August 1914 (318). He had previously served with the Senior Cadets and Citizen Force. He was described as a labourer, 5′ 7½″ tall, weighing 137 lbs, with fair complexion, blue eyes, fair hair and his religious denomination was Methodist. He was assigned to A Company on 21st August and embarked aboard HMAT A11 *Ascanius* at Adelaide on 20th October. Frederick was wounded by a gunshot to the foot at Gallipoli between 25th and 29th April 1915 and was evacuated aboard HMT *Clan McGillivray* to Tigne Convalescent Hospital, Malta, arriving on 4th May. He returned to Gallipoli on 25th July but was admitted to hospital with ear trouble on 27th July and was transferred to Mudros aboard HMS *Clacton*. He was transferred to No.1 Australian General Hospital, Heliopolis, Egypt on 31st July and was invalided to Australia aboard HT *Ulysses* from Port Said on 3rd September, suffering from shell shock and deafness. He arrived on 30th September. A medical report on 4th October concluded that complete deafness in his right ear was over a year old and was not caused by neglect, misconduct or due to military service, although it may have been aggravated by it. Frederick was discharged from 7th Australian General Hospital medically unfit with chronic suppurative otitis media on 30th October. He married Grace Douglas Wildy (1894–1979) in 1916. They had two daughters – Doreen Joy Johnston 1918 and Betty Douglas Johnston 1921. They divorced in 1930 and Grace married Harrold/Harold Arthur Gilbert (1895–1967) in 1931. Frederick served again in the early days of the Second World War (S212479).
- Thomas Edmund Johnston (18th July 1895–11th November 1924) enlisted in 10th Battalion AIF at Morphetville, SA on 19th August 1914 (323), the day after his brother, Frederick. He had two years' previous service with the Senior Cadets and one year and two months in 79th and 74th Infantry. He was described as a dentist mechanic, 5′ 5½″ tall, weighing 127 lbs, with dark complexion, blue eyes, dark hair and his religious denomination was Church of England. He was assigned to A Company on 21st August and embarked aboard HMAT A11 *Ascanius* at Adelaide on 20th October. Thomas landed at Gallipoli on 25th April 1915. He was taken ill with influenza on 28th April and was evacuated to Alexandria. He embarked there aboard RMS *Franconia* for Sedd el Bahr, Gallipoli on 14th May and rejoined the Battalion on 17th May. He was taken ill again and rejoined the unit on 20th July. On 23rd August he

was treated at 1st Australian Casualty Clearing Station for diarrhoea and was evacuated to Mudros. He arrived at Alexandria, Egypt aboard HMHS *Assaye* on 27th August and was treated for dental rheumatism, influenza, dyspepsia and debility. He was transferred to No.2 Australian General Hospital, Ghezireh, Cairo with dyspepsia and defective teeth (broken dental plate) on 30th August. He had lost about twenty pounds since enlisting. Thomas was transferred to Mena House, Cairo suffering from influenza on 5th October and returned to duty on 23rd October. He forfeited a day's pay for being absent without leave on 28th October. Thomas was attached to 4th Australian Field Ambulance at Serapeum on 25th January 1916 and transferred from 10th Battalion as a staff sergeant to the Army Medical Corps Dental Service as a dental mechanic on 28th January. He transferred to Base Details, Zeitoun on 19th February. On 1st June he embarked at Alexandria and disembarked at Marseille on 9th June. He transferred to 13th Australian Field Ambulance from 37th Dental Unit on 20th June and was detached to 2nd Australian Field Ambulance on 22nd July. On 8th August he transferred to ADMS 1st Australian Division. He was admitted to 13th Australian Field Ambulance with tonsillitis and influenza on 13th September and rejoined his unit on 17th September. On 1st January 1917 he was a member of No.34 Dental Unit attached to 13th Australian Field Ambulance. He was admitted to No.56 Casualty Clearing Station 3rd–7th May. Thomas transferred to 59th Dental Unit on 23rd May. He was admitted to 39th General Hospital, Le Havre 27th August–18th November suffering from gonorrhoea. On 1st March 1918 he transferred to the Australian Army Medical Corps, Dental Service in England and was attached to No.4 Command Depot, Hurdcott on 26th March. He joined 54th Dental Unit, Hurdcott on 30th March and No.2 Camp, Parkhouse, near Bulford pending return to Australia on 17th October. He moved to Devonport on 28th October and embarked aboard HT *Somerset* on 4th December for Special 1914 Leave. While aboard he was ill with influenza 6th–9th December and was appointed canteen sergeant on 27th December. Thomas disembarked on 15th January 1919 and was discharged on 20th March. He married Beatrice Ruby Addison (1895–1981) in 1919. They had a son, James Hardie Johnston, in 1920. Beatrice married Oliver George Smithers (1896–1966), born at Chertsey, Surrey, England, in 1928.

- James Coragan/Corrigan Johnston (9th August 1862–1915), born at Murray Scrub, Angaston, SA, married Florence Emma Phillips (28th November 1891–25th February 1971) on 18th January 1909 at the Methodist Manse, Strathalbyn, SA, where she was born. He died at Williston and she at Hackney, SA. They had three children:
    - John James Johnston (23rd July 1909–23rd May 1974).
    - Dorothy Grace Johnston (19th July 1911–24th August 1965) married Charles Stewart Powell (1903–41) in Adelaide in 1935.
    - Robert Douglas Johnston (28th May 1913–9th September 1988).

Troops at Blackboy Hill Camp. The Hill was named after Australian native black boy plants, which dominated the site. In April 1919 the camp was used as a fever hospital to treat Spanish flu. The site was used again during the Second World War. The camp has been mainly covered by St Anthony's Primary School and Church, Greenmount Primary School and housing. The remaining area has been left as a memorial to the troops who trained there.

When James' mother died, he was brought up by one of his half-sisters. He moved to Western Australia in 1914 with his brother, William. He carted timber and built fences in the Katanning area before becoming a vigneron at Caversham, WA. James tried to enlist in SA at the outbreak of the Great War but was rejected because he was below the minimum height. He tried several times to enlist again but was rejected until the standard was relaxed.

James enlisted in Perth, WA on 29th September 1916 and was posted to Blackboy Hill Camp (3244). He was described as 5′ 3″ tall, weighing 127 lbs, with fresh complexion, brown eyes, light brown hair and his religious denomination was Methodist. He joined 7th Reinforcements, 44th Battalion on 16th November and 8th Reinforcements, 48th Battalion on 2nd December. On 23rd December he embarked with 8th Reinforcement Group at Fremantle, WA aboard HMAT A35 *Berrima*. He disembarked at Devonport, Devon on 16th February 1917 and moved to Salisbury Plain, Wiltshire. He was posted to Camp Details Sutton Mandeville and 12th Training Battalion, Codford, Wiltshire on 6th March. On 26th March he reported sick with mumps and was admitted to Parkhouse Military Hospital, Salisbury Plain. His number was amended to 3244A on 7th April.

James was discharged to 12th Training Battalion on 13th April but reported sick on 18th April with bronchitis and pneumonia and was admitted to King

SS *Berrima* (11,137 tons) was launched in 1913 for P&O for the carriage of immigrants to Australia via Cape Town. She was requisitioned by the RAN in 1914 as HMAS *Berrima*, initially as an auxiliary cruiser. She transported two battalions of the Australian Naval and Military Expeditionary Force to the German New Guinea colonies in September. In October she was in the second ANZAC convoy to the Middle East and towed the submarine AE2. On 18th February 1917 she was torpedoed off Portland, Dorset, but was towed ashore and repaired, following which she was used to carry stores and munitions. *Berrima* returned to P&O service in 1920 until 1929 and she was broken up in 1930.

King George Hospital, Stamford Street, Waterloo, London. In 1914, it was a newly built warehouse for HM Stationery Office and was commandeered to be converted into a hospital, reputedly the largest in the country. The King opened it at the end of May 1915, the project having suffered from labour disputes and strikes. Convoys of wounded were brought by train to Waterloo Station nearby and transferred by tunnels to the hospital. The flat roof was converted into a garden with flowerbeds and shrubs, where patients could exercise. On Christmas Day 1916 the King, the Queen or one of their children visited every ward. The Hospital closed on 15th June 1919, having treated 71,000 patients. Today, it is the Franklin-Wilkins Building of King's College London.

Parkhouse Camp, between Bulford and Tidworth on Salisbury Plain.

George Hospital, Stamford Street, Waterloo, London on 1st May. He was transferred to 3rd Australian Auxiliary Hospital, Dartford, Kent on 27th June and was discharged to leave on 2nd July, to join No.4 Command Depot, Codford on 5th July. He transferred to the Overseas Training Brigade, Perham Down, Wiltshire on 9th August and embarked at Southampton, Hampshire for Le Havre, France on 1st September. He joined 4th Australian Division Base Depot, Le Havre next day and 48th Battalion on 12th September.

James reported sick on 23rd January 1918 with pericarditis and bronchitis and was treated at 13th Australian Field Ambulance, No.2 Australian Casualty Clearing Station and 54th General Hospital from 27th January. He was evacuated to England and admitted to 2/1st Southern General Hospital, Dudley Road, Birmingham, Warwickshire on 22nd February. He was transferred to 1st Australian Auxiliary Hospital, Harefield on 11th March and was discharged to No.3 Command Depot, Hurdcott on 13th March. On 4th May he transferred to the Overseas Training Brigade, Sandhill Camp, Longbridge Deverill, Wiltshire and on 22nd May returned to France via Folkestone, Kent. He joined the Australian Infantry Base Depot on 24th May and rejoined the Battalion on 30th May. On 23rd July he reported sick with dysentery and was admitted to 12th Australian Field Ambulance and No.20 Casualty Clearing Station. He was transferred to No.12 Casualty Clearing Station on 25th July, No.55 Casualty Clearing Station on 31st July and to the Australian Corps Reception Camp on 5th August. James rejoined the Battalion on 20th August.

Awarded the VC for his actions at le Verguier, northwest of St Quentin, France on 18th September 1918, LG 26th December 1918. He returned from

In November 1914, Mr and Mrs Charles Billyard-Leake, Australians living in Britain, offered their home, Harefield Park House, to the Minister of Defence in Melbourne as a convalescent facility for the AIF. It became No.1 Australian Auxiliary Hospital in December 1914, the only solely Australian hospital in Britain. Hutted wards were built on the lawn and by May 1915 eighty beds were ready. The first patients arrived on 2nd June and by the end of that month the Hospital had 170 patients and more huts were built. In August the King and Queen visited, by when there were 362 patients. Growth continued with an artificial limb and an eye ward being added. By March 1916 the Hospital had 803 beds and that October had 960 patients. In November the facility also became a general hospital, complete with operating theatres and X-ray department. An Australian Red Cross store opened in December and a magazine was produced by the patients, the *Harefield Park Boomerang*. At its height the Hospital could accommodate over 1,000 patients. It gradually closed during January 1919 and in 1920 was sold to Middlesex County Council for a tuberculosis sanatorium. Today it is Harefield Hospital.

leave in Brussels on 3rd April 1919 and returned to Hurdcott, England on 29th April. The VC was presented by the King at Buckingham Palace on 31st May. James embarked aboard SS *Königin Luise* on 21st June and disembarked at Fremantle, WA on 3rd August. He was discharged in Perth, WA on 10th September 1919.

SS *Königin Luise* was built in 1896 by Vulcan Shipbuilding Corporation, Stettin, Germany for the North German Lloyd Line, Bremen and was used on the Australia, Far East and North Atlantic routes. When war broke out she avoided being interned in neutral ports and was laid up in Germany. After the war she was allocated as reparations to the United Kingdom. On her third London–Australia voyage on 8th September 1920, she collided at Lisbon with SS *Loughborough*, which sank. In 1921 she was sold to the Orient Steam Navigation Co and renamed *Omar*. In 1924 she was sold to the Byron Steamship Co of London, was renamed *Edison* and operated the Piraeus–New York service until scrapped in Italy in 1935 (State Library of Queensland).

James took up a block of land in Swan Valley, near Perth and cultivated vines, citrus and stone fruit. When fruit was in season he would pick and pack all day and then get a few hours sleep, before taking the produce to market in a spring cart, a round trip of thirty miles. The horse knew the route home and he would catnap before arriving in time for breakfast and a new day's work.

James Woods married Olive Adeline Wilson (16th October 1899–26th October 1986), born at Manly, NSW, on 30th April 1921 at Caversham Methodist Church, Perth, WA. They lived there before moving to Swan Valley. When he retired, they settled at 25 York Terrace, Mosman Park, Claremont, Perth and had moved to 25 Watkins Road, Claremont by 1958. Olive was living at 21/31 Williams Road, Nedlands, WA in 1980. They had seven children:

- Gordon Park Woods (6th March 1922–5th October 1943) enlisted in the RAAF at Perth on 17th August 1941 (415295). He was commissioned as a pilot officer and was posted to 4 Operational Training Unit, Williamtown, NSW for flying training. He was killed on a training flight when his aircraft was lost at sea (Sydney Memorial, Sydney War Cemetery, Rookwood Necropolis, NSW).

The Sydney Memorial in Sydney War Cemetery is about seventeen kilometres west of Sydney. The War Cemetery is in the grounds of Rookwood Necropolis. The Memorial is one of several commemorating members of the Australian Army, Royal Australian Air Force and the Australian Merchant Navy who lost their lives in the southwest Pacific during the Second World War and who have no known grave. The 747 names on the Sydney Memorial were lost in the eastern and southern regions of Australia and in adjacent waters south of Latitude 20 degrees South.

- Norman James Woods (born 30th June 1923) enlisted in the RAAF on 14th September 1941 (415371). He reached the rank of warrant officer in 99 Squadron RAF and was discharged on 29th January 1946.
- Brian Stanley Woods (4th March 1926–29th October 2013) was granted a short service commission as a flight lieutenant in the Medical Branch of the RAAF on 20th September 1948 (297502). He was a dentist in 1954, living with his parents at 25 Watkins Road, Nedlands. He married Faye Hehir (c.1930–c.2010) in April 1954 at Wesley Church, Claremont. She was a secretary living at 200 Marine Parade, North Cottesloe, Fremantle at the time. They had a child.
- Vera Woods (born c.1930).
- Evan Wilson Woods (26th April 1932–16th June 2018) was a salesman in 1954, living with his parents at 25 Watkins Road, Nedlands. He married Pamela Rene White (c.1935–c.2020) c.1955 at Perth. He was a business manager in 1963, when they were living at 2 Brown Street, Claremont. He was a manufacturer's

representative by 1980, when they were living at 17 Thomas Street, Nedlands. They had four children:
- Michelle Marcia Woods (born c.1957).
- Nicole Adrienne Woods (5th August 1959–18th November 2012) never married.
- Glenn Wilson Woods (born c.1960).
- Simone Woods (born c.1962).
* Margaret Woods (born c.1935).
* Olive Raye Woods (born c.1937) was a stenographer in 1958, living with her parents.

Olive's father, Charles Henry Wilson (2nd May 1861–30th October 1951), born at Hotham, Victoria, was a mining engineer/geologist. He married Lily Augusta née Bennett (1862–12th September 1931), born at Manly, NSW, on 22nd February 1888 at the Congregational Church, Manly. They were living at Minnawarra, Caversham, WA in August 1914. Lily died at Swan, WA and Charles at Mosman Park, WA. In addition to Olive they had seven other children:

* Hubert Vivian Wilson (19th December 1888–17th June 1974), born at Carlton, Victoria, was a draughtsman. He travelled to the USA via Vancouver, British Columbia, Canada on 5th April 1909. Hubert married Olive Marian Dowie (28th August 1888–August 1978), born in Milwaukee, Wisconsin, USA on 5th June 1912 and they lived at 1212 Fairview Avenue, South Milwaukee. He became a naturalised US citizen on 10th June 1919. They both died at La Mesa, San Diego, California. They had three children – Lillian Olive Wilson (1913–2010), Frederick Hubert Wilson (1915–2015) and Lois Ruth Wilson (1924–2011).
* Norman Stanley Wilson (25th September 1890–29th July 1916), born at Hawthorn, Victoria, was a labourer when he enlisted in the AIF on 12th March 1915 (929), having served for two years in 18th Light Horse at Perth, WA. He was described as 5′ 8″ tall, weighing 145 lbs, with fresh complexion, brown eyes, brown hair and his religious denomination was Congregationalist. He was assigned to No.13 Depot Company and later to 6th Reinforcements, 16th Battalion. He embarked on HMAT A11 *Ascanius* at Fremantle on 29th June. He was transferred to 28th Battalion and embarked for Gallipoli aboard HT *Ivernia* at Alexandria, Egypt on 4th September. He was appointed regimental transport driver on 6th September and rejoined the Battalion on 12th October. Norman embarked on HMT *Ausonia* at Mudros on 6th January 1916 and disembarked at Alexandria on 10th January. He was appointed temporary corporal at Ismailia on 12th February. On 16th March he embarked at Alexandria and disembarked at Marseille on 21st March. Promoted corporal backdated to 12th February 1916 and temporary sergeant on 14th July. Norman was reported missing in action on 29th July. This was withheld from official casualty lists initially at the request

of his brother, Claude, until more definite information was available so as not to upset his mother unnecessarily. On 4th January 1917 a court of enquiry decided that he had been killed in action (Villers-Bretonneux Memorial, France).

- Irene Constance Wilson (2nd November 1892–18th April 1979), born at Broken Hill, NSW, was a schoolteacher. She married George Finlay Townsend (6th April 1889–14th December 1939), born at Frome, SA, on 31st October 1923 at the Methodist Church, Caversham, WA. He enlisted in N Group, Base Infantry AIF at Keswick, SA on 19th July 1915 (3048) and was assigned to 10th Reinforcements, 12th Battalion. He was described as a railway porter, 5′ 6¾″ tall, weighing 146 lbs, with fair complexion, grey eyes, brown hair and his religious denomination was Methodist. His next of kin was his mother, who had remarried as Mrs Katherine Marshall, living at Yongala Vale, via Terowie, SA. He embarked at Adelaide aboard HMAT A70 *Ballarat* on 14th September, arriving at Sarpi Camp, Lemnos on 4th December to join the Battalion. He disembarked from HMT *Lake Michigan* at Alexandria, Egypt on 6th January 1916. On 29th March he embarked at Alexandria and disembarked at Marseille, France on 5th April. He received gunshots to the back and left leg at Pozières on 24th July and was treated at No.3 Australian Casualty Clearing Station. He was moved by 29 Ambulance Train next day to 10th General Hospital, Rouen and on 26th July was evacuated to England aboard HMHS *St George* for admission to Reading War Hospital, Berkshire next day. He was transferred to 2nd Australian Auxiliary Hospital, Southall for convalescence on 14th November and was discharged on 16th November to No.2 Command Depot, Weymouth. On 24th January 1917 he went to France from Folkestone, Kent aboard SS *Princess Clementine*, joining 1st Australian Division Base Depot on 26th January and his unit on 7th February. He was admitted to 3rd Australian Field Ambulance on 13th March suffering from the old wound. He was transferred to No.45 Casualty Clearing Station next day, to 12th General Hospital, Rouen on 16th March and was discharged to Base Details on 19th March. He joined 1st Australian Division Base Depot on 29th March and was detached to HQ 3rd Australian Division for base duties on 12th May. He transferred to the Australian Employment Company on 11th November. George was granted leave in Britain 2nd-16th February 1918. He transferred to 23rd Company, 3rd Australian Division Train on 25th August and was attached to 3rd Australian Division Salvage Company on 31st August. He was appointed driver on 5th September and joined the Australian General Base Depot on 15th December. On 22nd December he reverted to private and returned to England on 31st December, joining No.2 Command Depot, Weymouth on 1st January 1919. He joined the Australian Army Service Corps Training Depot, Parkhouse Camp, Salisbury Plain on 12th February as a driver and the Overseas Training Brigade on 3rd March. George embarked aboard HMT *Armagh* at Devonport on 5th April and disembarked at Adelaide on 16th May. He was discharged on 8th July 1919 and returned to work on the Australian railways. Irene and George

lived at 13 Cross Roads, Edwardstown, SA. He was accidentally run over and killed by a train whilst on duty at Goyder, SA. George is named on the Adelaide South Australian Railways Honour Boards, the Peterborough War Memorial and the Terowie Institute Honour Board. Irene died at Monreith Aged Care Facility, 401 Portrush Road, Adelaide. They had four sons including:
  - Bruce Finlay Townsend (born 1st February 1925) enlisted in the RAAF on 16th March 1943 at Adelaide (122593) and was discharged as a leading aircraftman from 9 Transport and Movement Office on 17th April 1946.
  - Douglas George Townsend (born 12th May 1926) enlisted in the RAAF on 23rd February 1945 at Adelaide (457016 (O45678)) and was discharged as an aircraftman 2nd class from 1 Initial Training School, Somers, Victoria on 30th August 1945.
  - Graham Rosslyn Townsend (1927–18th March 1993) enlisted in the RAN on 21st May 1945 at Port Adelaide (PA5426) and was discharged as an able seaman from HMAS *Cerberus*, Victoria on 27th May 1947.
- Claude Manly Wilson (3rd March 1894–23rd March 1972), a vigneron/viticulturist, enlisted in 11th Battalion AIF at Helena Vale, WA on 17th August 1914 (373), was attested on 9th September and was assigned to A Company. He had served for two years and three months in 88th Infantry. He was described as 5′ 9″ tall, weighing 150 lbs, with fair complexion, brown eyes, dark hair and his religious denomination was Congregationalist. Promoted sergeant on 1st September. He embarked aboard HMT *Suffolk* on 2nd March 1915. He was wounded by a gunshot to the right thigh at Gallipoli on 25th April and was evacuated to Malta aboard HMT *Clan McGillivray* on 4th May, where he was admitted to the Convalescent Hospital, Tigne. He returned to duty on 9th June and embarked aboard HMT *Andania* for Egypt. On 14th June he embarked at Alexandria aboard HMT *Southland* and rejoined the unit at Gallipoli on 20th June. He was wounded on 1st August and was admitted to 1st Australian Casualty Clearing Station with a compound fracture of the thigh from bullet and bomb wounds. He was transferred to HMHS *Rewa* and disembarked at Alexandria on 6th August, for admission to 21st General Hospital, where a testicle was removed. He was transferred to 1st Australian General Hospital, Heliopolis, Cairo on 1st October and embarked aboard HMT *Kanowna* at Suez on 20th October for return to Australia. He was posted to 22 Depot on 26th September 1916 and joined No.5 Officer Cadet School, Duntroon on 14th October. On 4th January 1917 he joined No.1 Depot Battalion and passed Duntroon class III on 8th January. He was a sergeant at D3 Depot from 16th April. Claude was commissioned on 1st March 1918. He embarked at Sydney with a special draft of AIF officers aboard HT *Ormonde* on 2 March, disembarked at Suez on 4th April and disembarked at Southampton on 15th May. He went to France on 14th August via Southampton, joined the Australian Infantry Base Depot on 16th August and 16th Battalion on 21st August. Claude was detached to the Australian Corps Bombing School on

23rd October and was promoted lieutenant on 6th November. He was admitted to 51st Stationary Hospital with venereal disease on 28th November, transferred to 39th General Hospital and was discharged to Base Details on 9th January. He was granted leave to Britain 15th–25th January 1919. He returned to England on 31st March with 1915 personnel for return to Australia and joined No.4 Command Depot, Hurdcott on 1st April. He joined No.2 Group, Sutton Veny, Wiltshire on 10th June. He embarked aboard HT *Ormonde* on 16th June, disembarked in Australia on 1st August and was discharged on 31st August. George married Emily Maud Dawson (1895–4th April 1959), born at Lion Hill, WA, in 1920 in Perth, WA. Claude served in the Australian Army again, enlisting at Midland Junction, WA on 29th May 1941 (W40152) and was discharged as a captain from 7 Advanced Ordnance Depot, Australian Army Ordnance Corps on 15th August 1952. They had four children:
- Norman Francis Wilson (20th November 1919–2010) enlisted in the Australian Army at Perth, WA on 10th June 1940 (WX3970) and was discharged as a lieutenant from 2/6th Australian Field Regiment, Signal Section on 22nd November 1945.
- Joan Lillian Wilson (19th March 1922–13th May 1988) enlisted in the Australian Army at Claremont, WA on 31st July 1942 (W45816) and was discharged as a sergeant on 29th March 1946.
- Rosamond Olive Wilson (11th April 1923–2013) enlisted in the Australian Army at Claremont on 25th June 1942 (W45662) and was discharged as a corporal from HQ 12 Australian Lines of Communication Signals on 22nd January 1946.
- Colin Frederick Wilson (7th July 1924–30th December 2018) enlisted in the Australian Army at Perth on 1st August 1941 (WX33084 (W34288)) and was discharged as a corporal from 7 Australian Army Troops Company on 23rd April 1946.

- Leonard Gratton Wilson (13th August 1901–11th April 1990) enlisted as a boy 2nd class in the RAN (5596) on 14th March 1916 and was described as 5′ 4½″ tall, with brown hair, blue eyes and fresh complexion. Promoted ordinary seaman on 14th November 1918 and commenced adult service on 13th August 1919. He served on HMAS *Tingira* and *Penguin*. Leonard was sentenced by court martial on 11th May 1920 to twelve months imprisonment and he was dismissed from the service on 11th December 1920. Despite this he became a police constable. Leonard married Dunbar Duff (5th May 1906–29th June 1995), born at Station House, Port Soderick, Isle of Man, on 13th February 1926 at Guildford, WA. They were living at 19 Jubilee Street, South Perth, WA in 1931, at Albany, WA in 1943 and at Como, WA in 1954. He died at Dalkeith, WA and she at Craigwood Nursing Home, Como, WA. They had three children:
    - Peter Gratton Wilson (born and died 28th July 1926).
    - Dunbar Gratton Wilson (9th July 1927–27th February 2013).

- Leonard Gratton Wilson (1st March 1929–7th June 2014) was created an Officer of the Order of Australia for public service to science (Commonwealth of Australia Gazette 16th June 1979). He married Marion and they had several children.
* Septimus Wilson (7th-8th July 1905) born at Lithgow, NSW.
* Albyn Joseph Wilson (4th October 1907–21st January 1976) was a shopkeeper. He was a farmhand when he married Kathleen Margaret Makin (1912–2002), born at Bayswater, WA, in 1937. They lived at Camfield Road, Greenmount, Guildford, WA. He enlisted in the Australian Army at Claremont, WA on 24th February 1942 (W58007) and was discharged as a corporal on 3rd April 1947. By 1958 he was a bus driver and they were living at 6 Almondbury Street, Bayswater, WA. He died at 5 Balga Place, Koongamia, WA. They had two children.

An Anzac Dinner on 23rd April 1927, hosted by Lieutenant General Sir John Monash GCMG KCB VD, was attended by twenty-three VCs, including James Woods. For an unknown reason the Duke of York was not invited. James also attended the ANZAC Commemoration Service on 25th April 1927 at the Royal Exhibition Building, Melbourne in the presence of the Duke of York (future King George VI), with twenty-three other VCs. On 11th November 1929 James was entertained at a luncheon hosted by Colonel Sir William Campion KCMG DSO TD, Governor of Western Australia, at Government House, Perth to honour those VCs who could not attend the VC Dinner at the House of Lords in London. The other VCs attending included John Carroll, Clifford Sadlier and Hugo Throssell.

James' health suffered and he had to give up the farm in 1937. They moved to Perth, where he lived off a service pension, having been classified as a 'Totally

A group of Australian VCs at an Anzac Day parade in 1938. James Woods is sitting fifth from the left.

SS *Orcades* was the Orient Line's third ship of that name. Her maiden voyage from Tilbury to Australia commenced on 14th December 1948. In 1955 she began a world service westwards, departing London to New Zealand and Australia via the Panama Canal and returning to Britain via the Suez Canal. During the November 1956 Olympic Games in Melbourne she was used as an accommodation ship. She sailed her last cruises in 1972 and was broken up in 1973.

The grave of James and Olive Woods in Karrakatta Cemetery. He is one of eight VCs buried there.

Hollywood Repatriation Hospital was built in 1942 as 110 Military Hospital and became the Repatriation General Hospital, Hollywood in 1947. In 1994 it was purchased by Ramsay Health Care Group and became Hollywood Private Hospital. New wings in 2002, 2009 and 2016 added ten wards. It is the largest private hospital in Australia with 738 licensed beds, over 2,000 employees and 70,000 patients each year (Australian War Memorial).

and Permanently Incapacitated Pensioner'. He was President of the Caversham sub-branch of the Returned Sailors', Soldiers' and Airmen's Imperial League of Australia. He stopped a bolting horse and dray in the main streets of Guildford, WA by leaping at the horse's head and pulling it to a stop. James attended the VC Centenary Celebrations at Hyde Park, London on 26th June 1956, travelling on SS *Orcades* with other Australian VCs, who were part of the 301 Victoria Cross recipients from across the Commonwealth to attend.

James Woods died at Hollywood Repatriation Hospital, Claremont, WA on 18th January 1963 and is buried in Karrakatta Cemetery, Perth, WA (Wesleyan Section H-A Plot 1). He is commemorated in a number of other places:

- Australian Capital Territory
    - Woods Place, Canberra gazetted on 8th February 1978.
    - Commemorative display in the Hall of Valour, Australian War Memorial, Canberra.
    - Named on one of eleven plaques honouring 175 men from overseas awarded the VC for the Great War. The plaques were unveiled by the Senior Minister of State at the Foreign & Commonwealth Office and Minister for Faith and Communities, Baroness Warsi, at a reception at Lancaster House, London on 26th June 2014 attended by The Duke of Kent and relatives of the VC recipients. The Australian plaque is at the Australian War Memorial.
    - Australian Victoria Cross Recipients plaque on the Victoria Cross Memorial, Campbell, Canberra dedicated on 24th July 2000.
- Western Australia
    - The nineteen wards of Hollywood Private Hospital, Perth were named after VCs and GCs, including James Woods.
    - Plaque on Wall 3, Row C in the Garden of Remembrance at Karrakatta Cemetery, Perth.
    - Memorial plaque at the State War Memorial, King's Park, Perth, dedicated on 26th January 1996.
    - Plaque at Mosman Park, Bay View Terrace, Perth, dedicated in 2013.
    - Glen Eagles Commemoration Way Rest Area K is named after him on Albany Highway, Armdale.
    - Commemorative display at the Army Museum of Western Australia, Fremantle.
- Victoria
    - Victoria Cross Memorial, Springvale Botanical Cemetery, Melbourne.
- South Australia
    - JP Woods VC Anzac Day Medal was established in 2010 by the South Australia Community Football League, in partnership with the South Australian Department of Veterans' Affairs and the Returned & Services League. It is presented annually to the 'best on-field player' in the Adelaide Plains Football League Anzac Day match.
    - Victoria Cross Plaque, North Terrace, Adelaide.
    - Memorial at RSL HQ, Adelaide.
- New South Wales
    - Victoria Cross Memorial, Queen Victoria Building, George Street, Sydney, dedicated on 23rd February 1992 to commemorate the visit of Queen Elizabeth II and Prince Phillip on the occasion of the Sesquicentenary of

the City of Sydney. Sir Roden Cutler VC AK KCMG, Edward Kenna VC and Keith Payne VC were in attendance.
    ◦ Victoria Cross Recipients Wall, North Bondi War Memorial donated to Waverley on 27th November 2011 by The Returned & Services League of Australia.
    ◦ VC Memorial, Borella Road, Peards Complex, East Albury.
    ◦ VC Memorial, Ingleburn RSL Club, Sydney.
* Queensland
    ◦ Portrait painted by Graham Hocking in 1990 and held by the Nanango Returned and Services League.
* Communities and Local Government commemorative paving stones for the 145 VCs born in Australia, Belgium, Canada, China, Denmark, Egypt, France, Germany, India, Iraq, Japan, Nepal, Netherlands, Newfoundland, New Zealand, Pakistan, South Africa, Sri Lanka, Ukraine and United States of America were unveiled at the National Memorial Arboretum, Alrewas, Staffordshire by Prime Minister David Cameron MP and Sergeant Johnson Beharry VC on 5th March 2015.

In addition to the VC he was awarded the British War Medal 1914–20, Victory Medal 1914–19, George VI Coronation Medal 1937 and Queen Elizabeth II Coronation Medal 1953. His VC group was presented to the Australian War Memorial by his son, Norman and family, in November 1992 at a ceremony in the Western Front Gallery in front of Arthur Streeton's painting 'St Quentin'. The VC was received by the War Memorial councillor Sir William Keys and is displayed in the 'Hall of Valour' at the Australian War Memorial, Treloar Crescent, Campbell, Australian Capital Territory, Australia.

## SECOND LIEUTENANT FRANK EDWARD YOUNG
### 1/1st Battalion, The Hertfordshire Regiment

Frank Young was born on 2nd October 1895 at Cherat, North West Frontier Province, India (now Pakistan). His father, also Frank Young (27th March 1874–14th November 1952), was born at Houghton Regis, near Dunstable, Bedfordshire, as Frank Fensome. He enlisted in the Bedfordshire Regiment on 16th November 1889 and served at Shorncliffe Camp, Kent (3292). He gained the Army Certificate of Education 3rd Class on 19th March 1890 and 2nd Class on 17th June. Frank was promoted lance corporal on 16th May 1890, attended a regimental promotion course on 14th April 1891 and was

promoted corporal on 16th April. He injured his knee off duty on 30th October. On 19th May 1892 he was posted to the 2nd Battalion and passed the regimental promotion course for sergeant on 11th July. He suffered from synovitis of the right knee joint from a sprain off duty at Devonport, Devon on 5th October. Frank was promoted lance sergeant on 7th November 1892 and sergeant on 19th March 1893. He attended the School of Musketry, Hythe, Kent on 28th September. On 16th January 1894 he extended his service to complete twelve years and sailed for India with the 1st Battalion on 14th March. He saw action on the North West Frontier in October 1895 as part of the Chitral Relief Force (India Medal 1895–1902 with clasp 'Relief of Chitral 1895'). Frank sprained his right knee off duty again on 19th January 1897. He was promoted colour sergeant on 5th May 1899 and extended his service at Mooltan to complete twenty-one years on 21st July. He suffered from synovitis of the right knee again on 17th January 1902. He returned to England on 9th December and was posted to the permanent staff of 3rd Battalion on 5th January 1903. Frank gained a certificate as Inspector of Small Arms, Birmingham, Warwickshire on 13th February 1904 and was awarded the Army Long Service and Good Conduct Medal with gratuity in 1908. He was posted to the 1st Battalion, Hertfordshire Regiment on 31st October 1909 and was permitted to extend his service beyond twenty-one years on 2nd February 1910. Frank was appointed drill instructor with the Hitchin Company, 1st Hertfordshire.

Frank senior was mobilised in August 1914 and sailed for France on 5th November. He was appointed acting company sergeant major and acting regimental sergeant major on 15th February 1915 (later substantive from 29th January). He was mentioned in despatches for his actions during the Battle of Loos in September 1915 (LG 1st January 1916). Frank was invalided home on 12th April 1916, where he was appointed acting regimental sergeant major of 3/1st Battalion, North Camp, Halton Park, Tring on 16th April. He had applied for a commission on 15th December 1915 and attended No.6 Officer Cadet Battalion, Balliol College, Oxford and was commissioned into 3/1st Battalion, Hertfordshire Regiment on 4th August. His address was Chapel Street, Luton at the time. Appointed acting lieutenant on 17th April 1917. He suffered from albuminuria from July 1918 and was admitted to Manor House Hospital, Folkestone, Kent through Shorncliffe Military Hospital, Kent on 6th August. A medical board at Shorncliffe on 9th September found him fit for Home Service and he was to report to the Town Commandant of Folkestone that day to be appointed Assistant Commandant, No.3 Rest Camp, Folkestone as an acting captain. He was living at 22 Grimstone Gardens, Folkestone at the time. A medical board at Shorncliffe on 13th November found him unfit for General Service permanently but fit for Home Service. A medical board at Shorncliffe Military Hospital on 8th April 1919 found him unfit for General Service permanently but fit for garrison and labour units abroad, with his disability assessed at under 20%. Frank was disembodied on 18th November and he relinquished acting captain. He retired on 19th May 1921, having reached the age limit for his rank, and retained the rank of captain. He was living at Pirton Cottage, Pirton, near Hitchin, Hertfordshire at the time. Frank married Sarah Ellen 'Nellie' Searle née Burgoyne (5th October 1872–25th December 1960), born at Brixham, Devon, at Stoke Damerel Register Office on 19th February 1894. She was a domestic cook in 1891, living with her sister, Rosina Sheppard, at Stoke Damerel, Devon. They were living at Elm Villa in Verulam Road, Hitchin in 1911 and at 46 Wood Avenue, Folkestone in 1918. Later they lived at 139 Dolphins Road, Folkestone and were at 141 Dolphins Road in 1939, by when he was a clerk for the collector

Paleolithic, Bronze Age and Iron Age remains have been found around Houghton Regis, including the hill fort at Maiden Bower. The village is mentioned in the Domesday Book. The actor Gary Cooper was born and went to school there. The village character changed drastically when a massive London overspill estate was constructed in the 1950s and 60s.

of taxes. Frank senior subsequently died there. Sarah was living at 29 Sutherland Avenue, Leeds, Yorkshire at the time of her death at St James Hospital, Burmantofts, Leeds. Frank junior had six siblings:

- Isabella Nellie 'Nell' Young (30th December 1897–1988) was born at Ferozepore (now Firozpur), Punjab, India. She married Frank Walter Hartley (31st August 1895–4th September 1970), born at Leeds, Yorkshire, in 1919 at Hitchin, Hertfordshire. Frank was a Civil Service telegraph messenger in 1911, living with his mother at 3 Gledhow Terrace, Harehills, Leeds. Isabella was living at 29 Sutherland Avenue, Leeds in 1939. Frank was a Post Office overseer in 1945. They were living at 2 Sedge Rise, Tadcaster, Yorkshire at the time of his death there. Her death was registered at York. They had a daughter:

The India Medal was approved in 1896 for issue to officers and men of the British and Indian Armies. It was awarded for various minor campaigns in India, chiefly for the North-West Frontier in the period 1895-1902, and replaced the India General Service Medal 1854. Each campaign was represented by one of seven clasps:

- Defence of Chitral 1895 (3rd March – 13th April 1895).
- Relief of Chitral 1895 (7th March – 15th August 1895).
- Punjab Frontier 1897–98 (10th June 1897 – 6th April 1898).
- Malakand 1897 (26th July – 2nd August 1897).
- Samana 1897 (2nd August – 2nd October 1897).
- Tirah 1897–98 (2nd October 1897 – 6th April 1898).
- Waziristan 1901–02 (23rd November 1901 – 10th March 1902).

Multan, now in Pakistan, is a major cultural and economic centre of southern Punjab. Its history dates back 5,000 years. It was besieged by Alexander the Great in 326 BC and became an important trading centre in medieval Islamic India. It attracted many Sufi mystics in the 11th and 12th centuries, when it was known as the City of Saints, and there are many Sufi shrines there. The Mughals captured Multan in 1557 and in 1627 the city was encircled by walls. Under Mughal rule, Multan enjoyed 200 years of peace and prosperity, during which the city became

an important agricultural, textile manufacturing, currency minting, tile-making and commercial centre. However, its fortunes were badly affected by silting and shifting of the river and the waning of the Mughal Empire following the death of Emperor Aurangzeb in 1707. Its importance dwindled to that of a regional trading town and it came under Afghan rule. In 1772, Sikh forces captured the city but it reverted to Afghan rule in 1778. At the Battle of Multan on 2nd March 1818 control was wrested back by the Sikhs but its trading importance continued to decline. In 1848 local Sikhs murdered two British emissaries leading to the Multan Revolt and subsequent Siege of Multan. The rebellion spread and led to the Second Anglo-Sikh War, which resulted in the fall of the Sikh Empire in February 1849. On 22nd January 1849 the British breached the walls of Multan Fort and the city surrendered. Between the 1890s and 1920s a vast network of canals was constructed in the Multan region and throughout much of the Punjab. Following the independence of Pakistan in 1947, the minority Hindus and Sikhs migrated to India and some Muslim refugees from India settled in the city.

  - Eileen Nellie Hartley (28th July 1920–6th April 1991), born at Hitchin, was a sorting clerk and telegraphist in 1939. She married Granville Roberts (12th September 1915–29th April 1970), born at Pontefract, Yorkshire, in 1941 at Leeds. He was a Post Office telephone fitter in 1939, when they were living with his parents at 20 Ravenscar Avenue, Leeds. They were living at 11 Woodlands Avenue, Tadcaster at the time of his death at Brent, Greater London. She was living at 44 Stonefield Place, Birstall, Batley, Yorkshire at the time of her death there. They had three children – Suzanne Roberts 1946, John C Roberts 1947 and David Leslie Roberts 1951.
- Louisa Ruth Young (born 31st December 1899) was born at Mooltan, India.
- Albert James Young (3rd November 1904–1985), a twin with Percy, was born at Kempston, Bedfordshire. He married Ruby Edith Maxted (25th July 1910–22nd January 1976), born at Capel le Ferne, Kent, in 1933 at Dover, Kent. Albert was a motor mechanic. By 1939 he was a chauffeur and they were living at Sunny Bank, Dorking, Surrey. They were living at 9 Clarence Road, Capel le Ferne at the time of her death there. His death was registered at Dover. They had two children:
  - Brian J Young (born 1936) married Gillian Freeman in 1958 at Folkestone, Kent. They had two sons – Stephen C Young 1960 and Robert C Young 1961.
  - Jane Young (born 1947).
- Percy Oliver Young (3rd November 1904–23rd May 1981), a twin with Albert, married Margery Florence Monk (22nd May 1908–29th May 1997), born at

Sittingbourne, Kent, in 1932 at Milton, Kent. He was a garage service manager in 1939, when they were living at 139 Dolphins Road, Folkestone, next door to his parents. They were living at 33 Kettlewell Close, Woodloes Park, Warwick at the time of his death there. Her death was registered at Canterbury, Kent. They had two sons:
  - David Young (29th August 1934–March 2002) married Beryl D Truelove (born 1934) in 1955 at Canterbury, where she was born. They had three sons – Michael Young 1956, Adrian Young 1959 and Paul A Young 1961.
  - Richard Young (born 1936).
- Leslie Lewis Young (18th September 1907–17th October 1948) married Rose Victoria Holmes (22nd January 1917–3rd January 2010), born at West Ham, London, in 1938 at East Ham, London. He served in the Merchant Navy during the Second World War. They were living at 11 Walpole Road, East Ham at the time of his death at 5 Collingham Gardens, Earls Court, London. Rose married Bertram Cudbill (19th October 1924–1984) in 1955 at West Ham. He was a hat manufacturer's brusher in 1939, living with his parents at 31 Dongola Road, West Ham. They were living at 11 Walpole Road, East Ham in 1965 and both of them subsequently died at Colchester, Essex.
- Margery Muriel Young (born 12th August 1910) was born at Hitchin, Hertfordshire.

Aston Clinton lies in the Vale of Aylesbury at the foot of the Chilterns and at the intersection of two Roman roads, Akeman Street and Icknield Way. After the Romans the Saxons settled there and, prior to the Norman invasion, the village was under the patronage of Edward the Confessor. Aston appears in the Domesday Book of 1086 as *Estone*. By 1237 the manor was owned by the de Clinton family and the village subsequently became *Aston de Clinton*. The estates also passed through the Montacute, Hastings, Barrington, Gerard and Lake families. The car manufacturer Aston Martin took the first part of its name from the village, having great success in the Aston Clinton Hill Climb competition. The 1962 film *Lolita* was filmed in the village and the rock band *Marillion* formed there in 1979. Aston Clinton House seen here, also known as Green Park, was completed by Anthony Nathan de Rothschild in 1853. Workers' cottages, two schools and a village hall were also built under Rothschild patronage. During the Great War, Aston Clinton House was lent to the War Office. In September 1914 it was the HQ of 21st Division, a New Army formation that formed and trained in Buckinghamshire at Tring and on the Halton and Aston Clinton estates. By the outbreak of the Second World War, the house was the Green Park Hotel. It was used by the electronics company, EKCO, for radar research and development and the main house became a hospital for war wounded. Later it was a boys' prep school, where Evelyn Waugh began his teaching career. It was briefly a hotel again until it was demolished between 1956 and 1958. Today the estate is a residential training centre for young people. The only remaining original buildings are the stables.

Frank's paternal grandfather, James Young (9th June 1830–24th February 1917), a straw bonnet maker born at Aston Clinton, Buckinghamshire, married Emma née Paul (6th June 1830–30th March 1875), born at Sandridge, Hertfordshire, on 23rd July 1850 at Luton, Bedfordshire. They were living at Adelaide Terrace, Luton in 1851 by when Emma was a straw bonnet sewer. They had moved to 89 Albert Road, Luton by 1861. James married Sarah née Fensom/Fensome (1853–78) in late 1875 at Luton. Sarah had given birth to her son, Frank, on 27th March 1874 and, although not confirmed it is most likely that James Young was the father. Sarah's death almost certainly resulted from complications with the birth of an unnamed son, who also died. James married Louisa Ruth Dear (c.1836–99) in 1879 at Luton, where she was born. They were living at 86 Chapel Street, Luton in 1881, by when he was employing one man and five girls. Louisa died at Christchurch, Hampshire. James was living at Mount Pleasant, Harlington, Dunstable, Bedfordshire in 1911 and subsequently died there. In addition to Frank, James had eight other children from his first two marriages:

- Maria Young (March 1851–1852), born and died at Luton.
- Elizabeth 'Lizzie' Young (1852–2nd December 1937) married William Weatherhead (25th December 1859–16th November 1930) in 1882. William was running a hatters' machine manufacturing firm in Luton in 1911, when they were living at 4 Dumfries Street and later at 32a Conway Road. Lizzie was living at 42 Conway Road at the time of her death there. They had five children:
    - Lily Weatherhead (1883–16th February 1959) was a milliner's forewoman in 1911. She married William J Pearce (15th October 1898–1984) at Luton in 1937.
    - William Henry Weatherhead (17th February 1885–6th January 1958).
    - Fanny Weatherhead (25th September 1886–9th November 1974) married Percy William Reynolds (1887–1939) on 25th June 1910 at Union Church, Luton. They had two children – Olive Fanny Reynolds (born 18th March 1911) and Haydn Percy Eric Reynolds (born 21st October 1915). Percy was a motor mechanic (motorcycle fitter), living at 101 Stuart Street, Luton when he enlisted in the Army Service Corps (M2/18/855) on 2nd June 1916 and joined at Grove Park on 7th June. He was described as 5′ 6″ tall and weighed 196 lbs. He served at the London Motor Transport Repair Depot and transferred to Camberwell on 27th January 1917. He was medically downgraded to B2 on 8th September and was awarded the good conduct badge on 2nd June 1918. He transferred to the Class Z Reserve on 16th March 1919 from the Dispersal Unit, Purfleet.
    - Sydney James Weatherhead (1888–1927) was a hatter's machinery maker in 1911.
    - Percy Weatherhead (2nd August 1895–22nd November 1974) was a jeweller's apprentice in 1911. He married Ethel Jones (c.1896–1939) in

1916. They had seven children – Percy FW Weatherhead 1918, Ronald L Weatherhead 1920, Margaret M Weatherhead 1921, Unice E Weatherhead 1923, William J Weatherhead 1925, Rosemary B Weatherhead 1931 and Sheila D Weatherhead 1936. Percy married Evelyn Miller nee Charlton (1902–51) in 1941. She had married Reginald H Miller in 1927.

- James Edward Paul Young (27th February 1859–16th September 1938) married Kate Smith (24th September 1863–1st September 1946), born at Eastern Maudit, Northamptonshire, on 21st February 1882 at Luton. They emigrated to Australia, arriving in Brisbane on 10th March 1885 and lived in Queensland for a while until settling in New South Wales. He was a gardener in 1915, when they were living at Luton, 5th Avenue, Campsie, NSW. He died at Lewisham and she at Burwood. They had nine children:
  - Jeanette Buffa Young (7th October 1882–12th September 1968), born at Luton, married Herbert J Irwin (1883–1963), born at Dungog, NSW, in 1906 at Rockdale, NSW. He died at Rockdale and she at Kogarah. They had five children – Irene B Irwin 1907, Elsie K Irwin 1909, Jeanette D Irwin 1911, Edna H Irwin 1915 and Herbert C Irwin 1920.
  - Annie Kate Young (8th December 1883–11th April 1974).
  - James Alexander Young (17th January 1886–6th March 1887), born and died in Queensland.
  - Isabelle Florence Young (born 3rd March 1888) is believed to have married Robert Henry Simmons at Rockdale, NSW in 1938.
  - Edward Charles Young (1st January 1891–1958), born at Burwood, NSW and died at Taree, NSW.
  - Sydney Bond Young (19th January 1895–28th September 1985), born at Queanbeyan, NSW, enlisted in the AIF on 9th August 1915 (3968). He had been rejected previously for compulsory training due to a weak heart. He was a bricklayer, apprenticed to S Patrick in Rockdale for five years, and was described as twenty-one years and eight months old, 5' 7¾" tall, weighing 139 lbs, with fresh complexion, blue eyes, black hair and his religious denomination was Church of England. He joined B Company, 6th Battalion at Holdsworthy on 30th August, transferred to 12th Reinforcements, 4th Battalion on 24th September, to C Company, No.1 Battalion on 1st January 1916, to E Company, No.1 Battalion on 1st March and later to D Company, 36th Battalion. Sydney embarked at Sydney on 13th May and disembarked at Devonport on 9th July. He went to France from Southampton on 22nd November. On 18th January 1917 he was wounded by a gunshot in the back and was admitted to 10th Australian Field Ambulance and No.2 Casualty Clearing Station next day. He was transferred to 8th Stationary Hospital, Wimereux aboard 24 Ambulance Train on 22nd January. On 25th January he was evacuated to England from Boulogne and was admitted to 3rd Australian General Hospital, Brighton. He transferred to York Place Military Hospital,

Brighton on 16th February and 1st Australian Auxiliary Hospital, Harefield on 22nd March. Sydney was granted leave 2nd-17th April then reported to No.3 Command Depot, Hurdcott, Wiltshire. He transferred to 63rd Battalion at Windmill Hill Camp, Perham Down, Wiltshire on 27th April and attended the School of Musketry, Tidworth 3rd-28th July, qualifying first class with a fair working knowledge of the Lewis gun. On 19th September he transferred to 36th Battalion on joining the Overseas Training Brigade and returned to France from Southampton on 25th September. He joined 3rd Australian Division Base Depot, Rouelles next day and was taken on strength of 36th Battalion on 11th October. Sydney was granted leave in Britain 4th-21st February 1918 and transferred to 34th Battalion (1433) on 30th April for attachment to HQ 9th Australian Brigade. On 22nd August he was injured when a wagon ran over his left great toe and he was admitted to 10th Australian Field Ambulance. Next day he was transferred to No.7 Casualty Clearing Station and to 2nd Canadian General Hospital on 24th August. He was evacuated to England aboard HMHS *Grantully Castle* on 4th September and was treated at 1st Southern General Hospital, Edgbaston, Birmingham 5th September–14th October. He was granted leave 15th-29th October and then reported to No.1 Command Depot, Sutton Veny, Wiltshire. A medical board there found him fit for General Service on 6th December. Sydney embarked aboard HT *Mamani* at Liverpool on 21st December and disembarked in 3rd Military District in Australia on 4th February 1919. He was transferred to 2nd Military District and was discharged as a lance corporal on 3rd April 1919.

- Henry George Paul Young (5th February 1898–9th September 1990) enlisted in 12th Reinforcements, 13th Battalion at Holdsworthy on 24th August 1915 (3980). He gave his age as eighteen years and six months and declared previous service in the Australian Navy, having purchased his discharge. He was described as a jeweller's assistant, 5′ 10″ tall, weighing 130 lbs, with fresh complexion, blue eyes, dark brown hair and his religious denomination was Congregationalist. He embarked on HMAT A29 *Suevic* at Sydney on 22nd December. He was confined to camp for three days at Zeitoun, Egypt for disorderly conduct on parade on 22nd February 1916. On 4th March he was taken on strength of 13th Battalion at Tel-el-Kebir. He embarked at Alexandria on 1st June and disembarked at Marseille on 8th June. On 5th July he was wounded by a gunshot to the right ear (arm in some documents) and was admitted to 3rd Canadian General Hospital, Boulogne on 7th July. Next day he was evacuated to England aboard HMHS *St David* from Boulogne and was admitted to Norfolk War Hospital, Norwich on 9th July. He was transferred to No.1 Australian Auxiliary Hospital, Harefield on 18th July with otitis medea and was granted leave 17th-25th August, then reported to No.2 Command Depot, Weymouth. He had £-/2/- stopped from his pay for

loss of kit at Weymouth on 9th September. On 12th October he transferred to No.1 Command Depot, Perham Down, Wiltshire. He embarked aboard HMAT A31 *Ajana* at Portland on 17th October suffering from otorrhoea and disembarked at Melbourne on 8th December. He was discharged from 2nd Military District on 10th January 1917 and was awarded a pension of £1 per fortnight, amended to 15/- from 16th August. Henry married Elsie M Chatburn in 1923 at Canterbury, NSW, where she was born.
- Percy Robert John Young (1900–3rd October 1945) married Gladys A Kurtz (born 1901) in 1923 at Glebe, NSW, where she was born.
- William Ivor Claude Young (1903–12th May 1949) married Margaret J Marshall in 1924.

- Sarah Young (1st January 1862–11th August 1960) married James Runcieman (27th July 1864–10th November 1933), born at Widford, Chelmsford, Essex, at Luton in 1884. They were living at Christchurch, Southampton in 1901, when James was a manager of a market garden. They emigrated to New Zealand, where they both died at Birkenhead, Auckland. They had six children, all born at Luton except Chrissy:
  - Sarah Runcieman (born and died 1885).
  - Florence Runcieman (born 1886) was a dressmaker's apprentice in 1901.
  - Fred Runcieman (born and died 1889).
  - May Runcieman (born 1890) married John Hall in New Zealand in 1914. They had a stillborn child in 1918.
  - Elsie Runcieman (1891–1960) married Cyril Hubert William Lewis (born 1893), born in Birmingham, England, in New Zealand in 1916. They had a son, Cyril James Lewis, in 1917.
  - Chrissy Runcieman (born 1898), born at Christchurch, Hampshire, married William Thomas Smith in New Zealand in 1920.

- William Young (12th October 1863–18th November 1937) married Catherine Brant (1866–21st October 1941) in 1899 at Louth, Lincolnshire, where she was born. He was a poultry breeder in 1891, when they were living at Upper Stopsley, Luton. They had moved to 4 Russell Street, Luton by 1901 and he subsequently died there. Catherine was living at 19 Cutenhoe Road, Luton at the time of her death there. They had five children:
  - William James Young (1890–8th August 1966).
  - Catherine Ella Young (1st September 1891–1973) married Emil T Maier (1888–1920) at Luton in 1914. They had a daughter, Kathleen M Maier in 1916.
  - Isabella Constance Young (1893–1953) married Major Harrison Haworth (23rd February 1895–1970), born at Blackburn, Lancashire, at Luton in 1919. They had a son, Harrison R Haworth, in 1926.
  - George Edwin Young (born 1894).
  - Lilian Irene Louise Young (3rd March 1900–1970) married Leonard William Butcher (18th July 1900–1986) at Luton in 1921.

- Charles Edwin Young (26th October 1868–1942) married Mary Elizabeth Ribchester (6th March 1878–5th May 1955), born at Lancaster, Lancashire, in 1897 at Skipton, Yorkshire. He was a railway shunter for the Midland Railway in 1901, when they were living as visitors at 5 Milton Street, Skipton, North Riding of Yorkshire with Mary's parents, Thomas Ribchester (1856–1932), a railway engine driver, and Alice née Bonney (1852–1929). Charles was a railway goods guard in 1911, when they were living at 9 Pinfold Lane, Skerton, Lancaster. By 1939 they were living at 81 Halton Road, Lancaster, where they subsequently died. They had six children:
    - Elizabeth Alice Young (1898–22nd August 1959), born at Skipton, married Victor Ridding (1901–1960), born at St Olave, London, at Lancaster in 1924. They both died at Lancaster. They had a daughter, Joan Ridding, in 1925.
    - Albert Young (24th August 1899–1977), born and died at Lancaster.
    - Nellie Young (13th November 1905–1997).
    - Frank Fensome Young (23rd June 1910–1979) married Alice Roocroft (born 1909) at Lancaster in 1937. They had a daughter, Barbara Young, in 1940.
    - Lilian Young (1913–18).
    - Leslie Young (born 1915).
- Anne Maria Young (born 1877), born at Luton, married William How Dunning (1867–1942), born at Dorchester, Dorset, in 1904 at Ampthill, Bedfordshire. His death was registered at Dorchester. They had a daughter:
    - Doris Mabel Dunning (15th September 1906–17th October 1956) married William AC Venn (1st August 1898–1978), born at Cardiff, at Bournemouth in 1931. They had two children – Shirley A Venn 1942 and Graham C Venn 1945. Her death was registered at Bournemouth. William married Winifred SM Dickenson née Clemens (born 1911), in 1957 at Southampton, where she was born. She had married Cuthbert R Dickenson at Bristol in 1935.
- An unnamed boy born and died in 1878.

His maternal grandfather, John Pitman Burgoyne (15th August 1841–1894), a fisherman, was born at Brixham, Devon. He married Susan née Searle (1843–November 1912), born at Totnes, Devon, on 4th November 1866 at Lower Brixham. They were living at Overgang, Brixham in 1871 and 1881. By April 1891 he was a master aboard the trawler *Speedwell*, when they were living at Middle Street, Brixham. Susan was living with her children, Michael and Sophia, at 33 Higher Street, Brixham in 1911. In addition to Sarah they had seven other children:

- Rosina Burgoyne (1867–1954), born at Brixham, married Frank Sheppard (1867–1944), a butcher, born at Broad Chalke, Wiltshire, at Devonport on 9th October or November 1890. He was serving in 3rd Dorset when he enlisted in the Dorset Regiment for regular service at Dorchester, Dorset on 20th June 1888 (2708). He was described as 5′ 4″ tall, weighing 126 lbs, with florid complexion, hazel

Brixham in Devon, at the southern end of Torbay, was originally two separate communities – Cowtown on top of the hill, where the farmers lived, and a mile away around the harbour was Fishtown, where the fishermen and seamen lived. Although some Bronze Age and earlier evidence exists, the

first settlement was Saxon. In the Domesday Book, the population of *Briseham* was thirty-nine. William of Orange (William III) landed there on 5th November 1688 at the start of the Glorious Revolution. The road from the harbour to where the Dutch made their camp is still called *Overgang*, which is Dutch for passage. The Burgoynes were living there in the 1870s and 1880s. The main church in the town is St. Mary's, the third built on the site of a Celtic burial ground. All Saints' Church was founded in 1815 and one of its vicars, the Reverend Francis Lyte, composed the hymn *Abide With Me*. The British Seaman's Boys' Home for the orphaned sons of seamen was founded in 1863 and closed in 1988. The Torbay and Brixham Railway arrived in February 1868 and closed in May 1963. The town became popular as a holiday destination and several holiday camps were built in this area. Limestone and iron were mined in the area. Ochre was also found there. It was boiled with tar, tallow and oak bark to be painted on to the sails of the fishing boats to protect them and gave them their distinctive colour. Ochre was also used to make paint from about 1845, which was the first substance found in the world that could stop cast iron from rusting. However, fishing was the lifeblood of the town. In the Middle Ages it was the largest fishing port in the southwest. By the 1890s there were 300 vessels in Brixham and a few of the famous old sailing trawlers have been preserved. A storm on the night of 10th January 1866 prevented the fishing boats getting back into harbour. The beacon on the breakwater was swept away and in the darkness they could not determine their position. Fifty vessels were wrecked and more than one hundred lives were lost. The citizens of Exeter raised money to set up the Royal National Lifeboat Institution's Brixham lifeboat. Smuggling was more lucrative than fishing and some novel methods were developed to evade the Revenue men. On one occasion, during an outbreak of cholera, the smugglers drove their cargo from the beach in a hearse drawn by horses with muffled hooves, accompanied by supposed mourners. Since Tudor times Brixham has played a role in defence. On Berry Head was a gun battery to protect naval ships victualling in the harbour. Napoleon spent a few days anchored off Brixham, whilst waiting to be taken to exile on St Helena. Brixham is the site of one of only seven surviving Emergency Coastal Defence Batteries set up around the coast in 1940. There were originally 116. A ramp and piers were built on the breakwater to load landing craft for the invasion of Normandy in June 1944.

Totnes, at the head of the estuary of the Dart, is the administrative centre of the South Hams District of Devon. Its history dates back to at least 907, when the first castle was built. A Benedictine priory was founded in 1088. By the 12th century it was an important market town. By 1523, Totnes was the second richest town in Devon, and sixteenth in the whole of England. In 1553, Edward VI granted Totnes a charter allowing the former priory to be used as the Guildhall and a school. In 1624, the Guildhall became a magistrate's court (until 1974) and was used for soldiers' billets during the English Civil War, during which Oliver Cromwell visited for discussions with the Parliamentary commander-in-chief, Thomas Fairfax. Until 1887, the Guildhall was also the town prison. Today, the town is a centre for music, art, theatre and natural health.

eyes, dark brown hair and his religious denomination was Church of England. He was posted to the 2nd Battalion on 5th October and gained the Army Certificate of Education 3rd Class on 24th June 1889. He was promoted lance corporal on 20th September, returned to the ranks on 13th May 1890 and was awarded good conduct pay of 1d per day on 20th June. Frank transferred to the Ordnance Store Corps on 17th October 1890 and was discharged to the 1st Class Army Reserve on 24th March 1894. They lived at Stoke Damerel. Frank was recalled for service during the Second Boer War on 9th October 1899 and sailed for South Africa on 3rd November. He saw action in Transvaal and Natal and was awarded good conduct pay of 2d per day on 5th January 1900. Rosina was living at 96 Priory Road, Portswood, St Denys, Southampton at the time of the 1901 Census. Frank returned to England and was discharged on 19th June 1901. A gratuity of £5 for active service was issued on 31st August. Rosina was visiting her sister, Sarah and family, at the time of the 1911 Census. By 1914 he was a cab driver and they were living at 118 Poole Road, Bournemouth, Hampshire. Frank enlisted in 7th Hampshire at Bournemouth on 8th August 1914 (1929 later 305628). He was appointed temporary acting corporal on 6th October and was later substantive on the same date. Posted to India on 9th October, he was promoted lance sergeant on 17th June 1916 and joined 1/7th Depot on 1st January 1918. He departed India on 28th August 1919 and returned to England on 16th October, where he was posted to 176th Territorial Force Depot. He was discharged no longer physically fit for war service on 28th November 1919. They had no children and both of their deaths were registered at Hitchin, Hertfordshire.
- John Pitman Burgoyne (1871–72).
- Irene Burgoyne (1876–1936) married Harry Leonard Lewis (16th September 1877–30th May 1967), a general labourer, on 17th July 1898 at the Parish Church, Lower Brixham. They were living at Bay View Steps, Brixham in 1911. They had five children:
  - Blanche Rosina Lewis (born 1898).
  - John 'Jack' Henry HS Lewis (1900–27).
  - Henrietta 'Hettie' Lewis (4th April 1906–1973) married Francis H White (1908–52) in 1932.
  - William Ernest Sidney Lewis (19th May 1909–1981) married Ivy Vinola R Davies (9th October 1909–1981) in 1931. They had two children – John S Lewis 1932 and Pamela K Lewis 1941.
  - Harry Leonard Lewis (born 1912).
- Petera Burgoyne (3rd December 1877–1947) married Sidney Albert Maddick (19th August 1875–1st April 1952), a fisherman, on 28th May 1901 at the Parish Church, Lower Brixham. They were living at 1 Dashpers Road, Brixham in 1911 and he was absent at the time of the Census that year. He served in the Merchant Navy during the Great War. In 1939 he was skipper of a steam trawler and they were living at 23 Starbuck Road, Milford Haven, Pembrokeshire. His death was

registered at Haverfordwest, Pembrokeshire. She was living at 7 Prescelly Place, Milford Haven at the time of her death there. They had four children:
- Gladys Ellen Maddick (31st July 1902–1979) married Herbert Matthew Kingston (8th October 1900–14th May 1988) in 1923. They had six children – Phyllis P Kingston 1924, Roy S A Kingston 1926, Reginald HM Kingston 1928, Harriett G Kingston 1929, Margaret R Kingston 1937 and John B Kingston 1946. Herbert was serving in 424th Coastal Regiment RA TA (1660021) on 6th June 1947. It was redesignated 424th Heavy Anti-Aircraft Regiment TA on 1st September 1948 and he was discharged on 5th June 1949.
- Vera Rosina Maddick (26th August 1903–14th April 1995) married John Frederick Pulford (17th June 1900–21st July 1977) in 1926. They had a daughter, Beryl P Pulford, in 1931.
- Gwendoline Petera Sheppard Maddick (31st August 1906–1997) married Stanley G Hughes (1904–41) in 1927. They had a son, William SA Hughes, in 1931. Gwendoline married William G Thomas in 1949.
- Doris May Maddick (born 1908) married Tom Mowthorpe (14th January 1907–1980) in 1931. They had three children – Donald M Mowthorpe 1933, Marie P Mowthorpe 1935 and Betty R Mowthorpe 1941.

- Sophia Pitman Burgoyne (14th August 1880–1919) never married.
- Eli Samuel Burgoyne (May–19th September 1882).
- Michael Murray Burgoyne (12th January 1884–1941) was a mason's labourer in 1911, living at 33 Higher Street, Brixham as head of household with his widowed mother and sister, Sophia. He owned a smack fishing vessel in 1914 and was living at 8 Trafalgar Terrace, Brixham. He enlisted in the Royal Naval Reserve (DA683) at Milford Haven on 8th August 1914, described as 5′ 9″ tall, with ruddy complexion and blue eyes, while living at 23 Starbuck Road, Milford West, Pembrokeshire. He served aboard numerous vessels including HMS *Syringa* 8th August 1914, *Halcyon* 21st January 1915, *Blenheim* 22nd January, *Beatrice* 2nd February, *Albion* 1st April, *Osiris* 21st April, *Europa* 1st July, *Peony* 29th January 1916, *Europa* 15th December, *Admirable* 17th December, *Vivid* 31st March 1918, *Pekin* 1st April and *Nairn* at Peterhead, a requisitioned auxiliary, from 20th May. He spent seven days in the cells and forfeited seven days' pay on 9th June 1915 but was granted the good conduct badge on 23rd August 1917. Michael was demobilised on 25th January 1919. He was awarded a war gratuity of £26/10/-, paid on 4th April 1919, naval prize money of £18/15/- at Milford Haven on 1st January 1923 and the Great War medal trio. He later lived with Isabella McDonald Webber née Hubbard (13th April 1895–1974) after she left her husband, Ernest. She was born at 31 Broad Street, Peterhead, Aberdeenshire, Scotland and married Ernest Webber (5th November 1884–21st May 1941) in 1913 at Hull, East Riding of Yorkshire, where he was born. When she died in 1974, her year of birth was recorded as 1893. Ernest and Isabella had two children – Joan Webber 1915 and

James MH Webber 1921. Ernest enlisted in the Royal Naval Reserve (DA9235) on 25th October 1915, described as 5′ 8″ tall, with fair complexion and blue eyes. He joined the cruiser HMS *Pelorus* on 10th November. On 9th February 1917 he joined HMS *Wallington*, Auxiliary Patrol Base at Grimsby and served aboard HMS *Vivid III*, *Cormorant* and *Kingfisher*. Ernest was demobilised from HMS *Attentive III* at Dover on 8th January 1919. He was awarded £18/15/- prize money on 16th August 1922. Isabella and her mother left Hull and settled at Haverfordwest, Pembrokeshire, leaving her two children with their father, Ernest. Isabella moved in with Michael Burgoyne. Ernest was a general labourer in 1939, living at 10 Malvern Avenue, Kingston-upon-Hull. He had moved to 155 Plane Street, Kingston-upon-Hull and was a firewatcher at the time of his death on 21st May 1941 at Orange Shed, Albert Dock, Kingston-upon-Hull. Isabella and Michael had five children, all registered under Isabella's married name at birth, but they became Burgoynes thereafter:
- Jessie Eleanor Webber (7th April 1925–1984), a twin with Michael, married James G Crawford (11th April 1923–1988) in 1945. They had a daughter, Joan E Crawford, in 1949.
- Michael Murray Webber (1925–57), a twin with Jessie, married Frances W Taylor in 1949. They had three children – Frances A Burgoyne 1950, Susan M Burgoyne 1953 and Michael R Burgoyne 1955. He died at sea off Scotland and his death was registered at Kilninian and Kilmore, Isle of Mull, Argyllshire. Frances married Gerald D Forde in 1960. They had a daughter, Julie E Forde, in 1962.
- Susan Martha Webber (1926) married Stephen J Holmes in 1946. They had two children – Stephen M Holmes 1947 and Isabella Holmes 1953.
- Frederick Webber (born 13th April 1928) was a twin with Harry.
- Harry Webber (13th April 1928–1984), a twin with Frederick, married Violet F Kyle (born 1919) at Southwark, London in 1972.

Frank was educated in regimental schools and later at Kempston Boys School, Bedfordshire. He worked initially as an errand boy for WB Moss & Sons Ltd of Bancroft, Hitchin, Hertfordshire before moving to London and working at the Orleans Club in St James Street. At the time of the 1911 Census he was a page, living at 29 King Street, St James Street, London. He returned to Hitchin to work at the Hitchin Electrical Power Station, Whinbush Road and was planning to study electrical engineering as a career.

Frank enlisted, with his father's permission, in the Hitchin Company, 1st Hertfordshire Regiment (TF) (1285 later 265062) on 26th November 1909 and was appointed a boy bugler on 1st May 1910. He was just 5′ 3½″ tall. He attended annual training at Ipswich 31st July–7th August 1910, at Thetford 30th July–13th August 1911 and at Worthing 4th–11th August 1912. He re-engaged for one year on 25th November 1913 and was embodied on 5th August 1914, joining 1/1st Battalion at

The Bedfordshire Middle Class Public School Co Ltd was created in 1867 to build a school, which opened two years later in Ampthill Road, Kempston. The design was open to public competition, which was won by Frederick Peel of London. The building, of red brick, stood three storeys high and the front was about one hundred yards long. Over 300 boys were eventually accommodated but the school opened with just seventy boys. Of these, sixty were farmers' sons and the remainder were from the families of tradesmen and other businessmen. Almost half came from outside the county. The peak of 315 boys was attained in 1870 but the school was too cramped and about 200 was the most desirable number. In 1875 the school changed its name to Bedford County School. The school had a mortgage debt as a result of the cost of building exceeding estimates. In 1898 this debt was £3,000 and Bedford County School Ltd (formerly Bedfordshire Middle Class Public School Co Ltd) was wound up. The buildings and contents transferred to the Reverend Farrar for £10,000. He introduced electric light and hot water for the dormitories, built a new library and cricket pavilion and improved the sanatorium and chapel. A School Corps formed in 1900, which became part of the Officers' Training Corps in 1907. That year the school changed its name to Elstow School, although the whole site was within the boundary of Kempston. Cricket was taken very seriously and the school was included in the *Wisden Cricketers Almanacs* of the period. One of its pupils, Percy William Sherwell (1880–1948), played for Transvaal and in thirteen test matches for South Africa as captain. The school closed in 1916, partly due to the Great War, when the buildings were requisitioned as a military college and the numbers of boys attending from overseas fell dramatically. Farrar sold the buildings in 1920 to the Cosmic Crayon Co and in 1922 they were leased in part by Taylor's, the box makers. The buildings were demolished in the 1960s to make way for the offices of Robinson Rental, later Granada TV Rentals, and were later used by Central Bedfordshire Council.

Stowlangtoft, Bury St Edmunds. Although he volunteered for service abroad, he was unable to proceed on medical grounds and transferred to 2/1st Battalion when 1/1st Battalion left for France on 6th November. He was promoted sergeant on 17th December. An operation corrected some physical disabilities and he left for France from Southampton on 20th January 1915, arriving next day, to rejoin 1/1st Battalion. His father was also serving in the unit as a company sergeant major. At the time, the Battalion was part of 4th (Guards Brigade) and became known as the 'Hertfordshire Guards'. After completing five years' service with the TF he was granted leave in England on 31st August.

WB Moss & Sons Ltd, retail and wholesale grocers, were based in Hitchin, Hertfordshire. William Benjamin Moss established a grocer's shop in Hitchin c.1870 and by 1878 had moved to premises on the High Street. Two years later a second store opened on Nightingale Road. By 1908 there were additional shops in Baldock, Bancroft, and Letchworth. In the 1920s more shops were added in Kimpton, Shefford, Buntingford and Royston. The company was in business until at least 1939. The picture shows the Moss shop in Golden Square, Hitchin, the half-timbered building at the far end.

Frank playing tennis before the war (Richard Young).

The Orleans Club was damaged in an air raid in November 1940 but continued to function. In the Little Blitz, Pall Mall suffered significant incendiary damage on 22nd February 1944. The following night four high explosive bombs hit the area between Jermyn Street and Pall Mall. Extensive destruction and damage was caused, including an ARP warden post, which resulted in the death of four wardens. Another five people were killed. The area between King Street and Pall Mall was almost completely destroyed. Damaged buildings included the Carlton Club, the London Library, St James's Theatre, the Marlborough Club and the Orleans Club. The latter was completely destroyed as seen in the picture. On 31st December 1945 the Windham, Orleans and Marlborough Clubs amalgamated to form the Marlborough–Windham Club. However, rising costs and falling membership forced it to close in December 1953.

Warrant officers and NCOs of 1/1st Hertfordshire taken at Noeux-les-Mines in June 1915. Sergeant Frank Young is standing on the left and his father, RSM Frank Young, is sitting in the middle.

Frank re-engaged for the duration of the war on 25th November. He volunteered for a bombing instructor's course at the Central Bombing School, Rouen and was attached to Central Training Staff, No.1 Training Battalion Depot on 19th January 1916. He was admitted to 9th General Hospital, Rouen not yet diagnosed on 3rd April and was discharged on 9th April to join No.1 Infantry Base Depot. He was readmitted on 13th April and was evacuated to England aboard HMHS *St Andrew* on 4th May. He was treated at the Welsh Metropolitan War Hospital, Whitchurch, Cardiff 6th May–20th July and was granted leave 21st–31st July. Frank was attached to 3rd Company, 3/1st Hertfordshire Regiment at Halton Camp, Wendover near Aylesbury, Buckinghamshire on 1st August and was granted a £15 bounty on 19th September.

Frank was recommended for a commission and commenced training at No.6 Officer Cadet Battalion, Trinity College, Oxford in January 1917. He was commissioned on 26th April and was posted to 3/1st Battalion at Halton Camp, where he joined his father. On 11th July the Battalion combined with 5th (Reserve) Battalion, Bedfordshire Regiment there. The new unit moved to Crowborough Camp, Sussex that autumn. Frank was attached to the Royal Flying Corps/Royal Air Force, spending six weeks on ground training at Reading, Berkshire, before moving to Sleaford, Lincolnshire for flying training. He crashed his aircraft and was severely shaken. As a result he requested a return to his old unit. He rejoined 5th (Reserve) Bedfordshire at Crowborough on 10th July 1918. He was in Hitchin in September for two days' leave and returned to France on 5th September from Folkestone, Kent to rejoin 1/1st Hertfordshire. His father was at Folkestone to see him off. Frank rejoined the unit on 12th September and sent a field postcard home on 17th September, which was to be his last communication to his parents. **Awarded the VC for his actions at Havrincourt on 18th September 1918, LG 14th December 1918.** The VC was presented to his parents by the King in the ballroom at Buckingham Palace on 1st March 1919.

Frank was killed during the VC action. He was buried in an unmarked grave close to where he fell by men of 1/5th Manchester on 27th September. Second Lieutenant Johann Friedrich Georg Schlund, Wiltshire Regiment, serving with No.209 Prisoner of War Company at Vélu after the war, was aware that Frank's grave had not been located. A fellow officer mentioned that he had discovered the burial of a British officer and Schlund asked for details. The other officer handed over an identity disc for Second Lieutenant FE Young. Schlund was taken to the burial site and arranged for a wooden

Halton Camp.

Hitchin War Memorial outside St Mary's Church (Roll of Honour).

Franks' grave in Hermies Hill British Cemetery.

cross to be erected and the grave to be tidied before writing to Frank's parents. His father had been to France previously in an attempt to find the grave. Frank's remains were reinterred in Hermies Hill British Cemetery, France (III B 5). He is commemorated in a number of other places:

- Hertfordshire
    - Frank Young Court, Bedford Road, Hitchin.
    - Plaque, Church of the Holy Saviour, Radcliffe Road, Hitchin.
    - Hitchin War Memorial, St Mary's Church, Hitchin.
    - A Department for Communities and Local Government commemorative paving stone was dedicated at Hitchin War Memorial on 18th September 2018.
    - Named on the memorial to No.4 Company, 1st Battalion, Hertfordshire Regiment outside the Army Reserve Centre, Bedford Road, Hitchin.
    - Regimental War Memorial, All Saint's Church, Hertford.
- Communities and Local Government commemorative paving stones for the 145 VCs born in Australia, Belgium, Canada, China, Denmark, Egypt, France, Germany, India, Iraq, Japan, Nepal, Netherlands, Newfoundland, New Zealand, Pakistan, South Africa, Sri Lanka, Ukraine and United States of America were unveiled at the National Memorial Arboretum, Alrewas, Staffordshire by Prime Minister David Cameron MP and Sergeant Johnson Beharry VC on 5th March 2015.

The Victory Medal (or Inter-Allied Victory Medal) was first proposed by French Marshal Ferdinand Foch as a common award for all the nations allied against the Central Powers. Regardless of nationality, each medal is 36mm in diameter, the ribbon is a double rainbow and the obverse shows winged victory (except Japan and Siam where winged victory has no relevance). For British Empire forces the medal was issued to all who received the 1914 or 1914–15 Star and to almost all who received the British War Medal. The British alone struck 6,335,000 Victory medals. These three medals were known as Pip, Squeak and Wilfred after a popular newspaper comic strip. To qualify for the Victory Medal recipients had to be mobilised for war service and have entered a theatre of war between 5th August 1914 and 11th November 1918, plus Russia 1919–20 and mine clearance in the North Sea until 30th November 1919. Those Mentioned in Despatches wore an oakleaf on the Victory Medal ribbon as shown here.

- Named on The Ring of Remembrance (Ring of Memory) at Ablain-Saint-Nazaire, France, inaugurated on 11th November 2014, which commemorates the 576,606 soldiers of forty nationalities who died in Nord-Pas-de-Calais in the Great War.
- Plaque on the boardwalk around Lochnagar Crater, Somme, France.

In addition to the VC he was awarded the 1914–15 Star, British War Medal 1914–20 and Victory Medal 1914–19. The medals were presented to the Regiment by his siblings in 1957. The VC is held by the Bedfordshire & Hertfordshire Regimental Museum, Wardown Park Museum, Luton, Bedfordshire.

# Sources

The following institutions, individuals and publications were consulted:

## Regimental Museums

The following Museums and Regimental Headquarters kindly provided information:

Buffs Regimental Museum, Canterbury; Hertford Regiment Museum, Hertford; Light Infantry Office (Yorkshire), Pontefract; Museum of the Royal Leicestershire Regiment, Leicester; The Tank Museum.

## Individuals

The following individuals provided information and assistance:

Doug and Richard Arman, Susan Bavin, Laurence Calvert, David Fletcher, Terry Hissey, Mrs SJ Hoeft, David Hunter, Ian Hunter, Tom Johnson, Margaret Johnston, Alan Jordan, Diana Kennedy, Paul Lee, Steve Lee, Dawn Lewis, Alasdair Macintyre, Robert Mansell, John McNamara, Peter Myers, Iain Stewart, Vic Tambling, Vic Whittle, Valerie Wilding, Lt Col Les Wilson MBE, Richard Young.

## Record Offices, Libraries and Local Museums

Local studies information was obtained from the following Record Offices, Libraries and Museums:
    Birmingham Central Library, Leicester County Record Office.

## Newspapers

The following newspapers helped, either by supplying information directly or by printing an appeal:
    Leicester Mercury; Hereford Times.

## Divisional Histories

Listed in numerical order:
    The 18th Division in the Great War. Capt G H F Nichols. Blackwood 1922.
    A History of the 38th (Welsh) Division. Editor Lt Col JR Munby CMG DSO 1920.
    The 47th (London) Division 1914–19. Editor A H Maude. Amalgamated Press 1922.

## Brigade Histories

The 54th Infantry Brigade 1914–18 – Some Records of Battle and Laughter in France. E R. Gale & Polden 1919.

## Regimental/Unit Histories

Works appear by Regiment in precedence order:
The Buffs (East Kent Regiment)
    Historical Records of the Buffs, East Kent Regiment, Volume III 1914–19. Col R S H Moody. Medici Society 1922.
The Bedfordshire Regiment
    The 16th Foot, A History of the Bedfordshire and Hertfordshire Regiment. Maj Gen Sir F Maurice. Constable 1931.
    The Story of the Bedfordshire and Hertfordshire Regiment Volume II – 1914–58. Compiled by Lt Col T J Barrow DSO, Maj V A French and J Seabrook Esq. Published privately 1986.
The Royal Welsh Fusiliers
    That Astonishing Infantry, The History of the Royal Welsh Fusiliers 1689–1989. M Glover.
    Regimental Records of the Royal Welsh Fusiliers (23rd Foot), Volume III 1914–18 France & Flanders. Compiler Maj C H Dudley Ward. Forster Groon 1928.
The East Surrey Regiment
    History of the East Surrey Regiment, Volume II 1914–17 and Volume III 1917–19. Col H W Pearse & Brig Gen H S Sloman. Medici Society 1924.
The Oxfordshire and Buckinghamshire Light Infantry
    Regimental War Tales 1741–1919, Told for the Soldiers of the Oxfordshire and Buckinghamshire Light Infantry. Lt Col A F Modder-Ferryman & Lt Col R B Crosse. Slatter & Rose 1942.
    The Story of the 2/4th Oxfordshire and Buckinghamshire Light Infantry. Capt G K Rose. Blackwell 1920.
The Northamptonshire Regiment
    The Northamptonshire Regiment 1914–18. Regimental Historical Committee. Gale & Polden.
    Four VCs in Forty Months, The Proud Record in World War One of the 6th (Service) Battalion The Northamptonshire Regiment. G Moore. G Moore 1979.
The King's Own (Yorkshire Light Infantry)
    History of the King's Own Yorkshire Light Infantry in the Great War, Volume III 1914–18. Lt Col R C Bond. Percy Lund, Humphries 1930.
The Highland Light Infantry
    Proud Heritage, The Story of the Highland Light Infantry, Volume III 1882–1918. Lt Col L B Oates. House of Grant 1961.
Machine Gun Corps
    Machine Guns, Their History and Tactical Employment (Being also a History of the Machine Gun Corps 1916–22). Lt Col G S Hutchinson. MacMillan 1938.

Australian Imperial Force
   Official History of Australia in the War of 1914–1918, Volume IV – The Australian Imperial Force in France, 1917. 11th Edition 1941.
   They Dared Mightily. Lionel Wigmore, Jeff Williams & Anthony Staunton 1963 & 1986.
   Tales of Valour from The Royal New South Wales Regiment. Maj Gen GL Maitland 1992.
   The Story of the Fifth Australian Division. Capt AD Ellis MC. Hodder & Stoughton 1920.
   The Fighting Thirteenth, The History of the Thirteenth Battalion A.I.F. Thomas A White. 1924.
   The Story of a Battalion, Being a Record of the 48th Battalion A.I.F. W Devine. 1919.
New Zealand
   The New Zealand Division 1916–1919. A Popular History Based on Official Records. Col H Stewart CMG DSO MC. Whitcombe & Tombs Ltd, Auckland 1921.
   The Official History of the New Zealand Rifle Brigade (The Earl of Liverpool's Own). Compiled by Lt Col WS Austin DSO. LT Watkins Ltd, 115 Taranaki Street, Wellington 1924.

**General Works**

A Bibliography of Regimental Histories of the British Army. Compiler A S White. Society for Army Historical Research 1965.
A Military Atlas of the First World War. A Banks & A Palmer. Purnell 1975.
The Soldier's War 1914–18. P Liddle. Blandford Press.
Into Battle 1914–18. E Parker. Longmans 1964.
The Times History of the Great War.
Topography of Armageddon, A British Trench Map Atlas of the Western Front 1914–18. P Chasseaud. Mapbooks 1991.
Before Endeavours Fade. R E B Coombs. Battle of Britain Prints 1976.
British Regiments 1914–18. Brig E A James. Samson 1978.
Northamptonshire and the Great War 1914–1918. W H Holloway. The Northampton Independent 1923?
Leeds in the Great War 1914–1918. Leeds Libraries and Arts Committee 1923.

**Biographical/Autobiographical**

The Dictionary of National Biography 1901–85. Various volumes. Oxford University Press.
The Cross of Sacrifice, Officers Who Died in the Service of the British, Indian and East African Regiments and Corps 1914–19. S D and D B Jarvis. Roberts Medals 1993.
Australian Dictionary of Biography.
Whitaker's Peerage, Baronetage, Knightage & Companionage 1915.
The Roll of Honour Parts 1–5, A Biographical Record of Members of His Majesty's Naval and Military Forces who fell in the Great War 1914–18. Marquis de Ruvigny. Standard Art Book Co 1917–19.

The Dictionary of Edwardian Biography – various volumes. Printed 1904–08, reprinted 1985–87 Peter Bell Edinburgh.
Dictionary of Canadian Biography.
Valiant Hearts. Atlantic Canada and the Victoria Cross. John Boileau. Nimbus Publishing, Halifax, Nova Scotia 2005.
David Ferguson Hunter VC, The Man and the Medal. Ian Hunter.
Donald Dean VC: The Memoirs of a Volunteer & Territorial from Two World Wars. Edited by Terry Crowdy. Pen & Sword 2010.

**Specific Works on the Victoria Cross.**

The Register of the Victoria Cross. This England 1981 and 1988.
The Story of the Victoria Cross 1856 – 1963. Brig Sir J Smyth. Frederick Muller 1963.
The Evolution of the Victoria Cross, A Study in Administrative History. M J Crook. Midas 1975.
The Victoria Cross and the George Cross. IWM 1970.
The Victoria Cross, The Empire's Roll of Valour. Lt Col R Stewart. Hutchinson 1928.
The Victoria Cross 1856 – 1920. Sir O'Moore Creagh and E M Humphris. Standard Art Book Company, London 1920.
Heart of a Dragon, VC's of Wales and the Welsh Regiments 1914–82. W Alister Williams. Bridge Books 2006.
For Valour, The Victoria Cross, Courage in Action. J Percival. Thames Methuen 1985.
VC Locator. D Pillinger and A Staunton. Highland Press, Queanbeyan, New South Wales, Australia 1991.
The VC Roll of Honour. J W Bancroft. Aim High 1989.
A Bibliography of the Victoria Cross. W James McDonald. W J Mcdonald, Nova Scotia 1994.
Canon Lummis VC Files held in the National Army Museum, Chelsea.
Recipients of the Victoria Cross in the Care of the Commonwealth War Graves Commission. CWGC 1997.
Victoria Cross Heroes. Michael Ashcroft. Headline Review 2006
Monuments to Courage. David Harvey. 1999.
Beyond the Five Points – Masonic Winners of The Victoria Cross and The George Cross. Phillip May GC, edited by Richard Cowley. Twin Pillars Books, Northamptonshire 2001.
Our Bravest and Our Best: The Stories of Canada's Victoria Cross Winners. Arthur Bishop 1995.
A Breed Apart. Richard Leake. Great Northern Publishing 2008.

**Works on Other Honours and Awards.**

Recipients of Bars to the Military Cross 1916–20. J V Webb 1988.
Distinguished Conduct Medal 1914–18, Citations of Recipients. London Stamp Exchange 1983.
Recipients of the Distinguished Conduct Medal 1914–1920. RW Walker.

The Distinguished Service Order 1886–1923 (in 2 volumes). Sir O'Moore Creagh and E M Humphris. J B Hayward 1978 (originally published 1924).
Orders and Medals Society Journal (various articles).
The Old Contemptibles Honours and Awards. First published 1915. Reprinted by J B Hayward & Son 1971.
Burke's Handbook to the Most Excellent Order of the British Empire. A Winton Thorpe (Editor). Burke Publishing Co Ltd, London 1921.
South African War – Honours and Awards 1899–1902.
Honours and Awards of the Indian Army: August 1914–August 1921. 1931.

## University and Schools Publications

The OTC Roll – A Roll of Members and Ex-members of the OTC Gazetted to Commissions in the Army August 1914–March 1915. Tim Donovan 1989.

## Official Publications and Sources.

History of the Great War, Order of Battle of Divisions. Compiler Maj A F Becke. HMSO.
History of the Great War, Military Operations, France and Belgium. Compiler Brig Gen Sir J E Edmonds. HMSO. Published in 14 volumes of text, with 7 map volumes and 2 separate Appendices between 1923 and 1948.
Unit War Diaries in the Public Record Office under WO 95
Military maps in the Public Record Office under WO 297.
Medal Cards and Medal Rolls in the Public Record Office under WO 329 and ADM 171.
Soldier's Service Records in the Public Record Office under WO 97, 363 and 364.
Officer's Records in the Public Record Office under WO 25, 76, 339 and 374.
RAF Officer's Records in the Public Record Office under Air 76.
Navy Lists.
Army Lists – including Graduation Lists and Record of War Service.
Air Force Lists.
Home Guard Lists 1942–44.
Indian Army Lists 1897–1940.
India List 1923–40.
Location of Hospitals and Casualty Clearing Stations, BEF 1914–19. Ministry of Pensions 1923.
London Gazettes
Census returns, particularly for 1881, 1891 and 1901.
Service records in the National Archives of Australia.
Service records from the Library and Archives of Canada.
Service records in Archives New Zealand.
Officers and Soldiers Died in the Great War.

**Reference Publications.**

Who's Who and Who Was Who.
The Times 1914 onwards.
The Daily Telegraph 1914 onwards.
Kelly's Handbook to the Titled, Landed and Official Classes.
Burke's Peerage.

**Internet Websites**

History of the Victoria Cross – http://www.victoriacross.org.uk/vcross.htm – Iain Stewart.
Trenches On The Web – www.worldwar1.com
Commonwealth War Graves Commission – https://www.cwgc.org/
Free Births, Marriages and Deaths – www.freebmd.com
Memorials to Valour – http://www.memorialstovalour.co.uk
Scotland's People – https://www.scotlandspeople.gov.uk/
The Long, Long Trail – https://www.longlongtrail.co.uk/
Australian births, marriages & deaths:
   New South Wales – https://familyhistory.bdm.nsw.gov.au/
   Queensland – https://www.familyhistory.bdm.qld.gov.au/
   South Australia – https://www.genealogysa.org.au/
   Tasmania – https://linctas.ent.sirsidynix.net.au/client/en_AU/names/
   Victoria – https://my.rio.bdm.vic.gov.au/
   Western Australia – https://www.bdm.justice.wa.gov.au/
Canadian births, marriages & deaths:
   British Columbia – http://search-collections.royalbcmuseum.bc.ca/Genealogy
   New Brunswick – https://archives.gnb.ca/Search/VISSE/Default.aspx?culture=en-CA
   New Zealand births, marriages & deaths – https://www.bdmhistoricalrecords.dia.govt.nz/search

**Periodicals**

This England magazine – various editions.
Coin and Medal News – various editions.
Journal of The Victoria Cross Society – no longer published
Gun Fire – A Journal of First World War History. Edited by AJ Peacock – no longer published
Stand To – journal of the Western Front Association.

# Useful Information
## (Some details may be affected by Brexit)

**Accommodation** – there is a wide variety of accommodation available in France and Belgium. Search online for your requirements. There are also numerous campsites, but many close for the winter from late September.

**Clothing and Kit** – consider taking:

- Waterproofs.
- Headwear and gloves.
- Walking shoes/boots.
- Shades and sunscreen.
- Binoculars and camera.
- Snacks and drinks.

**Customs/Behaviour** – local people are generally tolerant of battlefield visitors but please respect their property and address them respectfully. The French are less inclined to switch to English than other Europeans. If you try some basic French, it will be appreciated.

**Driving** – rules of the road are similar to UK, apart from having to drive on the right. If in doubt about priorities at junctions, always be prepared to give way to the right, unless otherwise indicated, particularly in France. In many areas, particularly rural, you have to give way to vehicles coming in from the right, even from apparently minor roads onto major routes. Obey laws and road signs – police impose harsh on-the-spot fines. Penalties for drinking and driving are heavy and the legal limit is lower than UK (50mg rather than 80mg). Most Autoroutes in France are toll roads. In rural areas the speed limit is 80kph but in many places the old 90kph signs remain. The red-framed name board at the entrance to a village or town automatically imposes a 50kph speed limit.

> **Fuel** – petrol stations are only open 24 hours on major routes and larger supermarkets. Payment by credit/debit card in automatic tellers is increasingly becoming the norm. The cheapest fuel is generally at hypermarkets.

**Mandatory Requirements** – if taking your own car you need:
Full driving licence.
Vehicle registration document.
Comprehensive motor insurance valid in Europe (Green Card).
European breakdown and recovery cover.
Letter of authorisation from the owner if the vehicle is not yours.
Spare set of bulbs, headlight beam adjusters, warning triangle, UK sticker, high visibility vest and breathalyzer. Requirements do vary, so check before departing. An emission quality sticker is required if driving in Paris or certain other cities.

**Emergency** – keep details required in an emergency separate from your wallet or handbag:
Photocopy passport, insurance documents and EHIC/GHIC (see Health below).
Mobile phone details.
Credit/debit card numbers and cancellation telephone contacts.
Travel insurance company contact number.
Who to contact in an emergency.

**Ferries** – the closest ports are Boulogne, Calais and Dunkirk. The Shuttle is quicker, but usually more expensive.

## Health

European Health Insurance Card – entitles the holder to medical treatment at local rates. Apply online at www.ehic.org.uk/Internet/startApplication.do. It is issued free and is valid for five years. You are only covered if you have the EHIC with you when you go for treatment. Since Brexit, EHIC is being gradually replaced by a Global Health Insurance Card (GHIC).

Travel Insurance – you are also strongly advised to have travel insurance. If you receive treatment get a statement by the doctor (*feuille de soins*) and a receipt to make a claim on return.

Personal Medical Kit – treating minor ailments saves time and money. Pack sufficient prescription medicine for the trip.

Chemist (*Pharmacie*) – look for the green cross. They provide some treatment and if unable to help will direct you to a doctor. Most open 0900–1900 except Sundays. Out of hours services (*pharmacie de garde*) are advertised in Pharmacie windows.

(Some details may be affected by Brexit)

Doctor and Dentist – hotel receptions have details of local practices. Beware private doctors/hospitals, as extra charges cannot be reclaimed – the French national health service is known as *conventionné*.

Rabies – contact with infected animals is very rare, but if bitten by any animal, get the wound examined professionally immediately.

**Money**

ATMs – at most banks and post offices with instructions in English. Check your card can be used in France and what charges apply. Some banks limit how much can be withdrawn. Let your bank know you will be away, as some block cards if transactions take place unexpectedly.

Credit/Debit Cards – major cards are usually accepted, but some have different names – Visa is Carte Bleue and Mastercard is Eurocard.

Exchange – beware 0% commission, as the rate may be poor. The Post Office takes back unused currency at the same rate, which may or may not be advantageous. Since the Euro, currency exchange facilities are scarce.

Local Taxes – if you buy high value items you can reclaim tax. Get the forms completed by the shop, have them stamped by Customs, post them to the shop and they will refund about 12%. Brexit may change this.

**Passport** – a valid passport is required.

**Post** – postcard stamps are often available from vendors, newsagents and tabacs.

**Public Holidays** – just about everything closes and banks can close early the day before. Transport may be affected, but tourist attractions in high season are unlikely to be. The following dates/days are public holidays:

1 January
Easter Monday
1 May
8 May
Ascension Day
Whit Monday
14 July
15 August
1 & 11 November
25 December

In France many businesses and restaurants close for the majority of August.

**Radio** – if you want to pick up the news from home try BBC Radio 4 on 198 kHz long wave. BBC Five Live on 909 kHz medium wave can sometimes be received. There are numerous internet options for keeping up with the news.

**Shops** – in large towns and tourist areas they tend to open all day. In more remote places they may close for lunch. Some bakers open Sunday a.m. and during the week take later lunch breaks. In general shops do not open on Sundays and those that do have limited hours.

**Telephone**

> To UK – 0044, then delete the initial 0 and dial the rest of the number.
>
> Local Calls – dial the full number even if within the same zone.
>
> Mobiles – check yours will work in France and the charges.
>
> Emergencies – dial 112 for medical, fire and police anywhere in Europe from any landline, pay phone or mobile. Calls are free.
>
> British Embassy (Paris) – 01 44 51 31 00.

**Time Zone** – one hour ahead of UK.

**Tipping** – a small tip is expected by cloakroom and lavatory attendants and porters. Not required in restaurants when a service charge is included.

**Toilets** – the best are in museums and the main tourist attractions. Towns usually have public toilets where markets are held; some are coin operated. Otherwise on the battlefields facilities are sparse. Finding a local café may be the best option, although they are closing as rapidly as British pubs.

# Index

Notes:
1. Not every person or location is included. Most family members named in the Biographies are not.
2. Armed forces units, establishments, etc are grouped under the respective country, except for Britain's, which appear under the three services – British Army, Royal Air Force and Royal Navy. Royal Naval Division units appear under British Army for convenience.
3. Newfoundland appears under Canada although not part of it at the time.
4. Cemeteries/Crematoria, Cathedrals, Churches, Hospitals, Museums, Schools, Ships, Trenches, Universities and Commonwealth War Graves Commission appear under those group headings.
5. All orders, medals and decorations appear under Orders.
6. Belgium, Britain, France and Germany are not indexed in the accounts of the VC actions, as there are too many mentions. Similarly, England, Britain and United Kingdom are not indexed in the biographies.

Aachen, 95
Aaron VC, AL, 91
Abbassia, 71, 75, 151
Abbeyhill, 123
Abbotsford, Vic, 72
Abercarn, 160
Abercorn Memorials, Edinburgh, 129
Aberdeen, 128
    Prison, 128
Aberdeenshire, 128, 238
Abergavenny, 100
*Abide With Me*, 236
Ablain-Saint-Nazaire, 173, 244
Accident Services Review, 65
Acton, Sgt Arthur, 28
Adams, Pte J, 17
Addiscombe, 58
Adelaide, 199–203, 206–10, 212–13, 220–1, 225
Adriatic, 112
Afghanistan, 56, 229
Africa, 119, 170
Agincourt, Battle of, 93
Air Raid Precautions, 80, 83, 95, 163–4, 241
Aitken Colliery, 122
Aitken, Thomas, 122
Aitkenvale, Qld, 187
Akeman Street, 230
Albany, WA, 222
Albert, 126
Alberta, 120
Albion Park, NSW, 188
Alderney, 211
Aldershot, 80, 105, 107, 110–12, 165
Aldgate, SA, 201

Algiers, 111
Alexander the Great, 229
Alexandria, Egypt, 72, 94, 112, 139, 151, 181–2, 202, 207–208, 210, 213–14, 219–21, 233
Allan Leonard Lewis VC pub, Neath, 171–2
Allen, Lt Col AS, 75
Alloa, 117, 120
Alrewas, 78, 157–8, 226, 243
Altengrabow, 160
Alverstoke, 169
Ambrosia, 56
Amersham, 102, 167
Amesbury, 191
Amin, Idi, 114, 197
Ampthill, 235
Andrew VC, Cpl Leslie, 158
Angaston, SA, 212, 214
Anglo-Saxons, 187
Anglo-Soviet Trade Agreement, 109
Angus, 121, 127–8
Angus VC, William, 128
Antananarivo (Tananarive), 110
Antonine Wall, 211
Apiata VC, Cpl Willie, 157
Appleby-in-Westmorland, 175
Appledore, 102
Arab-Israeli War, 183
Archangel, 194
Archbishop of Canterbury, 63, 93, 115
Ardwick, 175
Ardwick-le-Street, 86
Argyllshire, 239
Armatree, NSW, 78
Armdale, WA, 225

Armstrong Whitworth & Co, 76, 193
Arncliffe, NSW, 188
Arnold, Dr Thomas, 62
Arras, 108
Arsenal FC, 204
Arthur Young McClelland Moores & Co, 124
Artois, 170
Ascension Farm, Spur, Valley & Wood, 22, 27–9
Ashford, 102
Ashton, 97
Aston Clinton, 230–1
Aston Martin, 230
Atcham, 176
Atkinson, Sir Harry, 131
Atkinson VC, A, 91
Auburn Carriage Co, 72
Auckland, 131–3, 136–8, 143–5, 153, 234
  High Court, 132,
Augusta, 111
Augustinians, 64
Aurangzeb, Emperor, 229
Australia, 58–9, 63, 66, 68–69, 74–5, 77–8, 98, 102, 105, 116, 119, 134, 157, 170–1, 182, 186, 188, 196, 199, 202, 206, 208, 213–15, 217–18, 220–22, 224, 226, 232–3, 243
Australian armed forces,
  Australian Army, 119, 203, 204, 218, 222–3
    Army Corps,
      Army Ordnance, 222
      Army Service Corps, 69, 203
      Australian Air, 71
      Australian Flying, 71
      Australian Imperial Force, 59, 70, 72–73, 208–209, 213, 217, 219, 221, 232
      Citizen Military Forces, 213
      Reserves, 73
    Australian Corps, 20–1, 32, 39
    Divisions,
      1st Australian, 20–1, 31–2, 214
      3rd Australian, 220
      4th Australian, 19–22
    Brigades,
      1st, 31–2
      3rd, 29, 31
      4th, 19, 21, 23, 25, 27–8, 31
      9th, 233
      12th, 19, 21, 23, 28–9, 31
      13th, 23
      14th, 23
      15th, 23
      16th, 23
    Cavalry,
      13th Australian Light Horse, 21, 72
      18th Australian Light Horse, 219
    Infantry Regiments/Battalions,
      1st, 232
      3rd New South Wales Imperial Bushmen, 71
      3rd Queensland Contingent, 105
      4th, 207, 232
      4th Training, 74
      6th, 232
      10th, 202, 209, 213
      11th, 221
      12th, 220
      12th Training, 215
      12th Victorian, 72
      13th, 19, 25–8, 68, 73–5, 233
      14th, 28–9, 31
      15th, 25–28
      16th, 25–7, 208, 219, 221
      28th, 219
      2/33rd, 203
      34th, 233
      36th, 232–3
      44th, 215
      45th, 21, 23, 28
      46th, 21, 28–32
      48th, 19, 21–3, 26, 29, 31, 199, 208, 215–16
      55th, 89
      63rd, 233
  Medical,
    1st Australian Auxiliary Hospital, Harefield, 59, 216–17, 233
    1st Australian Casualty Clearing Station, 207, 214, 221
    1st Australian Dermatological Hospital, Bulford, 75
    1st Australian Field Ambulance, 207
    1st Australian General Hospital, Heliopolis, 213, 221
    2nd Australian Auxiliary Hospital, Southall, 220
    2nd Australian Casualty Clearing Station, 216, 232
    2nd Australian Field Ambulance, 214
    Beach Dressing Station, 209
    2nd Australian General Hospital, Cairo/Ghezirah, 202, 207, 214
    3rd Australian Auxiliary Hospital, Dartford, 73–4, 202, 216
    3rd Australian Casualty Clearing Station, 135, 220
    3rd Australian Field Ambulance, 202, 220
    3rd Australian General Hospital, Abbassia/Brighton, 71, 232
    4th Australian Field Ambulance, 74, 214
    5th Australian Field Ambulance, 59
    5th Australian General Hospital, Melbourne, 71
    6th Australian Field Ambulance, 59
    7th Australian General Hospital, 202, 213
    10th Australian Field Ambulance, 232–3
    11th Australian Field Ambulance, 59
    12th Australian Field Ambulance, 74, 216

Index 257

13th Australian Field Ambulance, 74, 214, 216
15th Australian General Hospital, Torrens Park, 202
37th Dental Unit, 214
54th Dental Unit, 214
59th Dental Unit, 214
110 Military Hospital, 224
Anzac Casualty Clearing Station, 209
Australian Army Medical Corps, Dental Service, 214
Montazah Convalescence Depot, 71
Sultan's Palace Convalescence Hospital, Montazah, 207
Machine Gun Units,
  4th Australian Brigade Machine Gun Coy, 25
  5th Australian Machine Gun Bn, 20
  12th Australian Machine Gun Coy, 21
Royal Australian Artillery,
  3rd Australian Divisional Ammunition Column, 59
  3rd Australian Divisional Artillery, 59
  4th Field Artillery Bde, 70
  2/6th Australian Field Regt, 222
  8th Field Artillery Bde, 59
  10th Field Bde AFA, 21
  12th Bty, Field Artillery, 70
  14th Field Artillery Bde, 59
  19th Bty, Field Artillery, 70
  Field Artillery Reinforcements, 59, 70
  Reserve Bde Australian Artillery, Heytesbury/Larkhill, 59
Royal Australian Engineers,
  6th Field Coy, 210
  13th Field Coy, 21
Other units,
  1st Anzac Entrenching Bn, 69
  1st Australian Division Base Depot, Étaples, 207, 220
  1st Australian Division MT Coy, 69
  1st Australian Division Train, 69
  1st Australian Divisional Supply Column, 69
  1st Remount Unit, 71
  2nd AIF Depot, 203
  2nd Group, 75
  2nd Military District, 233–4
  3rd Australian Division Base Depot, Rouelles, 233
  3rd Australian Division Salvage Coy, 220
  3rd Australian Division Train, 220
    23rd Coy, 220
  3rd Military District, 59, 71, 233
  4 Australian Army Ordnance Depot, 205
  4th Australian Brigade Light Trench Mortar Bty, 25
  4th Australian Division Base Depot, 74, 216
  4th Australian Pioneer Bn, 21
  7 Advanced Ordnance Depot, 222
  7 Australian Army Troops Coy, 222
  7th Depot Units of Supply, 69
  12 Australian Lines of Communication Signals, 222
  12th Brigade Light Trench Mortar Bty, 21
  22 Depot, 221
  Australian Army Cadets, 72
  Australian Corps Reception Camp, 216
  Australian Employment Coy, 220
  Australian Flying Corps Laverton, 71
  Australian General Base Depot, Le Havre/Rouelles, 59, 69, 220
  Australian Infantry Base Depot, 209, 216, 221
  Balcombe Military Camp, 73
  Base Depot, Calais, 59
  Base Depot, Étaples, 220, 222
  Base Details, Zeitoun, 214
  Base Infantry AIF, 220
  D3 Depot, 221
  Details Camp, Moascar, 71
  Infantry General Base Depot, Tel-el-Kebir, 69
  No.1 Command Depot, Perham Down/Sutton Veny, 73–4, 233–4
  No.1 Depot Bn, 221
  No.1 Group, 69
  No.1 Home Training School, HQ Central Flying School, 71
  No.2 Camp, Parkhouse, 214
  No.2 Command Depot, Weymouth, 73, 202, 208, 220, 233
  No.2 Group, Sutton Veny, 222
  No.3 Command Depot, Hurdcott, 216, 233
  No.4 Camp, 75
  No.4 Camp, AASC Training Depot, Parkhouse Camp, 69
  No.4 Command Depot, Codford/Hurdcott, 59, 214, 216, 222
  No.13 Depot Coy, 219
  Overseas Base, 207
  Reinforcement Camp, Tel-el-Kebir, 69
  Reinforcement Camp, Zeitoun, 69
  Senior Cadets, 213
  Transport School, 202
Training Units,
  Australian Army Service Corps Training Depot, Parkhouse Camp, 220
  Australian Corps Bombing School, 221
  No.5 Officer Cadet School, Duntroon, 221
  Overseas Training Brigade & Depot, Longbridge Deverill/Perham Down, 59, 216, 220, 233
Australian Naval & Military Expeditionary Force, 215

Royal Australian Air Force, 71, 187, 201, 203, 218, 221
  1 Initial Training School, Somers, Vic, 221
  3 Transport & Movement Office, 203
  4 Operational Training Unit, 218
  9 Transport & Movement Office, 221
  99 Sqn, 218
  218th Sqn, 201
  Central Flying School, Laverton, 71
  Central Training Depot, Liverpool, 71
  Medical Branch, 218
  No.1 Aircraft Depot, 71
  No.1 Flying Training School, 71
  No.1 Station HQ, 71
  No.5 Repair & Servicing Unit, 187
Royal Australian Navy, 187, 203, 215, 221–2, 233
  HMAS *Berrima*, 215
  HMAS *Cerberus*, 221
  HMAS *Lonsdale*, 203
  HMAS *Melbourne*, 203
  HMAS *Penguin*, 222
  HMAS *Rushcutter*, 187
  HMAS *Tingira*, 222
  HMAT A11 *Ascanius*, 213, 219
  HMAT A12 *Saldanha*, 202
  HMAT A17 *Port Lincoln*, 209
  HMAT A18 *Wiltshire*, 72, 208
  HMAT A29 *Suevic*, 233
  HMAT A31 *Ajana*, 234
  HMAT A35 *Berrima*, 215
  HMAT A40 *Ceramic*, 72–73
  HMAT A44 *Vestalia*, 71
  HMAT A67 *Orsova*, 71
  HMAT A70 *Ballarat*, 69, 220
  HMAT D34 *Port Hacking*, 141
Australian Capital Territory, 77–8, 225–6
Australian Government, 73–4
  Commonwealth Ombudsman, 78
  Deputy Crown Solicitor, 78
  Ministry of Defence, 217
Australian Merchant Navy, 218
Australian Red Cross, 217
Austria, 95
Auxiliary Fire Service, 154, 163
Avesne, 108
Avocado Heights, NSW, 188
Awapuni, 149
Awoingt, 105
Aylesbury & Vale of, 230, 242
Ayrshire, 111, 188

Baden-Powell, Sir Robert, 182
BAE Systems, 189, 193
Baker, Lt Henry, 28
Balclutha, 152
Baldock, 240
Balkans, 61

Ballarat, Vic, 102, 206
Balmoral, NZ, 145
Baltic, 116
Bancroft, 240
Bandiana Army Camp, Vic, 77
Bangladesh, 100
Bangor, 184
Banks, Cpl John, 28
Banks, NSW, 188
Baptist Missionary Society, 100
Barclay Curle & Co, Glasgow, 111
Barden, 119
Barisal, 100
Barking & Dagenham, 92
Barlinnie Prison, 128
Barnsley, 81–3, 88
Baroness Warsi, 77, 157, 225
Barossa Valley, 199
Barrett, Richard, 131
Barrett VC, Lt John, 47, 49–50, 55–68
Barrossa Barracks, Aldershot, 80
Barrow & Calcutta Jute Co, 189
Barrow Hematite Steel Co, 189
Barrow-in-Furness, 147, 182, 186, 189–91, 193–4
  Corporation, 190–1
Barrow Shipbuilding Co, 189, 193
Barry, Sir Charles, 96
Barton, 176
Basrah, 94, 95
Basse Boulogne & South, 33, 35, 37, 39
Bassett VC, Cyril, 156
Basutoland, 111–12
Bath, 61
  Mayor, 61
Batley, 229
Batty, Sgt Al, 7
Bay of Islands, 153
Bayern/Bavaria, 124
Bayswater, 55, 61, 155
Bayswater, WA, 223
Beaminster, 168
Bear Hotel, Oswestry, 175
Beath, 120
*Beatles*, 125
Beaucamp Ridge, 8
Bechuanaland, 111–12
Beckenham, 196
Becket, Thomas, 93
Becontree, 91
Bedfordshire, 226, 229, 231, 235, 239, 244
  Central Bedfordshire Council, 240
Bedwellty, 160
Beeston, 92
Beharry VC, Sgt Johnson, 78, 157, 226, 243
*Being for the Benefit of Mr Kite*, 125
Beirut, 112
Beit Horon, 183

# Index 259

Beit Ur el-Foqa, 182, 183
Belfast, 162, 182
Belgium, 75, 78, 81–2, 89, 97, 116, 157, 161, 226, 243
Bellenglise, 47, 49–51
Bellicourt, 32, 35
Bellingen, NSW, 201
Benedictines, 236
Bengal, 100
Benjamin Post, 33, 35
Berela, NSW, 188
Berkhamsted, 101
Berkshire, 96, 166, 192, 195, 220, 242
Berlin, 56
Berne, 153
Berowra, NSW, 188
Berwickshire, 118
Besanko DCM MM, Sgt Cyril, 208
Betheron, 183
Bexley, 93, 95, 97, 100
Bexleyheath, 101, 154
Beynes, Norman, 51
Bickley, 100
Big Bill Copse, 22, 29
Billinge, 83
Billyard-Leake, Charles, 217
Bingham, 60
Binks, LCpl, 51
Birmingham, 60, 140, 162–3, 180, 207, 216, 227, 233–4
    Corporation Water Department, 180
Birstall, 229
Bishop Auckland, 62
Bishop of Fulham, 106
Bishop Rock, 211
Bisley Camp, 193
Bittern, Vic, 77
Black Sea, 116
Blackboy Hill & Camp, 215
Blackburn, 82, 192, 234
Blackpool, 81
Blacktown, NSW, 203
Blandford, 168
Blaxland, NSW, 188
Blendecques, 103
Bloomfield, Sir Reginald, 106
Blooming Rose pub, Hunslet, 86
Bloomsbury, 100–102
Blyth, 76
Boat pub, Boughrood, 160
Boer/South African Wars, 71, 105, 181, 237
Boggart's Hole, 10–12
Bologna, 112
Bolsheviks, 194
Bombay, 94, 101, 161
Bondi, NSW, 186–7
Bonnyrigg & Lasswade, 124

Boolaroo, NSW, 77
Boothby, SA, 201
Borden, 106
Borderer Ridge, 8
Bordertown, SA, 212
Boston, MA, 118
Boughrood, 160
Boulogne, 87, 97, 104, 108–10, 232–3
Bournemouth, 167–8, 235, 237
Bowden, 203
Bowral, NSW, 188
Box Hill, Vic, 188
Boy Scouts, 102, 138, 182
    1st Sittingbourne Tp, 102
Bradford, 81, 84, 91
Bradworthy, 167
Brandenburg-Prussia, 144
Brechin, 117
Brecknockshire, 163–4
Brecon, 160, 175, 179
Breconshire, 159
Bremen, 217
Brent, 229
Brentwood, 90
Bresin, 143
Bricket Lane, 56
Bridge of Allan, 124
Bridge of Dun, 128
Bridgewater, SA, 210
Bridgnorth, 102
Bridport, 154
Brighton, 87, 154, 186–7, 232–3
Brilley, 159, 164, 169, 171
Brisbane, 119, 232
Bristol, 87, 160, 163, 235
British Aerospace, 193
British Army (for Indian units *see* Indian Army), 58, 84, 89, 92, 102, 126, 164, 228
    Army Benevolent Fund, 113
    Army Certificate of Education, 226, 237
    Army List, 65, 106
    Army of Occupation, 87
    Army Reserves, 58
        1st Class, 237
        Class Z, 83, 165, 167, 190, 231
        Class Z (T), 169
        Militia, 175
        Supplementary Reserve, 127
        Territorial & Army Volunteer Reserve, 127
        Territorial Army Reserve of Officers, 65–6, 113, 196
    Commissions,
        Emergency, 195
        Regular, 195
        Short Service, 195
    Field Forces,
        British Expeditionary Force, 1, 46, 108

Chitral Relief Force, 227
Mediterranean Expeditionary Force, 94, 202
North Russia Relief Force, 194
Western Frontier, 181
General Headquarters BEF, 103, 107–108
Good Conduct Badge, 118
Kent Territorial & Auxiliary Forces Association, 113
Militia, 127, 175
Regular Army, 175
Territorial Force/Army, 87, 122, 123, 126, 127, 159, 178, 180, 181, 184, 192, 193, 198, 239, 240
Territorial Force/Army, Air Force & Auxiliary Forces Associations,
  City of London, 175
  Leicestershire & Rutland, 65
Armies,
  First, 1, 13, 51
  Second, 4
  Third, 1–2, 4, 13, 19–20, 39, 51
  Fourth, 1, 3–4, 13, 19–20, 32, 39–40, 47, 51
  Eighth, 112
Army Corps,
  III, 20, 32–3, 36, 51
  IV, 4, 43
  V, 4, 5, 39, 41, 43, 112
  VI, 4, 9
  IX, 20, 22, 28–9, 47, 51
  X, 111–12
  XI, 110
Corps,
  Army Service/Royal Army Service, 110, 117, 165, 169–70, 177, 231
  Army Stores, 237
  Auxiliary Military Pioneer Corps, 107–108
  Auxiliary Territorial Service, 123
  Intelligence, 196
  Machine Gun, *see* below
  Military Police, 139
  Pioneer, 107
  Royal Army Medical, *see* below
  Royal Army Ordnance, 111
  Royal Artillery, *see* below
  Royal Corps of Signals, 57, 123
  Royal Defence, 175
  Royal Engineers, *see* below
  Royal Flying, *see* below
  Territorial Force Nursing Service, 198
Divisions,
  1st, 20, 22, 28–9, 31, 47, 51
  2nd, 4, 9, 11, 23
  3rd, 45
  5th, 46
  6th, 47
  12th, 36, 38–9
  17th, 39–40
  18th, 19, 32, 34–7
  21st, 39, 230
  24th, 47
  32nd, 20
  33rd, 39
  37th, 4, 9, 11, 19, 43
  38th, 4, 19, 39–42, 193
  44th Home Counties, 107
  46th, 47
  47th, 117
  49th, 87
  52nd, 13
  57th, 13
  58th, 39
  62nd, 1, 4, 9, 44, 87
  63rd (Royal Naval), 80
  74th, 19, 32, 34, 181
Brigades,
  2nd, 20, 29
  4th Dismounted, 181
  4th Guards, 240
  8th, 45
  9th, 45
  9th Cavalry, 161
  50th, 40–2
  51st, 40
  52nd, 40
  53rd, 37
  54th, 19, 37
  55th, 37, 39
  63rd, 11, 46
  72nd, 47
  112th, 19, 43, 45–6
  113th, 41, 43
  114th, 40–3
  115th, 4, 5, 41–3
  137th, 49
  138th, 47
  139th, 47–8
  148th, 87
  155th, 13, 15–18
  156th, 15
  157th, 13, 18–19
  172nd, 13
  185th, 11
  186th, 9, 11–12
  187th, 1, 9, 11–12, 87
  229th, 33
  230th, 32
  231st, 19, 32–3, 36, 38, 181
  South Wales Mounted, 181
  Welsh Border Mounted, 181
Cavalry,
  7th Dragoon Guards, 160
  Imperial Yeomanry, 176, 181
    9th Bn, 181
    31st Coy (Montgomeryshire), 181

# Index

49th Coy (Montgomeryshire), 181
88th Coy (Welsh Yeomanry), 181
89th Coy (Montgomeryshire), 181
Montgomeryshire, 174, 180
Montgomeryshire Yeomanry, 176–7, 180–1
   1/1st, 180–1
   2/1st, 176, 181
   3/1st, 181
North Somerset Yeomanry,
   2/1st North Somerset Yeomanry, 167
Royal Dragoon Guards, 81
Welsh Horse Yeomanry, 181
West Kent Yeomanry, 97
Infantry,
   24th Regiment, 173
   Argyll & Sutherland Highlanders,
      7th Argyll & Sutherland Highlanders, 122, 126
      1/8th Argyll & Sutherland Highlanders, 126
   Bedfordshire, 226
      1st Bedfordshire, 227
      2nd Bedfordshire, 33, 37–8, 227
      5th (Reserve) Bedfordshire, 242
   Black Watch, 117
   Devonshire, 191
      1/5th Devonshire, 12
      16th Devonshire, 33
   Dorsetshire,
      2nd Dorset, 237
      3rd Dorset, 235
      4th Reserve Bn, 167
      Depot, 167
   Duke of Edinburgh's, 195
   Durham Light Infantry, 82, 161
      1st Durham Light Infantry, 162
      2nd Durham Light Infantry, 162
      1/9th Durham Light Infantry, 9
      14th Durham Light Infantry, 82, 161
      16th Durham Light Infantry, 82
      Depot, 82
   East Kent, 114
      4th East Kent, 97, 106–107
      1/4th East Kent, 101
      2/4th East Kent, 93–4
      3/4th East Kent, 93–4, 101
      1/5th East Kent, 94
      2/5th East Kent, 94
      3/5th East Kent, 94
      69th Provisional Bn, 97
      71st Provisional Bn, 97
   East Surrey,
      9th East Surrey, 51
   East Sussex, 114
   Essex,
      1st Essex, 43, 45–6
      1/8th (Cyclist) Essex, 167

   Hampshire, 114
      2/4th Hampshire, 9, 12
      7th, 237
      1/7th Hampshire, 237
   Herefordshire,
      1st Herefordshire, 181
   Hertfordshire, 244
      1st Hertfordshire, 19, 227, 239, 243
         Hitchin Coy, 227, 239
      1/1st Hertfordshire, 43, 45–6, 226, 239–42
      2/1st Hertfordshire, 240
      3/1st Hertfordshire, 227, 242
   Highland Light Infantry, 128, 160
      3rd Highland Light Infantry, 161
      5th Highland Light Infantry, 13, 15–19, 51
      1/5th Highland Light Infantry, 117, 125
      6th Highland Light Infantry, 15
      7th Highland Light Infantry, 15, 18
   Home Guard, 67, 128
      11th City of London (Dagenham/Essex) Bn, 91
   Irish Guards,
      2nd Irish Guards, 110
   King's (Liverpool),
      1st Volunteer Bn, 178
      3rd King's, 190
      10th King's (Liverpool Scottish), 190
      13th King's, 190
      Depot, 190
   King's Own Royal Lancaster,
      4th King's Own, 192
      2/5th King's Own, 81
   King's Own Scottish Borderers,
      4th King's Own Scottish Borderers, 15–18
   King's Own Yorkshire Light Infantry,
      2nd King's Own Yorkshire Light Infantry, 89
      2/4th King's Own Yorkshire Light Infantry, 9, 11
      5th & 1/5th King's Own Yorkshire Light Infantry, 1, 9, 11–13, 79, 87
   King's Shropshire Light Infantry,
      10th King's Own Shropshire Light Infantry, 35–6
   Leicestershire/Royal Leicestershire, 62, 65, 67
      4th Leicestershire, 47
      5th Leicestershire, 47–51, 55, 65–6
      1/5th Leicestershire, 62
      3/5th Leicestershire, 62
   Lincolnshire,
      5th Lincolnshire, 47, 49
   London,
      28th, 1/28th, 2/28th & 3/28th London, 55, 102–103
   Manchester,
      1/5th Manchester, 242

8th Manchester,
  No.5 Supernumerary Coy, 175
Middlesex, 114
North Staffordshire,
  1st North Staffordshire, 54
Northamptonshire, 171
  2nd (Home Service) Garrison Bn,
    Northamptonshire, 171
  6th Northamptonshire, 19, 37–9, 159,
    171
Prince of Wales's Royal Regiment, 114
Queen's Own (Royal West Kent), 107, 112
  3rd Royal West Kent, 104–105
  8th Royal West Kent, 104
  11th Royal West Kent, 103–104
Queen's Own Buffs, The Royal Kent
  Regiment, 112–13
  4th Queen's Own Buffs, 112
  11th Queen's Own Buffs, 113
Queen's Regiment,
  1st Queen's, 114
  2nd Queen's, 114
  3rd Queen's, 114
  5th Queen's, 114
Royal Berkshire, 195
  8th Royal Berkshire, 37
Royal East Kent, 112, 114
Royal Fusiliers,
  11th Royal Fusiliers, 37–9
  13th Royal Fusiliers, 43
Royal Highland Fusiliers, 128–30
Royal Munster Fusiliers,
  1st Royal Munster Fusiliers, 13
Royal Scots Fusiliers, 128
  4th Royal Scots Fusiliers, 17–18
  5th Royal Scots Fusiliers, 17–18
Royal Sussex,
  2nd Royal Sussex, 23
Royal Welsh Fusiliers,
  4th Reserve Bn, 181
  7th Royal Welsh Fusiliers, 181
  1/7th Royal Welsh Fusiliers, 177
  2/7th Royal Welsh Fusiliers, 174
  14th Royal Welsh Fusiliers, 43
  25th Royal Welsh Fusiliers, 19, 35–6, 38,
    173, 181
Royal West Kent (Queen's Own),
  2/4th Royal West Kent, 94
  2/5th Royal West Kent, 94
  7th Royal West Kent, 33, 37–8
  8th Royal West Kent, 47, 51, 54, 93
  10th Royal West Kent, 97
Royal West Sussex, 114
Seaforth Highlanders,
  1st Seaforth Highlanders, 124
Sherwood Foresters,
  6th Sherwood Foresters, 47–9, 51

South Staffordshire,
  6th South Staffordshire, 49
South Wales Borderers, 160
  1/1st Brecknockshire Bn, 159
  4th South Wales Borderers, 174–5
  10th South Wales Borderers, 42
Suffolk,
  1st Volunteer Bn, 160
  3rd Volunteer Bn, 160
  15th Suffolk, 32
Welsh, 58
  1st Welsh, 58
  13th Welsh, 40–3
  14th Welsh, 40–3
  15th Welsh, 41–3
  19th Welsh, 41
  24th Welsh, 33, 35
Welsh Guards,
  2nd Welsh Guards, 109–10
West Riding (Duke of Wellington's),
  2/4th West Riding, 9, 11
West Yorkshire,
  15th West Yorkshire, 86
Wiltshire, 191, 194–5, 242
  4th Wiltshire, 191
York & Lancaster,
  3rd York & Lancaster, 83
  2/4th York & Lancaster, 9, 11–12
  8th York & Lancaster, 8
Machine Gun Corps, 117, 193, 196
  2nd Battalion MGC, 10
  17th Battalion MGC, 40
  38th Battalion MGC, 41–3, 186
  62nd Battalion MGC, 9–10
  74th Battalion MGC, 33
  176th Machine Gun Coy, 193
  Guards Division MG Bn, 10
  Machine Gun Corps Base Depot, Camiers,
    193
  Machine Gun Depot, Grantham, 104
  Machine Gun School, Grantham, 193
Miscellaneous units,
  1st British Base Depot, 94
  1/1st Highland Cyclist Bn, 125
  1/2nd (47th) Division Ammunition Park, 117
  17th Army Auxiliary Coy, 165
  41st Divisional Train, 165
  47th Ammunition Sub Park, 118
  47th Division MT Coy, 118
  55 Area, 112
  57th Division MT Coy, 118
  68th Recruiting Area, 161
  71 Sub Area, 112
  121 Force, 110–11
  138th Brigade Light Trench Mortar Bty, 47
  176th Territorial Force Depot, 237
  187th Brigade Trench Mortar Bty, 10

Index  263

231st Brigade Light Trench Mortar Bty, 35
249th Signal Squadron (AMF(L), 138
310 Coy, 165
313th Protection Coy RDC, 175
317th Protection Coy RDC, 175
382nd MT Coy, 118
Central Bombing School, Rouen, 242
Dispersal Station, Fovant, 167
Dispersal Unit, Purfleet, 231
Dunfermline Territorials, 123, 124
East African Labour Group, 110
Expeditionary Force Canteen, Sharoban, 95
Force X, 111
Force Y, 111
Labour Corps Camp, Codford, 58
No.1 Dispersal Unit, Prees Heath, 165
No.1 District, 112
No.1 Infantry Base Depot, 242
No.3 Rest Camp, Folkestone, 227
No.4 AMPC Centre, Clacton, 107, 110
No.5 Group, AMPC, 107–08, 110–11
No.19 Group, AMPC, 111
No.39 Group, AMPC, 112
No.48 Group, AMPC, 111
No.209 Prisoner of War Coy, 242
Observer Coys, 175
Officers' Dispersal Unit, London, 98
Supernumerary Territorial Force Coys, 175
XXII Corps Cyclist Bn, 139–40
Royal Army Medical Corps/Army Medical Services, 65, 190, 196
  1st Auxiliary Hospital, Harefield, 208
  1st British Red Cross Hospital, Montazah, 71
  1st Northern General Hospital, 161
  1st Southern General Hospital, Edgbaston, 207, 233
  2/1st Southern General Hospital, Birmingham, 216
  2 Ambulance Train, 207
  2nd Convalescence Hospital, 135
  2nd Eastern General Hospital, Brighton, 161
  1/2nd London Field Ambulance, 140
  1/2nd South Midland Field Ambulance, 207
  2nd Welsh Field Ambulance, 94
  3 Casualty Clearing Station, 193
  3rd Convalescent Depot, Étaples, 151
  3rd East Lancashire Field Ambulance, 148
  3rd General Hospital, Le Tréport, 193
  4th Stationary Hospital, 165
  5th London General Hospital, 64
  5th Northern General Hospital, Leicester, 161
  6th Convalescent Depot, Camiers, 139
  7 Ambulance Train, 207
  7 Casualty Clearing Station, 233
  7th General Hospital, St Omer, 132, 137
  8th Stationary Hospital, Wimereux, 232
  9th (USA) General Hospital, Rouen, 59, 135, 242
  9th Stationary Hospital, Le Havre, 207
  10 Casualty Clearing Station, 59, 161
  10th General Hospital, Rouen, 148, 220
  11th Corps Rest Station, 193
  11th General Hospital, Camiers, 135
  12 Casualty Clearing Station, 216
  12th Convalescent Depot, 148
  12th General Hospital, Rouen, 207, 220
  15 Casualty Clearing Station, 202
  18 Casualty Clearing Station, 193
  18th Field Ambulance, 161
  18th General Hospital, 137, 207
  20 Casualty Clearing Station, 216
  20th Combined Field Ambulance, 94
  20th General Hospital, Étaples/Camiers, 161, 193
  21st Combined Field Ambulance, 94
  21st General Hospital, Alexandria, 221
  22nd Combined Field Ambulance, 94
  22nd General Hospital, Camiers, 139
  24 Ambulance Train, 207, 232
  24th General Hospital, 139
  29 Ambulance Train, 220
  30th General Hospital, 59, 65
  33 Ambulance Train, 139
  37 Ambulance Train, 59
  38 Casualty Clearing Station, 151
  39th General Hospital, 214, 222
  44 Casualty Clearing Station, 137, 207
  45 Casualty Clearing Station, 220
  51st Stationary Hospital, 222
  53 Casualty Clearing Station, 137
  53rd General Hospital, 202
  54th General Hospital, 202, 216
  55 Casualty Clearing Station, 216
  55th General Hospital, 148
  56 Casualty Clearing Station, 148, 214
  61 Casualty Clearing Station, 59
  63 Casualty Clearing Station, 148
  63rd Field Ambulance, 139
  128th Field Ambulance, 193
  129th Field Ambulance, 193
  130th (St John) Field Ambulance, 193
  133rd British General Hospital, Basrah, 94
  135th Combined Field Ambulance, 94
  138th Field Ambulance, 165
  140th Field Ambulance, 165
  Brighton Military Hospital, 161
  British Military Hospital, Münster, 124
  Cambridge Military Hospital, Aldershot, 105
  Citadel Military Hospital, Cairo, 94
  Convalescent Depot, Abbassia, 94
  Devonport Military Hospital, 73
  Exeter War Hospital, 59
  Fargo Military Hospital, Larkhill, 59

Fulham Military Hospital, 209
Furness Auxiliary Hospital, Harrogate, 97
General Military Hospital, Edmonton, 202
Kasr-el-Aini Hospital, Cairo, 94
Kent/52 Voluntary Aid Detachment, 103
King George Hospital, Waterloo, London, 215–16
Military Hospital, Hampstead, 137
Military Hospital, Newcastle upon Tyne, 162
Norfolk War Hospital, Norwich, 233
Orchard Military Hospital, Dartford, 74
Parkhouse Military Hospital, Salisbury Plain, 215
Prince of Wales' Hospital, London, 104
Queen Alexandra's Military Hospital, Millbank, 97
Reading War Hospital, 220
Red Cross Hospital, Longleat House, 170
Shorncliffe Military Hospital, 227
Tidworth Military Hospital, 141
Tigne Convalescent Hospital, Malta, 213, 221
VAD Hospital 32, Hayling Island, 137
Welsh Metropolitan War Hospital, Cardiff, 242
XV Corps Main Dressing Station, 151
York Place Military Hospital, Brighton, 232–33
Royal Artillery, 57, 97, 124, 196
  9th Anti-Aircraft Regt, 169
  107th Heavy Anti-Aircraft Regt, 169
  124th Heavy Anti-Aircraft Regt, 169
  207th Heavy Anti-Aircraft Training Regt, 169
  229th Anti-Aircraft Bty, 127
  332nd (Radnorshire) Field Bty (Howitzers), 181
  424th Coastal Regt TA, 238
  424th Heavy Anti-Aircraft Regt TA, 238
  No.4 Depot Bty RFA, 168
  Royal Artillery Institution, 58
  Royal Field Artillery, 168, 179
  Royal Garrison Artillery, 56
Royal Engineers, 37, 57, 125, 168
  1/2nd Cornwall (Fortress) RE TF, 58
  2/2nd Works Coy, 58
  182nd Tunnelling Company, 35
  468th Field Company, 47
  575th (Cornwall) Works Coy, 58
  No.5 Dem Train Depot RE, 58
  Western Army Troops Signal Coy, 178
  Western Telegraph Bn, 178
Royal Flying Corps, 242
Tank Corps,
  2nd Battalion, 21, 38
Training establishments/units,
  Inns of Court OTC, 101
  IV Corps Bombing School, 151
  No.1 Cadet Bn, MGC, Bisley, 193
  No.1 Training Battalion Depot, 242
  No.6 Officer Cadet Battalion, Balliol & Trinity College, Oxford, 227
  No.13 Officer Cadet Battalion, Newmarket, 151
  Officers' Training Corps, 62, 101, 240
  Royal Military Academy, Woolwich, 56–7
  Royal Military College/Academy, Sandhurst, 58
  School of Instruction, 171
  School of Musketry, Hythe, 227
  School of Musketry, Tidworth, 233
  Territorial Army Senior Officers' Course, Sheerness, 107
  Third Army School, 135
British Broadcasting Corporation, 63
British Columbia, 219
British Empire, 116, 126–7, 173, 244
British Government Departments/Ministries,
  Admiralty, 98, 131, 182, 211
  Communities & Local Government, 67, 78, 92, 116, 130, 157, 171, 184, 197, 226, 243
  Education & Science, 62
  Faith & Communities, 77, 157, 225
  Foreign & Commonwealth Office, 77, 157, 225
  House of Lords, 66, 114, 129, 197, 223
  Parliament, 64, 96, 211
  Pensions, 161–62
  Revenue & Customs, 124, 236
  War Office, 64, 107, 111, 170, 230
British India Steam Navigation Co, 111
British Journal of Surgery, 64
British Legion/Royal, 113, 197
British Red Cross Society, 61, 65
British Seaman's Boys' Home, 236
British Shipbuilders, 193
Brixham, 228, 235–8
Broad Chalke, 235
Broadmeadows Camp, 69–70, 72
Broadwinsor, 168
Brockenhurst, 135, 148
Brocton, 136
Broken Hill, 199, 202, 220
Bromley, 97, 102–103, 196
Brompton, 56
Bronze Age, 153, 183, 204, 228, 236
Brownlee, Gerry, 157
Broxton, 131
Brussels, 217
Bryngwyn, 159
Buckhaven, 120
Buckingham Palace, 62, 66, 75, 87, 91, 105, 114, 126, 129, 151, 171, 182, 185, 193, 197, 217, 242
Buckinghamshire, 102, 167, 230–1, 242
Buckley VC, Sgt Maurice, 19, 24–5, 27–8, 68–78
Builth Wells, 163–4
Buisson-Gaulaine Farm, 22, 29

Index 265

Bulford, Camp & Kiwi, 75, 135–8, 140–1, 150, 214, 216
Bulgaria, 105
Bull Post, 36
Bulwell, 62
Buntingford, 110, 240
Burma, 112
Burra, 128
Burrington, 58
Burstock, 168
Burton-upon-Trent, 90
Burwood, NSW, 232
Bury, Charles, 88
Bury St Edmunds, 160, 240
Butler VC, WB, 91
Butlins, 107
Byng, FM Julian, 4
Byron Steamship Co, 217

Caban-coch dam, 180
Cable Bay, 153
Cadeby Main, 87–8
Caen, 115
Café Royal, London, 66, 91, 115, 129, 155, 197
Cairo, 94, 112, 161, 202, 214, 221
Caister, 110
Caithness, 85
Calais, 59, 107, 109, 161
Calderdale, 81
Caledon Shipbuilding & Engineering Co, 98
California, 118, 219
Calvert VC, Sgt Laurence, 1, 11, 79–92
Camberwell, 231
Cambrai & Battle of, 9, 13, 19, 46, 105
Cambrian Hotel, Cardiff, 195
Cambridge, MA, 89
Cambrook, 2Lt Horace, 53–4
Camden, 61
Cameron, PM David, 78, 157, 226, 243
Camiers, 137, 139, 193
Campbell, ACT, 77–8, 225–6
Campbelltown, SA, 201
Campion, Col Sir William, 223
Campobasso, 112
Campsie, NSW, 232
Canada, 66, 78, 90, 116, 120, 157, 170, 178, 219, 226, 243
Canadian Armed Forces,
  Canadian Expeditionary Force, 178
  Brigades,
    5th, 19
  Infantry Regiments/Battalions,
    25th, 19
  Engineers, 178
    2nd Canadian Engineers Railway Bn, 178
    3rd Canadian Engineers Railway Bn, 178
    3rd Canadian Tunnelling Coy, 148

  Canadian Engineers Training Depot, 178
  Medical/ Royal Canadian Army Medical Corps,
    1st Canadian General Hospital, Étaples, 151
    2 Canadian Casualty Clearing Station, 139
    2nd Canadian General Hospital, 233
    3rd Canadian General Hospital, Boulogne, 233
    14th Canadian General Hospital, Eastbourne, 178
  Other units,
    H Wing, Witley, 178
    No.2 Canadian Discharge Depot, 178
    R Wing, 178
Canal du Nord, 1, 4, 13, 16, 32, 63
Canberra, 77–8, 225
Cannock, 176
Canterbury, 93, 95, 107, 113, 160, 230
Canterbury, NSW, 234
Canterbury, NZ, 138
*Canterbury Tales*, 93
Capability Brown, 170
Cape Colony, 175
Cape Town, 111, 215
Capel le Ferne, 229
Captain Swing Riots, 159
Capua, 112
Cardiff, 194–5, 235, 242
Carlton Club, 241
Carlton, Vic, 211, 219
Carmichael VC, John, 129
Carnegie, 123
Carnegie, Andrew, 118
Caroline Bay, 156
Carroll VC, John, 223
Carron Co, 211
Casemates Barracks, Gibraltar, 124
Caspian Sea, 116
Castlecliff, 143
Castleford, 80
Cat Post, 36
Catania, 111
Cathays, 195
Cathedrals,
  Hereford, 171
  Leicester, 67
  Newry, 204
  St Patrick's, Melbourne, 77
  St Peter's, Waikato, 133
  Westminster, 96
Catterick, 62
Caulfield South, Vic, 70
Cavendish, 56
Cavendish Dock, 194
Caversham, WA, 215, 219–20, 224
Celtic, 236
Cemeteries & Crematoria,

Brighton General Cemetery, Melbourne, 70, 76–7
Brookwood Cemetery, Woking, 101
Charing Crematorium, Kent, 116
Dunfermline Cemetery, 129–30
Emstrey Crematorium, Shrewsbury, 197
Gilroes Crematorium, Leicester, 67
Hamilton Park, Waikato, 133
Hawera, 156
Karrakatta Cemetery, Perth, WA, 224–5
Leeds (Holbeck) Cemetery, 86
Piako Cemetery, Morrinsville, 133
Rookwood Cemetery & Necropolis, Sydney, NSW, 218
St John's Churchyard, Hildenborough, 197
Salisbury (London Road) Cemetery, 191
South Essex Crematorium, Upminster, 91
Springvale Botanical Cemetery, Melbourne, 77, 225
Tunbridge Wells Cemetery, 54
Welsh Baptist Church Burial Ground, Welshpool, 183–4
Central Powers, 244
Chak Lala Camp, Rawalpindi, 94
Chambers, JE, 88
Chambers, Pte Keith, 28
Changi, 124–5
Channel Islands, 56
Charing Cross, 3, 8, 64
Charles Sturt City, SA, 201
Charmouth, 166–7
Chartered Institute of Taxation, 124
Chatham, 98, 100, 104
Checkers Inn, Montgomery, 174
Chelmsford, 234
Chelsea, 152
Cheltenham, Vic, 211
Chepstow, 81, 106
Cherat, 89, 226
Cherbourg, 107
Chertsey, 214
Cheshire, 131, 165, 177
Chester, 111
Chester, Pte, 17
Chesterfield, 62, 79
Chichester, 164
Chifley, NSW, 186
Chilterns, 230
China, 78, 157, 226, 243
China Navigation Co, 111
Chitral, Defence & Relief of, 228
Chorlton, 85
Christchurch, 231, 234
Christchurch, NZ, 146–7
Churches,
  All Saints, Brixham, 236
  All Saints, Denaby Main, 92
All Saints, Hertford, 243
Cairneymount, Maddiston, 123
Caversham Methodist, Perth, WA, 218
Christ Church, Frome, 167–8
Christ Church, Leeds, 84
Church of St Michael, Stamford, 66–7
Congregational, Manly, NSW, 219
Denaby Main Parish, 80
Falkirk Old Parish, 211
Garrison Church of St George, Woolwich, 58
Hampton Mill Parish, 166–7
Harrow Parish, 100
Holy Trinity, Adelaide, 202
Holy Trinity, Brompton, 56
Holy Trinity, Islington, 96
Holy Trinity, Karachi, 89–90
Holy Trinity, Kilburn, 155
Hunslet Parish, 85–6
Lillington, Warwickshire, 62
Llandrinio Parish, 176
Lower Brixham Parish, 237
Methodist Chapel, Klemzig, 201
Methodist Church, Caversham, WA, 220
Methodist Manse, Strathalbyn, SA, 214
Mount Rufus Congregationalist, Kapunda, SA, 200
North Church, Kelty, 119
Presbyterian, Goodwood, SA, 200
Priory Church, Great Malvern, 61
St Aidan, Leeds, 84
St Andrew & St George, Edinburgh, 124
St Andrew's Parish, Willesden, 154
St Anthony's, Blackboy Hill, 215
St Cuthbert, Hunslet Moor, 84
St George's Anglican, Gawler, SA, 200, 205
St George, Hanover Square, London, 60
St George, Leeds, 83
St George's Memorial, Ypres, 106–107, 116
St James', Doncaster, 79
St James, Whitehaven, 190
St John the Baptist, Tunstall, 99, 115–16
St John the Divine, Leicester, 65
St John's, Adelaide, 200
St John's Anglican, South Townsville, Qld, 187
St John's, Peshawar, 89–90
St Luke's, West Norwood, 196
St Margaret's, Leicester, 66
St Mary, Lifton, 56
St Mary's Anglican, Hawera, 152
St Mary Magdalen, Knighton, 66
St Mary's, Brilley, 171
St Mary's, Brixham, 236
St Mary's, Hawera, 132
St Mary's, Hitchin, 243
St Mary's, Walton-on-Thames, 137
St Mary's, Welshpool, 183
St Mary the Virgin, Hunslet, 84

# Index

St Matthew's, Hastings, NZ, 156
St Michael, Oxford, 166
St Michael's, Sittingbourne, 105
St Paul's, Aberdeen, 128
St Peter & St Paul, Mitcham, 187
St Peter & St Paul's, Whitney-on-Wye, 159, 171
St Peter's, Cardiff, 195
St Peter's, Hunslet Moor, 86
St Peter's, Leeds, 86
Saline Parish, Dunfermline, 127–8
Townhill Church of Scotland, Dunfermline, 119–20
Trinity, Adelaide, 206
Union, Luton, 231
Welsh Baptist, Welshpool, 183–4
Wesley Chapel, Sydney, NSW, 188
Wesley Church, Claremont, WA, 218
Wesleyan, Gawler, SA, 210
Wesleyan, Tataraimaka, 147
Whitley Memorial, New Plymouth, 140
Churchill, PM Winston, 121, 126, 194
Cistercians, 189, 204
Cité St Emilie, 47
Civil Defence, 67, 91
Civil Service, 228
Clackmannanshire, 117, 120
Clacton, 107, 110
Claerwen dam & river, 180
Claines, 61
Clare, SA, 199
Claremont, SA, 204
Claremont, WA, 201, 218, 222–3, 225
Clayton-le-Moors, 81
Cleckheaton, 86
Clerkenwell, 205
Clifford, 159
Clifton Hill, Vic, 59
Climpson, Sgt Leonard, 28
Clyde & Canal, 80, 211
Cobham, 104
Cockburn, Sir George, 87
Cockermouth, 189
Codford, 58, 74, 135, 137, 146, 150–1, 215
Coffs Harbour, NSW, 188
Colchester, 230
Cologne Farm, 31–2
Colonel Light Gardens, 203
Coma, WA, 222
Comines, 97
Commonwealth, 66, 89, 106, 113, 116, 224
Commonwealth/Imperial War Graves Commission,
  Bleuet Farm Cemetery, 81
  Choloy War Cemetery, 153
  Durnbach War Cemetery, 124
  Gordon Dump Cemetery, 210
  Grand Ravine British Cemetery, 44–5
  Hermies Hill British Cemetery, 243
  Houchin British Cemetery, 54
  Knightsbridge War Cemetery, 149
  Moeuvres Communal Cemetery Extension, 15, 18
  Oosttaverne Wood Cemetery, 104
  Ovillers Military Cemetery, 126
  Phaleron War Cemetery, 148
  Portsmouth Naval Memorial, 99
  Ste Marie Cemetery, Le Havre, 182–3
  Sydney Memorial, 218
  Villers-Bretonneux Australian National Memorial, 28, 208–209, 220
  Vis-en-Artois Memorial, 170–1
  Ypres (Menin Gate) Memorial, 82
Comrie Colliery, 126–7
Concord, NSW, 203
Congo Free State, 89
Conisbrough, 79–80, 87–9, 92
Connaught Rooms, Covent Garden, 115, 155, 197
Conservative Party, 172
Coogee, NSW, 186
Cook, Capt James, 131
Cook, NSW, 186
Cooker Quarry, 22–3
Cooperative Dairy Co, Te Kowhai, 133
Cooper, Gary, 228
Corey, Pte Ernest, 89
Corfe DSO, Lt Col Arthur, 104–105
Cork, 194
Cork, Co, 68
Cornell, Pte Aubrey, 28
Cornwall, 56, 106, 166
Coronet Post, 22, 27
Cortenwood Colliery, 88
Couillet Valley, 4
Counter-Reformation, 144
Covent Garden, 116, 155, 197–8
Coventry, 81
Cowdenbeath, 119, 123, 200
Craig-goch dam, 180
Crewe, 165
Crichton VC, James, 156
Cricklade, 191
Crimean War, 58
Cromer, 180
Cromwell, Oliver, 236
Cronulla, NSW, 188
Crook and Billy Row, 102
Crosby, 62–3
Cross VC, Arthur, 196
Crowborough Camp, 242
Croydon, 61, 99, 162, 186, 188
Crusaders, 183
Crystal Palace, 80, 105
Cubbington, 62
Culsalmond, 128

Cumberland, 189
Cumbria, 175, 189
Cuneo, Terence, 67
Cutler VC, Sir Roden, 78, 226
Cymbran, 163

Dagenham, 90–1
*Daily Mirror*, 116
Dalby, 119
Dalkeith, WA, 205, 222
Dalton-in-Furness, 189
Daly, SA, 199, 212
Danes, 204
Daniels VC, H, 91
Dannes-Camiers, 207
Darke, Sgt Frederick, 28
Dartford, 73, 93, 97, 100, 202, 216
Dartmoor, 58
David J Dunlop, 151
Daw Park, 203
Dawson, Sgt Albert, 28
Day DSC, Flt Sub Lt Harold, 173
DC Thompson, 121
De Rothschild, Anthony, 230
Dead Man's Corner, 2–5, 8–9
Dean Colliery, 117, 122, 126
Dean Copse, 21
Dean VC, Lt Donald, 47, 52, 93–117
Dean's Post, 52–4
Deccan, 161
Denaby & Cadeby Main Colleries Ltd, 86–7
Denaby & Main, 80, 86–8
Denmark, 78, 112, 114, 134, 157, 226, 243
  Royal House, 112–13
Dennistoun, 142
Denny, Pte Thomas, 28
Deputy Lieutenant, 65, 113
Derby, 101, 165
Derbyshire, 79, 101, 165
Devizes, 169
Devonport, 55, 69, 94, 135, 137, 146, 180, 214–15, 220, 227, 232, 235
Devonport, NZ, 145
Devonshire, 55–6, 58, 73, 90, 101, 166–68, 180, 215, 227–8, 236
Diamond Hill, 58
Dibgate Camp, 107
Dickens, Charles, 60
Diego Suarez (Antisiranana), 110
Dix Noonan Webb, 198
Doleful Post, 171
Domesday Book, 93, 115, 159, 228, 230, 236
Dominions, 116, 173
Donald, Capt William, 18
Doncaster, 80, 87
Dorchester, 167–8, 235
Dorchester Hotel, London, 91, 114, 129, 197

Dore & Bredwardine, 159, 163
Dorking, 95, 229
Dorsetshire, 154, 159, 166–8, 174, 191, 215, 235
Dorstone, 159
Douglas VC, HEM, 194
Doullens, 107–108
Dover, 93, 97–8, 107, 161, 229, 239
Down, Co, 186
Driefontein, 58
Dromore, 204
Drumheller, Alta, 120
Dublin, 206
Duke of Connaught, 196
Duke of Kent, 60, 77, 116, 157, 197, 225
Duke & Duchess of York, 128, 223
Dumbarton, 152
Duncan & Davies Ltd, 147
Duncan, Adam Viscount Camperdown, 121
Duncan, Cpl Joseph, 28
Dundee, 98, 119, 121–2
*Dundee Courier*, 125
Dunedin, 151, 155, 157
Dunfermline, 117–23, 125–30
Dunfermline Athletic FC, 123–4, 130
Dungog, NSW, 232
Dunkirk, 109
Dunolly, Vic, 70
Dunstable, 226, 231
Duntroon, 221
Durban, 110–11
Durham, Co, 62, 82, 102, 143
Durris, 127

Earl of Egmont, 131
Easington, 82
East African Airways, 114, 197
East Albury, NSW, 78, 226
East Ashford, 98
East Barnet, 163
East Ham, 230
East India Company, 58
East Preston, 100
Eastbourne, 162, 178
Eastern Maudit, 232
Eastry, 98
Eastwood, 100
Eaucourt l'Abbaye, 103
Eccles, 176
Eden Monaro, NSW, 186
Eder dam, 180
Edgbaston, 207, 233
Edinburgh, 124–5, 129, 131, 206, 211
Edmonton, 60, 162–3, 202
Edwards, Cpl Alfred, 28
Edwards VC, FJ, 114
Edwards VC, W, 91
Edwardstown, SA, 221

Eglinton Iron Works, 188
Egremont, 189
Egypt, 72, 75, 78, 86, 89, 94, 112, 132, 139, 148, 151, 157, 161, 181, 207, 210, 213–14, 219–21, 226, 233, 243
EKCO, 230
Elan River, Valley & Village, 179–80
Elan Valley Railway, 180
Elizabethans, 170
Ellery DCM, Sgt Frank, 5
Elliot VC, Rev'd Keith, 156–8
Elstree, 102
Eltham, NZ, 136, 148
Emergency Coastal Defence Batteries, 236
Engadine, NSW, 188
England Football Team, 189
England Rugby Team, 63
English Channel, 109
English Civil War, 68, 236
English Heritage, 96
Épehy & Battle of, 4, 13–14, 19, 32, 36–9, 47
Epping Forest, 103
Epsom, 167
Epstein, Jacob, 129
Erskine VC, John, 118
Essex, 90–1, 100, 102, 110, 154, 163, 192, 230, 234
Estaires, 139, 207
Étaples, 74, 104, 132, 135, 148, 150–1
Europe/an, 112, 125, 131, 172
European Tour (golf), 204
Evans Hotel, Dunolly, Vic, 70
Everton, 178
Ewshott, 150
Exeter, 168, 236

Fairbanks, Douglas, 60
Fairfax, Thomas, 236
Falkirk & Battles of Falkirk & Falkirk Muir 123, 210–11
Falmouth, 58, 106, 166
Fanque, Pablo, 125
Far East, 217
Faringdon, 96
Faversham, 105–106
Featherston & Camp, 136, 139, 146, 149
Felstrom, 143
Fenwick, Margaret, 121
Ferozepore, 228
Field Punishment No.2, 74, 139, 148
Fife, 117, 119–20, 122–3, 127–30, 200
Fife Coal Co, 122, 127
Fife Electric Power Co, 117
Fins & Ridge, 40–2
Fire Service, 67
First Jewish-Roman War, 183
Firth of Forth, 211

Fisher, G, 88
Fiskerton, 165
Fitzroy, NZ, 143–4
Fitzroy, Vic, 76–7, 212
Fixby, 84
Flanders, 4
Fleeceall Post, 39
Fleming, Pte John, 19
Flemington, Vic, 69
Flesquières, 10
Flinders, SA, 200
Flintshire, 164
Foch, Marshal Ferdinand, 1–2, 244
Foligno, 112
Folkestone, 69, 74, 107, 216, 220, 227–30, 242
Football Association Charity Shield & Cup, 204
Ford Motor Co, 90
Forden, 174, 177
Forest Row, 93
Forfar, 121
Forfarshire, 117, 119, 121
Forli, 112
Fort Bell, 24, 26
Fort Bull (Dyce), 24, 27
Fort Horsted, 104
Fort Lees, 24, 27
Forth Valley & Canal, 211
Fovant, 167
France, 56, 59, 62, 69, 74, 78, 81, 86–7, 89, 98, 103–104, 107, 109, 125–6, 133, 135, 137, 139, 148, 150–1, 153, 157, 161, 165, 170–3, 178–9, 182, 190–1, 193, 202, 208, 216, 220–1, 226–7, 232–3, 240, 242–4
Frankley Reservoir, 180
Frankston, 73
Freemasons, 113, 128, 155, 196
    Freemason's Hall, London, 116, 197, 198
    Heretaunga Lodge, 155
    St Luke's Lodge, 196
    St Michael Lodge, 113
    Sacdingbirna Lodge, 113
    Taranaki Lodge, 155
    Union Lodge, Dunfermline, 128–29
Freetown, 110
Fremantle, 215, 217–19
French Army, 110, 133
    First Army, 19, 47
French, FM Earl John, 106
Frickleton VC, Samuel, 156, 158
Frinton-on-Sea, 102
Frome, 166–8
Frome, SA, 201, 220
Frutigen, 153
Fulham, 90, 102, 106
Fullarton, SA, 206, 210
Furness Abbey, 189
Furness Railway, 189

Gainsborough, 83, 87
Gallipoli, 94, 182, 207, 209, 213, 219, 221
Galway, Co, 167
Garreg-ddu, 180
Gawler, SA, 199–200, 205–206, 209–10
Gaza, Third Battle of, 182
Gdańsk (Danzig), 144
GEC, 193
Geelong, Vic, 69
Geneva Convention, 110
Genoa, 80
George Hotel, Brecon, 160
German armed forces,
　Army, 109
　　Divisions,
　　　26th Infanterie, 12
　　　119th, 26
　　Regiments,
　　　2nd Guards, 37
　　　3rd, 46
　　　58th Infanterie, 26
　　　64th, 46
　　　396th, 46
　　　Jäger, 7
　Air Force/Luftwaffe, 189, 194
　Navy,
　　U-9, 80
　　U-97, 99
　　UC-74, 182
German Defence Ministry, 172
German New Guinea, 215
German War Cemetery, Maissemy, 22
Germany, 56, 78, 87, 95, 98, 124, 127, 143–4, 157, 160, 217, 226, 243
Gerrards Cross, 102
Ghezirah, 206
Gibraltar, 124
Gillick, Ernest, 170
Gippsland, Vic, 76–7
Giuseppe Miceli, 198
Glamorganshire, 169, 194–5
Glasgow, 110–11, 117, 125, 128, 130, 149
Glebe, NSW, 188, 234
Glen Innes, 140
Glen Parva Barracks, 67
Glenelg, SA, 203
Glenfield, NSW, 186
Global Demographics Ltd, 133
Glorious Revolution, 236
Gloucester, 61, 163
Gloucestershire, 87, 160
Glover, Sgt, 17
Glyndŵr, Owain, 174
Gommecourt, 62
Goodwood, SA, 201
Gorre, 62
Gort VC, Lt Col Viscount, 108

Gorton, 85
Gouzeaucourt, 1, 3–4, 6, 19, 40–2, 151, 193
Govan, 80
Goyder, SA, 221
Graceville, Qld, 119
Graham VC, Reginald, 196
Granada TV Rentals, 240
Grand Central Hotel, Belfast, 162
Grand Priel Wood, 31
Grand Ravin/e, 4, 44, 46
Grangemouth, 98, 123
Grant VC, John Gildroy, 156, 158
Granville Hotel, Ramsgate, 97
Gray, Pte W, 19
Grayndler, NSW, 186, 189
Great Malvern, 60–1
Great Marlow, 57
Great Western Railway & Hotel, 104, 169, 173
Greater London, 229
Greece, 105, 147–8, 182
Greenock, 110
Greenwich, 95
Greenwood OBE, John, 63
Greystanes, NSW, 188
Gricourt, 47
Grimaldi Bros, 152
Grimsby, 239
Grogan VC, GWStG, 194
Grouville, 56
Grove Park, 117, 169, 231
Guildford, 102, 162
Guildford, WA, 222–4
Guy, Sir Thomas, 64

Hackney, 97
Hackney, SA, 214
Haig, FM Sir Douglas, 2, 4
Hailsham, 176
Hailbeath, 119
Halifax, 80–1
Halton Park & Camp, 227, 230, 242
Hambledon, 95
Hamburg, 98
Hamilton, 160
Hamilton, Gen Sir Ian, 62, 182
Hamilton, NZ, 133, 144–5
Hamilton VC, John, 129
Hampshire, 80–90, 114, 137, 155, 162, 167–9, 216, 231, 234, 237
Hampstead, 60–1, 97, 101
Hampton Mill, 167
Hanzinelle, 75
Harefield, 59, 208, 216–17, 233
Harland & Wolff, 182
Harris, Rev'd RA, 210
Harris, William of Hayne, 56
Harrogate, 97, 133

# Index   271

Harrow, 93
Haslemere, 95
Hastings, NZ, 152–3, 156
Hatfield, 102
Havelock North, 152
Haverfordwest, 238–9
Havering, 90, 163
Havrincourt, Chateau Wood and Battle of, 1, 4, 9–13, 19, 44–5, 87, 242
Hawera, 131–4, 136, 147, 149, 152–3, 155–6
Hawke's Bay, 150, 152, 156
Hawthorn, SA, 209
Hawthorn, Vic, 219
Hay-on-Wye, 160, 169
Haydock, 83
Hayling Island, 137
Healey/Healy, Rfm Maurice, 6
Heathrow, 114, 197
Helena Vale, WA, 221
Helensburgh, NSW, 188
Heligoland Bight, Battle of, 80
Heliopolis, 71–2, 213, 221
Helmia, 181
*Help for Heroes*, 198
Hemel Hempstead, 55–6
Hendon, 101, 154–5
Henley Beach, SA, 201
Henry, Mayor Joseph, 89
Hereford, 164–5, 171–2
Herefordshire, 58, 159–60, 162–5, 171
Hermies, 10
Herne Hill, 93
Hertfordshire, 55–6, 63, 102, 110, 163, 167, 228, 230–1, 237, 239–40, 243
Hesdin, 103
Heudicourt, 42
Hever, 153
Heytesbury, 59
High Valleyfield, 120
Hildenborough, 194, 197
Hill 60, 58
Hill, Sgt R, 28
Hillingdon, 154
Hindenburg Line, Advanced & Support, 1, 3–4, 9, 13, 16–20, 23, 28–9, 31–2, 39, 45, 47, 51, 63
Hindmarsh, SA, 201, 205–206
Hinton VC, John, 156, 158
Hirsch VC, DP, 91
Hitchin, 228–30, 237, 239–40, 242–3
Hitchin Electrical Power Station, 239
HM Stationery Office, 216
Hobson, 152
Holbeck, 79, 85–6
Holborn, 100
Holbrook VC, Norman, 156
Holdsworthy, NSW, 232–3
Hollande, Pres François, 172

Hollingbourne, 97
Hollybush Inn, Hay-on-Wye, 160
Hollywood, 60
Holmescales, 178
Hong Kong, 111
Hornchurch, 90, 135, 137, 163
Hornsey, 163
Hospitals,
  Alfred, Melbourne, 70
  Allan Lodge Care Home, Bridge of Allan, 124
  Auckland, 134
  Bronllys, Brecon, 160
  Brook, Greenwich, 95
  Caulfield Repatriation, 71
  Chilton Croft Nursing Home, Sudbury, 56
  Craigwood Nursing Home, Coma, WA, 222
  Croydon General, 80
  Edgware General, Hendon, 155
  General Infirmary, Stafford, 176
  Gloucestershire Royal, Gloucester, 163
  Greenlane, Auckland, 132
  Guy's, London, 64
  Hereford County, 160
  Hereford County & City Lunatic Asylum, 165–6
  Hinckley & District, 64
  Hollywood Repatriation, Claremont, WA, 224–5
  Hospital de Monaco, 56
  Illoura Nursing Home, Norwood, Adelaide, 203
  King Edward VII, London, 104
  Langwarrin Venereal Disease Hospital, Frankston, Melbourne, 72–3
  Leicester City General, 64
  Leicester Isolation Hospital & Sanitorium, 64
  Leicester Royal Infirmary, 63
  Manor House, Folkestone, 227
  Melbourne Hospital, Vic, 71, 212
  Mendip Hospital, Wells, 167
  Monreith Aged Care Facility, Adelaide, 221
  Mount St Evins, Fitzroy, Vic, 76–7
  Newbridge, Salisbury, 168
  North Lonsdale, Barrow-in-Furness, 190
  Northern Hospital, Dunfermline, 129
  Orchard Hospital, Dartford, 74
  Paddington, 155
  Palmerston North, 142
  Park View Nursing Home, Bradford, 84
  Parkside Mental, SA, 206
  Pembury Hospital, Kent, 194
  Perth Royal infirmary, 128
  Priory Nursing Home, Wellington, 197
  Repatriation General Hospital, Daw Park, SA, 203
  Roose, Barrow-in-Furness, 191
  Roslyn Private Hospital, Arncliffe, NSW, 188
  Royal Sussex County, 186
  St James', Leeds, 228
  St Mary, Eastbourne, 162

St Thomas's, London, 62–4
St Vincent's, Fitzroy, 76
Shrewsbury, 174
Stratford, Inglewood, 147
Sunset, Dalkeith, WA, 205
Tenterden House Nursing Home, Bricket Wood, 56
Victoria, Kirkcaldy, 119
Westcliffe, 154
Woodend Hospital, Aberdeen, 128
Hotchkiss, 80
Hoth Frazer, 70
Hotham, Vic, 219
Houghton Regis, 226, 228
Huddersfield, 84
Hughes, Emlyn, 189
Hughes Bolckow Shipbreaking Co, 76
Hull, *see* Kingston
Hull VC, C, 91
Hulley, H, 88
Hulme VC, Alfred, 156, 158
Hummock Hill, SA, 200
Hunslet & Moor, 79, 83–6
Hunter VC, Cpl David, 13, 15–19, 51, 117–30
Hunter's Post, 15–18
Huntington, 165
Hurdcott, 59, 214, 216–17, 222–33
Hyde Park & Corner, London, 66, 91, 115, 129, 155, 196–7, 224
Hyde Park, SA, 208
Hythe, 227

*I Love a Lassie*, 126
Iceland, 65
Icknield Way, 230
Illinois Steel Corp, 118
Imperial London Hotels, 102
Inchy, 13, 15–18
India, 56, 78, 89–92, 94, 100–101, 112, 157, 159, 161, 226, 228–9, 237, 243
Indian Army, 92, 111, 228
 Indian Expeditionary Force D, 94
 School of Artillery, Kakul, 56
Inglewood, 131, 142–3, 147, 149–50
Inspector of Mines for Yorkshire & North Midlands, 88
Institution of Civil Engineers, 211
Interlaken, 153
Invercargill, 147
Ipswich, 239
Iraq, 78, 157, 226, 243
Ireland/Irish, 68, 70, 82, 89, 98, 161, 167, 170, 186, 194, 204–206
Irish Republican Army, 89, 194
Irish Sea, 99
Iron Age, 228
Iron Shipbuilding Co, 193

Isle of Man, 175, 222
Isle of Mull, 239
Isle of Wight, 101, 211
Islington, 163, 194
Ismailia, 151, 219
Israel, 183
Italy, 80, 111–12, 152, 165, 217

Jack, Simon, 63
Jacobites, 121, 204, 211
James Keiller & Sons, 121
James Martin & Co, 199, 200
Japan, 37, 78, 123, 131, 157, 226, 243–4
Japanese Navy, 110, 189
 *Mikasa*, 189
Jeddah, 111
Jennings OBE, Patrick, 204
Jersey, 56, 211
Jerusalem, 183
Jervois, 202
Jewish, 95, 144
Jewish Revolt, 183
Johannnesburg, 58, 175
Jones, Pte William, 18–19
Jordan, 183
Justice of the Peace, 113

Kaeo, 152
Kaitaia, 152
Kakul, 56
Kampala, 114, 197
Kanpur, 90
Kapa, James Joseph, 158
Kapunda, SA, 200
Karachi, 89–90, 94
Katanning, 215
Katoomba, NSW, 187
Kattschow, 144
Kay MBE, Benedict, 63
Keating, Lt Gen Tim, 157
Keighley, 81–3
Kelty, 119–20, 123
Kempston, 229, 240
Kenna VC, Edward, 78, 226
Kennedy DSO MC, Lt Donald, 5
Kensington, 60–61, 101
Kent, 54, 90, 93, 95–102, 105–107, 110, 113, 115–16, 120, 153–4, 160, 171, 194, 196–7, 202, 216, 220, 226–7, 229–30
 Special Constabulary, 102
Kent Town, SA, 212
Kenya, 110, 114, 197
Kenya Police Force, 195
Kenyatta, Pres, 114, 197
Ker VC, Allan, 196
Keswick, SA, 220
Keys, Sir William, 226

## Index

Khedivial Mail Steam Ship & Graving Dock Co, 151
Kidde, Revd John, 63
Kilburn, 155
Kilkenny, SA, 201
Kilninian & Kilmore, 239
Kilwinning, 188
Kimberley, Relief of, 58
Kimpton, 240
Kincardineshire, 127
King Alfred, 56
King Charles I, 118
King Christian V (Denmark), 112
King David II, 118
King Edward I, 118, 211
King Edward III, 189
King Edward VI, 64, 236
King Edward VII, 80, 126, 180
King Edward VIII, 184
King Edward the Confessor, 230
King Frederick IX (Denmark), 114
King George IV, 60
King George V, 62, 75, 87–8, 105, 113, 126, 128, 151, 171, 182, 193, 216–17, 242
King George VI, 91, 108, 208, 223
King Henry IV, 174
King Henry V, 93
King Henry VIII, 93
King James I & VI, 118
King Leopold II, 89
King Malcolm III, 118
King of the Belgians, 4
King Stephen, 189
King William III (William of Orange), 236
King's Cross Station, London, 96
Kingsford-Smith, NSW, 186
Kingseat, 117, 119–20, 126
Kingston-upon-Hull, 238–9
Kington, 159, 162, 164
Kirk, Alfred, 62
Kirkham, 178
Kiwi Polish Co, 138
Knight, 2Lt John, 104
Knockaloe, 175
Knoll Post, 39
Kogarah, NSW, 232
Koongamia, WA, 223

La Linea, 124
Lake Victoria, 114, 197
Lambeth, 64, 93, 101
Lanarkshire, 125
Lancashire, 57–8, 62, 81–3, 85, 97, 111, 147, 163, 174–8, 186, 189, 192, 212, 234–5
  Combination League, 179
Lancaster, 235
Lancaster Gate, 63

Lancaster House, London, 77, 157, 225
Langwarrin Internment Camp, 73
Larkhill, 59
Latton, 189
Lauder, Capt John, 126
Lauder, Sir Harry, 125–6
Lauenburg (Lebork), 143–44, 147
Laurent Barracks, Linton, NZ, 156
Laurent VC, Sgt Harry, 1, 3, 5–7, 131–58
Laverton, Vic, 71
Le Havre, 59, 104, 165, 182–3, 214, 216
Le Tréport, 193
Le Verguier, 19, 24–6, 38, 74, 216
League of Nations, 105
Leamington Spa, 55, 60–2, 67
Leeds, 79, 83–6, 91–92, 228–9
  City Art Gallery, 91
  School Board, 87
Leicester, 65–7, 161
  Siege of 1645, 68
Leicestershire, 65, 67, 96
  County Council, 67
Leigh-on-Sea, 100, 154
Leith, 128
Leith, Hull & Hamburg Steam Packet Co, 98
Lemnos, 220
Lempire, 32, 171
Lens, 51–2, 62, 104
Leominster, 160
Lepperton, 143
Letchworth, 240
Leverton, 96
Levin & Co, 155
Lewes Prison, 75
Lewis, A Neville, 130
Lewis VC, LCpl Allan, 19, 34, 38–9, 159–73
Lewisham, NSW, 232
Libya, 149
Lichfield, 176
Lifton, 55–6
Lihou, Sgt James, 28
Lillington, 62
Limerick, 194
Lincoln, 123
Lincoln's Inn, London, 101
Lincolnshire, 83, 96–7, 234, 242
Lindsay Colliery, 122
Linton & Military Camp, 142, 156
Lion Hill, WA, 222
Lisbon, 217
Little Bill Copse, 22, 29
Little Blitz, 241
Little Holbeck, 83
Liverpool, 57–8, 62, 111, 141, 146, 149, 163, 178, 190, 202, 233
Liverpool FC, 189
Livingston, 122

Llanddewi Rhydderch, 100
Llandeilo Graban, 169
Llandrindod Wells, 180–1
Llandrinio, 176–7
Llandysilio, 177
Llanfyllin, 177, 179
Llanganten, 163
Llanwrthwl, 179
Llanymynech, 176
Llewynolin, 173
Lloyd George, PM David, 184
Lochgelly, 117, 119
Lochnagar Crater, 244
Lochore, 120
Lochrin Autos, 124–5
Lockhart, Robert, 118
*Logan's Collection of Highland Bagpipe Music*, 130
*Lolita*, 230
London, 55–6, 58, 60, 61, 63, 66, 75, 77, 80, 90–3, 95–8, 100–102, 104, 106, 114–16, 118, 129, 133, 136, 140, 144, 150–2, 154–5, 157, 160, 162–3, 169, 173, 182, 186, 192, 194, 197–8, 205, 209, 211, 216–17, 223–5, 228, 230, 235, 239–40
   City of, 64, 211
   Library, 241
   East India Docks, 211
   Motor Transport Repair Depot, 231
   West India Docks, 211
Long Hope, 98
Longbridge Deverill, 69, 216
Longleat & Priory, 170
Loos & Battle of, 170, 227
Lord Ashcroft Victoria Cross Collection, 92, 198
Lord Michael Ashcroft, 92, 158, 198
*Lord of the Rings*, 114
Lough Neagh, 204
Louth, 234
Lowestoft, 97
Luton, 227, 231–2, 234–5, 244
Lutyens, Sir Edwin, 208
Lyme Regis, 159, 166–7
Lyndhurst, 167
Lyndoch, SA, 206
Lys, Battle of, 139
Lyte, Revd Francis, 236

Maadi, 202
Machine Gun Corps Memorial, 196
Machynlleth, 176
Madagascar, 110–11
Maddiston, 123
Mahimahi Contractors Ltd, 153
Maiden Bower, 228
Maidstone, 194
Maisemore, 60
Majunga (Mahajanga), 110
Malakand, 228

Malakoff Farm, 32
Malaysia, 81, 111
Malta, 80, 111, 221
Maltby Colliery, 87
Malvern, Vic, 68
Manawatu-Wanganui, 150
Manchester, 85, 175, 212
Manganui, 153
Mangorei, 140
Manly, NSW, 218–19
Maori, 131
Maplin Sands, 211
Marconi Marine, 193
*Marillion*, 230
Marks, 2Lt ROC, 5
Marlborough Club, 241
Marlborough-Windham Club, 241
Marne, Second Battle of, 139
Marquess of Bath, 170
Marsden, Lt Col TR, 20
Marseille, 161, 202, 207–208, 210, 214, 219–20, 233
Marton Chirbury, 174
Martyn, Cpl Henry, 28
Marylebone, 102
Mascot, NSW, 187–9
Massachusetts, 89, 118
Matupa, 152
Mauritius, 112
Maxim Nordenfelt Guns and Ammunition Co, 193
May Bros & Co, 199
May Copse, 39
Mayo, Co, 82
McDonald, Cpl William, 28
McFarlane, Pte D, 18–19
McKenna VC, E, 91
McNess VC, F, 91
Melbourne, 59, 68–73, 75–7, 188, 206, 217, 223–5
   City Council, 76
Melrose Abbey, 118
Mentone, Vic, 70
Merchant Navy, 56, 101, 230, 237
Merchant Taylors' Company, 63
Merionethshire, 174
Merton, 197
Mesopotamia, 94
Messines, Battle of, 104
Messrs Haythorne Davis & Co, 79
Metz, 8
Meurthe-et-Moselle, 153
Meuse-Argonne front, 1
M'Ewing, Cpl, 17
Mexborough, 84, 86
MI5, 189
Michael Ashcroft Trust, 198
Middle Ages, 115, 236
Middle East, 202, 215
Middlesbrough, 85

# Index 275

Middlesex, 60, 93, 100–101, 154–5, 162–3, 167, 202
   County Council, 217
Middleton, 83
Midland Junction, WA, 222
Midland Railway Co, 86, 165, 235
Midlothian, 123–4, 128, 206
Milford Haven, 237–8
Mill Spinney, 22, 24–6
Millbank, 97
Miller, Cpl Keith, 28
Milos, 182
Milstead, 97
Milton Regis & Creek, 93, 95–6, 99, 101, 106, 230
   Rural District Council, 105
Milwaukee, WI, 219
Mitcham, 186–7, 197
Mitchell, RQMS Jack, 28
Moascar, 71
Moe, Vic, 188
Moeuvres, 13, 15–18, 45, 51, 99, 125
Moggill, 119
Möhne Dam, 180
Mombasa, 110, 114, 197
Mompezat, Henri de Laborde de, 114
Monash, Lt Gen Sir John, 223
Monmouth, 164
Monmouthshire, 81, 100, 106, 160, 163, 168, 180
Mons, 58
Montazah, 71, 207
Monterey, 187
Montgomery, 173–4, 177, 179
Montgomeryshire, 173–4, 176–7
   Challenge Cup, 179
   League, 179
Montréal, 178
Mooltan/Multan, Battle, Fort, Revolt & Siege, 227, 229
Moonta, SA, 206
Moore, William, 187
Moore VC, MSS, 194
Moray, 118
Morecambe Bay, 189
Morphettville, SA, 202, 213
Morrinsville, 133, 138
Morris cars, 128
Morton, 123
Morwell, Vic, 77
Mosman Park, WA, 219
Mount Albert, 143
Mount Barker, SA, 201
Mount Crawford, SA, 199
Mount Eden, 145
Mount Fuji, 131
Mount Taranaki/Egmont, 131
Mount Waverley, Vic, 70
Mountain VC, A, 91

Mudros, 207, 209, 213–14, 219
Mughals & Empire, 229
Muiravonside, 123
Mulhill, Pte Terence, 18
Munhall, PA, 118
Münster, 124
Murchison Falls, 114, 197
Murrumbeena, 69
Museums,
   Army Museum of Western Australia, 225
   Australian War Memorial, 73–4, 77–8, 225–6
   Bedfordshire & Hertfordshire Regiment, 244
   British, 101, 187
   Dolphin Yard Sailing Barge Museum, Sittingbourne, 105
   Imperial War, 92, 129–30, 198
   National Army, Waiouru, NZ, 158
   Newarke Houses, Leicester, 68
   Queen Elizabeth II Army Memorial Museum, NZ, 158
   Royal Highland Fusiliers, 130
   Royal Leicestershire Regiment, 68
   Royal Welch Fusiliers, 185
   Rugby Football Union, Twickenham, 198
   Scottish Mining, 122
Mustapha, 207

Nairobi, 114, 197
Nanango, Qld, 226
Nant-y-Gro dam, 180
Napier, 135, 146, 156
Naples, 111–12, 152
Napoleon I, 236
Napoleonic Wars, 181
Natal, 237
National Coal Board, 88
National Health Service, 166
National Memorial Arboretum, Alrewas, 78, 157–8, 226, 243
National Provincial (Westminster) Bank, 91
Nauroy, 32
Naval Construction & Armaments Co, 193
Navy Hotel, Plymouth, 58
Nazis, 95, 144
Neame VC, Maj Gen Philip, 58
Neath, 169, 171–2
Nedlands, WA, 218–19
Needles, 211
Nellis, 2Lt Harry, 42
Nelson, NZ, 158
Neolithic, 118, 189
Nepal, 78, 157, 226, 243
Netherlands, 78, 157, 226, 236, 243
   Royal Netherlands Navy, 121
Netherton, 132–3
New Forest, 167
New Parkside, SA, 204

New Plymouth (Ngamotu), 131, 134, 139–40, 143–5, 147–9
New South Wales, 73, 78, 186–8, 201–203, 207, 218–20, 225–6, 232, 234
New York, 89, 118, 217
New Zealand, 78, 105, 116, 127, 131–3, 137–8, 140–1, 143–4, 146, 148–52, 155–8, 170, 196, 224, 226, 234, 243
New Zealand armed forces, 158
  National Military Reserve, 158
  New Zealand Army, 138
    Division, 1, 4, 9
    Brigades,
      1st NZ Brigade, 9
      3rd NZ (Rifles) Brigade, 1, 4, 9
      4th NZ Infantry Reserve, 135, 137
    Bns/Regts,
      Auckland Regt,
        1st Auckland, 9
      3rd NZ Contingent, 105
      4th Reserve, 135
      11th Taranaki Rifles, 136, 151
      11th Regt Territorials, 134
      14th Bn, National Reserve, 141
      Manaia Bn, 155
      Mounted Rifles, 139
      New Zealand Infantry, 147–8
        21st Bn, 149
      New Zealand Regt, 142
      New Zealand Rifle Bde, 132, 152
        1st NZ Rifle Bde, 4, 5, 7–8
        2nd NZ Rifle Bde, 1, 4–9, 131, 151
        3rd NZ Rifle Bde, 4
        4th NZ Rifle Bde, 4, 8
        5th Reserve Bn, 137, 146
        Depot, Brocton, 136
      Ranfurly Rifles, 146
      Taranaki Regt, 155
        1st Bn, 155
        2nd Bn, 141
        Coy, 100
      Trentham Regt, 132
        1st Bn, 132
        2nd Bn, 151
      Waikato Mounted Rifles, 139
      Wellington,
        1st Wellington, 135
          11th Taranaki Coy, 148
        3rd Reserve, Wellington, 135, 140
        3rd Wellington, 135–7
        4th Reserve Wellington, 137
      Wellington West Coast Regt, 155
        3rd Bn, 145
  Home Guard, 145, 155, 158
    Group No.8A, Home Guard, 155
  Interim Army, 141
  New Zealand Medical Corps/Medical, 149,
1st New Zealand Field Ambulance, 148, 150
1st New Zealand General Hospital, Brockenhurst, 135, 146, 148
2nd New Zealand Field Ambulance, 135, 150
2nd New Zealand Hospital, Walton-on-Thames, 136–7
3rd New Zealand Field Ambulance, 132, 135, 137
3rd New Zealand General Hospital, Codford, 146
4th New Zealand Field Ambulance, 135
New Zealand Convalescent Hospital, Hornchurch, 135, 137
New Zealand General Hospital, Abbassia, 151
HQ London, 150
Reserve Bn, Bulford, 150
New Zealand Stationary Hospital, Amiens, 132
New Zealand Expeditionary Force, 136, 151–2
New Zealand Regular Force, 141
Other units,
  2nd Anzac Reinforcement Camp, 151
  3rd New Zealand Entrenching Bn, 150
  5th Motor Transport Workshops, 141
  10th Coastal Regt RNZA, 141
  33rd Specialist Coy, 145
  35th Army Troops Salvage Coy, 141
  Auckland Machine Gun Coy, 4
  B Group, Codford, 151
  Base Depot, 141
  C Group, 137
  Camp Staff Linton, 141
  Construction Coy RNZE, 141
  General Base Depot, Étaples, 148
  Junior Cadets, 140
  National Military Reserve, 141
    12th Coy, 145
  New Zealand Army Service Corps, 147
  New Zealand Base Depot, Étaples, 132, 137, 148
  New Zealand Command Depot, Codford, 135, 137, 146
  New Zealand Cyclist Coys, 139
  New Zealand Discharge Depot, Torquay, 148
  New Zealand Division Lewis Gun School, 135
  New Zealand Infantry & General Base Depot, Étaples, 135, 139, 150–1
  No.1 NZ Entrenching Bn, 135
  No.3 NZ Entrenching Bn, 139–40
  Ordnance No.2 Sub Depot, 141
  Otago Machine Gun Coy, 4

Index    277

  Post & Telegraph Corps, 145
  Reserve Depot, Ewshott, 150
  Royal New Zealand Engineers, 142
  Senior Cadets, 140
  Wellington Machine Gun Coy, 4
 Permanent Defence Staff, 155
 Reserve of Officers & Supplementary List, 152, 155
 Retired List of Officers, 155
 Territorial Force, 140, 151–2
 Volunteers, 149
Royal New Zealand Air Force, 141, 153
 No.47 Sqn Air Training Corps, 155
Royal New Zealand Navy,
 HMNZT 33, 44, 53, 63 & 78 *Navua*, 151
 HMNZT 52 *Makoia*, 139
 HMNZT 71 *Port Lyttleton*, 136–7
 HMNZT 79 *Ruapehu*, 135
 HMNZT 82 *Pakeha*, 135
 HMNZT 86 *Maunganui*, 146
 HMNZT 92 & 110 *Ruahine*, 151–2
 HMNZT 94 *Arawa*, 137
 HMNZT 99 *Athenic*, 149
 HMNZT 100 & 108 *Ulimaroa*, 136, 140, 146
 Naval Auxiliary Patrol Service, 158
New Zealand Government, 131
 Defence, 157
 Governor General, 155, 157
 Parliament, 157
 Premier/Prime Minister, 131, 139
New Zealand Historic Places Trust, 156
New Zealand Merchant Navy, 158
New Zealand Post & Telegraph, 145, 157
New Zealand Shipping Co, 152
Newcastle, Alta, 120
Newcastle upon Tyne, 133, 161–2, 210
Newfoundland, 78, 157, 226, 243
Newington, 64, 96
Newport, 168
Newry, Raid on & Abbey, 204–205
 Town FC, 204
Newton Colliery, 83
Ngorongoro Crater, 114, 197
Nice, 69
Nightingale, Florence, 64
Noeux-les-Mines, 241
Nord-Pas-de-Calais, 172, 244
Norfolk, 101, 178, 180–1
Normanby, 134
Normandy, 112, 133, 236
Normans & Conquest, 56, 66, 204, 230
Normanton, 165
Norrie, Lt Gen Sir Willoughby & Lady, 155, 157
North Atlantic, 217
North Aylesford, 120
North Bondi, 78, 226
North Caulfield, 72

North Eastern Kenya, 195
North German Lloyd, 217
North Island, NZ, 131
North Melbourne, 68, 72
North Russia, 116, 184
North Sea, 109, 244
North Wales Heroes' Memorial, 184
North West Frontier & Province, 56, 91–2, 226–8
Northamptonshire, 232
Northcote, Vic, 59, 134, 211
Northern Ireland, 204
 Football Team, 204
 Troubles, 204
Northern Wars, 144
Northumberland, 65, 133, 210
Norval, Provost, 126
Norwich, 125, 233
Norwood, SA, 204, 206
Notre Dame de Lorette, 172
Nottinghamshire, 60, 62, 165
Nyeri, 114, 197

Oakley East, Vic, 70
Oatlands, Tas, 212
O'Brien, Cpl William, 5
O'Connor, Pte, 110
Offenders Prohibition Act, 203
Ohangai, 132
Old Pretender, 121
Oldbury, 195
Olympic Games, 224
Omagh, 161
Onehunga, 132
Opel, 123
Operation Ironclad, 110
Operation Steam Line Jane, 110
Opunake, 132, 149–50
Orange Free State, 175
Orchard Post, 33, 35
Order of Druids,
 Welshpool Lodge, 179
Orders, Decorations & Medals,
 1914 Star (Mons Star), 173, 198, 244
 1914/15 Star, 78, 92, 116–17, 158, 173, 198, 238, 244
 1939–45 Star, 117
 Africa General Service Medal 1902–56, 173
 Army Long Service & Good Conduct Medal, 227
 British Empire Medal, 113
 British War Medal 1914–20, 61, 67, 78, 92, 95, 116–17, 130, 142, 158, 173, 185, 198, 226, 238, 244
 Colonial Auxiliary Forces Long Service Medal, 127
 Colonial Police Medal, 195
 Defence Medal 1939–45, 67, 117, 198

Distinguished Conduct Medal, 19, 23, 28, 54, 63, 74, 78, 89, 208
Distinguished Service Cross, 99
Distinguished Service Medal, 99
Distinguished Service Order, 20, 28, 99, 104, 107, 110, 157, 223
Edward Medal, 88
Efficiency Decoration (Territorial), 65, 66, 68, 107, 113, 117, 127, 198
Efficiency Medal, 127, 130
Efficiency Medal (New Zealand), 127
George Cross, 88, 130
Imperial Service Medal, 126, 130
Imperial Service Order, 126
Imperial Yeomanry Long Service Medal, 184
India General Service Medal 1854–95, 228
India General Service Medal 1909–35, 92
India Medal 1895–1902, 227–8
Italy Star, 117
Khedive's Sudan Medal 1910, 172
King George V Silver Jubilee Medal 1935, 68
King George VI Coronation Medal 1937, 68, 92, 116–17, 130, 158, 198, 226
King's South Africa Medal, 58
Mentioned in Despatches, 92, 99, 105, 109, 112, 117, 161, 198, 244
Mercantile Marine War Medal, 95
Meritorious Service Medal, 28
Military Cross, 23, 42, 63, 89, 157
Military Medal, 17, 28, 54, 63, 87, 89, 92, 182, 185, 208
Militia Long Service Medal, 127
New Zealand War Service Medal 1939–45, 158
Order of Australia, 78, 223, 226
Order of Leopold (Belgium), 89, 92
Order of Leopold II (Belgium), 89
Order of St Michael & St George, 78, 131, 157, 223, 226
Order of the Bath, 107, 157, 223
Order of the British Empire, 63, 113, 117, 204
Order of the Crown (Belgium), 89
Order of the Dannebrog, 112–13, 117
Order of the Elephant (Denmark), 112
Order of the Garter, 197
Queen Elizabeth II Coronation Medal 1953, 68, 92, 117, 130, 158, 198, 226
Queen Elizabeth II Silver Jubilee Medal 1977, 116–17, 158
Queen's Gallantry Medal, 113
Queen's South Africa Medal, 58, 175
Royal Victorian Order, 157
Special Reserve Long Service & Good Conduct Medal, 127
Territorial Decoration, 66, 223
Territorial Efficiency Medal, 127, 182, 198
Territorial Force Efficiency Medal, 177, 184–5
Territorial Force War Medal, 198
Victory Medal 1914–19, 61, 67, 78, 92, 116–17, 130, 142, 158, 173, 185, 198, 226, 238, 244
Volunteer Long Service Medal, 127, 184
Volunteer Long Service Medal for India and the Colonies, 127
Volunteer Officers' Decoration, 66, 223
Volunteer Reserves Service Medal, 66, 127
War Medal 1939–45, 67–8, 117, 158, 198
Orient Line, 224
Orient Steam Navigation Co, 217
Orleans Club, 239, 241
Osborne, Maj Gen Edmund, 107
Oswestry, 174–5
United, 179
Otago, 138
Ottoman Empire, 183
Ovillers-la-Boisselle, 210
Oxenhope, 80–1
Oxford, 166, 227, 242
Oxfordshire, 166

Paardeberg, 58
Pacific, 67, 151, 218
Pacific & Orient Steam Navigation Co, 215
Pacific Steam Navigation Co, 182
Paddington & Station, 55, 60, 154, 173
Padua, 112
Paglieta, 112
Pakistan, 78, 89–90, 157, 226, 229, 243
Paleolithic, 228
Palestine, 182–3
Pall Mall, 241
Palmerston North, 140–1, 145, 150, 156
Panama Canal, 224
Pancras, 102
Papua New Guinea, 119
Paris, 74, 108
Parker Copse, 22–3
Parkhouse Camp, 69, 214, 216, 220
Parkside, SA, 205
Parliamentarians, 121, 236
Parry, Lt W, 23
Pattrick, Lt HB, 5
Payne VC, Keith, 78, 226
Payneham, SA, 201, 206
Pearson VC, J, 91
Pembrokeshire, 81, 237–9
Pen-y-garreg, 180
Penang, 81
Peninsular & Oriental Steam Navigation Co, 98
Pennington, SA, 203
Pennsylvania, 118
Penrhyndeudraeth, 174
Percheron, Daniel, 172
Percival, Lt Gen Arthur, 37
Perham Down, 73–4, 216, 233–4
Perlin, 147

Perth Prison, 128
Perth, WA, 215, 217–19, 222–3, 225
Perugia, 112
Peshawar, 89–90
Peterborough, SA, 221
Peterhead, 238
Phillips, Pte John, 18–19
Picardy, 170
Pickering, WH, 88
Piel Island, 189
*Pip, Squeak & Wilfred*, 116, 173, 244
Piraeus, 217
Pirton, 228
Ploegsteert, 103
Plumer, FM Lord, 106
Plumstead, 154
Plymouth, 56–9, 73, 90, 140, 151
Plympton, SA, 205
Point Cook, 71
Poland/ish, 144, 211
Polmont, 210–11
Pommern, 143
Pontefract, 229
Pontru, 23–4, 26
Pontruet, 23, 30, 32, 47–9, 51, 62
Pontypool, 100
Poole, 174
Poona, 161
Port Adelaide, 201, 203, 221
Port Augusta, 203
Port Chalmers, 151
Port Gawler, 199
Port Germein, 203
Port Glasgow, 151
Port MacDonnell, SA, 200
Port Pirie, SA, 203, 212
Port Said, 148, 213
Port Soderick, 222
Portadown, 186
Portland, 208, 215, 234
Post Office, 126, 211, 229
Potsdam Agreement, 144
Potter, John, 187
Poulter VC, A, 91
Powys, 174, 184–5
Pozières, 207, 220
Prees Heath, 165
Price DCM, Cpl TA, 23
Price, Lt RL, 25
Prince Arthur, 196
Prince of Wales, 103, 184
Prince Philip, 78, 113, 225
Prince Regent, 60
Prince, WH, 88
Princess Elizabeth, 114, 197
Princess Victoria, 60
Privy Councillor, 63

Prospect, SA, 201, 205–206
Prost, Philippe, 172
Provincial Surgical Club of Great Britain, 65
Prussian Confederation, 144
Puchevillers, 89
Punjab & Frontiere, 228–9
Purfleet, 231
Pylos, 148

Quadrilateral, 33, 35
Quarries, 33
Queanbeyan, NSW, 232
Queen Alexandra, 80, 180
Queen Elizabeth I, 56
Queen Elizabeth II, 78, 91, 180, 225
Queen Elizabeth, Queen Mother, 91
Queen Margrethe I (Denmark), 114
Queen Margrethe II (Denmark), 114
Queen Mary, 88, 128, 216 217
Queen Victoria, 60, 64, 93, 157
Queen Victoria Building, Sydney, 225
Queen Victoria Diamond Jubilee, 199
Queensland, 70, 105, 119, 187, 201, 226, 232
Quid Copse & Post, 33, 39

Radnor West, 160
Radnorshire, 160, 164, 179
Rafferty, Ronan, 204
Raleigh, Sir Walter, 187
Ramallah, 183
Ramsden, James, 189, 193
Ramsgate, 97
Randwick, NSW, 188, 207
Rawlinson, Gen Lord Henry, 4, 20
Rayleigh, 90
Rayne, 128
Raynes VC, JC, 91
Reading, 195, 220, 242,
Red Army, 144
Redfern, NSW, 186
Redhill, SA, 199, 210, 212
Reedy Creek, SA, 211
Reformation, Protestant, 118, 144, 153
Regent Hotel, Leamington Spa, 60–1
Regent's Park Barracks, London, 160
Reid, John, 118
Remuera, 153
Reninghelst, 103
Renmark, SA, 203
Returned & Services League of Australia, 78, 225–6
Returned Services Association (NZ), 157
Returned Soldiers & Sailors Imperial League of
 Australia, 224
Reykjavik, 65
Rhayader, 164
Rhyl, 178
Ribécourt, 44

Richmond & Park, 103
Rickmansworth, 167
Ridley, Harold, 64
Rimington, Dame Stella, 189
Ring of Remembrance, 172–3, 244
Ringwood, Vic, 188
River Canche, 109
River Dart, 236
River Nile, 114, 197
River Severn, 174
River Wandle, 187
River Wye, 159
*Roamin' in the Gloamin*, 126
Robert the Bruce, 118, 121, 125
Robinson, LCpl, 46
Rochdale, 177
Rochester, 104
Rochford, 90
Rockdale, NSW, 232
Rode, 167
Rodger, T Menzies, 130
Romans, 93, 183, 187, 211, 230
    Twelfth Legion, 183
Romford, 90, 163
Ronssoy, Wood & Spur, 19, 32, 34–8, 171, 182
Rose & Crown pub, Hunslet, 86
Rose Inn, Sittingbourne, 93
Rose Park SA, 204
Rosebury, NSW, 187
Ross, 159
Ross, Cpl I, 17
Rosyth, 98
Rotherham, 83, 86
Roundhay, 84
Rouelles, 59, 233
Rouen, 59, 103, 117, 135, 220, 242
Roupell VC, GRP, 114
Royal Academy, 129
Royal Air Force, 20, 92, 123, 242
    90 Sqn, 123
    101 Sqn, 153
    Administrative & Special Duties Branch, 61
    RAF Hospital, Changi, 124–5
    RAF Volunteer Reserve, 61, 123
Royal College of Surgeons, 65
Royal Danish Ballet, 114
Royal Exhibition Building, Melbourne, 223
Royal Leamington Spa, *see* Leamington Spa
Royal Mail Steam Packet Co, 182
Royal National Lifeboat Institution, 236
Royal Navy, 79, 80, 123, 159, 168, 189, 194, 196, 211
    7th Cruiser Squadron, 80
    Auxiliary Patrol Base, Grimsby, 239
    Commands,
        Dover, 109
        Nore, 109

First Lord of the Admiralty, 131
Mediterranean Fleet, 80
Reserves,
    Royal Fleet, 80
    Royal Naval Reserve, 98, 238–9
Ships,
    AT *Varsova*, 94
    HMA1 *Hermione/Mayfly* (airship), 192, 194
    HMHS *Assaye*, 214
    HMHS *Devanha*, 207
    HMHS *Dieppe*, 161
    HMHS *Dover Castle*, 101
    HMHS *Grantully Castle*, 233
    HMHS *Guildford Castle*, 59
    HMHS *Liege*, 193
    HMHS *Newhaven*, 137
    HMHS *Panama*, 135
    HMHS *Pieter de Coninck*, 202
    HMHS *Rewa*, 221
    HMHS *Salta*, 94
    HMHS *St Andrew*, 242
    HMHS *St David*, 148, 233
    HMHS *St George*, 220
    HMS *Aboukir*, 79–80
    HMS *Admirable*, 238
    HMS *AE2*, 215
    HMS *Albion*, 238
    HMS *Attentive III*, 239
    HMS *Beatrice*, 238
    HMS *Blenheim*, 238
    HMS *Canopus*, 79
    HMS *Clacton*, 213
    HMS *Cormorant*, 239
    HMS *Cressy*, 80
    HMS *Europa*, 238
    HMS *Formidable*, 98
    HMS *Furious*, 79
    HMS *Goliath*, 79
    HMS *Halcyon*, 238
    HMS *Hermione*, 194
    HMS *Hogue*, 80
    HMS *Holland I*, 189
    HMS *Kingfisher*, 239
    HMS *Marmara*, 98
    HMS *Nairn*, 238
    HMS *Osiris*, 238
    HMS *Pekin*, 238
    HMS *Pelorus*, 239
    HMS *Pembroke II*, 98
    HMS *Peony*, 238
    HMS *Prince George*, 79
    HMS *Queen Elizabeth*, 182
    HMS *Rodney*, 159
    HMS *Syringa*, 238
    HMS *Turbulent*, 147
    HMS *Victory*, 79
    HMS *Vimiera*, 109

Index    281

HMS *Vindictive*, 79
HMS *Vivid*, 238
HMS *Vivid III*, 239
HMS *Wallington*, 239
HMS *Westphalia (Cullist, Hayling, Jurassic & Prim)*, 98–9
HMS *Whitley*, 109
HMT *Andania*, 221
HMT *Arcadian*, 180
HMT *Armagh*, 220
HMT *Ausonia*, 219
HMT *Borda*, 207
HMT *Clan McGillivray*, 213, 221
HMT *Dilwara*, 110
HMT *Kanowna*, 221
HMT *Kildonan Castle*, 148
HMT *Lake Michigan*, 220
HMT *Maryland*, 202
HMT *Northland*, 94
HMT *Raranga*, 75
HMT *Southland*, 221
HMT *Suffolk*, 221
HT *Arawa*, 202
HT *Arcadian*, 132
HT *Ceramic*, 59
HT *Ivernia*, 219
HT *Longola*, 161
HT *Mamani*, 233
HT *Ormonde*, 221–2
HT *Simla*, 207
HT *Somerset*, 214
HT *Tunisian*, 139
HT *Ulysses*, 213
HT *Vasnu*, 94
Royal Naval Air Service, 98
Royal Naval Division, units appear under British Army
Royal Observer Corps, 67
Royal Welsh Warehouse of Newtown, 179
Royston, 240
Rugby World Cup, 63
Ruislip, 154
Runcie, Archbishop Robert, 63
Rüsselsheim am Main, 124
Russia, 244
Russo-Japanese War, 189
Ryder Cup, 204
Ryhope Colliery, 82

St Andrew's Golf Club, Yonkers, NY, 118
St Asaph, 164
St Clement, 127
St Cynfelin, 174
St Eloi, 104
St Giles, London, 93, 100–102
St Helena, 236
St James's Theatre, London, 241

St John Ambulance, 61
St Kilda, Vic, 134
St Leonards-on-Sea, 137
St Marylebone, 60, 133
St Olave, 235
St Omer, 103, 137
St Pancras, 60
St Patrick, 76
St Pol, 108
St Quentin, 19, 23, 216
St Quentin Canal, 32
St Quirinus, 153
St Thomas Becket, 64
Ste Émélie, 36
Ste Hélène, 47, 49, 51
Sadlier VC, Clifford, 223
Salford, 175–6
Saline, 123
Salisbury, 167–8, 191
Salisbury Plain, 69, 75, 215, 220
Samana, 228
San Diego, 219
San Vito, 112
Sanders VC, G, 91
Sandhurst, 58
Sandridge, 231
Sarpi Camp, 220
Savona, 152
Savoy Hotel, London, 115
Saxons, 56, 115, 230, 236
Saxony-Anhalt, 160
Scandinavia, 114
Scapa Flow, 98
Schlund, 2Lt Johann, 242
Schneider, Henry, 189
Schools,
   Arnold Lodge, Leamington Spa, 62, 67
   Baptist College, Pontypool, 100
   Berriew Road Boys' National, Welshpool, 179
   Christ Church Infants', Welshpool, 179
   Christian Brothers, Abbotsford, Vic, 72, 77
   Cockburn Higher Grade, Leeds, 86–7, 92
   Fernden Preparatory, Haslemere, 95
   Gawler Primary, 204
   Greenmount Primary, Blackboy Hill, 215
   Halbeath, Dunfermline, 122
   Hawera District High, Tarata, 151
   Kempston Boys', 239
   Laurence Calvert Academy, Leeds, 91
   Leamington Spa, 62
   Merchant Taylor's, Crosby, 62–3
   Municipal Technical School, Barrow-in-Furness, 192
   North Foreland lodge, Hampshire, 114
   Quernmore House, Bromley, 102–103
   Rowland Road Board, Leeds, 86, 89

Royal School for Daughters of Officers of the Army, 170
Rugby, 62
St Anthony's Primary, Blackboy Hill, 215
St Leonard's, Dunfermline, 122
St Margaret's, Polmont, 211
Salters Hill, West Norwood, 192
Serampore College, 100
Taunton, 101
Whitney-on-Wye, 169
Scotland, 28, 85, 111, 117–18, 126, 131, 142, 188–9, 200, 206, 210, 238–9
Scott, Capt Robert, 121
Scottish Court, 118
Seaford, 178
Seaview Downs, 203
Second Anglo-Sikh War, 229
Second World War, 58, 64, 73–4, 81, 89, 91, 97, 103, 107, 109, 118, 120, 123–4, 128, 138, 144, 160, 164, 168, 170, 189, 192, 203, 211, 213, 215, 218, 230
Second Taranaki War, 131
Secunderabad, 161
Sedd el Bahr, 213
Selfit School of Dressmaking, 147
Senegal, 111
Sensée River, 1
Serampore, 100
Serapeum, 210, 214
Serengeti, 114, 197
Serre, 86
Sessa, 112
Sexton VC, Sgt Gerald, *see* Buckley, Maurice
Seychelles, 112
*Sgt Pepper's Lonely Hearts Club Band*, 125
Shark Bay, 203
Shaw, Savill & Albion Co, 76
Shaw, Thomas, 170
Sheerness, 98, 171
Sheffield, 189, 193
Shefford, 240
Shepherd, Pte F, 28
Sheringham, 180
Sherwell, Percy, 240
Sherwood-Kelly VC, J, 194
Sherwood, Qld, 119
Shetland Islands, 128
Ships,
  *Alexandra*, 58
  Barque *Rienzi*, 206
  *Cedar*, 58
  *Duke of Devonshire*, 189
  *Jane Roper*, 189
  MS *Dilwara*, 111
  MS *Kuala Lumpur*, 111
  MS *Sobieski*, 110
  MV *Carnarvon Castle*, 112
  *Nino Bixio*, 147–8

  RMS *Aquitania*, 209
  RMS *Arcadian*, 182
  RMS *Franconia*, 111, 213
  RMS *Malwa*, 208
  RMS *Osterley*, 59
  RMS *Remuera*, 148
  RMS *Saxonia*, 210
  RRS *Discovery*, 121
  SS *Arundel*, 69
  SS *Atlanta*, 117
  SS *Auriga*, 152
  SS *Beltana*, 98
  SS *Berrima*, 215
  SS *Briton*, 150
  SS *Edison*, 217
  SS *Egra*, 95
  SS *Hororata*, 132
  SS *Ile de France*, 89–90
  SS *Ionic*, 137
  SS *Konig Friedrich August*, 69
  SS *Königin Luise*, 217
  SS *Loughborough*, 217
  SS *Mamari*, 136
  SS *Navua*, 151
  SS *Ocean Pride*, 111
  SS *Omar*, 217
  SS *Orcades*, 224
  SS *Ortona*, 182
  SS *Princess Clementine*, 220
  SS *Princess Victoria*, 74
  SS *Ratanga*, 76
  SS *Rimutaka*, 140
  SS *Roda*, 151
  SS *Ruahine*, 152
  SS *Saturnia*, 178
  SS *Taranaki*, 143
  SS *Ville d'Oran*, 111
  SS *Westphalia*, 98
  Trawler *Speedwell*, 235
  TSS *Jervis Bay*, 119
Shooters Hill, 95
Shorncliffe Camp, 226–7
Showgrounds Camp, Sydney, 73
Shrewsbury, 173–74, 197
Shropshire, 102, 166, 173–4, 176, 197
  League, 179
Siam, 244
Sicily, 111
Sidi Rezegh, 149
Sidmouth, 101
Sierra Leone, 110
Sikh Empire, 229
Simpson RN, Capt Salisbury, 98
Singapore, 37, 111, 124
Singer Sewing Machines, 85
Sir Robert Peel Inn, Hunslet, 84
Sisters of Mercy, 166
Sittingbourne, 93, 95–8, 102, 105–106, 113, 115–16, 230

Six Day War, 183
Skerton, 235
Skipper DCM, Sgt Thomas, 54
Skipton, 235
Sleaford, 242
Sling Camp, Bulford, 135–8, 140–1, 146, 150
Slough, 192
Smallburgh, 101
Smeed, Dean & Co, 96, 105
Smith & Guthrie, 124
Smith, Cpl, 45
Smuts, Gen JC, 105
Snarestone, 96
Soames, Olave St Claire, 182
Solihull, 163
Somers, Vic, 221
Somerset, 61, 106, 166–8
Somme, 151, 170, 244
Sotheby's, 198
South Africa, 58, 66, 78, 110, 157, 170, 173, 175, 181, 206, 226, 237, 240, 243
    Defence Force, 105
South America, 152
South Australia, 199–215, 220–1, 225
    Community Football Leaguge, 225
    Department of Veterans' Affairs, 225
    Railways, 202–21
South Devon & Tavistock Railway, 56
South Hams, 236
South of Scotland Electricity Board, 127
South Perth, WA, 222
South Russia, 116, 184
South Stoneham, 168–9
South Taranaki & Bight, 132
South Townsville, 187
South Wales, 169, 171
Southall, 220
Southampton, 59, 69, 75–6, 90, 101, 104, 107, 112, 117, 137, 165, 168–9, 216, 221, 232–5, 237, 240
Southborough, 154
Southend-on-Sea, 154, 192, 196
Southwark, 64, 239
Southwell, 165
Southwold, 176
Soviet Union, 109, 144
Spain, 124
Spalding, 97
Spanish Influenza, 215
Spencer, Sgt, 49–50
Spoil Heap, 2, 4
Sri Lanka, 78, 157, 226, 243
Stafford, 176
Staffordshire, 78, 90, 102, 157, 176, 226, 243
Stalag XI-A, 160
Start Point, 211
Staunton-on-Wye, 164
Steelend, 126
Stettin (Szczecin), 144, 217

Stirlingshire, 123–4, 210–11
Stockport, 177
Stockton-on-Tees, 143
Stoke Damerel, 55, 228, 237
Stowford, 56, 58
Strand, 95
Stratford, NZ, 147
Strathmore, Alta, 120
Stuarts, 121
Sturgess, Tom, 158
Sudbury, 56
Suez & Canal, 71–2, 132, 139, 148, 221, 224
Suffolk, 56, 91, 160
Sullivan VC, AP, 91
Sumner, Capt Wallace, 5
Sunderland, 82
Surrey, 61, 95, 101–102, 104, 162, 167–8, 178, 186, 188, 193, 214, 229
Surrey Iron Railway, 187
Sussex, 75, 87, 93, 100, 137, 154, 164, 178, 186, 242
Sussex Hotel, Eastbourne, 162
Sutherland, NSW, 189
Sutton Mandeville Camp, 215
Sutton-on-Trent, 62
Sutton Veny, 75, 222–33
Suvla Bay, 94
Swale & District Council, 95, 106
Swan, WA, 219
Swan, Hunter & Wigham Richardson Ltd, 109
Swan Valley, 218
Swanage, 191
Swaziland, 112
Sweden, 144
Swindon, 162
Swinford, 82
Switzerland, 153
Sydney, NSW, 72–3, 78, 98, 186, 188, 201, 218, 221, 225–6, 232–3
Syracuse, 111

Tadcaster, 228–9
Tait, Agnes 'Nan', 192
Takanini, 133
Tamaki, 132
Tamuna, 94
Tandey VC, Pte Henry, 61, 63
Tank, Mk V, 21
Tanta, 89
Tanzania, 114, 197
Taranaki, 131, 134, 140, 142–4, 150–1, 153
Taranto, 111
Tarata, 131, 142, 151
Taree, NSW, 232
Tarrant Gunville, 191
Tasmania, 212
Taunton, 61
Tavistock, 56
Tay Rail Bridge, 121

Te Kowhai, 133
Te Kuiti, 146
Tel-el-Kebir, 71, 208, 233
Telford, Thomas, 211
Templeux-le-Guérard, 33
Terminus Hotel, Eastbourne, 162
Terowie, SA, 220–1
Teutonic Knights, 144
Thames, 64, 93, 109
Thames, NZ, 144
Thatcher, PM Margaret, 62
*The End of the Road*, 126
*The Last Sumarai*, 131
*The Seven Heroes of Moeuvres*, 130
Thebarton, SA, 205
Thessaloniki, 182
Thetford, 181, 239
Thierru Copse, 22, 24–5
Thirteen Years War, 144
Throsk, 124
Throsk Community Enterprises Ltd, 124
Throssell VC, Hugo, 223
Thuringowa, Qld, 70
Thynne, Sir John, 170
Tidworth, 146, 162, 216, 233
Tigne, 221
Tilbury, 135, 150, 224
Timaru, 152, 156
Tipperary, 194
Tirah Campaign, 228
Tokaora, 132
Tolkien, JRR, 114
Tonbridge, 90, 97
Toowoomba, Qld, 119
Torbay, 236
Torbay & Brixham Railway, 236
Torquay, 137, 146, 148
Torrens Park, 202
Totnes, 235–6
Tottenham Hotspur FC, 204
Toukley, NSW, 188
Tower Bridge, 96
Tower Hamlets Spur, 104
Townhill, 117
Townsville, Qld, 187
Towyn, 174
Toxteth Park, 58
Toye VC, AM, 194
Transvaal, 237, 240
Traralgon, Vic, 188
Travelodge, 61
Treaty of Warsaw, 144
Treetops, 114, 197
Trenchard-Davies, Claude, 51
Trenches,
  African & Support, 4–9
  Bass Lane, 44
  Beux, 48
  Burton Lane, 44–5
  Canary, 51–3
  Cemetery Support, 16
  Chapel Wood Switch, 45
  Cheetham Reserve, 11
  Cinnabar, 53–4
  City & Support, 12
  Claud, 51–2, 54
  Cooker, 21
  Cut Lane, 45
  Dean, 21
  Derby, 45
  Etrepot, 31–2
  Femy, 45
  Forgan's, 48–51
  Fourmi, 20, 31, 48
  Gallichet, 48
  Hobart Street, 15, 17–19
  Hun, 25
  Kitten, 11
  Knat Avenue, 11
  Knights Bridge, 11
  Leduc, 48
  Lincoln Reserve, 8
  London & Support, 9, 11–12
  Mareval, 23
  Midland Reserve, 8
  Mile End Road, 11
  Pen, 30–2
  Potts Lane, 8
  Putney & Avenue, 11–12
  Queer Street, 11
  Railway, 11–12
  Ridge Reserve, 39
  Rifle Pit, 33
  Shaftesbury Avenue, 8
  Shropshire & Support, 11
  Snap Trench & Reserve, 4, 8–9
  Triangle, 33
  Twisted Alley, 51
Trentham, 132, 134, 136, 141, 145–6, 148–9
Trescault & Spur, 4, 9–11, 43, 45
Triangle Wood, 12, 44–6
Trimulgherry, 161
Tring, 227, 230
Trinity House, 211
Truelove, JR, 170
Tsavo National Park, 114, 197
Tudors, 236
Tunbridge Wells, 153–4
Tunstall, 93, 96–7, 100, 106, 113, 115–16
  Parish Council, 113
Turkey, 182
Turner, Capt HW, 26
Twickenham, 198
Two Wells, SA, 199, 209
Tyne, 109

Uganda, 114, 197
Ukraine, 78, 157, 226, 243

Ulverston, 190
Union Canal, 211
Union Steamship Co, 151
United Nations, 89
United States of America, 78, 89, 118, 125, 157, 219, 226, 243
Universities,
   Aarhus, 114
   Balliol College, Oxford, 227
   Bangor, 184
   De Montfort, 68
   Girton College, Cambridge, 114
   King's College, London, 64, 216
      Florence Nightingale Faculty of Nursing & Midwifery, 64
      School of Medicine & Dentistry, 64
   London School of Economics, 114
   Sorbonne, 114
   Trinity College, Oxford, 242
Unknown Warrior, 89
Upham VC, Charles, 156, 158
Upkeep mine, 180
Uplyme, 166
Upminster, 91
Upton-upon-Severn, 55, 60
Uralla, NSW, 186–87
Urenui, 147
Uruguay, 63
Uttar Pradesh, 90
Uxbridge, 154

Vadancourt, 47, 49–51
Van Wakeren, Ronald, 158
Vancouver, 219
Vaulx-Vraucourt, 87
Vauxhall Bridge, 211
VC10 aircraft, 114, 197
Vélu & Wood, 9, 242
Vendelles, 24
Verwood, 168
Vichy France, 110
Vickers & Sons, 189, 192–3
Vickers Armstrong, 193
Vickers Armstrong Shipbuilders Ltd, 193
Vickers Ltd, 193
Vickers Ltd Shipbuilding Group, 193
Vickers, Sons & Maxim Ltd, 182, 193–4
Victor Harbour, 203
Victoria, 59, 68–70, 72, 76–7, 102, 134, 188, 206, 211–12, 219, 221, 225
   Ministry of Conservation, 73
   State Electricity Commission, 188
   State Government, 73
Victoria Barracks, Sydney, 73
Victoria Cross & George Cross Association & Reunions, 66, 91, 114–15, 129, 155, 197
Victoria Cross Centenary 1956, 91, 115, 129, 155, 197, 224

Victoria Cross Dinner, House of Lords 1929, 66, 114, 129, 197, 223
Victoria Cross Garden Party, 66, 91, 114, 129, 197
Victoria Cross Roads, 22, 29
Victory Day, 91, 114, 129, 197
Vienna, 95
Vikings, 189
Villawood, NSW, 186, 188
Villeret, 24, 31
Villers-Bretonneux, Second Battle of, 208
Viscount Weymouth, 170
Von der Leyen, Ursula, 172
Von Mohl, Kaptlt Hans, 99
VSEL, 193
Vulcan Shipbuilding Corp, 217

W Denny & Bros, 152
Waikato, 133, 144, 146
Waiouru, 158
Waipawa, 145
Waipukurau, 150
Waitara, 131
Waitotara, 132
Wakefield, 84
Walduck's Hotel, Bloomsbury, 100–102
Wales, 159, 173, 184
Walker, James, 211
Wallace, William, 125, 211
Wallis, Barnes, 180
Wallsend, 109
Walton-on-Thames, 136, 137
Walton-on-the-Hill, 178
Wanbi, SA, 203
Wandsworth, 93, 95
Wanganui, 136
Wangaratta, Vic, 188
Wantage, 166
Wapping, 103
War Bonds, 87, 126
War Service Badge, 59
Ward VC, C, 91
Wareham, 69, 191
Waring VC, LSgt William, 19, 34–6, 173–85
Warrington, 212
Warrnambool, Vic, 72
Warwick, 61, 164, 230
Warwickshire, 55, 60–2, 67, 81, 162–3, 216, 227
Warwickshire County Cricket Club, 60
Waterloo & Station, London, 216
Watford, 55–6, 63
   FC, 204
Wath Rescue Service, 88
Watling Street, 93
Watson, NSW, 186, 188–9
Watt, James, 211
Watton, 178
Waugh, Evelyn, 230
Waverley, NSW, 186, 188

Waziristan, 56, 92, 228
WB Moss & Sons, 239–40
Wellington, 102, 134–8, 140, 143, 145–6, 149, 155, 157, 197
Wellington Arch, London, 196
Wellington Barracks, London, 91
Wells, 167
Welshpool, 173–7, 179–81, 183–5
   Reserves, 179
   Town Council, 185
Wemyss, 120
Wemyss Barracks, Canterbury, 113
Wendover, 242
Werribee, Vic, 70
West Bank, 183
West Bromwich, 102
West Derby, 58, 174, 177–8
West Dulwich, 186, 194
West Germany, 124
West Ham, 230
West Hartlepool, 82
West Indies, 182
West Maling, 97
West Norwood, 192, 196
West Woodyates, 168
Westcliffe-on-Sea, 154
Western Australia, 199, 201, 203, 205, 215, 217–25
   Government House, 223
   Governor, 223
   State War Memorial, 225
Western Cape, 206
Westminster, 56, 89, 102, 162
Weston-super-Mare, 106
Westown, 147
Weymouth, 73, 168, 202, 208, 220, 233–4
Whangamomona, 148
Wharfedale, 80
Wheaton Aston, 176
Whitby, 87, 211
White VC, J, 91
White Russians, 194
White VC, 2Lt William, 19, 40, 42–3, 186–98
Whitehaven, 189–90
Whitley, 178
Whitley Bay, 65
Whitney-on-Wye, 159, 171
Whittington, Richard, 64
Whyalla, SA, 200
Wick, 85
Wicks, Pte Edward, 28
Wigston, 67
Willesden & Green, 154
William the Lion, 121
Williamites, 204
Williamson, Herbert, 88
Williamtown, NSW, 218
Williston, 214
Wilson VC, ECT, 114

Wiltshire, 59, 69, 74–5, 136–7, 141, 162, 167–70, 189, 191, 215–16, 222, 233–5
Wimereux, 108, 232
Winch, Sgt W, 88
Winchester, 155
Windmill Hill Camp, 233
Windygates, 120
Wingate, 82
Wingham, NSW, 186
Wirrabara, SA, 201
Wisconsin, 219
Wisden Cricketers Almanac, 240
Wodonga, Vic, 77
Wolf Rock, 211
Wood, Derwent, 196
Wood Green, 163
Wood MM, Cpl Edward, 6
Wood Road, 3, 7–8
Woodbridge, 91
Woods VC, Pte James, 19, 30–1, 199–226
Woodville Gardens, SA, 203
Woolwich, Royal Arsenal, Common & Garrison, 56–7, 95
Worcester, 61–2
Worcestershire, 55, 60–1, 195
Worshipful Company of Butchers, 61
Worth Valley, 81–3
Worthing, 239
Wren, John, 76
Wren, Sir Christopher, 170
Wrexham, 183
Wycheproof, Vic, 188
Wyeside, 159
Wyken, 166

Yak Post, 37
Yass, NSW, 203
Yeovil, 168
Yongala Vale, SA, 220
Yonkers, 118
York, 87, 162, 228
York, SA, 203
Yorketown, SA, 206
Yorkshire, 62, 79–81, 83–7, 133, 228–9, 235, 238
   East Riding, 238
   North Riding, 235
   West Riding, 79, 81, 92
Yorkshire Bank, 10
Young VC, 2Lt Frank, 19, 44–6, 226–44
Ypres, 87, 103, 106–107, 116, 161
Ypres League, 106
Ypres Veterans, 113
Ytres, 9

Zebra Post, 37, 39
Zeitoun, 214, 233
Zulu War, 173